Developments in the European Union

Developments in Politics

Laura Cram, Desmond Dinan and Neill Nugent (eds)
DEVELOPMENT IN THE EUROPEAN UNION

Patrick Dunleavy, Andrew Gamble, Ian Holliday and Gillian Peele (eds)
DEVELOPMENTS IN BRITISH POLITICS 5

Peter A. Hall, Jack Hayward and Howard Machin (eds)
DEVELOPMENTS IN FRENCH POLITICS (Revised edition)

Gillian Peele, Christopher Bailey, Bruce Cain and B. Guy Peters (eds)
DEVELOPMENTS IN AMERICAN POLITICS 3

Martin Rhodes, Paul Heywood and Vincent Wright (eds)
DEVELOPMENTS IN WEST EUROPEAN POLITICS

Developments in the European Union

Edited by
Laura Cram,
Desmond Dinan
Neill Nugent

St. Martin's Press
New York

DEVELOPMENTS IN THE EUROPEAN UNION

St. Martin's Press, Scholarly and Reference Division,
175 Fifth Avenue, New York, N.Y. 10010

First published in the United States of America in 1999

This book is printed on paper suitable for recycling and made from fully managed and sustained forest sources.

Printed in Great Britain

ISBN 0–312–22532–6 clothbound
ISBN 0–312–22533–4 paperback

Library of Congress Cataloging-in-Publication Data
Developments in the European Union / edited by Laura Cram, Desmond Dinan and Neill Nugent.
p. cm.
"Developments in politics"—Prelim. page.
Includes bibliographical references and index.
ISBN 0–312–22532–6 (cloth). — ISBN 0–312–22533–4 (pbk.)
1. European Union. 2. European Union countries—Politics and government. I. Cram, Laura. II. Dinan, Desmond, 1957–
III. Nugent, Neill.
JN30.D48 1999
341.242'2—dc21

99–22005
CIP

Contents

PART 3 POLICIES AND POLICY OBJECTIVES

PART 4 KEY ISSUES

PART 5 CONCLUSIONS

List of Tables and Figures

Tables

Figures

Preface

In keeping with the spirit and rationale of the *Developments* series, the focus of this book is on recent developments in the European Union. The background and context of developments are explained as appropriate, but they are not examined in depth.

Since the Treaty on European Union came into effect in 1993, there has been a problem with the use of the terms 'European Community' and 'European Union'. This arises from the fact that the Treaty incorporated what had formerly been called the European Community – which actually consisted of three Communities – into the European Union, and also renamed the European Economic Community, which was the most important of the three Communities, the European Community. To try to minimize confusion, the practice adopted in this book has been to use European Union wherever possible and to use European Community only when it is absolutely necessary for reasons of historical or legal accuracy.

Another, more recent, problem in writing about the EU is how to deal with the numbering of the articles of the Treaties on which the Union is based. The 1997 Treaty of Amsterdam, which came into effect in 1999, provided for a renumbering of the articles of the Treaty on European Union and the Treaty Establishing the European Community, with the consequence that numbers that had over the years become very familiar to EU practitioners and observers no longer have their former applications. For example, the rules for the conduct of external trade negotiations are no longer based on Article 113 of the European Community Treaty but rather on Article 133. Our approach is to use the new article numbers, but also to give the old numbers when it seems important or helpful to do so.

In order to help readers keep up with the constant and rapid evolution of the EU, our publishers are creating a web page for this book and related titles which will provide information on key developments – such as changes in the composition of the European Parliament and of the Commission – and links to selected other internet resources. The address is

http://www.macmillan-press.co.uk/politics/EU

We would like to thank all the contributors for producing what we believe to be high-quality work and for meeting deadlines. Our thanks also go to our publisher, Steven Kennedy, for his strong support and good-humoured encouragement.

Laura Cram
Desmond Dinan
Neill Nugent

Notes on Contributors

Michael Baun is Pizer Associate Professor of International Relations at Valdosta State University. He is the author of *An Imperfect Union: The Maastricht Treaty and the New Politics of European Integration* and of many articles and book chapters on European and German Politics.

Michael Calingaert, a former US diplomat and European director of a US trade association, is executive director of the Council for the United States and Italy, guest scholar at the Brookings Institution, and Political Section member of the Free University of Brussels' Institute of European Studies. He is the author of two books on European integration.

Laura Cram is Lecturer in Politics at the University of Sheffield. She has published several articles and book chapters on the the EU policy process and is the author of *Policy-Making in the European Union: Conceptual Lenses and the Integration Process*. She is currently completing a book on social policy and the EU.

Desmond Dinan is Associate Professor in the Institute of Public Policy, George Mason University, and is also Visiting Fellow at the Netherlands Institute of International Relations, Clingendael, The Hague. He is the author of *Ever Closer Union: An Introduction to European Integration* (2nd edn) and editor of the *Encyclopedia of the European Union.*

Kevin Featherstone is Professor of European Studies and Jean Monnet Professor of European Integration Studies at the University of Bradford. He has co-authored *The United States and the European Union: Partners in Transition* and *Negotiating the Maastricht Treaty: The Dynamics of Economic and Monetary Union.*

Fiona Hayes-Renshaw is a freelance researcher and copy-editor working in Brussels. She has worked at the College of Europe in Bruges, the Royal Institute of International Affairs in London, and the secretariat of the European Round Table of Industrialists in Brussels.

Her publications include several articles on COREPER and the EU Permanent Representations and she is the co-author of *The Council of Ministers*.

Martin Holland is Associate Professor of Political Science at the University of Canterbury, New Zealand. He was formerly Jean Monnet Fellow at the European University Institute, Florence, and Alexander von Humboldt Fellow at the Arnold Bergstraesser Institut, Freiburg. His many publications include *European Community Integration*, *European Union Common Foreign Policy: from EPC to CFSP Joint Action and South Africa*, and *Common Foreign and Security Policy: The Record and Reforms* (editor).

Brigid Laffan is Jean Monnet Professor of European Politics at University College Dublin. She has published numerous articles and book chapters on different aspects of European integration. Her books include *Integration and Co-operation in Europe* and *The Finances of the European Union.*

Finn Laursen is Professor and Head of the Thorkil Kristensen Institute at South Jutland University Centre, Esbjerg. He was formerly at the European Institute of Public Administration, Maastricht. He has published widely on EU trade issues and on the EU's relations with Central and Eastern Europe.

Sonia Mazey is a Fellow of Churchill College and a Lecturer in the Faculty of Social and Political Sciences, University of Cambridge. She is the author of numerous articles and books on French politics, regional politics, European integration, and the role of women in the European policy process.

Paul McAleavey completed his doctorate on the implementation of the European Regional Development Policy at the European University Institute in Florence. Since 1995 he has worked in DGV of the European Commission, focusing on employment policy and the structural funds.

John McCormick is Associate Professor of Political Science at the Indianapolis campus of Indiana University. His recent publications include *Acid Earth: The Politics of Acid Pollution* (3rd edn) and *Understanding the European Union.*

James Mitchell is Professor of Politics at the University of Sheffield. His books include *Conservatives in the Union* and *Strategies for Self-Government*. In addition, he has written many articles, focusing primarily on territorial politics. He is currently completing books on regions and regionalism in the EU and on devolution in the UK.

Karlheinz Neunreither is Professor at the University of Heidelberg and a former senior official in the Secretariat of the European Parliament. He has co-edited *Institutional Dynamics and Prospects for Democracy in the European Union.*

Neill Nugent is Professor of Politics and Jean Monnet Professor of European Integration at Manchester Metropolitan University. His recent publications include *The Government and Politics of the European Union* (4th edn), and *At the Heart of the Union: Studies of the European Commission* (editor)

Jeremy Richardson is a Professorial Fellow at Nuffield College and Director of the Centre for European Politics, Economics and Society, University of Oxford. He is the author of numerous articles and books on public policy and is the editor of the *Journal of European Public Policy.*

Emek Uçarer is Assistant Professor of International Relations at Bucknell University, Pennsylvania. Her recent publications include *Immigration into Western Societies: Problems and Policies* (co-edited), and articles on international and European migration.

Daniel Wincott is Lecturer in Political Science and International Studies at the University of Birmingham, where he is also Deputy Director (Research) of the Graduate School of European Studies. He has published a number of articles on the legal/political analysis of European integration. His *Politics, Law and European Integration* is scheduled to be published in 2000.

List of Abbreviations

ACP	African, Caribbean and Pacific Countries
ASEAN	Association of South East Asian Nations
ASEM	Asia–Europe Meeting
BEST	Business Environment Simplification Task Force
BSE	Bovine Spongiform Encephalopathy
CAP	Common Agricultural Policy
CCP	Common Commercial Policy
CDU	Christian Democratic Union (Germany)
CEECs	Central and Eastern European Countries
CEEP	European Centre of Enterprises with Public Participation
CET	Common External Tariff
CFCs	Chlorofluorocarbons
CFSP	Common Foreign and Security Policy
CIS	Customs Information System
CMEA	Council of Mutual Economic Assistance
COM	Commission Document
CoR	Committee of the Regions
COREPER	Committee of Permanent Representatives
CORINE	Coordinating Information on the Environment
CSU	Christian Social Union (Germany)
DECODE	Designing the Commission of Tomorrow
DG	Directorate General
EAGGF	European Agricultural Guidance and Guarantee Fund
EAP	Environmental Action Programme
EBRD	European Bank for Reconstruction and Development
EC	European Community
ECB	European Central Bank
ECJ	European Court of Justice
Ecofin	Economic and Finance Ministers
ECSC	European Coal and Steel Community
ECU	European Currency Unit
EDU	European Drugs Unit
EEA	European Economic Area *also* European Environmental Agency
EFTA	European Free Trade Association

EIB	European Investment Bank
EMI	European Monetary Institute
EMS	European Monetary System
EMU	Economic and Monetary Union
EP	European Parliament
EPC	European Political Cooperation
EPP	European People's Party
ERDF	European Regional Development Fund
ERM	Exchange Rate Mechanism
ESC	Economic and Social Committee
ESDI	European Security and Defence Identity
ESF	European Social Fund
ETF	European Training Foundation
ETUC	European Trade Union Confederation
EU	European Union
FDI	Foreign Direct Investment
FTA	Free Trade Agreement
GATS	General Agreement on Trade in Services
GATT	General Agreement on Tariffs and Trade
GDP	Gross Domestic Product
GSP	General System of Preferences
IGC	Intergovernmental Conference
IGS	Inspectorate-General of the Services
IMPEC	EU Network for the Implementation and Enforcement of Environmental Law
JHA	Justice and Home Affairs
MAP	Modernization of Administration and Personnel Policy
MEP	Member of the European Parliament
Mercosur	Southern Core Common Market
MFA	Multi-Fibre Arrangements
MFN	Most Favoured Nation
NAFTA	North Atlantic Free Trade Area
NATO	North Atlantic Treaty Organization
NGO	Nongovernmental Organization
NIC	Newly Independent Country
NIS	New Transatlantic Agenda
NTA	Non Tariff Barrier
NTB	Non Tariff Barrier
NTM	New Transatlantic Marketplace
OECD	Organization for Economic Co-operation and Development

OJ	Official Journal of the European Communities
OPEC	Organization of Petroleum Exporting Countries
PCA	Partnership and Cooperation Agreement
qmv	qualified majority vote/voting
QR	Quantitative Restriction
RECHAR	Community Initiative Programme for the Conversion of Coal Mining Areas
SEA	Single European Act
SEM	Single European Market *also* Sound and Effective Management
SLIM	Simplifying Legislation Relating to the Internal Market
TCN	Third Country National
TEC	Treaty Establishing the European Community
TEU	Treaty on European Union
T of A	Treaty of Amsterdam
TRIM	Trade-Related Investment Measure
TRIP	Trade-Related Aspects of Intellectual Property Rights
UK	United Kingdom
UN	United Nations
UNICE	Union of Industrial and Employers' Confederations of Europe
US/USA	United States of America
VER	Voluntary Export Restraint
WEU	Western European Union
WTO	World Trade Organization

Map of EU member states and applicant states

PART 1

Introduction

1

Reconciling Theory and Practice

LAURA CRAM, DESMOND DINAN AND NEILL NUGENT

This book focuses on developments in the European integration process and, more especially, developments in the European Union (EU). The chapters which follow cover a wide variety of topics and issues. The purpose of this first chapter is to lay a foundation for these following chapters by outlining key underlying questions.

The first question is what should be the focus of study when examining and attempting to explain European integration and the EU? The second question is to what extent has there been a shift in the balance of power within the EU in recent years, especially in respect of the intergovernmental/supranational balance? The third question – and the one that is given most attention in this chapter – is what conceptual and theoretical approaches are most useful for examining the nature of the integration process and the character and functioning of the EU?

European Integration and the European Union: What is to be Studied and Explained?

Since the European Communities were founded in the 1950s, there has been an ongoing debate in Western Europe about the direction and the way in which European integration should proceed. Many of the central issues in this debate have persisted over time, as can be seen by the focus in the current debate on updated versions of long-asked questions. For example, should the EU remain primarily an arena for economic/technical cooperation or should political and security cooperation become 'mainstream' EU activities? Should the EU continue to widen by increasing the number of its member states or should it focus on deepening through strengthening its institutions and embracing more policy areas? If there is to be institutional strengthening, how much power should be delegated to EU institutions and what degree of autonomy should they be allowed? And how involved should the EU citizenry be in decisions taken at the EU level?

In practice, 'macro' questions such as these are usually resolved through processes of compromise in which complex package deals, containing something for everyone, are brokered between the member states, the EU institutions and various interests at the EU level. This internal horse-trading allows the EU to move forward, albeit often slowly and painstakingly. Many factors may affect these compromises and deals. For example: external factors, from the impact of globalization to security tensions in the Middle East; intra-European factors, such as the desire or need for economic cooperation with neighbouring European countries and the relative power enjoyed by different EU member states; internal or domestic factors, such as the need to respond to internal political needs and pressures; the current popularity of European ideals and the perceived desirability of cooperation in Europe; and the role of key individuals, be they in favour of or opposed to European integration.

The ways in which macro questions of this sort are approached and answered by practitioners, and the factors that influence them, are central to an understanding of what the EU is and what it may become. The many issues associated with such questions are therefore of great interest to scholars concerned with the study of European integration.

However, the study of European integration and the EU cannot be limited to 'big' questions. More routine and humdrum issues must also be studied. This is because within the EU a host of different sorts of actors – institutional and noninstitutional, governmental and nongovernmental, and transnational, national, regional, and local – are involved in a wide variety of 'everyday' political and policy activities. Such activities are, in many respects, similar to those that occur at the national level, with ongoing political debate and contestation, and with policies constantly being initiated, developed, negotiated, implemented and evaluated. To give just three examples of the range of such 'normal' political and policy activities in the EU: there are many organizational power struggles between and within

EU institutions; there are conflicting policy pressures of many kinds – for instance, some actors want competition policy to be be applied more rigorously, while others advocate a more flexible approach; and much policy activity is more technical than political in nature – as is largely the case with the almost daily adjustments that need to be made to the implementing rules and regulations of the Common Agricultural Policy (CAP).

There is thus no shortage of subjects and issues for European integration scholars to examine. They range in character from the overall nature of the integration process to the features of particular EU institutions, decision-making processes, and policy areas. In seeking to conduct their examinations, two problems in particular face European integration scholars. The first is that their subject material is ever changing. Whenever a scholar thinks that the essence of the subject – be it the integration process as a whole or a specific EU policy or process – has been captured, a new development occurs and the project has moved on. The second is that conceptual and theoretical tools are needed to direct and inform enquiry.

The next section illustrates 'the moving target' problem; the following section explores how conceptual and theoretical tools have been developed and applied.

The Changing Balance of Power in the EU: Supranationalism and Intergovernmentalism

The extent to which supranational procedures and institutions have developed at the EU level is generally considered to be one of the distinguishing features of the EU, setting it apart from other international organizations. Since the transfer of responsibilities to supranational institutions implies the placing of constraints on national sovereignty – that is, restrictions on the ability of member states to act independently and on their own initiative – the debate over the balance of power within the EU between supranational and intergovernmental actors is fundamentally important to an understanding of both the distribution and balance of power at the EU level and between the EU level and the member states.

'Supranational' implies the existence of a power above or beyond the level of the nation-state enjoying some degree of autonomy from national governments. Thus, when EU member states create a supranational body or procedure, they delegate a range of tasks that they expect to be performed without constant references back to them for approval. Inevitably, the creation of such tasks places some constraints on the sovereignty and powers of member states since they no longer have full control over the outcomes of the supranational institutions or the procedures that they have created. The most important supranational institutions in the EU are: (i) the European Commission, which is obliged to act in the 'European' rather than any national interest, enjoys the right to initiate new policies and, in some cases – for example, competition policy – has the right to take binding decisions which do not have to be approved by member states; (ii) the European Parliament (EP), which is directly elected by the European public, is autonomous from the governments of the member states, and enjoys the power of co-decision with the member states (meeting collectively in the Council of Ministers) on many important aspects of policy; and (iii) the European Court of Justice (ECJ), which has consistently developed and ensured the supremacy of EU legislation over any contradictory provision within the member states' legal systems. Even within the Council, which is generally considered to be dominated by member state interests, certain aspects of supranationalism have developed, most notably through the widespread availability of qualified majority voting (qmv), which prevents any single member state from vetoing a policy which is not in its national interest.

As more areas of policy activity are transferred to the EU level, and as qmv and co-decision are used more extensively, the importance of the supranational aspect of the EU becomes ever more apparent. A key question for scholars, therefore, is why do member states choose to extend their activities at the EU level given that it means a curtailment of their own autonomy? As will be seen below, some scholars argue that member states have found themselves caught up in a process from which they cannot easily extricate themselves, even when it would be in their interest to do so. Rather like a fly in a web, they find themselves more and more entwined with their EU partners and more and more influenced by the supranational institutions at every turn. Other scholars, however, argue that far from losing control over the integration process, member states have decided that a certain trade off between autonomy and influence is worthwhile. Thus, having a little less autonomy over certain policy decisions is acceptable if it results in having greater international power as part of a major economic trading bloc. A challenge for those who study the

EU is to determine which of these positions or, indeed, the many variations on these positions – is best supported by the evidence.

In assessing the balance between supranationalism and intergovernmentalism in the EU, it is important to distinguish clearly between the phenomenon of intergovernmentalism from the theoretical approach of the same name considered below (see pp. 10–11). When applied to actors or processes at the EU level, the terms intergovernmental and intergovernmantalism simply imply that the institution, actor or process is dominated by the national governments of the member states and that the main focus is on the protection of national interests. This can best be explained through concrete examples. One very obvious instance is the fact that the treaties establishing and amending the foundations on which the EU is based have to be agreed and ratified by all member states. Another example is the use of unanimous voting in the Council, which still applies to certain types of decisions (see Chapter 7) and which, by allowing any member state to exercise a veto, is a clear case of the dominance of national interests and of member states maintaining tight control over decision-making. The almost invariable use of unanimity in the European Council, where member states are represented at the highest political level, serves a similar purpose. A quite different example of the continuing importance of intergovernmentalism is the way in which the implementation of EU legislation – primarily the responsibility of national authorities – is, despite the legal supremacy of EU law, often very slow and inadequate, reflecting the ability of national interests to corrupt EU processes.

The balance between the supranational and intergovernmental aspects within the EU is precarious and constantly shifting. For those trying to understand the development of the EU the nature of this balance helps to provide a yardstick against which the various turning-points in the development of European integration can be measured. How, for example, do the three founding treaties of the 1950s compare? Did the 1966 Luxembourg Compromise mark a shift towards greater intergovernmentalism? How can the extension of competences and powers of EU institutions in the 1986 Single European Act (SEA) be explained? Did the establishment of two new-pillars in the 1992 Maastricht Treaty – one on foreign and security policy and one on justice and home affairs policy – represent a return to intergovernmental power? And how does the 1997 Amsterdam Treaty affect the supranational intergovernmental balance?

Making Sense of the EU: Different Approaches

As has been indicated above, there are many dimensions to the study of European integration and the EU. But how are these dimensions to be examined? This section provides an introduction to some of the key theoretical and conceptual approaches that have been developed to further the study of the process of European integration and the nature and functioning of the EU.

There are many such approaches and they can be presented in different ways. They can, for example, be divided into categories on the basis of what they are seeking to analyse and explain. One such categorization (used by Nugent, 1999) is to distinguish between: grand theory – which seeks to explain the integration process as a whole; middle range, or meso, theory – which seeks to explain aspects of the functioning of the EU (most middle-range theory focuses particularly on policy processes); and conceptualizations – which seek to capture the essence of the EU in conceptual terms.

The approaches are not divided into categories here. Rather, a more historical framework is used, so as to show how theoretical and conceptual debates have developed and how the component parts of the debates have been closely intertwined. The examination that follows does not seek to be exhaustive, but rather seeks to provide an introduction to some of the key authors and texts that have influenced theoretical and conceptual debates.

Functionalism

The roots of European integration theory are usually traced back to David Mitrany's 1943 book *A Working Peace System*. Mitrany hoped that the functionalist method would help to overcome the conflicts inherent in competing national systems which he felt led inevitably to war. Basically, Mitrany argued that increasing cooperation between countries in functional areas where they could pool their technical expertise would eventually lead to a desire for greater technical/ functional cooperation in wider areas and would result in lasting habits of cooperation between nations. As this functional cooperation 'spilled over' from one area to another, the incentive to go to war with partners would diminish and a 'working peace system' would prevail. Mitrany himself was opposed to European integration as he felt this would just create a national bloc writ large. However, functionalism as a theory was highly influential both for the development of subsequent theories of European integration, such as neo-functionalism, and as the method employed by two of the key architects of the European project, Jean Monnet and Robert Schuman, when they were establishing the European Coal and Steel Community (ECSC) in the early 1950s.

Transactionalism

Developed by Karl Deutsch and his colleagues (1957, 1966), the transactionalist approach is also referred to as the communications school of thought. This approach was based on extensive comparative research on how political communities and a sense of identity are developed. Deutsch *et al.* focused primarily on the manner in which increased interaction between European peoples, as transactions between European countries intensified, would contribute to an increased sense of mutual responsiveness between previously disparate populations. It was argued that as a result of a complex learning process, in which shared symbols, memories, values and norms were allowed to develop, individuals in Europe would eventually begin to view themselves as a people with a shared sense of identity. Under these conditions, the process of European integration would flourish.

The transactional approach was heavily criticized in the late 1960s because an increasing level of transactions did not seem to have led to any discernable increase in mutual responsiveness between European peoples. However, Deutsch's insights continued to be important for the development of neo-functionalist theory and in recent years a number of scholars have begun to return to transactionalism and to revise Deutsch's work in response to current developments.

Neo-functionalism

Developed originally by Ernst Haas (1958), and later by scholars such as Lindberg (1963), Lindberg and Scheingold (1970) and Schmitter (1970), the neo-functionalist approach to European integration focused on the process through which integration could be expected to proceed. Drawing on and developing some of the insights of Mitrany's functionalism (particularly the aspects of incremental spill-over) and Deutsch's transactionalism (particularly concerning the importance of a political community), Haas attempted to derive a comprehensive theory of European integration that would not only describe the processes taking place in the ECSC, but would also help to predict how the process of European integration might be expected to progress. Haas emphasized the importance of experts, interests, supranational institutions and technical expertise rather than national politicians in the process of integration. He refined Mitrany's concept of spill-over to encompass three distinct elements: technical/functional spill-over, political spill-over, and geographical spill-over.

It was through these three elements that the process of integration could be expected to progress. Technical/functional spill-over referred to the process by which cooperation in one agreed area (for example, agriculture) would require further cooperation in a second, related area (for example, food hygiene standards) in order to be successful. Political spill-over referred to the shift in the expectations and activities of individuals which might be expected to emerge in reponse to the new policies emerging at the European level. For example, as policies began to affect people more directly, they might begin to lobby at the European Community (EC) level or join a transnational interest group, thus changing their previous pattern of activities and shifting their expectations away from the national level. Geographical spill-over referred to the impact which the Community had on non-member states, not least by altering existing trade patterns. As excluded states felt the effect of the economic giant on their doorstep, they would increasingly be inclined to join the Community.

Neo-functionalism seemed to capture the essence of European integration fairly well until the mid-1960s, when the actions of the French President Charles de Gaulle reminded scholars of the important role an individual national leader could play in slowing up the various processes of spill-over. By the early 1970s, when the oil crises struck and world economic recession set in, the inexorable processes of spill-over through which the nation-state would eventually become irrelevant were much less apparent. Scholars, accordingly, sought a theoretical approach that could account for the impact of external shocks and the continued importance of national governments within the integration process.

Intergovernmentalism

Intergovernmentalism emphasizes the central role of national governments in the integration process and is associated with the work of Stanley Hoffmann (1966). Hoffmann produced an insightful critique of the neo-functionalist approach in which he argued that the nation-state and national governments were considerably more 'obstinate' than they were 'obsolete'. There were a number of potential brakes upon the kinds of spill-over that Haas had identified: brakes that would stop national governments from becoming an irrelevance in the process of European integration. Hoffmann reminded scholars of the importance of the international system and the role that national governments played in defending the interests of their peoples within this system. He argued that national governments might allow a certain degree of spill-over to take place in areas of 'low politics' (economics and welfare policies) where such spill-over did not threaten their vital interests and indeed where cooperation might enhance their position within the international environment. However, in areas of 'high politics' (such as foreign policy, security and defence) national governments would be much more wary and would swiftly put a stop to any attempts to encourage spill-over. Thus, for Hoffmann, spill-over was not inexorable; rather, he saw it as a process that national governments tolerated when it suited them and could bring to an abrupt halt when it did not.

Interdependence

Although not focused directly on Europe, from the early 1970s some of the insights of scholars working in the general field of international relations began to have a major impact on European integration theory. Of particular importance was work on the concept of international interdependence undertaken by Robert Keohane and Joseph Nye (1974 and 1977). Interdependence theorists emhasized the roles played by a diverse range of actors on the international scene: from fragmented nation-states, through multinational corporations, to dynamic international institutions. The interactions between these actors in an international context were viewed as important in influencing their preferences and desires in international negotiations. Thus, in international bargains and negotiations the history of previous interactions and the nature of current interdependencies were considered to be an important aspect of how actors weighed up the costs and benefits of further collaboration. Some of the insights of this approach have been incorporated into the thinking of scholars working within both the neo-functionalist and the intergovernmentalist traditions. In the current work of new institutionalist scholars (see below), a similar emphasis on historical interactions between actors and the development of norms and values can also be discerned.

Domestic Politics

By the late 1970s a number of scholars had tired of what were increasingly seen as unsatisfactory attempts to create 'grand theories' of European integration. The focus of their research shifted to particular aspects of the integration process and to examining how the tools of political analysis developed in the national context to analyse domestic political processes could be applied to the European level. This was perhaps the first step towards the study of the EC, and later the EU, as a system of governance. It was pioneered by scholars such as Wallace, Wallace and Webb (1977) and Bulmer (1983) who reminded other scholars of the important influence that domestic politics within the various member states continued to exert on decision-making processes and decisional outcomes. Crucially, Bulmer criticized the continued focus of scholars on the 'supranationalism versus intergovernmentalism' debate and urged them instead to examine linkages between the domestic and EC levels. Bulmer argued that scholars should not make the mistake of assuming that continued focus on the EC as a special kind of international organization precluded the use of important analytical tools developed in the domestic context.

Building on Neo-functionalism

The 're-launching' of European integration in the mid-1980s via the Single European Market (SEM) programme and the SEA prompted a new wave of theorizing about the nature of the integration process, as scholars sought to explain the new surge of integrationist advance.

The roots of what soon became a revised debate on European integration can easily be traced to the traditional divide between neo-functionalists and intergovernmentalists: were national governments the driving forces behind the integration process or not? Sandholtz and Zysman (1989), incorporating some of the key insights of the neo-functionalist approach, argued not. It was, they argued, the Commission acting as a policy entrepreneur, with the support and help of a transnational industrial coalition favouring the creation of a single market, that managed to persuade national governments of the benefits of collaborating to bring such a market about. Thus, the key role identified by Haas for the Commission and economic interests was reexamined. As well as drawing on some of the insights of the neo-functionalists, however, Sandholtz and Zysman also incorporated aspects of the 'domestic politics' approach and recognised the importance of the changing international and domestic climate in creating an opportunity for the Commission to act. Meanwhile, the critical role played by European business elites – in setting the agenda for the 1992 project, in mobilizing support, and in overseeing its implementation – identified by Sanholtz and Zysman (1989) and by Green Cowles (1995), represented a significant advance on Haas' original theory and introduced some new elements to the debate.

Liberal Intergovernmentalism

In contrast to Sandholtz and Zysman's interpretation of the SEA, Andrew Moravcsik (1991) drew on the tradition of intergovernmentalist thought and argued that the key determinants of the negotiation of the SEA were the inter-state bargains struck between the three most powerful member states: Britain, France and Germany. Moravcsik also stressed the importance of domestic politics, arguing that it was the convergence of national interests between these three states that had made bargains at the level of the 'lowest common denominator' possible. For Moravcsik, the activities of the Commission and the transnational industrial interests were peripheral to the real bargaining process which took place between the three big member states.

Moravcsik (1993, 1998) has since developed this argument further, stressing the important role played by the EU in helping national governments to sidestep the many constraints placed upon them by domestic societal interests. Far from national governments being caught up in a process that they cannot control at the EU level, national governments have, he argues, often used the EU as a scapegoat to give them more room for maneuver within their domestic political environment. Such compromises and bargains as are contained in 'historic' intergovernmental agreements are made largely because they benefit the key national governments involved in the negotiations; a series of side-payments are used to buy off the weaker member states.

Multi-level Governance

Developed initially in the context of his study of the structural policy of the EU, Marks' (1992) concept of 'multi-level governance' is now widely used to describe how the EU functions and to identify the various forces which contribute to the EU's continuing development as a system in which actors at various levels – local, regional, national, transnational and international – are intimately involved in a process of governance. In contrast to state-centred approaches to European integration, this approach emphasizes the fluid and open-ended nature of the EU system within which a broad range of actors have the potential to play an influential role.

A particular point argued by Marks in his original formulation of multi-level governance was that as subnational actors and the institutions of the EU, particularly the Commission, developed closer links with one another, it was possible that they would begin to undermine the dominant role of national governments within the EU policy process. This point has been debated vigorously by EU scholars, with many questioning whether multi-level governance has indeed led to a reduced role for national governments.

Comparative Politics and Public Policy Approaches

During the 1980s increasing attention was paid to developing empirical studies of the functioning of the EU and by the 1990s there was a major revival of interest in the study of the EU policy process, both to illuminate how the EU operates as a system of governance and to bring some of the insights from studies of public policy development to bear on the process of European integration more generally. Three major edited collections – by Sbragia (1992), Wallace and Wallace (1996), and Richardson (1996a) – encouraged the application of theories of comparative politics and those derived from the study of public policy at the national level to developments within the EU. Along with a host of academic articles, these have contributed significantly to the development of a new strand of thinking in the area of EU studies.

There is, for example, now an extensive literature on the role played by interest groups in the EU (Greenwood *et al.*, 1992; Mazey and Richardson, 1993; Greenwood, 1997). This has been used and developed by scholars examining the role of policy networks (Peterson, 1995) and epistemic communities (Richardson, 1996b) within the EU policy process. To what extent are decisions now taken by tightly knit networks of actors rather than simply by national governments? Having worked together within an epistemic community, do experts begin to develop a shared language or sense of priorities? These are amongst the many questions being explored by scholars working on the EU policy process.

Studies of agenda-setting, decision-making and the implementation and enforcement procedures within the EU policy process have all led to a more complete understanding of how the EU functions and the relative power of the various actors involved. A series of studies examining specific policy areas or the roles played by the supranational EU institutions have emerged. By the early 1980s, for example, it was increasingly recognised that in a treaty-based organization such as the EU, the role of law and of the European Court of Justice had a vital role to play in explaining both the process of European integration and the day-to-day functioning of the EU as a system of governance. Pioneered by scholars such as Weiler (1982) and Stein (1981), there are now few who would dispute the very important place of the study of law and the ECJ in the study of the EU. A number of scholars have continued to develop this strand of EU research and there is now a wealth of literature detailing the various ways in which law and the ECJ contribute to making the EU what it is today (see Weiler, 1991; Garrett, 1992; Burley and Mattli, 1993; Alter and Meunier-Aitsahalia, 1994; Wincott, 1995; Dehousse, 1998). Scholars have also sought to illuminate the role played by the Commission in the policy process as an agenda-setter (Peters, 1994; Pollack, 1995); as a promoter of a regulatory regime at the EU level (Majone, 1989; Cram, 1993; Bulmer, 1994); as a provider of leadership (Nugent, 1995); and as an entrepreneurial actor intent on enhancing its role and powers (Majone, 1993; Cram, 1997). Similarly, studies of the European Parliament have examined its power as an agenda-setter (Tsebelis, 1994) and illuminated its different influence across policy sectors (Judge et al., 1994).

The increasing understanding of the complex politics of the EU that has been yielded by these studies is both useful in itself and helps to answer wider questions concerning the key forces and actors which influence the process of European integration.

New Institutionalism

One of the most influential approaches derived from the field of comparative politics to be applied to the study of the EU in recent years is that of new institutionalism. In particular, the variant of new institutionalism known as 'historical institutionalism' has become an increasingly popular approach to explaining the functioning of the EU and to help understand the process of European integration.

Drawing on the work of scholars such March and Olsen (1989) and Thelen and Steinmo (1992), the starting-point for the insights provided by historical institutionalism is that institutions at the EU level do not simply provide an arena within which EU politics are conducted. Rather, they themselves play an important role in shaping the norms, values and conventions shared by actors involved at the EU level (see, for example, Bulmer, 1994; Armstrong and Bulmer, 1998). Although the national governments of the member states are recognised by historical institutionalists as key actors, responsible for major EU decisions such as treaty revisions, it is argued that the basis on which governments make such decisions is affected by the history of their participation in the EU. This notion of the importance of the history of participation is a key feature of historical institutionalism. Employing terms such as 'lock in' and 'path dependency', Pierson (1996), for example, seeks to demonstrate the constraints which have emerged over time on EU actors, and especially the autonomous actions of member state governments as a result of their involvment in the EU.

Building on Transactionalism

An interesting recent development in integration theory is a reassessment by a number of scholars of the contribution made by Deutsch and the transactionalist school to the study of European integration. For example, Sandholtz and Stone Sweet (1998) have advanced a theory of integration taking into account exchange (or transactions) between transnational actors, the role of supranational organizations, and the institutionalization of certain behaviours through the elaboration of rules. Thus, rather than simply examining the background conditions that are necessary for integration to occur – the main focus of Deutsch's work on the EU – Sandholtz and Stone Sweet also try to explain the process through which integration might be expected to take place. The focus in their work on interests, rules and supranational institutions is also reminiscent of the work of Haas and the neo-functionalists.

Concluding Remarks

Most academics would agree with Hodges (1972) that a successful theory of European integration should be able to *describe* the processes taking place at the European level, be able to *explain* why these particular processes have emerged in the manner and at the time they have, and be able to *predict*, under specified conditions, what processes and forms will emerge in the future. This is a challenge to which few approaches to European integration have managed to rise. It has become increasingly clear that the range of factors that must be incorporated into any convincing account of the integration process is daunting. Indeed, by the 1970s few scholars attempted to develop an all-encompassing 'grand theory' of European integration. Most began to focus more on the 'day-to-day' functioning of the EC as a system of governance, examining internal processes and institutional structures within the EC and focusing less on the 'nature of the beast'.

Since the early the 1990s, studies focusing on the EU policy process and the EU as a system of governance have mushroomed. At the same time, however, some scholars have attempted once again to generate broader theories of European integration while others have sought to integrate studies of the 'day-to-day' policy process with the insights of some of the 'grand theories' with a view to understanding the integration process more generally. As always in the study of politics, there are many competing interpretations of the same process and the same empirical information.

For those who study European integration and the EU, a vital task is thus to try to gather empirical information on the functioning of the EU against which the theoretical and conceptual approaches can be assessed. The following chapters of this book should help readers to integrate theoretical and empirical material and thus help them to develop a fuller understanding of how the EU has reached its current stage of integration and where it might be headed in the future.

References

Alter, K. and Meunier-Aitsahalia, S. (1994) 'Judicial Politics in the European Union: European Integration and the Pathbreaking Cassis de Dijon Decision', *Comparative Political Studies*, vol. 26, pp. 536–61.

Armstrong, K. and Bulmer, S. (1998) *The Governance of the Single European Market*. Manchester: Manchester University Press.

Bulmer, S. (1983) 'Domestic Politics and EC Policy-Making', *Journal of Common Market Studies*, vol. 21, pp. 349–63.

Bulmer, S. (1994) 'The Governance of the European Union: A New Institutionalist Approach', *Journal of Public Policy*, vol. 13, pp. 351–80.

Burley, A. and Mattli, W. (1993) 'Europe Before the Court: A Political Theory of Legal Integration', *International Organisation*, vol. 47, pp. 41–76.

Cram, L. (1993) 'Calling the Tune Without Paying the Piper? Social Policy Regulation: The Role of the Commission in European Union Social Policy', *Policy and Politics*, vol. 21, pp. 135–46.

Cram, L. (1997) *Policy-Making in the EU: Conceptual Lenses and the Integration Process*. London: Routledge.
Dehouse, R. (1998) *The European Court of Justice*, Basingstoke: Macmillan.
Deutsch, K. *et al.* (1957) *Political Community: North Atlantic Area*. New York: Greenwood Press.
Deutsch, K. (1966) *Nationalism and Social Communication,* 2nd ed, Cambridge, MA: MIT Press.
Garrett, G. (1992) 'International Cooperation and Institutional Choice: The European Community's Internal Market', *International Organisation,* vol. 46, pp. 533–60.
Green Cowles, M. (1995) 'Setting the Agenda for a New Europe: The ERT and EC 1992', *Journal of Common Market Studies,* vol. 33, pp. 501–6.
Greenwood, J. (1997) *Representing Interests in the European Union*. Basingstoke: Macmillan.
Greenwood, J., Grote, J. and Ronit, K. (1992) *Organised Interests and the European Community*. London: Sage.
Haas, E. (1958) *The Uniting of Europe*. Stanford: Stanford University Press.
Hodges, M. (ed.) (1972) 'Introduction' in *European Integration*. London: Penguin.
Hoffmann, S. (1966) 'Obstinate or Obsolete? The Fate of the Nation State and the Case of Western Europe', *Daedalus*, vol. 95, pp. 892–908.
Judge, D., Earnshaw, D. and Cowan, N. (1994) 'Ripples or Waves: the European Parliament in the European Community Policy Process', *Journal of European Public Policy,* vol. 1, pp. 27–52.
Keohane, R. and Nye, J. (1974) 'Transgovernmental Relations and the International Organisations', *World Politics*, vol. 26, pp. 39–62.
Keohane, R. and Nye, J. (1977) *Power and Interdependence: World Politics in Transition*. Boston: Little, Brown.
Lindberg, L. (1963) *The Political Dynamics of European Economic Integration*. Oxford: Oxford University Press.
Lindberg, L. and Scheingold, S. (1970) *Europe's Would-Be Polity: Patterns of Change in the European Community*. Englewood Cliffs, NJ: Prentice-Hall.
Majone, G. (1989) 'Regulating Europe: Problems and Prospects', *Jarbuch zur Staats- und Verwaltungswissenschaft*, vol. 3. Baden-Baden: Nomos Verlagsgesellschaft.
Majone, G. (1993) 'The European Community: Between Social Policy and Social Regulation', *Journal of Common Market Studies,* vol. 31, pp. 153–69.
March, J. and Olsen, J. (1989) *Rediscovering Institutions: The Organisational Basis of Politics*. New York: The Free Press.
Marks, G. (1992) 'Structural Policy in the European Community', in A. Sbragia (ed.), *Euro-Politics: Institutions and Policy-Making in the 'New' European Union*. Washington: The Brookings Institution pp. 191–224.
Mazey, S. and Richardson, J. (1993) *Lobbying in the European Community*. Oxford: Oxford University Press.
Mitrany, D. (1943; repr. 1966) *A Working Peace System*. Chicago: Quadrangle.
Moravcsik, A. (1991) 'Negotiating the Single European Act: National Interests and Conventional Statecraft in the European Community', *International Organisation*, vol. 45, pp. 19–56.

Moravcsik, A. (1993) 'Preferences and Power in the European Community: A Liberal Intergovernmentalist Approach', *Journal of Common Market Studies*, vol. 31, pp. 473–524.
Moravcsik, A. (1998) *The Choice for Europe*. London: UCL Press.
Nugent, N. (1995) 'The Leadership Capacity of the European Commission', *Journal of European Public Policy*, vol. 2, pp. 603–23.
Nugent, N. (1999) *The Government and Politics of the European Union*, 4th edn. Basingstoke: Macmillan.
Peters, B. (1994) 'Agenda-Setting in the European Community', *Journal of European Public Policy,* vol. 1, pp. 9–26.
Peterson, J. (1995) 'Decision-Making in the European Union: Towards a Framework for Analysis', *Journal of European Public Policy,* vol. 2 pp. 69–93.
Pierson, P. (1996) 'The Path to European Integration: A Historical Institutionalist Perspective', *Comparative Political Studies,* vol. 29 pp. 123–63 .
Pollack, M. (1995) 'Creeping Competence: The Expanding Agenda of the European Community', *Journal of Public Policy,* vol. 14, pp. 97–143.
Richardson, J. (eds) (1996a) *Policy-making in the European Union*. London: Routledge.
Richardson, J. (1996b) 'Policymaking in the EU', in J. Richardson (ed.), *Policy-making in the European Union*. London: Routledge pp. 3–23.
Sandholtz, W. and Stone Sweet, A. (eds) (1998) *European Integration and Supranational Governance*. Oxford: Oxford University Press.
Sandholtz, W. and Zysman, J. (1989) '1992: Recasting the European Bargain', *World Politics,* vol. 42, pp. 95–128.
Sbragia, A (ed.) (1992) *Euro-Politics: Institutions and Policy-Making in the 'New' European Union*. Washington: The Brookings Institution.
Schmitter, P. (1970) 'A Revised Theory of Regional Integration', *International Organisation,* vol. 24, pp. 836–68.
Stein, E. (1981) 'Lawyers, Judges and the Making of a Transnational Constitutions', *American Journal of International Law,* vol. 70, pp. 1–27.
Thelen, K. and Steinmo, S. (1992) 'Historical Institutionalism in Comparative Politics', in S. Steinmo, K. Thelen and F. Longstreth (eds), *Structuring Politics: Historical Institutionalism in Comparative Analysis*. Cambridge: Cambridge University Press pp. 1–32.
Tsebelis, G. (1994) 'The Power of the European Parliament as a Conditional Agenda-Setter', *American Political Science Review,* vol. 88, pp. 128–42.
Wallace, H., Wallace, W. and Webb, C. (1977; repr. 1983) *Policy-Making in the European Community*. Chichester: Wiley.
Wallace, H. and Wallace, W. (eds) (1996) *Policy-Making in the European Union*. Oxford: Oxford University Press.
Weiler, J. (1982) 'Community, Member States & European Integration: Is the Law Relevant?', *Journal of Common Market Studies*, vol. XXI, pp. 39–56.
Weiler, J. (1991) 'The Transformation of Europe', *Yale Law Journal*, vol. 100, pp. 2403–83.
Wincott, D. (1995) 'Institutional Interaction and European Integration: Towards an Everyday Critique of Liberal Intergovernmentalism', *Journal of Common Market Studies*, vol. 33, pp. 597–609.

PART 2

The Political System

2

The European Council and the Council of Ministers

FIONA HAYES-RENSHAW

The Council – a term used in this chapter to cover the entire Council hierarchy from the European Council to the Council Secretariat – is arguably the most important and probably the most misunderstood of the EU's institutions (Hayes-Renshaw and Wallace, 1997, p. 1). Three major events have shaped its composition, role and functioning since the early 1990s. The first was implementation of the Treaty on European Union (TEU), or Maastricht Treaty, in November 1993, which resulted most obviously in the Council officially changing its name to the Council of the European Union (*Official Journal*, L281(8)). The second was enlargement of the EU in 1995 (when Austria, Finland and Sweden joined), necessitating some adjustments to the composition of the various levels of the Council and the necessary threshold for achieving a qualified majority in the Council proper.

The third major event was the 1996–7 Intergovernmental Conference (IGC) – culminating in the Amsterdam Treaty – that sought to make the EU more effective, open, democratic and responsive to its citizens. With regard to the Council, the IGC considered the scope of qualified majority voting (qmv), the threshold for a qualified majority, and the weighting of votes among member states. Considered a 'bitter disappointment' even by some of its signatories (Duff 1997, p. xxvii), institutionally the Amsterdam Treaty was an adaptation to the past rather than a provision for the future in the sense that a number of Council-related problems were not addressed, consideration being postponed until the next IGC.

The Council Hierarchy

The European Council

From being a body originally created in 1974 as a forum for informal 'fireside chats' among the political leaders of the member states, the European Council has developed into a very different political animal indeed. Its meetings are now accompanied by the type of fanfare that it initially strove hard to avoid, attracting large national delegations and a huge media following. Because of the people involved and the importance of many of the issues being discussed, expectations surrounding meetings of the European Council are high; consequently, when no agreement is reached on a particular issue, European Councils are hailed by the watching media as a 'failure' and the very future of European integration is brought into question.

The 1990s saw the European Council play a central role in the construction of Europe because of its intimate involvement with preparations for enlargement of the EU, Economic and Monetary Union (EMU), and the institutional reform proposals discussed at the 1996–7 IGC. Great expectations for the work of the European Council grew steadily over the years as its stature and role steadily increased. Article D of the TEU required the European Council to 'provide the Union with the necessary impetus for its development, and to define general political guidelines', thereby giving it an integrating remit for the first time, and officially recognizing it as the motor of European integration, constituting the apex of the Council hierarchy for all areas of EU activity, both supranational and intergovernmental. The Amsterdam Treaty followed suit, confirming the European Council as the chief source of the impetus for the integration of Europe. With a certain malicious pleasure, Duff (1997, p. 128) notes that 'The European Council will be primarily responsible for making a success of the modest set of arrangements in the field of foreign and security policy. It is a diverting thought that they who are responsible for the Treaty of Amsterdam will now have to make it work.'

Paradoxically, the European Council is not legally an institution of either the EC or the EU. Rather it exists and acts in many respects as a 'super Council', composed as it is of the Heads of State (in the case of France and Finland) and Government of each of the member states, assisted by their Foreign Ministers and by the President and one other member of the Commission. Since 1988, the President of the European Parliament (EP) has attended the opening session of each summit to give the EP's perspective on the various agenda items. In recent years, Finance Ministers have also been part of national delegations, meeting in the margins of the European Council to advise their political leaders on major economic and financial issues, and to indicate their support for the conclusions reached.

The European Council convenes once towards the end of each presidency in the presidency country, and extraordinary sessions may be convened as and when the need arises. The heads of State and Government, with Foreign Ministers, meet with a minimum of officials – a total of about 40 people are in the room altogether, far fewer than the 100 or more attending in a normal Council meeting. Other members of the national delegations wait in adjoining rooms for news of what is going on in the meeting. They are briefed at intervals by relatively junior officials allowed into the room to carry messages to and from the principal participants, and by their respective political leaders during breaks in the meeting.

The intergovernmental nature of the European Council is more marked than that of the sectoral Councils. Indeed, the European Council is not subject to the decision-making procedures and rules that bind the Council. Thus, as a general rule, the European Council does not vote. Normally, it discusses an agenda item until a general consensus has been reached, even if this requires a certain amount of package-dealing, log-rolling and side-payments. Such an approach often results in general conclusions and declarations of principle, leaving the details to be worked out later at a lower level of the Council hierarchy. The more intergovernmental nature of the European Council also means that the EP is marginalized from its work, being at best consulted and at worst merely informed about its deliberations. Nor does the European Court of Justice (ECJ) have jurisdiction over the activities of the European Council.

Despite its elevated position in the hierarchy, the European Council is normally unable to take legally binding decisions; as a general rule, only the Council of Ministers can do so. This has not prevented the European Council from carving out a niche for itself at the very heart of the EU. Thus, for example, it was at the Copenhagen European Council in June 1993 that the official agreement to enlarge the EU to include the Central and Eastern European countries was reached and the conditions for their accession were agreed. Similarly, the starting date for accession negotiations was decided at the Luxembourg European Council in December 1997. To take another example, the final negotiation sessions leading to the Treaties of Maastricht and Amsterdam took place at the Maastricht European Council in December 1991 and the Amsterdam European Council in June 1997, respectively.

The Council of Ministers

Legally, there is a single Council, but in practice it meets in many different configurations (see Table 2.1). Each Council consists of 'a representative of each member state at ministerial level, authorised to commit the government of that member state' (Article 203, formerly Article 146, TEU). This usually means a minister from each of the member states with national responsibility in the area being discussed, but it also allows regional ministers to sit in Council, an important step for those member states, such as Germany, with powerful regional authorities. Each minister is supported by a delegation consisting of national officials, whose job it is to provide advice and background information during meetings. In the event that a minister is unable to attend a meeting, he or she may be represented by another member of the delegation, often the Brussels-based Permanent Representative, although the existing quorum rule demands that eight ministers be present in order for a legal decision to be taken. The Commission is represented as of right at every meeting of the Council (unless the Council decides otherwise), acting in effect as a sixteenth delegation in the Council's deliberations. The Council normally meets at its headquarters in Brussels, but in April, June and October it meets in Luxembourg.

The TEC states that the role of the Council is to 'ensure coordination of the general economic policies of the member states', and that the Council has 'power to take decisions' (Article 202, ex Article 145). As such, the Council may normally only act on the basis of a proposal from the Commission and after consulting, cooperating or co-deciding with the EP (the relevant procedure determines the method of voting, whether unanimity, simple majority or qualified majority). Relations between the Council, Commission and EP are consequently close, if not always consensual. In fulfilling its role as an EU institution, the Council is guided by its internal rules of procedure, the most recent version of which was adopted on 6 December 1993 (*Official Journal*, L304 (1)). The increasing complexity of the Council and its working methods may be gauged from the fact that, when the Council's original internal rules of procedure were first published in

TABLE 2.1 *Sectoral composition and frequency of Council sessions*

	1980	*1990*	*1997*
Agriculture	14	16	11
General Affairs	13	13	14
Ecofin	9	10	11
Fisheries	7	3	2
Budget	3	2	2
Environment	2	5	4
Transport	2	4	4
Social Affairs	2	3	5
Energy	2	3	3
Development	1	4	2
Education	1	2	2
Justice and Home Affairs	1	1	3
Internal Market	—	7	3
Industry	—	4	2
Telecommunications	—	2	3
Consumer Affairs	—	2	2
Health	—	2	2
Culture	—	2	2
Research	—	2	2
Catastrophe Protection	—	1	—
Tourism	—	1	1
Trade	—	1	—
Others	3	—	—
Total	60	91	81

Source: Annual Reports of the Council.

1979, they took up three pages in the *Official Journal*, whereas the 1993 version took up eight pages (Schloh, 1998, p. 102).

The number of meetings of the Council has increased dramatically over the years with the extension of the scope of the EC and then of the EU. Each presidency tries to schedule at least one meeting of every Council during its period in office. Three formations – the General Affairs Council (composed of the Foreign Ministers), Economic and Financial Affairs Council (ECOFIN), and Agriculture Council – meet on average about once a month; the others meet less frequently (see Table 2.1). There are differences in style and attitude among the various formations, due to the personalities involved and the issues being discussed, but proceedings tend on the whole to be tough and businesslike, aiming for an agreement including the largest possible number of participants.

There is an informal hierarchy among the Councils, the apex of which used to be occupied by the General Affairs Council. In recent years, however, ECOFIN appears to be in the ascendent. This may be due in part to the importance of the economic and financial issues raised by the introduction of EMU, but may also reflect the fact that certain Foreign Ministers seem not to take the General Affairs Council seriously. Some regularly fail to turn up, or merely turn up for the informal part of the meeting (usually a lunch), leaving their Permanent Representative to represent them at the formal meeting.

The Senior Preparatory Bodies

Given the impermanence of the Council – the fact that its many formations meet only intermittently and then only for a day or two, and that its members are busy government ministers often incapable of dealing efficiently or effectively with the technical details of the dossiers under discussion – the need for permanent administrative and preparatory bodies is obvious. Whereas the General Secretariat provides administrative support, most of the substantive work is done by working groups, whose work in turn is reviewed by more senior preparatory bodies that act as a filter for the Council.

The most senior and respected of these groups is the Committee of Permanent Representatives (COREPER) which, as its name implies, is a permanent fixture, both in Brussels and in the Council hierarchy. In fact it is made up of two committees: COREPER II is composed of the Permanent Representatives (senior civil servants of ambassadorial rank from the Foreign Ministries of each of the member states); COREPER I is composed of their deputies, also senior civil servants. Each committee has its own areas of responsibility, preparing the work of the relevant Councils. As a general rule, COREPER II tends to deal with the more political issues, while the more technical dossiers are the preserve of COREPER I. In preparing the work of the Council, COREPER uses the so-called A- and B-point procedure, according to which the Council's agenda is divided into two parts: issues appearing in Part A are understood to have been the subject of agreement at COREPER or even working-group level and can be adopted by the ministers without discussion; issues appearing in Part B, by contrast, have yet to be resolved and require the active input of ministers.

The Permanent Representatives and their deputies have seen their role and functions grow during the 1990s. With the construction of the pillar system under the Maastricht Treaty and the consequent extension of the Council's activities, COREPER's responsibilities increased almost overnight. The Amsterdam Treaty further extended the EU's competence, with the result that COREPER once again saw its role expand. At the same time, enlargement brought new members into what had traditionally been a small, all-male, elitist group. This meant a process of adaptation for both parties. The newcomers had to come to terms with the rules of the game and get to know the other members. Established members have also had to learn to work with the new members, some of whom have brought different philosophies and attitudes to the group.

The Permanent Representatives also head up the national delegations (Permanent Representations) in Brussels, which are staffed by officials from a range of national ministries who attend meetings in Brussels in their areas of competence and report back to their bosses in the capital. The number of ministries represented in the permanent representations has increased over the years in line with the expansion in the scope of the EU's activities, but a large number are common to most permanent representations.

Until the early 1990s, the EC's senior preparatory bodies consisted of COREPER; the Special Committee on Agriculture (SCA); the Article 113 Committee (now the 133 Committee), responsible for external trade and tariff negotiations and policy; and the Political Committee, which oversaw the preparation of all foreign policy issues dealt with under the intergovernmental system of the pre-Maastricht European Political Cooperation (EPC). The creation of the three pillars of the EU under the Maastricht Treaty brought the CFSP (which replaced EPC) and cooperation on Justice and Home Affairs (JHA) within COREPER's purview. However, the main preparatory work in these two areas is undertaken by the Political Committee for the CFSP and by the so-called K.8 Committee (formerly the K.4 Committee) for the JHA.

The Political Committee prepares the work of the General Affairs Council as well as the discussions and conclusions of the European Council on issues of foreign policy arising under the CFSP pillar. It is composed of the political directors of the foreign ministries of each of the member states, who oversee the work of specialized working groups. The working methods of the Political Committee have changed since the advent of the CFSP, bringing them more into line with those of COREPER and the Community method. For example, the Political Committee has started to hold most of its monthly meetings in Brussels, instead of in the country holding the Council presidency. Moreover, each national delegation dealing with CFSP matters normally now includes an official from the national permanent representation in Brussels, in order to facilitate coordination between EC and CFSP matters. A number of EC and formerly EPC working groups have been merged to form CFSP groups in order to avoid duplication of work, and the seating arrangements at Political Committee meetings have been altered to place the Commission opposite the presidency, as is the case in COREPER meetings (Hayes-Renshaw and Wallace, 1997, pp. 92–3).

The K.8 Committee, which prepares meetings of the JHA Council, is composed of senior officials responsible for various aspects of internal security from the national ministries responsible for justice and home affairs. Since its inception under the Maastricht Treaty, the JHA hierarchy has been criticized for being cumbersome and overcrowded. Steps to counter the inherent weaknesses of the third pillar were taken under the Amsterdam Treaty, with the title of the third pillar being altered, some issues being moved to the first pillar, and the three original steering groups being abolished (see also the section on the pillar structure below, and Chapter 13).

One other senior preparatory body that ought to be mentioned is the Economic and Financial (ECOFIN) Committee, which came into existence on 1 January 1999, at the start of the third stage of EMU, to assist the ECOFIN Council in its work. It is thought that this committee may eventually take over responsibility for preparing the Council's work in this area in the same way as the SCA has done for the Council of Agriculture Ministers (Nicoll, 1994, pp. 195–7).

The Working Groups

Every working day, hundreds of national officials from the capitals or permanent representations of the 15 member states of the EU converge on the Council's Brussels headquarters. They participate as experts and representatives of their national ministries in meetings of specialized working groups, which constitute the broad base of the Council hierarchy and the backbone of the entire system of European integration. It is here that most of the substantive work, which later allows ministers to take decisions in Council, takes place. There is no official register of working groups, although lists of working groups are drawn up from time to time by the Council Secretariat. In addition, each presidency draws up a list of the groups which will meet during its term in office, as it must provide a chairperson for each one, in addition to a national delegation. In any event, any list quickly becomes out of date, because some working groups are only set up for a short period or in order to deal with a particular issue, while others are permanent, and meet on a regular basis. There are about 150 working groups in operation at present, although numbers fluctuate.

The working groups are created by and answerable to COREPER. The individual members of the groups act as the representatives of their national ministries, discussing Commission proposals article by article, articulating the point of view of their member states and attempting to reach agreement among themselves on as much of the dossier as possible, covering both general and technical issues. Their aim is to reduce as much as possible the number of issues to be discussed at the higher (and more senior) levels of the Council hierarchy. The result of their deliberations is sent to COREPER in the form of a report that details areas where agreement has been reached and where problems remain, with some indication of the positions and concerns of the various member states, including any proposed amendments. These reports form the basis for discussions in subsequent COREPER meetings, where agreements reached at the lower level are normally accepted without discussion, and the debate continues on those points where the working group has failed to achieve a consensus. The dossier may subsequently be sent back to the working group by COREPER for further discussion on technical points. Representatives of the Commission attend all working group meetings to defend their proposal, which constitutes the negotiating text.

The working groups cover all areas of EU activity, and their number has increased in line with the new areas of competence assumed by the EU. No voting takes place in the working groups. Instead, discussion continues (normally in all the working languages with simultaneous interpretation) until such time as the chairperson judges that a consensus in favour of a certain outcome has been reached, or that nothing further can be achieved by continuing the discussion at this level. It may take one or more meetings to reach that stage. A certain esprit de corps is noticeable among working groups that meet regularly, allowing the delegates to get to know one another well enough to appreciate their differing points of view and to try to settle their differences amicably.

The Council Secretariat

A good book is waiting to be written on the General Secretariat of the Council, whose shadowy existence until the 1990s belied the importance of its contribution to the life of the Council in particular and the EU in general. One example of its influence is that officials from the Council's Legal Service provided over 90 per cent of the draft articles used as a basis for negotiation in the 1996–7 IGC (Stubb, forthcoming). The Secretariat and the role of its Secretary General were first officially recognised by the Maastricht Treaty, and are now enshrined in Article 202 (ex Article 151) TEC. The Secretariat is a staunchly apolitical body working closely with the Presidency to ensure that the Council fulfils its obligations under the Treaties, and that the work of the Council proceeds smoothly.

On a day-to-day basis, Secretariat officials provide vital logistical and technical support, keeping the work of the Council flowing by ensuring that deadlines are met, meetings are properly and efficiently organized and conducted, and a record of all proceedings is produced. Senior officials may also become involved in the negotiating process, in their capacity as assistants to the Presidency. The Secretariat organizes and documents the work of over 100 ministerial and over 200 subministerial meetings every year.

The Secretariat is divided into ten administrative units, known as Directorates General (DGs). One is responsible for administration; the others are organized on a functional basis according to the Councils they serve. The extension of the EU's activities in the aftermath of the Maastricht Treaty, combined with the 1995 enlargement, resulted in a major reorganization of the Secretariat. The scope of the External Relations DG was extended to cover CFSP, incorporating the formerly independent EPC Secretariat. The old DGs were split up to create a new DG dealing with the environment and consumer protection, and a DG covering economic and social cohesion. Finally, an entirely new DG was set up to cover JHA matters.

A large number of new posts was created in the Council Secretariat in 1995 to make room for officials from the new member states, each of which was entitled to a certain number of posts at all levels in the Secretariat. Despite this staff increase, the Secretariat is still small, consisting of about 2,500 independent international civil servants, recruited by open competition from among the nationals of the member states.

The Secretariat is headed by a Secretary General, appointed by the Council acting unanimously. Although there is no set tenure for the position, appointments tend to be long term (the Council Secretariat has had only four Secretary Generals since its inception). The position is also an increasingly important one, given the expanding responsibilities of the Council. The character of the Secretary General clearly affects how the Secretariat is perceived: a Secretary General who emphasizes the purely administrative aspects of the job – organizing meetings, taking minutes, translating, photocopying and distributing documents – would preside over a very different Secretariat to that headed by someone who believes that the Secretariat can and should play a more political role, getting involved in drafting, compromise-building and decision-making, in cooperation with and even on behalf of the presidency.

Respect for the perceived neutrality of the position of Secretary General is reflected in the fact that the Amsterdam Treaty provided that the Secretary General will become the High Representative for CFSP, and will assist the Council by contributing to both the formulation and implementation of policy. In so doing, the Secretary General will assist the President of the Council, and will work closely with the newly created post of Vice-President of the Commission responsible for external affairs. The Secretary General will also oversee the work of a new Policy Planning and Early Warning Unit for CFSP.

The Amsterdam Treaty provided for the creation of the post of Deputy Secretary General responsible for administration and internal coordination. These everyday activities have been somewhat lacking in the Secretariat in recent years, causing some overlap and confusion between different areas of Secretariat and Council activity. As a result of the Amsterdam Treaty, the Schengen Secretariat (consisting of about 60 people) has been incorporated into the Council Secretariat. With all these changes and increased responsibilities, it is clear that much more will be heard of the Council Secretariat in the future.

The Presidency

Originally, the office of the Presidency of the Council was viewed as an administrative device to ensure coordination at all levels of the Council's work, but over time its importance has increased in line with the growing global power and influence of the EU. Although more than a symbolic post, the Presidency does not confer a free hand on the holder; the Presidency must work within the constraints imposed on it both by its colleagues and by the system itself. As the formal representative of the Council *vis-à-vis* the other institutions and the outside world, the role of the Presidency has become more proactive and increasingly important in line with the increasing number of areas for which the EU is responsible.

The Maastricht Treaty added to the formal responsibilities of the Presidency by granting it the role of representing the EU for the CFSP. This has led to fears about the ability of prospective small and micro member states to cope with the demands of the Presidency, giving rise to unsettling discussions about relations between large and small member states in general. Thus far, the formal equality and balanced rotation of the Presidency have been maintained, and small member states wish to retain the status quo (Laffan, 1997, p. 300).

Each member state, no matter what its size, exercises the role of President for a period of six months, according to a pre-defined rotation system. Since the beginning of 1998, the rotation system has sought to ensure that the 'Troika' (the current, preceding and subsequent Presidencies who work together to provide continuity and coherence between presidencies) contains at least one larger member state, and no more than one new member state. Although it has not been possible to ensure this all the time, the new role foreseen by the Amsterdam Treaty for the Council Secretariat's Secretary General in the CFSP will undoubtedly help.

The question of the length of each Presidency is still a matter for discussion, with some larger member states proposing longer presidencies for themselves and regional groupings for the smaller member states. Other member states favour team Presidencies. The idea of electing a President of the Union for external policies has also been mooted. For the moment, the status quo remains, but the next enlargement may provide an opportunity for the question to be settled one way or the other.

For the incumbent member state, exercising the role of President means fielding two delegations for every meeting in the Council hierarchy – one to chair and run the meeting, the other to represent the national position. The Presidency is required to be neutral and impartial, so steps must be taken to distance itself from the national delegation, although this is not always easy, possible, or perhaps even desirable. As with all difficult jobs, experience counts. By 1998, each of the original six member states had exercised the role of president ten times, constituting a solid cadre of experienced officials. Those who have joined more recently are gaining experience quickly, and profiting from the many years' experience of officials in the Council Secretariat, who spend large amounts of time with officials and in the presidency capital in advance of the Presidency itself, briefing the officials whose job it will be to chair meetings and keep the Council in business for six months.

There are many contacts between Presidency officials and ministers and the EP both before and during the Presidency, and a report is presented to the EP at the end of the Presidency's six-month term. It has now also become commonplace for a new Presidency to invite the Commission to its capital for a first meeting with the government, in order to discuss the political objectives and priorities it wishes to pursue during its Presidency. Over the six-month period, a trialogue consisting of the Presidents of the Council, Commission, and EP meets regularly to attempt to iron out any difficulties that may affect the necessary cooperation between the three institutions. The Presidency therefore operates at the very centre of both the Council and the wider institutional system of the EU.

The Pillar Structure

One of the chief innovations of the Maastricht Treaty was the creation of three 'pillars' (a term which does not appear in the Treaty, but has become common usage): pillar one covering the European Communities; pillar two covering the CFSP; and pillar three covering JHA. In terms of the Council's work, the main difference between the three pillars, and the issues to be dealt with under each of them, is that issues falling within pillar one are subject to Community procedures – that is, proposal from the Commission, an input from the EP and other consultative bodies, a pre-determined and detailed decision-making procedure culminating in voting by unanimity or qmv, and judicial review by the ECJ. The work of pillars two and three, on the other hand, is intergovernmental, with the EP being largely excluded, decisions being taken by consensus or unanimity, and the ECJ being denied the ability to review the decisions taken.

The CFSP (pillar two), although intergovernmental and lying outside the framework of the EC, has nevertheless assumed some of the characteristics of Community decision-making. In principle, decisions on the CFSP are taken by unanimity; and abstention by individual member states does not prevent unanimity being achieved. Through the use of 'constructive abstentionism' that was established by the Amsterdam Treaty, a member state may permit a proposal to be adopted without itself being bound to apply it; if more than one third of the member states attempt to utilize this opt-out clause for a particular proposal, it will not be adopted. There is some overlap between the structures of pillars one and two, with the General Affairs Council, which forms the apex of the second pillar, also operating in pillar one. COREPER is responsible for preparing the work of the Foreign Ministers under the first pillar, but must avoid stepping on the toes of the Political Committee, which prepares the work of the Foreign Ministers when dealing with the CFSP. Continuity in the CFSP system is provided by the Council Secretariat and the Presidency.

While the second pillar is generally thought to have worked satisfactorily, there has been criticism of the third pillar. Cooperation in JHA has suffered from four major deficiencies: a lack of objectives, weak definition, a paucity of appropriate instruments and an absence of driving force (Duff, 1997, p. 19). The JHA hierarchy has also been criticized for containing too many layers, with the result that the Amsterdam Treaty provided for the abolition of the original three steering committees. Also under the Amsterdam Treaty, the third pillar was re-named Police and Judicial Cooperation in Criminal Matters, and areas such as immigration and asylum policy – hitherto dealt with under this pillar – were moved to pillar one, although they were to be subject to decision-making by unanimity for a transitional period of five years before the introduction of qmv.

Decision-Making and Voting

Decision-making procedures in which the Council is involved are explained in Chapter 7. Perhaps their most important feature (as regards the Council) is that the Council's ability to impose its views has declined over the years as the powers of the EP have increased. Many types of decision which used to be taken by the Council alone are now taken jointly by the Council and the EP. In consequence, close cooperation between the two institutions is required if there is to be effective EU decision-making.

Voting in the Council is a particularly vexed question concerning EU decision-making. There are two main aspects to this: the use of qmv rather than unanimity, and the mechanism of qmv itself – that is, the weighting of votes between the member states and the threshold for a qualified majority. In the early days of the EC, unanimity was the method by which decisions were taken in the Council, except in the Budget Council which has always operated on the basis of majority voting. The pre-ordained movement to qmv at the end of the transition period sparked off the infamous Empty Chair Crisis of 1965–6, which resulted in the Luxembourg Compromise (a de facto acknowledgment of a member state's right to exercise a national veto).

The Single European Act (SEA) of 1986 started the process of moving away from unanimity except for issues of major political and constitutional importance. The Maastricht Treaty extended the number of issues to be decided by qmv, and the Amsterdam Treaty continued this trend for matters falling under the first pillar. According to the Amsterdam Treaty, qmv may also be used for certain issues under the CFSP pillar, subject to the ultimate right of a member state to apply an 'emergency brake' to block a decision – a provision viewed by some as a revival of the Luxembourg Compromise under another name. Under the third pillar, the implementation of binding decisions, which themselves are to be agreed by unanimity, will be by qmv.

On the occasion of each enlargement, the voting mechanism was adapted to account for the accession of new member states, without altering the original, fundamental principles underlying it. Consequently, small member states continued to be overrepresented *vis-à-vis* larger ones and the threshold for a qualified majority remained at about 70 per cent of the total (see Hösli, 1996). A decision was taken during each set of accession negotiations as to the number of votes it was to be allocated under qmv, and the threshold for a qualified majority was altered in line with these decisions. For the best part of 40 years, this approach was followed without too much discussion.

In 1994, however, the qmv mechanism was the subject of much heated debate during the enlargement negotiations with European Free Trade Area states, with Britain and Spain demanding that the level of the blocking minority be retained at 23 votes, instead of rising to 26 as warranted by a purely mechanical adjustment of the system. The effect of such a decision would have been to raise the threshold for the formation of a qualified majority from 71 per cent to 78 per cent. The ensuing row resulted in the so-called Ioannina Compromise, under which the threshold for a blocking minority was unofficially raised to 26. It was initially intended that the Ioannina Compromise would remain in force only until the 1996–7 IGC, but because of member states' inability to agree on revised voting figures, it will continue in force, at Spanish insistence, until the next enlargement (Duff, 1997, p.133).

The debate over the threshold for a qualified majority exposed underlying tensions between large and small (or, as some commentators prefer to call them, more and less populated) member states which had always existed, but had seldom risen to the surface with such vehemence. Large member states were concerned that their relative weight was in decline, and that they could be outvoted by the smaller member states – particularly in light of prospective enlargements which would introduce more small and medium-sized member states into the EU (Laffan, 1997, p. 301). The weight of the large member states in the total population of the Community declined only slightly between 1957 and 1997 (from 87 per cent in the EC of six member states to 79 per cent in the Union of 15). The weight of their votes, on the other hand, had weakened considerably – from 70.59 per cent in 1957 to 55.17 per cent in 1997. In addition, a significant gap exists between the percentage of votes required for a qualified majority (71 per cent) and the minimum population required to attain this qualified majority (58 per cent of the total population) (Sauron, 1998, pp. 76–7).

The idea of re-weighting the votes allotted to each of the member states for the purposes of qualified majority voting is now firmly on the table. It was discussed during the 1996–7 IGC, but finally deferred, in part because enlargement was not thought likely to happen as soon as originally expected. The Amsterdam Treaty stipulated that there will be no change in the weighting of votes in the Council until the next enlargement. At that stage, a solution that compensates the five largest member states for giving up their right to nominate a second Commissioner must be found. This could entail either a complete revision of voting weights or a 'dual majority' requirement, which would mean a resolution would require both a majority of votes and a majority of population. Either way, a solution acceptable to all member states will be extremely difficult to find.

Today, there is more information on the use of qmv in the Council than heretofore, and the very fact of having recourse to it has changed the style of negotiation within the Council. Frequently, the aim is still consensus via compromise and drafting dexterity (Nicoll, 1994, p. 193), except in the case of the Budget Council, where voting is and always has been the norm; the use of qmv in other sectoral Councils, however, is frequently a case of last resort rather than a regular practice.

Transparency

The issue of transparency, while rumbling around for some time in Community affairs, only became politically important following difficulties encountered in the ratification of the Maastricht Treaty in 1992. Following complaints about the so-called 'democratic deficit' in the EU, it was agreed that 'something had to be done'. Member states moved swiftly to diffuse criticism of the Council's opaque working methods, culminating in agreement by the European Council in Edinburgh in December 1992 on a number of transparency measures. The three most notable measures are as follows:

1. *More information about voting in the Council is made available to the public.* Article 202 (formerly Article 151) TEC was amended to read: '. . . when the Council acts in its legislative capacity, the results of votes and explanations of votes as well as statements in the minutes shall be made public'. Details of votes cast are now published in the *Bulletin of the European Union* every month, with dissenting delegations being identified. The Commission's annual *General Report* also contains some general information on voting in the Council. Explanations of votes are included in the press release issued after each Council meeting, subject to agreement by the Council; this agreement is almost always forthcoming. Statements from delegations on legislative acts are included in the minutes of the meetings and may also be published in the press release, unless the Council decides otherwise (in other words there is a presumption that they will be published). The fact of having their voting records and statements published has made delegations more careful about what they say and do during meetings in the Council hierarchy.

2. *Members of the public are allowed to make written applications for specific Council and Commission documents.* Implementation of this decision has not been easy because the decision on whether to grant

public access to a document is made on the basis of a simple majority in the relevant Council. Given the differing traditions of and attitudes towards transparency in each of the member states, it is not surprising that some favour transparency at European level more than others. In fact, the existence of a small majority opposed to granting public access to Council documents makes it difficult to reach agreement on the matter. This negative attitude towards public access to Council documents may change in time as familiarity with the new procedures grows. Difficulties also arise because many requesters do not always know what documents are in existence, but a new *Register of Council Documents* produced by the Council Secretariat should help. Thus the procedure for allowing public access to documents, while laudable, is still experiencing problems and needs to be improved.

3. *Subject to a unanimous vote, some meetings or parts of meetings of the Council may be held in public (that is, televised).* However, the Council has refused to allow the televising of votes, preferring to show orientation debates on work programmes or major new legislative programmes, which tend to be less interesting or illuminating to those who want to know how the Council reaches its decisions. The argument made by the Council against allowing the televising of votes was that negotiations within the Council would be affected by the presence of television cameras, something which strikes a chord with at least one senior Commission official (Sverdrup, forthcoming).

While welcome as a first step in what will obviously be a long process, measures to increase transparency in the Council's working methods have been criticized for failing to live up to the spirit in which they were proposed, and for merely paying lip-service to the notion of transparency while doing little to increase openness in practice. Much remains to be done before the general public feels that it has gained an insight into what really happens inside the Council, but the Council has moved a long way in a short time for such a secretive institution, and should perhaps be given more credit for what it has achieved.

Flexibility

The notion of flexibility (or 'closer cooperation' as it is styled in the Amsterdam Treaty) is not new to the member states of the EU. It has existed in several guises over the years as a means of allowing some member states to proceed with a particular form of cooperation or integration in advance of the others. The Schengen Agreements are a case in point, and other examples include the partial membership of the exchange rate mechanism (ERM) and the UK opt-out from the social chapter of the Maastricht Treaty. The innovative aspect of the Amsterdam Treaty as far as flexibility was concerned was that it was accorded legal status and therefore institutionalized as a basic principle in the Treaties. A legal device now exists to prevent further integration being achieved only at the rate of the slowest or least integrationist member state. (From a different standpoint, the flexibility provisions may be viewed as a useful means for a recalcitrant member state to avoid being drawn into deeper integration in certain sensitive areas.)

A majority of member states may now be authorized by a Council decision to use the institutions of the Union to develop 'closer cooperation' between themselves in a particular area of first or third pillar activity. Decisions on the use of flexibility will be taken by qmv, but an 'emergency brake' may be applied by a member state to block the decision. No similar provision for flexibility applies under the CFSP pillar, because the new 'constructive abstention' procedure in pillar two make such a provision unnecessary (Government of Ireland, 1998, p. 29). It remains to be seen how much the new provisions will actually be used in practice, as certain areas will be excluded completely, and the use of the mechanism is circumscribed by a number of detailed conditions. It also remains to be seen how flexibility will affect the organization of the work of the Council hierarchy.

Conclusion

The 1990s have been a decade of change for the Council. Some of these changes have been outside its control, but have necessitated other changes on its part to deal with the altered circumstances in which the Council finds itself. The Council's membership has increased by one quarter, with all the adjustments which that implies. The areas over which it has competence have increased, necessitating the expansion and reorganization of the Council Secretariat, including the incorporation of two smaller secretariats (for CFSP and Schengen). The Council has seen greater legislative power being granted to the EP, demanding more cooperation between the two institutions at all levels. Despite these changes, the basic nature of the Council has remained unchanged; it is still the place where the member states' and the EU's interests meet and have to be reconciled.

The process of deepening and widening the competences and integrationist nature of the EU continued in the Amsterdam Treaty, even if it did not go as far as some member states would have liked. Indeed, the Amsterdam Treaty may well be remembered more for its missed opportunities than for the objectives it achieved. Because of a number of issues unresolved at Amsterdam, another IGC will be convened before the next enlargement in order to take what will inevitably be difficult decisions on the political and institutional reform of the EU.

In the meantime, there is a need to consolidate what has been achieved, and to gather forces for future battles – for battles there will be. Agreement was not reached on institutional matters in Amsterdam because the issues involved are of fundamental importance to the member states, and go to the very core of their beliefs. Until now, member states have been content merely to tinker with the original, basic mechanisms of Council voting when enlargement has necessitated it. The extent and implications of the next and subsequent enlargements are so far-reaching that tinkering will no longer suffice. It is likely, therefore, that some very unpopular decisions will have to be made, not least about the internal functioning of the Council. In the meantime, given its central role in the EU and the recent, far-reaching extension of its powers, interest in the Council and what it does is increasing. The Council would do well to harness such interest, in order to gain some public understanding of its work and impressive output.

Guide to Further Reading

The two main books on the Council are Hayes-Renshaw and Wallace (1997) and Westlake (1996). The principal arguments and conclusions of the former are summarized in Hayes-Renshaw and Wallace (1995). For insiders' views, see de Bassompierre (1988) – slightly dated but still relevant; van Schendelen (1996) – on the workings of the Agriculture Council; de Zwann (1995); and Lewis (1998).

References

Bassompierre, G. de (1988) *Changing the Guard in Brussels: An Insider's View of the EC Presidency*. New York: Praeger.
Duff, A. (ed.) (1997) *The Treaty of Amsterdam: Text and Commentary*. London: Federal Trust.
Duff, A., Pinder, J. and Pryce, R. (eds) (1994) *Maastricht and Beyond: Building the European Union*. London: Routledge.
Government of Ireland (1998) *Treaty of Amsterdam White Paper*. Dublin: Government of Ireland.
Hayes-Renshaw, F. and Wallace, H. (1995) 'Executive Power in the European Union: The Functions and Limits of the Council of Ministers', *Journal of European Public Policy*, vol. 2, no. 4, pp. 559–82.
Hayes-Renshaw, F. and Wallace, H. (1997) *The Council of Ministers*. London: Macmillan.
Hosli, M. (1996) 'Coalitions and Power: Effects of Qualified Majority Voting on the Council of the European Union', *Journal of Common Market Studies*, vol. 34, no. 2, pp. 255–73.
Laffan, B. (1997) 'The IGC and Institutional Reform of the Union', in G. Edwards and A. Pijpers (eds), *The Politics of European Treaty Reform: The 1996 Intergovernmental Conference and Beyond*. London: Pinter, pp. 288–305.
Lewis, J. (1998) 'Is the "Hard Bargaining" Image of the Council Misleading? The Committee of Permanent Representatives and the Local Elections Directive', *Journal of Common Market Studies*, vol. 36, no. 4, pp. 479–504.
Nicoll, Sir W. (1994) 'Representing the States', in A. Duff, J. Pinder and R. Pryce (eds), *Maastricht and Beyond: Building the European Union*. London: Routledge, pp. 190–206.
Sauron, J–L. (1998) 'Le Traité d'Amsterdam: une réforme inachevée?', Recueil Dalloz, 8e Cahier, Chronique, pp. 69–78.
Schloh, B. (1998) 'The Presidency of the Council of the European Union', *Syracuse Journal of International Law and Commerce*, vol. 25, pp. 93–119.
Stubb, A. (forthcoming) 'Negotiating Flexible Integration in the Amsterdam Treaty', in K. Neunreither and A. Wiener (eds). *Amsterdam and Beyond: Institutional Dynamics and Prospects for Democracy in the European Union*. Oxford : Oxford University Press.
Sverdrup, U. (forthcoming) 'Precedents and Present Events in the EU: An Institutional Perspective on Treaty Reform', in K. Neunreither and A. Wiener (eds), *Amsterdam and Beyond: Institutional Dynamics and Prospects for Democracy in the European Union*. Oxford: Oxford University Press.
van Schendelen, M.P.C.M. (1996) 'The Council Decides: Does the Council Decide?', *Journal of Common Market Studies*, vol. 34, no. 4, pp. 531–48.
Wallace, H. (forthcoming) 'Flexibility: A Tool of Integration or a Restraint on Disintegration?', in K. Neunreither and A. Wiener (eds), *Amsterdam and Beyond: Institutional Dynamics and Prospects for Democracy in the European Union*. Oxford, Oxford University Press.
Westlake, M. (1996) *The Council of the European Union*. London: Cartermill.
Zwann, J. (1995) *The Permanent Representatives Committee: Its Role in European Union Decision-Making*. Den Haag: Elsevier.

3

The Commission

LAURA CRAM

Scholars of European integration and of the EU policy process invariably ask a number of key questions: Who runs this process? Which actor or set of actors is most influential within it? To what extent are intergovernmental actors, particularly the member states, in control, or is it the case that supranational actors and institutions also have an important role to play? A considerable amount of attention inevitably focuses on the role played by the Commission. Is the Commission simply the servant of the member states or does it have a degree of autonomous influence at the EU level?

Allegations of fraud and inefficiency within the Commission in 1998–9, culminating in an attempted motion of censure in the European Parliament (EP) in January 1999 and, ultimately, in the mass resignation of the College of Commissioners on 15 March 1999, attracted extensive press coverage in the member states and bear testimony to the degree of public importance which has been attributed to this bureaucracy. What has, however, received less public attention has been the ongoing effort within the Commission to reform its internal management structures including those concerning financial controls, internal audits and the evaluation of resource management.

This chapter introduces the key debates about the Commission's place in the EU system and briefly reviews the changing role played by the Commission. It is argued that the Commission is best understood as a bureaucracy with a mission: a body charged by the founding treaties to promote the integration process. In order to carry out this mission it must have the support of the member states, the other EU institutions, the European public, and a dedicated and loyal staff. Since 1995, a crucial aspect of the Commission's attempts to retain the dwindling support of these four groups has been an ongoing effort to reform its internal structures and activities. This reform effort, and the problems it has encountered, is examined below.

Introducing the Commission

The term Commission refers to both the Executive Commission – better known as the College of Commissioners – and/or the Administrative Commission.

Composed of 20 Commissioners drawn from the member states (two from each of the five largest member states and one from each of the other states) but sworn to operate independently of them, the College serves a five-year term of office. Presided over by the President of the Commission, the College is the Commission's supreme decision-making body. Each Commissioner has his/her own policy portfolio, and is assisted by a cabinet (private office) composed of seven members plus support staff whose job it is to keep the Commissioner well briefed. The College meets weekly to discuss Commission business; these meeting are coordinated by the Secretariat-General of the Commission.

The Administrative Commission is commonly referred to as the Commission Services. It consists of just over 20,000 officials and support staff and is responsible for the day-to-day administration of Commission tasks and for generating proposals that are eventually considered by the College. The Administrative Commission is divided into 24 Directorates General (DGs), each dealing with a different policy area (for example, agriculture or competition policy) as well as 15 or so specialized services such as the Legal Services, the Statistical Services and the Inspectorate-General of the Services (IGS) (see Table 3.1).

Understanding the Changing Role of the Commission

The Commission plays key formal roles in the EU policy process: carrying out the tasks of initiating policy; creating legislation; representing the EU abroad; acting as a watchdog to ensure implementation of EU policies; and taking responsibility for the administration of Commission programmes. These are all roles specified for the Commission by member states in the various treaties establishing the EU. However, the Commission also plays important informal roles, including acting as broker of interests, gatherer of research and information, formulator of deals that are acceptable to the Council and the European Parliament (EP), and encourager of whistle-blowers to report failures to implement EU legislation. It is these roles that are most controversial and that raise questions about the relative influence of the Commission as a supranational actor. To

TABLE 3.1 *Directorates General and Special Services of the Commission*

Directorates General	
DG I	External Relations: Commercial Policy and Relations with North America, the Far East, Australia and New Zealand
DG IA	External Relations: Europe and the New Independent States, Common Foreign and Security Policy and External Missions
DG IB	External Relations: Southern Mediterranean, Middle and Near East, Latin America, South and South-East Asia and North-South Cooperation
DG II	Economic and Financial Affairs
DG III	Industry
DG IV	Competition
DG V	Employment, Industrial Relations and Social Affairs
DG VI	Agriculture
DG VII	Transport
DG VIII	Development
DG IX	Personnel and Administration
DG X	Information, Communication, Culture, Audiovisual
DG XI	Environment, Nuclear Safety and Civil Protection
DG XII	Science, Research and Development
DG XIII	Telecommunications, Information Market and Exploitation of Research
DG XIV	Fisheries
DG XV	Internal Market and Financial Services
DG XVI	Regional Policies and Cohesion
DG XVII	Energy
DG XIX	Budgets
DG XXI	Taxation and Customs Union
DG XXII	Education, Training and Youth
DG XXIII	Enterprise Policy, Distributive Trades, Tourism and Cooperatives
DG XXIV	Consumer Policy and Consumer Health Protection
Main Special Services and Units	
Secretariat-General of the Commission	
Inspectorate-General	
Legal Service	
Forward Studies Unit	
Joint Research Centre	
Spokesman's Service	
Translation Service	
Joint Interpreting and Conference Service	
Statistical Office	
Information Directorate	
European Community Humanitarian Office	
European Supply Agency	
Office for Official Publications of the European Communities	

Note: Situation in March 1999.
Source: Commission homepage <http://europa.eu.int/comm/dgs_en.htm>

what extent is the Commission simply doing its job, as specified by the member states, and to what extent has it expanded the roles given to it and become an influential actor in its own right?

Scholars from the intergovernmentalist school, for example, Moravscik (1993), argue that the activities of the Commission are largely inconsequential when it comes to examining major advances in European integration. Thus, intergovernmentalists argue that major treaty changes are the result of bargains struck between key member states, with the Commission playing only a marginal role. From their point of view, the Commission exists to aid the member states in their collective endeavours; should the Commission attempt to overstep the mark, member states will simply rein it in.

Over the years, there have certainly been a number of challenges and threats to the roles played by the Commission, and pressures have been placed on it by member states to curtail its activities. Developments in the institutional structures and decision-making processes of the EU have had a particular impact. So, for example, the establishment of the European Council in 1974 provided a new source of initiative for policies, thereby undermining the monopoly held by the Commission in this area. The introduction of the cooperation and co-decision procedures with the Single European Act (SEA) and the Treaty on European Union (TEU) enhanced the role of the EP in relation to the Commission. The new pillar structure introduced by the TEU allowed a parallel decision-making process to develop in the areas of the Common Foreign and Security Policy (CFSP) and Justice and Home Affairs (JHA), in which the Commission's role was marginalized. Meanwhile, the introduction of concepts such as subsidiarity and transparency have been, in considerable part, a response to constant criticisms of what has been seen by many to be an overactive Brussels bureaucracy. There is thus no doubt that it is possible for member states to restrict the range of activities delegated to the Commission.

For many observers, however, the debate is less clear cut. For neofunctionalists such as Haas (1958), the role of the Commission was always crucial to any understanding of European integration. Increasingly, scholars of the EU as a system of governance have supported this view, seeing the Commission as a body with a somewhat ambiguous role. As Usher (1994, p. 149) argues, 'as a civil service, the Commission would naturally give way to its political masters. As an independent political animal, the Commission is keen to extend its power and play a politically strategic role in setting the goals of the Community itself'.

There is now an extensive literature on the role and functioning of the Commission in theory and in practice (see, for example, Coombes (1970), Christiansen (1996, 1997), Cini (1996), Cram (1993, 1997), Edwards and Spence (1994), Majone (1993), Nugent (1995, 1997), Peters (1992, 1994), and Pollack (1994, 1997)). Scholars have variously argued that the role played by the Commission has to be given serious consideration. Based on observations of the activities of the Commission within the EU policy process, they have argued that the Commission's role is both complex and potentially of far-reaching importance.

The Commission, it is argued, has used its various roles within the policy process – for example, as 'agenda-setter' (Peters, 1994; Pollack, 1994) or as 'broker of interests' (Mazey and Richardson, 1994) – to maximize its range of competences and hence the degree of influence which it is able to exert. The Commission, it has been argued, acts as a 'purposeful opportunist' (Cram, 1993, 1997), and has learned to maximize its room for manouevre in the policy process while attempting to avoid direct conflict with the member states. As the Commission has matured as a bureaucracy (Christiansen, 1996), it has learned ever more sophisticated means of expanding its competences in areas where it is difficult for the member states to rein it in – such as ones popular with European publics or where there are no obvious costs to the member states. The long-term effects of these activities can be to lock the member states into commitments that they might not initially have chosen themselves. In this way, the Commission, it is argued, may have some influence on the process of European integration more generally.

This analysis should not, however, lead the reader to believe that the Commission can become complacent about its role in the EU system. On 15 March 1999 the Santer Commission (1995–1999) resigned in response to the findings of a Committee of Independent Experts charged, at the instigation of the European Parliament, to investigate *'Allegations Regarding Fraud, Mismanagement and Nepotism in the European Commission'*. The Committee focused in its report on the College of Commissioners and the 'question of the "specific responsibility" of the Commission as a body and of Commissioners individually in a range of specific cases' (Committee of Independent Experts, point 1.1.6). Although the Committee did not find that any individual Commissioners had gained from fraudulent dealings involving EU monies, it concluded that there were 'instances where Commissioners or the Commission as a whole bear responsibility for instances of fraud, irregularities or mismanagement in their services or areas of special responsibility' (Committee of Independent Experts, point 9.2.3). Although President Santer protested that 'on the basis of a tiny number of cases of fraud and malfunctioning, which did indeed merit criticism, the committee's report paints a picture of total absence of responsibility on the part of the institution and its officials' (Santer, 16 March 1999), the full Commission resigned unanimously, accepting collective responsibility for these failures.

As these events testify, it is thus not only the member states which the Commission needs to keep on side. Increasingly, close attention must also be paid to the expectations of other EU institutions (particularly the EP) and to the views of the European public. In seeking to satisfy these 'constituencies', the Commission must deal with a number of factors that present a potential threat to its credibility and effectiveness:

- The member states agreed at the Berlin European Council in March 1999 to put forward the former Italian Prime Minister, Romano Prodi, as President designate to replace Santer at the head of the Commission. However, the replacement of the post-March 1999 'caretaker' Commission with the new 'millennium' Commission (a complex task that is underway at the time of writing) will have major implications for the future credibility and efficiency of the Commission. The role of the EP is now crucial in the appointment of replacement members. While Prodi fought to hold off pressure from the EP for a rapid reappointment process (by May 1999), claiming that this would simply lead to an inefficient and opaque selection process, the EP has made its mark as a force to be reckoned with in this area.
- Meanwhile, the Commission continues to contend with its own internal dynamics. It does not always act in a consistent or coherent manner. The Commission is a 'multi-organisation' (Cram, 1994, 1997) with fierce internal conflicts (Christiansen, 1997). There may be in-fighting between different DGs or, indeed, between the President of the Commission and a particular DG (Ross, 1995). The process by which issues get accepted onto the agenda of the executive Commission is in itself complex, and requires a significant degree of policy entrepreneurship on the part of those within the various DGs. These complex internal dynamics mean that no simple solution to the criticisms of the Committee of Independent Experts is likely to be found.
- The contribution of the Commission's high-calibre staff – a staff traditionally committed to achieving the 'mission' of the Commis-

sion – has been crucial to the development of the Commission's role. Increasingly, however, there are problems within the staff body of the Commission and new pressures are constantly being brought to bear. The prospect of the EU expanding in size to over 20 member states, for example, presents logistical and political problems, such as how to integrate new officials without disrupting the career prospects of existing officials. Staff morale within the Commission is already low, with officials working under extreme stress, with promotion prospects being limited by rigid staff regulations, and poor procedures for planned career development. The high profile criticism of the College of Commissioners and, by implication, of Commission administrators has not helped to boost morale in any sense.

- Finally, the European public has sometimes contradictory views and expectations of the Commission. High profile coverage of Commission fraud along with the extensive myths about EU employment practice and salary packages, along with very public recruitment fiascos (*Financial Times*, 22/9/98) all contribute to public distrust of the Commission. Yet, as Commission activity extends into more areas of public policy, public expectations also increase and create new pressures for Commission action. This is even evident in areas like the Common Foreign and Security Policy (CFSP) where, although the Commission has few powers, the public still criticises it for being ineffective. How to straddle the gap between public expectations and the powers delegated to the Commission is thus a major dilemma.

To maximize its influence the Commission needs to maximize also its internal coherence and efficiency, as well as ensuring that it has the support and commitment of its staff. At the same time, as has just been noted, to maintain its range of powers the Commission needs to be seen to respond to the demands of the member states, of the other EU institutions and of the European publics. It was for this reason that, during the 1996–7 IGC, Commission President Santer sought to fend off an attack by the German Government on the Commission's right of initiative by declaring that the Commission would bring forward proposals for its reform before the end of his Presidency (*European Voice*, 16–22 April 1998, p. 9). The reform process that was initiated concerned every level of the Commission hierarchy, from the role of the President of the Commission, to the structure and functioning of the College of Commissioners, to the administration of the Commission services.

The involvement of the member states in the high-profile reform of the Executive Commission is examined below, but particular attention is then paid to the reform process within the Administrative Commission. This latter process has been rather overlooked in the literature. Yet as Cini (1996, p. 217) has noted, 'questions such as those affecting personnel policy and managerial weakness are as important if not more important than how many commissioners there are, the dividing up of portfolios, and the other "big" issues of the day'. This point was strongly reinforced by the findings of the Committee of Independent Experts who lamented the lack of internal controls within the administrative framework of the Commission. Indeed, one of the key objections from the outgoing President Santer was that he had 'hoped that the Committee of Independent Experts might have attached appropriate significance to the very substantial reforms carried out by this Commission since 1995 and the ambitious programme announced to Parliament last January' (Santer, 16 March 1999). Ultimately, the lessons which emerged from the reform process under Santer and how they are implemented may have fundamental implications for the future credibility and effectiveness of the Commission and, in the long term, for the debate concerning the relative importance of intergovernmental and supranational actors within the EU.

The Reform Process: The Executive Commission

The process of attempting to reform the Executive Commission predates the crisis over the Santer Commission and has involved the governments of the member states engaging in extensive and high-profile discussions and negotiations. Decisions involving changes to the functioning and structure of the College have very obvious political implications and also require treaty amendments. The Commission's role in this process is necessarily more limited than its role in implementing reforms of the Administrative Commission. Nevertheless, the Commission has been an active contributor to the reform process. Thus, in March 1997 the Commission adopted a Communication to the IGC on the 'Composition, Organization and Operation of the Commission' (Commission, 1997b). In this communication it highlighted four questions to be addressed in relation to the rationalization of the College, as well as stressing the importance of reforms within the Administrative Commission:

1. *The composition of the Executive Commission.* Debate on reform of the Commission amongst national leaders frequently focuses on the size of the College. This is a very sensitive political debate, and is one that is only likely to be exacerbated by the prospective enlargement of the EU to over 20 member states around 2004–5. In the Commission's own words: 'above a certain number of Members, the Commission's efficiency suffers. Below a certain number, its legitimacy suffers' (Commission, 1997b). The communication suggested that Commission membership should be confined to one representative per member state. A procedure should also be created to allow for a review of Commission membership above a certain number.

2. *The role of the Commission President.* The communication recommended that the EP formally approve the Commission President. This, it was argued, would give greater legitimacy to the office of the Presidency. The Commission also stressed the importance of the President's role not only in designating the responsibilities of the various members of the College but also in determining who those members should be.

3. *The organization of the Executive Commission and the allocation of portfolios and responsibilities.* On this point the Commission sought to mark out its turf in relation to the member states renegotiating the Treaty at the IGC. It was recognised that enlargement would require a reassessment of portfolios which took into account the political need for a balance between member states. However, the Commission communication specifically stated that, while a rationalization of portfolios was required to improve the efficiency and coherence of the Commission, this was not a matter for the Treaty but for the Commission's Rules of Procedure.

4. *The Operation of the Executive Commission and the number and functions of Vice-Presidents.* One of the Commission's suggestions for the improved functioning of the College was better use of the role of Vice-President. In particular, the Commission communication to the IGC proposed the creation of a Vice-President for 'External Affairs', able to act as the 'special interlocutor' of the Foreign Ministers. In addition, a Vice-President for 'Economic and Financial Affairs' was suggested and also a possible third Vice-President with special responsibility for 'Integration Policies and the Interests of Citizens'.

The Commission's proposals were discussed in the IGC and some were addressed in the Amsterdam Treaty. A decision on the thorny issue of the size of the College was postponed until nearer the time of the next enlargement, but the basis of a possible settlement was identified, with the five states which currently have two Commissioners each indicating that they would agree to having only one if the weighting of votes in the Council is readjusted in their favour. The role and status of the Commission President were bolstered by the Amsterdam Treaty: the EP is now required to approve the President designate (Article 214, TEC); the other Members of the Commission must be approved (if not chosen) by the President (Article 214); the Commission is to work under the political guidance of the President (Article 219); and the President is to have broad discretion in the allocation and reshuffling of tasks within the College throughout a Commission's term of office (Declaration 32). It is under these new rules that the 'millennium' Commission is to be appointed and function. In Declaration 32 the 'Conference also notes the Commission's intention to undertake in parallel a corresponding reorganisation of its departments. It notes in particular the desirability of bringing external relations under the responsibility of a Vice-President'.

The Reform Process: the Administrative Commission

The reform of the Administrative Commission initiated under the Santer Commission was formally launched in 1995 as a joint initiative led by Erkki Liikanen, the Finnish budget, personnel and administration Commissioner, and Anita Gradin, the Swedish Commissioner with responsibility for financial controls and the combating of fraud. The reform process comprised three key projects: Sound and Efficient Management (SEM 2000), Modernisation of Administration and Personnel Policy (MAP 2000), and Designing the Commission of Tomorrow (DECODE). Each of these projects is examined below. Together these modernizing projects sought to alter the management culture of the Commission by inculcating the principles of sound financial management; by clarifying the responsibilities of various actors within the Commission; and by decentralising certain aspects of internal decision-making, in particular those concerning the organisation and functioning of individual DGs which had hitherto been carried out by DGIX (Personnel).

While these very sensitive internal projects took shape, the renegotiation of the Maastricht Treaty during the 1996–7 IGC, together with discussions and conflict over proposed reforms to the Statute of Service for Commission employees, at various times overshadowed and even threatened to hijack the reform process within the Commission. Meanwhile, the whole discussion took place within the context of the Santer Commission's ethos of 'doing less but doing it better', which was intended to reinvent the Commission as a leaner and more efficient machine. It remains to be seen how much of this reform effort will survive the crisis and resignation of the Santer Commission. Certainly, however, each of the parallel reform developments have important implications for the overall success of the reform process and for the future role and structure of the Commission.

'Legislate Less to Act Better'

The theme of 'Legislate Less to Act Better' provided the backdrop for the entire restructuring process. Focusing on producing fewer proposals for legislation and improving consultation mechanisms, 'for the Commission this also means acting in a different way, in order to be more efficient in its role in a changing Europe' (Commission, 1998, p. 1). Simplification, recasting and consolidation were the buzzwords, each describing a method by which the Commission sought to streamline its legislative output. The Commission was amending its General Guidelines for Legislative Policy to ensure that the principles of subsidiarity and proportionality were fully incorporated. Meanwhile, a series of measures and task forces were put into place to ensure that streamlining and consultation took place.

The message from Santer was that the Commission had been spreading itself too thin. There was, it was argued, a need for the delegation of administrative tasks and for the definition of priority areas for action that would make for a leaner, more effective management structure rather than an unwieldy administration. This message came through clearly in the Commission's *Agenda 2000* declaration: 'managing a high level of integration will require a thorough re-evaluation of the Commission's executive and management functions and a change in its administrative culture' (Commission, 1997a: Part One, V).

Sound and Efficient Management (SEM 2000)

The first major management initiative of the Santer Commission, SEM 2000, was launched in 1995 under the guidance of Commissioners Liikanen and Gradin. The main aim of this project was to ensure that the Commission complied with the basic principles of sound financial management. Thus, issues of financial controls, internal audits, public procurement, monitoring and evaluation of resource management all came under scrutiny.

The first and second phases of the SEM 2000 project focused on internal Commission measures with the aim of making the real cost of political decisions clearer. This move was intended to prevent irresponsible policy formulation that ignores the financial rules in place. Phase 3 of SEM 2000, meanwhile, concerned partnership with the member states. Some progress concerning the relationship between the Commission's Financial Controller and counterparts in the member states as well as on the collection of 'own resources' was made in this area.

The response of Commission staff to these changes was mixed. While few were opposed to the SEM reforms *per se*, and indeed many aspects of the reforms were seen as an inevitable response to the pressures on public services everywhere, many were unhappy about the way in which the reforms were implemented within the Commission. While some aspects of the reforms were seen by Commission staff to have strengthened individual DGs, providing stronger central coordination and allowing some resource units to develop a better overview of how the individual DG functioned, in other respects the transition period was hard. Many officials felt that time was not always saved since new layers of bureaucracy and internal controls emerged to meet the SEM 2000 demands. Meanwhile, the top-down introduction of the SEM 2000 programme and continued questions about the real commitment of those at the top to better resource management and to more transparent decision-making also had some negative effects on staff morale.

Modernization of Administration and Personnel Policy (MAP 2000)

On 30 April 1997 the Commission approved the general principles of the MAP 2000 programme. These formed the second major step in the reform process. Spearheaded by Commissioner Liikanen and Secretary-General Carlo Trojan, the aim of MAP 2000 was to simplify administrative procedures and decentralize power over personnel matters and administration from DGIX to other Directorates-General and services throughout the Commission.

Phase 1 (1997/98) of the MAP 2000 project was set up to simplify in-house administrative procedures and to give responsibilities over these matters to services other than DGIX. To achieve this, 25 specific measures were adopted. These delegated some very important powers to the DG level: power over certain resources; flexibility over the DG's organization chart; responsibility for internal staff mobility within DGs; the power to recruit auxiliary staff; some resources for staff training; the right to draw up a schedule of vacant posts; and direct on-line management of leave and absences. The proposals also aimed to speed up the payment of expense claims from within and outside the DGs. Equally, however, the measures transferred a number of responsibilities to the DGs. For example, for mail sorting; for reducing the use of translation and interpreting services; and for reducing the cost of telecommunications. At the same time, officials were encouraged to make more use of Europa (the Commission's internet server); Europa Plus (the Commission's intranet); and electronic mail to reduce the paper trail within the Commission. Finally, department and staff representatives were urged to assume a greater responsibility in the area of social dialogue within the Commission.

This last point is not insignificant. As with the SEM 2000 project, the MAP 2000 reforms were felt by many working on the ground in the Commission to be imposed from on high with insufficient staff involvement or consultation. It proved impossible to obtain the agreement of staff unions. Although some very significant powers have been decentralised as a result of the MAP 2000 reforms, many Commission staff found the reform process to be poorly handled and somewhat disempowering. Meanwhile, the rather clumsy handling of parallel discussions over the reform of the staff regulations only served to exacerbate this problem (see below).

Phase 2 (1998/99) of the MAP 2000 project aimed to ensure that the vertical delegation of responsibility within individual DGs was carried out and that increased responsibility for the management of administrative resources was fully transferred to individual DGs. The internal discord which had been generated during the introduction of Phase 1 reforms led to an increased focus on staff involvement in Phase 2.

Five high-level reflection groups, established to assess the necessary next steps for MAP 2000, produced a joint report in early 1998 on how to move reform forward, suggesting that a coordinated consultative effort was required to elicit the participation of the Commission staff in the process. By that time, however, the leaking of a confidential management document advocating far-reaching changes in a whole range of staffing issues (the so-called Caston paper) made something of a mockery of the stated commitment to staff involvement in and empowerment by the reform process, and threatened to derail the MAP 2000 project altogether. Learning that such management discussions were taking place 'in secret' only added to the suspicions of many officials about the real objectives of the new tranche of reforms in MAP 2000 and posed a serious threat to the continuation of the project.

Designing the Commission of Tomorrow (DECODE)

The third key aspect of the reform process took the form of a screening exercise known as DECODE, carried out in 1998. A project very much driven by Trojan, the screening exercise was intended to provide information about the variety of tasks carried out within the various DGs and services, the ways and means by which these tasks were performed, and the current deployment of resources within the Commission. This data was to provide a basis for future decisions about the reorganization of Commission services, the priorities to be pursued by the Commission, the possible delegation of certain administrative tasks to specialist agencies, and the potential creation of common services cutting across traditional sectoral boundaries within the Commission. Proposals contained in the final report were to be implemented by late 1999, leaving the new improved Commission in place for the start of 2000.

Given the delicate political context in which this project was launched – just as Commission staff were being subjected to a glut of top-down reforms – a key feature of the DECODE project was the effort made by Trojan to take the Commission staff with him. A number of detailed messages were circulated to all Commission employees explaining the reasoning behind the project, how it was to be implemented and who was directly involved in the screening exercise. Inevitably, some scepticism persisted within the staff body. Some asked whether this screening exercise would reflect the outcome of a truly consultative process or whether the results of the exercise would simply be used to rationalize a set of priorities already agreed by some in the higher echelons of the Commission. In the event, the resignation of the Santer Commission raises much bigger questions about whether the results of the exercise will be used at all or whether they will be forgotten as a new reform effort is launched by the new Commission.

Reform of the Staff Statute of Service

Deliberations about the role and functioning of the Commission at the IGC did not focus solely on the Executive Commission. Fundamental debates concerning the efficiency of the Commission provoked Santer to declare that the Commission would also bring forward proposals for reform of the staff statute before his Commission left office. This was a clear case of 'reform or be reformed', and placed the difficult issues of employment rights, salaries, pensions and job security squarely on the agenda.

Having recently criticized the implementation of the SEM 2000 and MAP 2000 projects for lack of staff consultation, many staff and the staff unions were wary of these proposed reforms. The Statute of Service is something of a bible for European civil servants. Drawn up in 1962, the staff regulations detail the rights and responsibilities of Commission staff (Cini, 1996, p. 122). The regulations not only specify the pay scales, pension and insurance schemes, and social benefits due to Commission staff, but also lay out the career structure within the administration. 'Although they have been modified almost 80 times over the years, they still essentially reflect the rigid structure created in a very different era when there were just six member states' (*European Voice*, 16–22 April 1998, p. 9). Reform may have been inevitable, even overdue; but it needed to be tackled with some sensitivity.

Even if handled well, the timing of this debate could hardly have been worse. Already wearied by the imposition of the SEM 2000 and MAP 2000 reforms, Commission staff were also becoming nervous about the ten-yearly discussions with member states regarding the periodic adjustments of the salaries and employment conditions of all European civil servants. This process, known as the 'Method', is to take place in the year 2000. In this context it is perhaps unsurprising that the inept handling of the debate over the staff regulations, culminating in the leaking of the Caston paper, led to a Commission staff strike on 30 April 1998 – the first strike of Commission officials since 1991. It was less the content of the report than the discovery by staff and unions that Caston had been working on this document for six months 'in secret' that provoked the strike (*European Voice*, 7–13 May 1998, p. 6).

Conclusion: The Reform Process and the Future of the Commission

With the collapse of the Santer Commission, reform of the Commission has become one of the priority issues in debates over the 'millennium' Commission and is likely to be a key feature of the next IGC. A major question is whether the lessons of the reform process reviewed here will be learned and built upon or whether they will simply be swept aside as a new tranche of reforms are launched and the new broom seeks to sweep the Commission clean. For all the Santer Commission's failings, it is ironic that the Commission which sought to introduce some of the most far-reaching and unsettling internal management reforms should be remembered only for its failures in this respect. There are a number of lessons which new reform efforts might usefully learn from the attempts at Commission reform reviewed in this chapter.

First, implementation of the reforms was not easy. Although the 1996/97 IGC reached agreement on some reform of the functioning of the College, the big issue – the future size of the College – was left unresolved. The inability of member states to reach a deal on this issue, which was closely tied to the issue of national voting strengths in the Council, was one of the main failures of the IGC. Meanwhile, the various internal projects to reform the Administrative Commission were disrupted by a variety of events – for example, the leak of the Caston paper and a Commission staff strike. Reforms were plagued by low staff morale and the feeling that they were largely an imposition from above. In the long term, this needs to be dealt with as human resources are vital to the successful functioning of the Commission. Resolution of these internal administrative reforms will continue to be an important development and one that will be watched closely by scholars interested in the extent to which the Commission is able to act as an autonomous actor within the EU.

Second, reform of the Commission must satisfy a wide range of audiences and competing demands: to appear more transparent and responsive to citizens; to decentralise administrative decision-making; to improve staff skills, motivation and career development; and to become more efficient. Member states, the EU institutions, the European public, and Commission staff (administrators as well as managers) need to be satisfied by these reforms. Even if the reforms are considered to be a success by the standards of one group, they are unlikely to please everyone. For example, a better public profile involving bringing the Commission closer to the people of Europe may not be welcomed by all of the member states. Similarly, a revised career structure may appeal to bright, ambitious officials but is unlikely to thrill 'job for lifers'. There is a real risk of reform overload which could have a further negative effect on staff morale, particularly if the restructured Commission is not a noticeable improvement on the status quo. In short, to realise the aims of the restructuring process, the Commission needs not only to take its own staff along with it but also the European public, the other EU institutions and the member state governments.

Finally, member states must ask themselves what they really want from the Commission. A reformed Commission may expose some of the anomalies in the existing Commission/member state relationship which some member states might prefer to remain obscured. Dinan (1997, p. 197) recommended that the Commission 'should attempt to educate public opinion about the stranglehold that member states have on key aspects of the Commission's structure and staff policy'. This is precisely what had begun to happen. For example, one Commission communication stated that 'recent experience has shown that the desire to simplify, repeatedly expressed by European Ministers, is sometimes at odds with their attitude to simplification proposals on the table' (Commission, 1998, p. 5). This whole process raises questions. Do member states really want a leaner more efficient Commission or does the current ambiguity and relative inefficiency rather suit them?

Guide to Further Reading

For a detailed account of the role and functions of the European Commission, see Nugent (1999). Cini (1996) provides a useful overview of the functions and history of the Commission as well as of its organisations, internal processes and management. There are a number of good edited collections covering various aspects of the Commission's role: see for example, Edwards and Spence (1994) and Nugent (1997). For detailed discussions on the relative autonomy of the Commission, see Cram (1993, 1997) and Pollack (1994, 1997).

References

Christiansen, T. (1996) 'A Maturing Bureaucracy', in J. Richardson (ed.), *European Union: Power and Policy-Making*. London: Routledge, pp. 77–95.

Christiansen, T. (1997) 'Tensions of European Governance: Politicized Bureaucracy and Multiple Accountancy in the European Commission'. *Journal of European Public Policy*, vol. 4, pp. 73–90.

Cini, M. (1996) *The European Commission*. London: Macmillan.

Commission (1997a) Agenda 2000, in *Bulletin of the European Union*, Supplement 5/97.

Commission (1997b) Commission Communication to the IGC, 5 March 1997, in *Bulletin of the European Union*, 3/1997: point 1.1.

Commission (1998) *Legislate Less to Act Better: The Facts* (COM (1998) 345 final).

Committee of Independent Experts (1999) *First Report on Allegations Regarding Fraud, Mismanagement and Nepotism in the European Commission* (15 March 1999). Brussels: European Commission.

Coombes, D. (1970) *Politics and Bureaucracy in the European Community*. London: Unwin.

Cram, L. (1993) 'Calling the Tune Without Paying the Piper? Social Policy Regulation: The Role of the Commission in European Union Social Policy', *Policy and Politics*, vol. 21, pp. 135–46.
Cram, L. (1994) 'The European Commission as a Multi-Organization: Social Policy and IT Policy in the EU', *Journal of European Public Policy*, vol. 1, pp. 195–217.
Cram, L. (1997) *Policy-Making in the European Union: Conceptual Lenses and the Integration Process*. London: Routledge.
Dinan, D. (1997) 'The Commission and the Reform Process', in G. Edwards and A. Pijpers (eds), *The Politics of European Treaty Reform*. London: Pinter pp. 188–211.
Drake, H. (1995) 'Political Leadership and European Integration: The Case of Jacques Delors', *West European Politics*, vol. 18, pp. 140–60.
Edwards, G. and Spence, D. (eds) (1994) *The European Commission*. Harlow: Longman.
Haas, E. (1958) *The Uniting of Europe*. Stanford: Stanford University Press.
Majone, G. (1993) 'The European Community: Between Social Policy and Social Regulation', *Journal of Common Market Studies*, vol. 31, pp. 153–69.
Mazey, S. and Richardson, J. (1994) 'The Commission and the Lobby', in G. Edwards and D. Spence (eds), *The European Commission*. London: Longman pp. 169–87.
Moravcsik, A. (1993) 'Preferences and Power in the European Community: A Liberal Intergovernmentalist Approach', *Journal of Common Market Studies*, vol. 31, pp. 473–524.
Nugent, N. (1995) 'The Leadership Capacity of the European Commission', *Journal of European Public Policy*, vol. 2, pp. 603–23.
Nugent, N. (ed.) (1997) *At the Heart of the Union: Studies of the European Commission*. Basingstoke: Macmillan.
Nugent, N. (1999) *The Government and Politics of the European Union*, 4th edn. Basingstoke: Macmillan .
Peters, B. G. (1994) 'Agenda-Setting in the European Community', *Journal of European Public Policy*, vol. 1, pp. 9–26.
Peters, B. G. (1992) 'Bureaucratic Politics and the Institutions of the European Union', in A. Sbragia (ed.), *Euro-Politics: Institutions and Policy-Making in the 'New' European Union*. Washington: The Brookings Institution pp. 75–122.
Pollack, M. (1994) 'Creeping Competence: The Expanding Agenda of the European Community, *Journal of Public Policy*, vol. 14, pp. 97–143.
Pollack, M. (1997) 'Delegation, Agency and Agenda Setting in the European Community', *International Organization*, vol. 51, pp. 99–134.
Richardson, J. (1993) 'Doing Less by Doing More: British Government 1979–93', in *A New Role for the State?*. Vienna: Bundesministerium fur Finanzen (HG).
Ross, G. (1995) *Jacques Delors and European Integration*. Oxford: Polity Press.
Santer, J. (1999) 'Statement by President Jacques Santer the Day After the Resignation of the Members of the Commission', 16 March. Brussels: European Commission.
Usher, J. (1994) 'The Commission and the Law' in G. Edwards and D. Spence, (eds), *The European Commission*. London: Longman pp. 146–68.

4

The European Parliament

KARLHEINZ NEUNREITHER

In terms of size, internal structure and functioning, composition, and above all political role, the European Parliament (EP) has changed more radically than any other EU institution in recent years. Although this chapter will concentrate on the evolution of the EP since the beginning of the 1990s, the EP's emerging legislative role must be traced back to 1987, when implementation of the Single European Act (SEA) greatly increased the EP's involvement in EU decision-making. Both the Treaty on European Union (TEU) and the Amsterdam Treaty continued that trend, which has affected not only inter-institutional relations but also internal EP political dynamics.

The TEU and Amsterdam Treaty revisions, together with the accession of Austria, Finland and Sweden in 1995, are the major events that changed the European Parliament's role in the 1990s. But it would be erroneous to limit our approach to a number of modifications of legal texts. Often, links between seemingly isolated elements are equally important. Thus the EP receives more attention from the media and from lobbyists because of its increasing legislative power; the EP uses budgetary prerogatives to try to shape policy; and committees of inquiry are changing the EP's relationship with the Commission. Clearly, the EP's political role is complex, and even in a relatively short chapter it should be seen as such.

This chapter will explore the evolution of the EP's functions, composition, rhythm of work, and internal structures. European elections, the mandate of Europarliamentarians (MEPs), and MEPs' links with European citizens and with national and transnational parties will also be discussed.

Legislative Powers

The EP is now commonly regarded as a co-legislator with the Council. Yet this is a relatively recent development: for many years, the EP was excluded from effective participation in the legislative process. Indeed, Jean Monnet's original design for the European Coal and Steel Community (ECSC) included only two decision-making institutions: the High Authority (predecessor of the Commission) and the Council. The Assembly (now the EP) and the Court were intended to provide political and legal control, but nothing more. The Treaty of Rome that established the European Economic Community (EEC) gave the EP only a vague and virtually powerless right to deliver opinions on certain legislative proposals, which the Council could accept or reject. This was the so-called consultation procedure.

Although the legislative system evolved slowly, with the EP trying above all to force the Commission to incorporate parliamentary amendments into the Commission's own proposals, the original design prevailed for many years. Even the SEA left the basic provisions unchanged: the EP would exercise the powers of 'deliberation and control' conferred upon it by the Treaty (original Article 137 TEC). In other words, the cooperation procedure that was created by the SEA and that gave the EP greater legislative influence was not specifically mentioned as an additional and new category of parliamentary power (original Article 149, changed by the TEU to Article 198c, now Article 252, TEC). It was not until the TEU that the old Monnet restrictions were finally lifted with the introduction of the co-decision procedure (Article 251, ex Article 189b, TEC). Characteristically, the Amsterdam Treaty did not enumerate the EP's new legislative functions either, dropping the words 'deliberation and control' and declaring instead that the EP exercises the powers 'conferred upon it by this Treaty' (Article 189, ex 137, TEC). It is consistent with this approach that the terms 'co-decision procedure' and 'cooperation procedure' are not formally mentioned in the EC Treaty. Instead, they are timidly spoken of as the 'procedure referred to in Article 251' (ex Article 189b) or 'Article 252' (ex Article 189c).

Despite the reluctance of some member states to increase the EP's powers, treaty reforms have triggered the most important changes in the EP's role during the last decade. The effects of treaty reform on the EU institutional balance, and also within the EP itself, have been enormous. The SEA provided for an enhanced form of parliamentary participation – the cooperation procedure – in a limited number of areas, mostly linked to the single market programme. Under the procedure, the EP was asked to deliver opinions on the draft legislative proposals of the Commission, just as in the classical, relatively powerless, consultation procedure. The Council would then deliberate, possibly taking into account EP amendments. When it agreed on texts – by adopting 'common positions' – the Council sent proposals back to the EP for a second reading. The EP could amend or reject texts, but only by a majority of all its members, whether present or not.

To put this innovation in perspective: the EP now has 626 members; 314 MEPs therefore constitute an absolute majority. If, at a particular time, only 80 per cent of MEPs – that is, about 500 of them – are present in the chamber, almost 63 per cent of that number would have to vote in favour in order to be able to amend or reject a common position; if only 70 per cent are present – that is, about 440 MEPs – almost 72 per cent would have to vote in favour in order to be able to amend or reject a common position. In other words, the cooperation procedure could well have left the EP with no influence whatsoever, because the EP could rarely form such relatively large majorities. Once it amended a common position in the second reading stage, the EP would ask the Commission formally to incorporate its amendments into the Commission's own proposal. The Council could then adopt the final text, by qualified majority vote (qmv) if it did not deviate from the Commission's text, by unanimity otherwise.

For the EP, this new procedure presented perhaps the most serious institutional challenge in its history. For many years, and especially since the advent of direct elections in 1979, the EP had sought a gradual increase in its legislative role. Were it now unable to form the necessary majorities, those who had opposed an increase in its role would certainly have seen their convictions confirmed. Thus the introduction of the cooperation procedure, limited in scope and in influence though it was, forced the EP to undertake a major revision of its functioning. The ensuing TEU and Amsterdam reforms, which included important legislative changes – notably the introduction and enhancement of co-decision – built on the internal mechanisms and procedures put in place by the EP in the post-SEA period.

The EP needed to change in at least three ways to meet the challenge presented by the new legislative procedure established by the SEA. Firstly, it had to develop much closer cooperation between political groups, and above all between the two largest of them, the Party of the European Socialists (PES) and the European People's

Party (EPP) or Christian Democrats, who together accounted for about 55–60 per cent of the EP's membership. Secondly, it had to react more rapidly to legislative proposals (the EP had only three months to respond to the Council's common position, a time much too short to elaborate a completely new approach on a complex subject, but just long enough to see how the Council treated the EP's amendments from the first reading and to decide how best to proceed). Thirdly, it had to exert greater pressure on the Commission to convince it to take over as many EP amendments as possible, thus forcing the Council into the difficult position of being able to reaffirm its common position only by unanimity.

The key word in this new situation was 'cooperation', both internally and in dealings with other institutions. The ambitious single market programme included a considerable increase in legislative work in order to meet the 1992 deadline. For the first time, annual legislative programmes were presented, including an indicative timetable for proposals in various sectors. The EP introduced a system of monthly updating of work in progress in its various committees. Most proposals were assigned not just to a single standing committee, but to other relevant committees as well. This added to the complexity of coordination, the bulk of which was done by the Conference of Committee Chairmen.

The transformation of the EP into a cooperative working institution that could handle complicated procedures impressed the other institutional actors. Thus it was in the immediate aftermath of the SEA that the new role of the EP was shaped, in terms of both internal adaptation and external recognition. These were years of sowing: the Maastricht and Amsterdam treaties were the harvest. The major innovation of the Maastricht Treaty – the introduction of co-decision – meant that if the EP amended or rejected a legislative proposal the Council could no longer override the EP. In the case of amendments, the Council could either accept them or try to change them through negotiation with the EP.

As a result, a true bicameral system came into existence in respect to the making of EU legislation. As in most bicameral systems – be they the US Congress or the German Federal Parliament – a solution would have to be found if the two chambers were deadlocked. The institutional solution in the EU consists of a conciliation committee: a joint adhoc committee composed of 15 members from the Council (one for each member state) and an equal number of MEPs. As Neill Nugent shows in Chapter 7, where the co-decision procedure is described in detail, this committee meets when the Council feels unable to adopt a position taken by the EP in its second reading. Its only task is to provide a compromise text that has to be agreed upon by each of the delegations, and then approved by the two institutions (without possibility of further amendment). If either the Council or the EP fail to agree, the legislative proposal fails. Despite a number of procedural criticisms, such as lack of confidentiality and occasional differences of opinion between the EP delegation and the EP as a whole, the conciliation committee has proved to be successful.

The Amsterdam Treaty streamlined the co-decision procedure, most importantly by making it possible to adopt a legislative act at the first reading if everybody involved in the process agrees. The EP is enthusiastic about this new feature, which could enhance its involvement in the pre-legislative phase of decision-making. It remains to be seen, however, whether the Commission – and above all the Council – will engage in a process that could boost the EP's influence in return for an acceleration of decision-making under co-decision.

Budgetary Powers

The 'power of the purse' is often quoted as the origin of parliamentarianism. This has two dimensions: what comes in and what goes out. In modern democracies, the income side (revenue) has become politically more important: 'no taxation without representation' is a slogan to incite rebellion; nobody would rebel to demand greater budgetary scrutiny.

In the EU, the two sides of the purse are neatly separated for political reasons. Member states insist on the exclusive right to determine how much should go into the common budget; only on that condition do they concede some power to the EP (a partial form of co-decision) over how it should be spent. The formal justification is that the 'own resources' of the EU are not its 'own' after all, and that the EU budget is predominantly composed of direct contributions from the member states that are authorized by national parliaments. Consequently, the granting of budgetary power to the EP in 1970 and 1975 has been limited to the spending side.

The literature on the EU budget tends to emphasize the EP's limitations, thereby underestimating two important factors that have emerged over the last years: the embeddedness of expenditures in multi-annual programmes to which the EP is a full partner; and the leverage that budgetary authority provides in other areas, such as comitology or external EU programmes.

The EP has been adroit in extending its budgetary influence. This is nowhere more clearly demonstrated than in the way that it has sought to break down the distinction in the budget between 'compulsory' and 'non-compulsory' expenditure. The official reason for this distinction – that many budget items (staff salaries, rents for buildings, etc.) are determined by previous legal or other binding decisions – does not make sense in practice. The real purpose of the distinction is to minimize the EP's influence in a number of sensitive areas, above all agricultural spending, because the EP has much less say over 'non-compulsory' items. Under these circumstances, the EP's strategy has been, firstly, to challenge the justification of the budgetary classification and, secondly, to try to question the classification item by item in order to increase the size of the non-compulsory side. Inevitably, this has resulted in permanent quarrels with the other arm of the budgetary authority, the Council. A temporary truce was reached via an inter-institutional agreement in 1993 that clarified the application of the principle of the 'maximum rate of increase', a treaty provision (Article 272.9 TEC) that constitutes a 'brake' against rapid increases of non-compulsory expenditures. This agreement should have been reviewed in the intergovernmental conference (IGC) that preceded the Amsterdam Treaty, but the issue was merely referred back to the two institutions with a request for a new agreement in 1999 when, in any case, a new financial perspective would have to be decided upon for the period until 2006 (a perspective for 2000–6 was agreed at the March 1999 Berlin European Council meeting and is being considered by the EP at the time of writing).

What are the prospects for the EP's budgetary powers? As the Amsterdam Treaty has confirmed, the EU is not yet in a mood for basic reform. The EP, however, has been pressing (and is likely to continue to press). First, it wants a say – possibly in the form of an extension of co-decision – on the revenue side of the budget. It believes that taxation, levies, or other revenues should be approved by the EP. The less 'direct' parts of the EU budget, those which flow through national budgets, should also be included in its remit. The contrary argument, that national parliaments already agree to these, is not seen as being convincing, not least because there are already many EU activities in which both national parliaments and the EP are involved, for example in the assent procedure concerning external agreement with third countries that include financial obligations.

Second, the EP is likely to continue its campaign for the abolition of the division between compulsory and non-compulsory expenditure, which was never fully justified and became obsolete as the EP emerged as a responsible co-legislator. In practice, the EP's overall approach is to try to extend co-decision to all policies that incur major expense, above all agriculture, thereby exposing the budgetary consequences of such policies. There are already some tentative steps in this direction: for a number of years, the Commission has included in an annex to its legislative proposals an estimate of the proposals' financial consequences. Nevertheless there is much scope for improvement; it remains to be seen whether the next IGC will take up these matters.

Control of the Commission

The original text of the treaties conferred on the EP the powers of 'deliberation and control'. If deliberation is understood as the right to take up any subject for discussion – a right that some national parliaments would very much like to have – what does control mean?

The EP defines control as political oversight and scrutiny of another institution. Due to the wide range of its activities, the Council is difficult for the EP to target as an object of control. In any case, the Council has been extremely reluctant to involve itself with the EP in a way that would give the appearance of possible parliamentary control over its affairs. Nevertheless, a good working relationship has developed between the EP and the Council in recent years; indeed, this has been one of the outstanding elements in EU institution building during the last few years. Not only does the Council answer written and oral questions and participate in plenary question time, but it also uses the EP as a forum to announce Council Presidency programmes and to report on progress at the end of each Presidency. In addition, the EP invites ministers into standing EP committees to discuss major legislative proposals. It is likely that this cooperation will intensify following implementation of the Amsterdam Treaty.

The Commission, rather than the Council, is the obvious 'object' of parliamentary control. Its special relationship with the EP is evident in the classic treaty provision, dating from the ECSC Treaty, that the EP can dismiss the Commission as a whole by a motion of censure that is carried by a two-thirds majority of the votes cast and which represents a majority of all MEPs (Article 201, TEC). This is, of course, the ultimate weapon, and one that the EP is extremely reluctant to use. It did, however, come close to doing so in January 1999 when the Commission was perceived as reacting only slowly and reluctantly to charges of mismanagement, nepotism, and fraud. It was only because President Santer agreed to the establishment of a special investigatory committee and to the creation of new Commission working practices that the motion of censure that was tabled was not passed – through 232 MEPs still voted in favour of it, 293 voted against, and 27 abstained. As was shown in Chapter 3, the special committee's report subsequently led to the resignation of the Santer Commission in March 1999.

In 1997 the EP employed a variation of its censure powers when it passed a 'conditional censure'. This occurred in the wake of the BSE crisis, when the EP stopped short of passing a formal vote of censure but approved a resolution requiring the Commission to adopt certain measures to improve food safety policy and reserved the right to check whether its requirements were put to practice. The use of this device of conditional censure illustrates how the EP is always very adept in interpreting its formal powers in innovative ways and applying them to its advantage.

Beyond its censure powers, the EP has sought to develop a variety of elements of control and oversight in order to be able to evaluate closely the activities and performance of the Commission. These elements are now well established, and range from the Commission's almost permanent participation in plenary debates (including presentations of work programmes and other policy orientations) to extensive exchanges in all committees, especially those having legislative or budgetary powers. As the BSE example showed, the post-TEU committees of inquiry are another instrument of parliamentary control of the Commission. Despite the co-responsibility of the member states for the administration of EU policies, it is above all the Commission that has to respond directly to the MEPs questions and concerns about such matters.

The Maastricht Treaty substantially increased the EP's say in the nomination of the Commission (that is, both the President and the College of Commissioners). Article 214 TEC, revised by the TEU, stipulated that the President would still be nominated by common accord of the national governments, but with the EP playing a consultative role. Although the EP's advise would be legally non-binding, there was no doubt that in practice governments would be unable to confirm a candidate rejected by the Parliament.

The new procedure was first used in July 1994, when the confirmation of Jacques Santer proved to be a stormy event. The EP had no problem with Santer personally: as Prime Minister of Luxembourg he had extensive EU experience; he was a leading member of the EPP; and he was a former MEP. But the EP wanted to express its frustration with the European Council which had, under pressure from the UK, rejected the first candidate, Belgian Prime Minister Jean-Luc Dehaene, for allegedly being too 'federal'. In the event, Santer was approved by the EP by a narrow margin (260 votes for, 238 against), but he might not have been had national governments not lobbied the political groups.

The EP scored a surprising success in the next phase of the nomination procedure for the Santer College, with all Commissioners-designate appearing before the respective standing EP committees in January 1995. This proved a difficult ordeal for some of them. Newcomers seemed too hesitant, and observers had the impression that they followed guidelines from the Commission services about not making promises they could not keep – above all on the sensitive issue of whether they thought that the Commission should systematically incorporate amendments from the EP in the co-decision or cooperation procedures. By contrast, the 'old hands' (Commissioners up for reappointment) had learnt how to 'play the game' and avoided answering critical questions directly. As a result, four new Commissioners received mixed or even negative reviews from their respective committee. In the final vote, however, Parliament approved the Commission 'as a body'.

It is difficult to gauge the precise political impact of the 1994 and 1995 nomination processes. They have, however, clearly enhanced the political stature of the Commission, and they may well have contributed considerably to the Commission paying much more attention to EP concerns, even with regard to its internal structure and functioning. But where do we go from here? The Amsterdam Treaty again changed the procedure, with the nominee for President now officially subject to a vote of approval in the EP. In addition, the President-designate's position is strengthened with regard to the selection procedure for the College of the Commission (Article 214.1 and 2, TEC). Doubtless the EP will also keep in mind during the confirmation procedure that the President, once confirmed, will have an enhanced policy role (Article 219 TEC stipulates that the Commission shall work under the President's 'political guidance').

Parliament and the Citizen

As a representative body, a parliament must maintain and develop a permanent dialogue with those it is supposed to represent. In a world inundated with information, the EP must make itself heard in order to assure citizens that it exists and that it actively represents their interests. Are EU citizens aware of the EP's existence and, if so, what do they think of the EP? One answer can be found in Eurobarometer, the Commission-based public opinion survey, which periodically contains a chapter on how EU citizens perceive the EP. Public awareness of the EP varies considerably, not surprisingly peaking (at 60–70 per cent) just before direct elections. Awareness varies greatly from country to country, with Finland (69 per cent) and Luxembourg (64 per cent) ranking highest, and Britain and Ireland (33 per cent) lowest. These figures may seem low, but more people have heard about the EP than about any other EU institution. A substantial number of those (47 per cent) who are aware of the EP's existence think that the EP is important. Indeed, many people (38 per cent) want the EP to have a more important role (Eurobarometer 48, Autumn 1997; chapter 5.1).

The increased powers of the EP since implementation of the TEU seem to have had a substantial effect on citizen awareness. It is true that most legislative areas subject to co-decision are not very exciting for the public at large, but there are a number of non-legislative areas where the EP is garnering support. For example, about 500 groups participated in hearings on the 1996–7 IGC organized by the EP. In most national political systems, parliaments thrive not so much in the legislative field but as forums for clashes between political parties, and above all between government and opposition. Since this possibility does not exist in the EU, and as there is no coherent group labelled the 'European public', the EP has had to explore new ways of demonstrating its relevance (Neunreither, 1998).

One way has been the formalization by the TEU of the right of citizens to send complaints on EU affairs directly to the EP in the form of petitions (Article 194, TEC). Even before that, the EP had set up a petitions committee but this lacked legal standing. The possibility to petition a parliament is one of the classical rights of citizens; in the EU, this right is not restricted to EU citizens but extends to all residents and even legal persons (that is, companies or organizations) having their registered office in one of the member states. The petition must concern a matter that comes within the EC's field of activity and the author(s) must be directly affected by it.

Elections and Composition

Since 1979, MEPs have been directly elected. They represent 'the peoples of the States brought together in the Community' (Article 189 TEC), not a hypothetical European people. This wording has not only stimulated academic debate about whether a European 'demos' exists (Weiler, 1997), but has also raised questions about the organization and the political impact of elections: at present, national political parties are responsible for the selection of candidates, the campaigns are influenced more by domestic issues than European ones, and even the electoral laws are matters of national competence.

Elections to the EP – which cannot be dissolved – take place every five years during the month of June. Participation is significantly lower than in national elections, except in those countries (Belgium, Greece, Italy and Luxembourg) where voting is obligatory. This is easy to understand: in a national context, parliamentary elections determine the composition of the next government; provide a unique opportunity for the opposition to challenge the majority; are generally highly personalized, with the current head of government standing against a challenger for the most powerful political post in the land. These elements are all absent in the EU system: EP elections do not bring a political group or individual to power, either in the Council or in the Commission.

The June 1994 direct elections confirmed a long-term participatory trend: despite the EP's greater powers, voter turnout continued to decline. Overall participation was only 56.4 per cent, compared to 58.4 per cent in 1989, and 63.0 per cent for the first elections in 1979. The decline was especially strong in countries that traditionally favour integration, such as Germany (from 65.0 per cent in 1979 to 58.0 per cent in 1994), Ireland (from 63.6 per cent to 44.0 per cent), and the Netherlands (from 57.8 per cent to 35.6 per cent). Only in those countries where voting is obligatory did participation stay above 70 per cent.

The 1999 elections will show whether the disappointing 1994 result was due to a reaction against the TEU, and especially to the unpopularity of EMU, or whether the long-term trend will continue. On the one hand the EP has had a number of opportunities to make its voice heard on controversial public issues in recent years, for instance on BSE and on tobacco advertising. On the other hand national political parties still run the show and are reluctant to use their transnational party federations to 'Europeanize' the EP elections by drawing up joint lists, including candidates from other member states, putting forward prominent politicians, and the like. Given that the mandate of the Commission now coincides (with a six-month delay due to the nomination procedure) with that of the EP, and given the circumstances of the resignation of the Santer College, some political groups may make an issue of the Commission's composition and political role in their electoral campaign.

The composition of the EP itself is the result of a compromise reflecting the weight and size of member states while guaranteeing a minimum representation for smaller countries. Thus the EP has 99 German MEPs (each representing about 820,000 inhabitants); 87 MEPs from the UK, France, and Italy respectively (each representing about 660,000 inhabitants); 64 Spanish MEPs (each representing about 610,000 inhabitants); 31 MEPs from the Netherlands and 25 from Belgium and Greece respectively (each representing about 450,000 inhabitants); 25 Portuguese MEPs, 22 Swedish, 21 Austrian, 16 Danish and 16 Finnish (each representing about 350,000 inhabitants); 15 Irish MEPs (each representing about 240,000 inhabitants); and six MEPs from Luxembourg (each representing about 65,000 inhabitants).

There are two major issues concerning the future composition of the EP: its overall size and the electoral procedure. The increasing number of MEPs (410 at the time of the first direct elections; 626 today) has become a major concern. The EP feels that it would lose its efficiency and finally its effectiveness if its membership continued to increase at the same rate. As a result, the EP decided that, regardless of further enlargement, the total number of MEPs should not exceed 700. This was confirmed in the Amsterdam Treaty (Article 189, TEC). By implication, the distribution of seats will have to be re-examined before future rounds of enlargement, with larger member states likely to demand a levelling out of the present distortions in the ratio of MEP to population, and smaller member states insisting that their present numbers are not reduced. The Amsterdam Treaty requires for the first time that all future adaptations of the number of MEPs must ensure 'appropriate representation of the peoples' (Article189.2). Inevitably, each group of states will use this stipulation to try to bolster its case.

The electoral system is also undergoing major change after a long period of stalemate. The original EEC Treaty had called for a 'uniform procedure' in all member states, and had invited the EP to submit proposals to that effect. The EP made several efforts to do so, but national government resistance to uniformity prevented progress. Apart from major differences between those who favoured proportional representation and others – mainly the British – who defended the simple majority (first-past-the-post) system, questions about electoral thresholds and lists (should they be open or closed, national or regional?) proved too contentious. The Amsterdam Treaty did not do much more than fudge the issue, by declaring that the electoral system should be 'in accordance with principles common to all Member States' (Article 189.4).

Nonetheless, the EP acted on this provision even before the Amsterdam Treaty came into effect. A report approved by the EP in July 1998 (Anastassopoulos Report, 1998) included a Draft Electoral Act, which went to the Council for a decision (by unanimity). If passed by the Council, the electoral act will be forwarded to member states for inclusion in their national electoral laws. The EP's proposal reflects the difficulties of reaching agreement on even a limited number of principles. While the main suggestions of the original report were adopted (notably the provision that the electoral system should be based on proportional representation), the final text was full of conditions and qualifications, making its transmission into national laws much more flexible and stretching somewhat the idea of strict common principles. The EP set the 2004 elections as a general deadline for the application of the common procedures, but on the sensitive issue of whether to reserve seats for 'European' as opposed to national lists, the EP may present an additional proposal that would come into force only in 2009.

An accompanying EP resolution raised a number of related points. For instance, the EP would prefer to make regional constituencies obligatory, but only for member states whose populations exceed 20 million inhabitants (smaller member states could maintain national lists). Even if elected in regions, MEPs should not consider themselves representatives of their constituencies, but of the 'peoples of the States brought together in the Community' (Articles 189 and 190 TEC). This sounds self-evident, but could trigger a much wider debate about who an MEP really represents: his constituents, national party, or a hypothetical EU entity? With the proposed establishment of transnational elements within national representations, this much-neglected question acquires a new dimension (Neunreither, 1999).

Changes to the EP's composition and electoral system were greatly facilitated by the change of government in the UK following the May 1997 general election. The new Labour Government created a total of ten pluri-member EP constituencies of four to 11 members each for England, Scotland, and Wales (in addition to the unique three-member constituency which was already in existence in Northern Ireland). With its regional basis, this configuration comes close to what the EP wants to see as a general rule. France is now the only large member state that does not have some form of regional list system. Prime Minister Jospin was forced by his coalition partners in June 1998 to withdraw a reform draft law for the next elections that would have replaced the national list system with regional constituencies. The impasse in France may eventually be resolved, but it was not done in time for the 1999 elections.

Political Groups

The internal power structure of the EP is largely dominated by the political groups which not only select candidates for leadership positions – the President, the Vice-Presidents, Quaestors, Committee Chairmen, etc. – and influence the nomination of senior staff, but also organize the EP's agenda and plenary sessions. Political groups are conspicuous in parliamentary debates in Strasbourg or Brussels: following introductory remarks by a committee rapporteur and by representatives of the Commission or Council, spokesmen take the floor to present the political groups' views on any given issue. Only then are individual speakers called upon, according to a formula agreed by the political groups.

At the time of writing (early 1999), the EP has eight political groups, which is a relatively low number when put in historical perspective. Changes among the political groups are common and reflect, amongst other things, the evolution of the party system in the member states. So, for example, the arrival in the EP in 1994 of members of Silvio Berlusconi's Forza Italia, Bernard Tapie's Radical Alliance, and Philipe de Villiers' Europe des Patries resulted in the formation of EP groups. At the same time, four of the political groups that had existed before the 1994 elections were not re-elected in sufficient strength to continue their separate existence.

TABLE 4.1 *Political groups in the European Parliament (July 1998)*

	Belgium	*Denmark*	*Germany*	*Greece*	*Spain*	*France*	*Ireland*	*Italy*
PES	6	4	40	10	21	16	1	19
EPP	7	3	47	9	30	11	4	35
ELDR	6	5			2	1	1	4
UFE				2		18	7	4
EUI/NGL				4	9	7		4
Greens	2		12				2	4
ERA	1				2	12		2
I-EN		4				10		
IND	3					12		15
Total	25	16	99	25	64	87	15	87

Note:
PES: *Party of European Socialists.* Socialist parties from all 15 member states.
EPP: *European People's Party.* Christian Democrats, British Conservatives, Irish Fine Gael, Forza Europa.
ELDR: *European Liberal, Democratic and Reformist Group.* The largest contingent is from the Netherlands. It also includes two British Liberals and one Irish Independent.
UFE: *Union for Europe.* French Gaullists, Irish Fianna Fáil, Greek 'Political Spring' party, three centre party Portuguese MEPs, two Dutch members who crossed the floor from the PES and EPP groups.
EUL/NGL: *Confederal Group of the European United Left/Nordic Green Left.* Representatives of Green/Left parties from Denmark, Finland, Greece, Italy, Spain and Sweden. Members of Communist parties from France, Greece and Portugal. One Irish member.

The new legislative procedures created by treaty reform have triggered important changes in the nature and working methods of the political groups. As already mentioned, the cooperation and later co-decisions procedure require absolute majorities and these can only be achieved by groups – and especially by the two largest groups – working closely together. Close cooperation between the PES and the EPP was quickly established and soon spread to other areas, including nominations for internal leadership positions. As a result, the Presidency of the EP now rotates between the two groups, and no other political force – on the left or right – has been able to change this. Most smaller groups feel marginalized, with the consequence that joining one or other of the large groups is attractive. The concentration process began on the right with the Spanish Alianza Popular leaving a small conservative group and joining the EPP. The

Luxembourg	*Netherlands*	*Austria*	*Portugal*	*Finland*	*Sweden*	*United Kingdom*	*Total*
2	7	6	10	4	7	61	214
2	9	7	9	4	5	18	200
1	10	1		5	3	2	41
	2		3				36
			3	2	3	1	33
	1	1		1	4	1	28
1						2	20
	2					1	17
		6				1	37
6	31	21	25	16	22	87	626

Greens: Green parties from nine member states.
ERA: *European Radical Alliance.* French Radical Party, two Scottish Nationalists, two Italian Radicals, Spanish and Belgian regionalists, one former Green from Luxembourg.
I-EN: *Independent Europe of the Nations Group.* French members from 'Europe des Nations', Danish anti-marketeers, two Dutch members from smaller parties, one Ulster Unionist.
IND: The rest of the EP is made up of independents, including French and Belgian National Front members and Italian 'Liga Nord'.

Note: The information on this page will be regularly updated on the Macmillan EU web site at <http://www.macmillan-press.co.uk/politics/EU>

British Conservatives soon followed suit. On the left, the Communist group split, with the more reformist part joining the Socialists.

Although this process could continue, it is evident that the addition of smaller groups of MEPs with a distinctly different political background does not strengthen the coherence of the large groups, which have already become mini-parliaments of their own, spending considerable time preparing common positions before plenary sessions. Up to now, the multinational groups have done a remarkable job of moulding individual MEPs, often elected without any experience outside their own country, into a political family where compromises are a fact of life. But there is a limit: only in plenary sessions can the public debate take place and can the Commission and Council be scrutinized. Group meetings cannot substitute for this; they are necessary preparatory stages and should remain so.

Committees and Delegations

The EP has inherited from the continental – and also the American – propensity to work via permanent or standing committees. Everything that could conceivably be dealt with by the EP falls under the competence of these committees, which officially examine only questions referred to them by the EP. In practice, incoming documents – legislative proposals and the like – go directly to the committee responsible as well as to other relevant committees. The committee responsible nominates a rapporteur who prepares a draft report, taking into account the contributions of other committees. The position of rapporteur is highly desirable, especially if a report is likely to receive a lot of publicity. While each committee is formally responsible for nominating its own rapporteurs, group whips and their staffs follow closely the appointment of rapporteurs and are likely to intervene on occasion.

In addition to its standing committees, the EP occasionally establishes temporary committees to examine specific questions. Some of these have been especially important, such as the ones on German reunification and reform of the Structural Funds. The TEU added a new dimension by officially creating committees of inquiry. Although the EP hoped that these would become powerful instruments of parliamentary scrutiny, inter-institutional negotiations among the EP, Council, and Commission revealed considerable differences of opinion as to the scope and operation of such committees. Some member states evidently regretted what they had signed in the TEU and blocked all progress on the most important question of witnesses. The agreement finally reached, after almost two years of negotiation, did not satisfy the EP but at least allowed a start to be made. However, this will not prevent a re-examination of the basic questions involved and a revision of the inter-institutional agreement (Shackleton, 1998).

Besides committees, inter-parliamentary delegations play an important role in the life of the EP. They were first set up in the framework of association agreements with Greece and Turkey in the early 1960s in order to assure a link between the EP and the parliament of the associated country. Inter-parliamentary delegations are made up of an equal number of MPs from both sides, with a mixed chairmanship and secretariat. Their scope was expanded in the 1970s to cover first the United States, then Latin America and elsewhere. The 1980s saw a thorough, perhaps too far-reaching, systematization of these contacts with the result that practically the whole world is now covered by no less than 21 such delegations. Some, like the one dealing with the US Congress, are politically important; others are relatively insignificant and underworked

In the framework of Europe Agreements and similar agreements establishing close relations between the EU and third countries, interparliamentary delegations have been upgraded to the more impressive sounding 'joint parliamentary committees'. Not only has this resulted in an undesirable increase in meetings and travel, but it has also caused a segmentation of the EP's approach to international affairs, making it more difficult for the EP to advocate regional solutions where appropriate.

Framework of Activities

The EP has developed structures for its activities that have proved remarkably stable and extremely difficult to change, even though they contain some dysfunctional elements. The most dysfunctional of these elements has concerned the various locations of the EP. Since the launch of the ECSC, the Parliament has held its plenary sessions in Strasbourg. For many years the EP did not even have own administrative buildings there, but used the premises of the Council of Europe. Only in the 1980s were the first administrative buildings opened; a separate new chamber for the EP was not added until 1998.

The EP Secretariat was never permanently based in Strasbourg, but in Luxembourg, on the pretext that it was functionally indispensable to remain close to the first EC executive, the ECSC High Authority. In truth, the EP's administrative management felt that they would never gain independence while staying too close to the Council of Europe's then-powerful bureaucracy in Strasbourg. The EP Secretariat could and should have moved to Brussels when the EEC became operational in 1958, but it hesitated and, when the three executives of the ECSC, the EEC, and Euratom merged in 1967, Luxembourg asked for compensation for the departure of High Authority staff to Brussels. The Council decided that only parliamentary committees – and by implication political groups – would meet in Brussels; the seat of the new joint executive – the EC Commission – would be in Brussels; the EP Secretariat would remain in Luxembourg; and plenary sessions would continue to take place in Strasbourg. The inefficiency created by this split has been considerable, but the host countries have resisted attempts to change them. The TEU confirmed the arrangement in the form of a declaration, as did the Amsterdam Treaty in the form of a protocol.

In the meantime, the working requirements of the EP have changed substantially, and the facilities available to the EP have improved accordingly. Working conditions in Brussels have been upgraded, with buildings constructed for meetings of committees and political groups and to provide office space for MEPs and staffers. Of the EP's 3,500 EP staff (not counting the groups' staff of about 700 and a large number of private assistants to MEPs), about 1,000 are based in Brussels. The others, including most of the purely administrative and translation services, are still in Luxembourg.

As well as MEPs and their assistants, more than 1,200 EP staff move to Strasbourg for plenary sessions. Add to this Commissioners and their staff, members of the Council and the Council Secretariat, journalists, lobbyists, official visitors from outside, and a plethora of visitor groups, and the logistical problems faced by this mid-sized town and its surroundings readily become apparent. Yet the Treaty must be respected, despite the fact that a majority of MEPs would prefer to have all parliamentary activities concentrated in Brussels. The Amsterdam Treaty stipulates that 12 plenary sessions each year must be held in Strasbourg, while 'additional' plenaries (in 1998 there were four such sessions of two days each) may be held in Brussels.

Another area where the EP has had difficulties changing established patterns is in its internal rhythm of work. The traditional cycle is that two weeks of each month are reserved for committee meetings, the third for political group meetings, and the fourth for the plenary session. Many MEPs complain that this does not provide enough time for contacts with constituents and national parties, or for other obligations. Various proposals have been made to block out at least a few 'white weeks' during the year when no meetings would be held, but both the increasing workload and the diverging interests of members have foiled all attempts to do so.

Conclusion

In terms of the evolution of EU institutions since the early 1990s, the EP's development has been especially dynamic. Looking at the institutional triangle of EU decision shaping and making – Commission–

Council–EP – the EP has emerged from its former role of junior partner and has firmly established itself as a co-legislator, a forceful arm of the budget authority, and a body of democratic control.

Within the EP, this greater dynamism has been accompanied by a thorough reorganization of working methods, including many elements of planning and cooperation that also affect relations between the political groups. The most apparent sign of this is the increasing importance of the two largest groups – the PES and the EPP – and the partial marginalization of the smaller ones. A number of minor groups have reached the logical conclusion and joined one of the larger groups, thereby weakening the latter's internal coherence.

The positive performance of the EP during the development of the single market programme (1987–2) when, for the first time, it was entrusted with limited, but nevertheless real, legislative power, led to a recognition by the other institutional actors – the Commission and even more so the Council – of a new parliamentary role. Simply put, the cooperation procedure led to a cooperative Parliament. Some observers regret this key development, fearing that the EP has lost its soul by becoming too pragmatic and efficient. Be that as it may, the EP has been rewarded in both the TEU and Amsterdam Treaty with an extension of its powers, mainly in the legislative field but also in some other areas, such as the nomination of the Commission. The post-TEU years have revealed a Parliament that uses its new functions cleverly and often maximizes its influence by combining diverse instruments, such as committees of inquiry and threats to sack the Commission, or budgetary authority and legislative involvement in certain policy areas.

The EP's growing institutional influence is not necessarily matched by an improvement in Parliament's relations with the EU's citizens. It is true that the media have paid increasing attention to the EP and that interest groups have discovered the EP's usefulness. But public awareness of the EP has advanced only slowly. If anything, people have become more critical towards all EU institutions since the post-Maastricht debates. There is still a long way to go. The EP needs allies to develop a European political consciousness. Unfortunately, the European party federations that should see the EP as a prime arena of activity have so far been of little help. Their role may, however, increase if the national political parties, which still dominate the public political debate, can overcome their reluctance and open the way for a real European discourse. They certainly have no shortage of subject-matter: the euro and its economic and political implications, employment policy, enlargement, the environment, internal security, and so on.

One of the EP's major tasks in the years to come will be to convince ordinary people that the EU can provide solutions to policies and problems, and that Parliament matters. In so doing, it is in a position to build on the substantial progress that it has made in recent years.

Guide to Further Reading

Most general books on the EU, and especially on its institutional system, include a chapter on the EP. Corbett, Jacobs and Shackleton (1995) and Westlake (1994) provide the most knowledgeable and comprehensive overviews of the EP. Corbett (1998) gives an insider's account of the EP's role in EU constitution-building since the early 1980s. Useful books on European political parties and EP political groups include Hix and Lord (1997), Blondel *et al.* (1998), and Morgan and Tame (1996). Marsh and Norris (1997) gives a detailed academic study of political representation within the EP. On democracy in the EU, see Chryssochoou (1998). For a more sociological approach to the EP, see Abelès (1992).

References

Abelès, M. (1992) *La vie quotidienne au Parlement Européen*. Paris: Hachette.

Anastassopoulos Report (1998) *Minutes of sitting of 15 July 1998*, Part II, Doc. PE 271.049, Brussels: European Parliament.

Blondel, J., Sinnott, R., and Svensson, P. (1998) *People and Parliament in the European Union*. Oxford: Clarendon Press.

Chryssochoou, D. (1998) *Democracy in the European Union*. London and New York: I. B. Tauris.

Corbett, R. (1998) *The European Parliament's Role in Closer EU Integration*. Basingstoke: Macmillan.

Corbett, R., Jacobs, F., and Shackleton, M. (1995) *The European Parliament*. 3rd edn. London: Cartermill.

Hix, S. and Lord, C. (1997) *Political Parties in the European Union*. Basingstoke: Macmillan.

Marsh, M. and Norris, P. (eds) (1997) 'Political Representation in the European Parliament', special issue of *European Journal of Political Research*, vol. 32, no. 2, pp. 153–289.

Morgan, R. and Tame, C. (eds) (1996) *Parliaments and Parties*. Basingstoke: Macmillan.

Neunreither, K. (1998) 'Governance Without Opposition: The Case of the European Union', *Government and Opposition*, vol. 33, no. 4 , pp. 419–44.

Neunreither, K. (1999) 'Political Representation in the European Union: A Common Whole, Various Wholes, or Just a Hole?', in K. Neunreither and A. Wiener (eds), *Institutional Dynamics and Prospects for Democracy in the European Union*. Oxford: Oxford University Press.
Shackleton, M. (1998) 'The European Parliament's New Committees of Inquiry: Tiger or Paper Tiger?', *Journal of Common Market Studies*, vol. 36, no. 1 (March 1998), pp. 115–30.
Weiler, J.H.H. (1997) 'Legitimacy and Democracy of Union Governance', in G. Edwards and A. Pijpers (eds), *The Politics of European Treaty Reform*. London: Pinter. pp. 249–87.
Wessels, W. and Diedrichs, U. (1997) *A New Kind of Legitimacy for a New Kind of Parliament – The Evolution of the European Parliament*. Eiop papers 1997, at: http://eiop.or.at/eiop/texte/1997-006a.htm
Westlake, M. (1994) *A Modern Guide to the European Parliament*. London: Pinter.

5

The Court of Justice and the Legal System

DANIEL WINCOTT

Questions about the judicial or political activism of the European Court of Justice (ECJ) have been the subject of extensive academic and political debate in recent years. The closely related question of the extent to which the Court has made an autonomous contribution to the integration process – that is, a contribution beyond the one the member states have authorized it to make – has also animated scholarly analysis. This chapter will consider whether the increase in intensity is a product of increased judicial activism or of changes in the environment within which the Court operates. While academic analysts have begun to clarify the role played by the ECJ, a more nuanced understanding of the Court and European law is still required if the issue of judicial activism is to be addressed. Specifically, the Court (and law) need to be considered in a broader context than has been typical thus far and the relationship between structure and agency should be made the subject of explicit analysis.

Too often the Court has been analysed as a more or less autonomous actor, without paying due attention to the structures which facilitate, but also constrain, its activity. Rather than being wholly impersonal, these structures are created and maintained (consciously or unconsciously) by the activity of agents. For example, while in one sense the Court itself is (partially) constrained by the structure of European Community law, from another perspective it is an author of that law. Moreover, the tendency has been to focus on the Court as an actor, rather than placing it in the context of the law and of wider aspects of the European political economy (but see Wincott, 1995b and Armstrong and Shaw, 1998). The ECJ should be analysed as an actor in the development of the Community legal order and the European policy process, emphasizing the importance of the context within which it acts and its relationships with other actors.

In this chapter the various key actors within the European legal system are identified, before a description of the organization of the European legal system is presented. Successive sections analyse: the ECJ, European law and the European Community/European Union (EC/EU) system of governance; the Court and EC policy-making; the Maastricht and Amsterdam Treaties, particularly in so far as they include measures to rein in the Court; and political and legal dimensions of European constitutionalism. Finally, questions about the relationship between judicial activism and changes in the environment of the Court are considered.

Before moving on to the body of the argument, a brief description of the structure of the EU is in order. The Treaty on European Union (TEU) founded the European Union on three 'pillars', together with some overarching provisions common to the Union as a whole. The first of these pillars was based on the three long-established European 'communities': the European Coal and Steel Community (ECSC); the European Atomic Energy Community (Euratom); and the European Economic Community (EEC). The ECJ's jurisdiction was largely confined to this pillar made up of the original three 'communities', as modified by subsequent treaties. In other words, the second and third pillars of the treaty – those concerned with Common Foreign and Security Policy (CFSP) and Justice and Home Affairs (JHA) – were for the most part beyond the remit of the Court, as were its general provisions on 'European Union'. For this reason, unlike other chapters in this book, the discussion that follows is mainly focused on the EC and EC law, rather than the EU.

Before the Treaty on European Union (also known as the Maastricht Treaty), major treaty revisions, including the Single European Act (SEA), *altered* the treaties which created the original three communities. These communities can be commonly (if somewhat informally) described, first as the 'European Communities' and later as the 'European Community'. The TEU created the European Union, which encompassed the original communities, alongside the other two pillars. Cutting against the grain of earlier conventions, the TEU deleted the 'Economic' from the EEC, renaming it as the 'European Community'. Somewhat confusingly, together the EC, ECSC and Euratom are widely known as the Community pillar of the EU. The Treaty of Amsterdam revised the TEU rather than replacing it, with one of the most significant revisions being the reconstitution of the JHA pillar as Police and Judicial Cooperation in Criminal Matters.

Actors in European Law

There are a number of courts within the EU itself. The most important of these is the European Court of Justice, which regards itself as the ultimate arbiter of the meaning of European Community law – a sort of supreme court for the EC. Other EC courts include the Court of First Instance and the Court of Auditors. The Court of Auditors is part of the structure of financial accountability with the EC. The Court of First Instance was created by the SEA in order to ease the caseload of the ECJ. It is concerned mainly with competition policy and cases concerning the EC/EU's own staff. It is important to note at this point that the European Court of Human Rights is *not* an institution of the EU, although many otherwise well-informed commentators apparently remain confused on the matter. It was created by the European Convention on Human Rights, a treaty quite separate from those which constitute the EU.

Judges in the Court of Justice are appointed by the member states (one from each state) for a term of six years. Within this period states cannot remove a judge. The Court sits in 'chambers', so not all judges consider every case. In principle, however, each judgement is a decision of the whole Court. Decisions are taken by a simple majority, but no votes or dissenting opinions of any sort are published. These features of the Court are important, as they are the institutional parameters within which the Court negotiates its degree of autonomy from other actors, particularly the member states. The debate over the level of independence that the European institutions traditionally designated as 'supranational' can achieve has been a key issue recently (see Cram, 1993; 1997; Garrett, 1992; Pollack, 1997). In the last few years the Court has joined the Commission as an important focus for this debate. Some analysts did claim 'all-or-nothing' positions – *either* the institutions were wholly constrained by the preferences of the member state *or* they were entirely independent. More often, subtle analyses of the degree of autonomy were mis-read or caricatured as if they were making all-or-nothing claims (an example is Cram's 1993 article which is as much concerned with the constraints on, as with the autonomy of, the Commission). Be that as it may, more recently something of a convergence has taken place, perhaps especially in relation to the Court, with most scholars agreeing that extreme positions are implausible. The consensus is that debate should focus on the degree of independence that the Court (and the Commission) can achieve, or actually achieve during a particular period – a subject on which important disagreements remain (see Cram, 1997; Pollack, 1997; Alter, 1998b; Mattli and Slaughter, 1998).

After the judges themselves, the next most important officers of the ECJ are its Advocates-General. The role of an Advocate-General is to sum up the legislation, case law and evidence relevant to a particular case some time before the Court actually makes its judgement. These 'opinions', which are published before the Court makes its decision, are not binding, although the Court does follow them more often than not. As a result of the secrecy which surrounds the process by which the ECJ comes to a judgement, and the relatively brief, and sometimes gnomic, terms in which it explains its judgments, the opinions of the Advocates-General are an important source of information on the reasoning behind a judgement. Moreover, they can serve as a vehicle for 'testing out' ideas about the development of the law, without committing the full authority of the law to them. New ideas can be transmitted to a wide legal audience through these opinions, and the tone of any subsequent debate may indicate whether or not a legal innovation will be favourably received.

European law is not hermetically sealed off from national law. A significant part of the Court's role is to attempt to ensure that when policies are agreed, they are implemented – that when the states have decided to integrate, they do so. National courts have come to play a key role in this process. As we shall see in more detail below, references from national courts requesting that the ECJ clarify a point of European law has become the largest source of its cases. Two points are worth making here. The first is that the relationship between the ECJ and national courts is a cooperative one – at least in the sense that the European Court has little or no power to ensure that national courts follow its advice. Secondly, within a national legal system, a court might make references to the ECJ to enhance its position *vis à vis* other national courts or other branches of the government. Karen Alter (1998a) has shown that the lower a court is in the national hierarchy, the more likely it is to make more references to the ECJ. We might expect higher courts, and particularly those charged with constitutional responsibilities, to be less sanguine about the encroachment of the ECJ on their jurisdiction. However, a higher court which changes a low court decision that is based on an ECJ judgement risks politicizing the law to the detriment of all courts. While the various national constitutional courts have generally developed an effective working relationship with the ECJ, there is considerable evidence that they do not wholly accept the principle that the ECJ should have supreme jurisdiction over them. On the other hand, even relatively high courts can deploy the ECJ and European law to gain leverage over the executive and legislative branches of government. The development or extension of 'judicial review' of the government provides these courts with important incentives to cooperate with the ECJ (Alter, 1997; Burley and Mattli, 1993; Weiler, 1993, 1994).

The other European institutions all play some role within the European legal system. Even beyond their parts in the legislative process, all institutions have rights of some sort to take cases before the ECJ. One of the tasks of the Court is to define and maintain the appropriate 'balance' between these institutions. Of these other institutions perhaps the most important is the Commission, and particularly its legal service, which acts as a political bell-wether for the Court (Stein, 1981, p. 25; Mattli and Slaughter, 1998, p. 181). Equally, the governments of the member states have been important, both individually and collectively through the Council and in inter-governmental conferences (IGCs). The representations of the states and the Council in individual cases give the Court an indication of their views, although it is worth noting that even when they have objected strongly in the course of a case, the states have not generally sought to challenge the validity of the Court's judgements once they have been made. Since the 1980s, however, the states seem to have become increasingly canny about the Court. They have, for example, sought to restrict the scope of the Court to some extent, through successive treaty revisions. Sometimes states have even redefined particular lines of authority in case-law (the most notable example is the so-called 'Barber Protocol' attached to the TEU, in which the states attempted to constrain the Court's interpretation of gender equality in pensions law by attaching a particular interpretation of the Treaty in a legally binding protocol).

Finally, both lawyers and litigants have played an important part in the development of European law. Until recently, experts in EC law in universities and in practice were generally sympathetic to the 'project' of European integration and particularly of its legal dimension. As a consequence a body of legal commentary grew up around the Court which supported and protected it. The goal of 'integration' (or at least a version of it) was enscribed in the language of European law. Other actors had to engage with the Court in its own language, given the importance of technical discourse in the law, and therefore on its terms. Another key facet of the development of European law concerns the manner in which it has drawn individual and institutional litigants (other than the Community institutions and the states) into the European legal process, albeit largely though national courts. Litigants of this sort have played a role as decentralized monitors of the implementation of European law. This role may appear especially important where significant groups or agencies feel cut off from access to the state, and seek to use the European level as an additional avenue of pressure.

The Organization of the European Legal System

As with the EU in general, it is crucial to remember that the European legal system is not static. Not only has the dynamic development of the Union produced changes in the law, the legal system itself has been transformed, and is likely to continue to change in the future. This is not the place to set out fully the dynamics of this transformation (see Weiler, 1991). It is sufficient to make two points here. First, the historical transformation of the European legal system altered it from a relatively conventional form of international law into something new. Although this 'new legal order' is probably not best understood as a form of state law, it is at least debatable whether it can still be classified within the category of 'international law'. While conventional international law is strictly binding only on states, European law has developed binding effects on individuals as well. The second point that needs to be made is that the Court of Justice has played a central, strategic role, albeit acting within significant constraints, in the development of this legal system – and indeed the development of this system seems to have been the Court's primary objective (see the discussion in Wincott, 1995a; Alter, 1996, 1998a).

Conventional accounts of the development of European law describe two doctrines or principles of European law – direct effect and supremacy – as key to the development of the new legal order. Neither principle was written into the EEC Treaty: both became a part of Community law through the case law of the ECJ. If a European rule is directly effective then, whether or not it has been (adequately) implemented by any state or all states, individuals can rely on it directly as law. Although we would usually expect member states to pass legislation implementing European rules – unlike conventional international law which needs to be implemented by national legislation – directly effective Community rules do not require implementation to become law. Supremacy is a logical corollary of direct effect. If national implementing legislation is no longer a requirement for European rules to be effective, then the possiblity of conflict between European and national law exists. The principle of supremacy means that in the event of such a conflict European law prevails.

Although direct effect and supremacy are usually described as distinct principles of Community law, logically and historically they are closely bound up with one another. Both were initially stated by the Court in the mid-1960s (direct effect in the 1963 *Van Gend* case and supremacy in the 1964 case *Costa* v. *ENEL*). As a matter of logic, the Commission's legal service, several member states and even the Advocate-General in *Van Gend* all thought that direct effect and supremacy were so closely related that they could not be separated (Stein, 1981; Wincott, 1995a). The Court, perhaps as a matter of political tactics, did divide them, holding back from a decision on supremacy until after it had 'tested the water' on direct effect. A closer look at the notion of direct effect shows it has taken a number of distinct forms in various different contexts. Most legal textbooks suggest that the Court created a doctrine of direct effect in the *Van Gend* case, which it subsequently developed in other directions. *Van Gend* suggested that some provisions of the Treaty of Rome could be directly effective. In the 1970s the Court argued that the most significant form of secondary legislation – the directive – could be directly effective, a move which proved controversial with some member states. However, the direct effect of treaty provisions is much more comprehensive than that of directives. Treaty provisions can be directly effective on relationships between individuals as well as between the individuals and the state (that is, they have horizontal and vertical effects), whereas directives can only have the latter sort of effect (that is, only vertical direct effect). These characteristics of direct effect might suggest that it is more a technique for ensuring that European law is adequately implemented and enforced than a coherent legal 'principle' with significance on a par with that of 'supremacy' (compare the discussion of direct effect and supremacy in Weiler, 1994 and Shaw, 1993).

If the transformation of European law was partly a matter of the development of case law, it was also crucially premised on the development of new legal procedures – particularly those which concerned the manner in which cases could come before the Court. The basis of the system as it seems to have been conceived initially was that the various Community institutions and the member states would be the main litigants before the Court. The Commission was initially envisaged as having the key role in monitoring the implementation of Community law within the member states, using the Court as an important arena within which recalcitrant states could be sanctioned. Individuals had very limited direct access to the Court. Although these procedures have played a role, they have been partly eclipsed by the striking development of an apparently innocuous provision of the EC Treaty – Article 234 (previously Article 177) – which allowed national courts to refer questions of European law to the ECJ. This 'preliminary reference' procedure has been transformed into a means by which individuals have access – albeit indirectly – to the Court of Justice and to European law. It has worked in partnership with 'direct effect' to make individuals important potential players within the European legal system. In effect individuals have become decentralized monitors of the implementation and enforcement of Community law. In conjunction with Article 10 of the Treaty (which enjoins states to cooperate fully in processes of integration), the transformation of Article 234 has also been instrumental in drawing national courts into the European legal system. As a consequence, national courts have developed into 'European' courts of a sort (Maher, 1994). Rather than having one, later two, centrally located and overloaded European courts, the 'European legal system' has been dramatically expanded in scope. In addition to the direct impact of the legal system, the existence of a comparatively well developed legal system can change the terms of political debate and the position of individuals even without pursuing cases through the courts. For example, advice from the Commission might be sufficient to resolve a legal dispute, without it ever going to court.

The ECJ, European Law and the EC/EU System of Governance

Neither the European legal system nor the wider EU has a powerful coercive capacity: the capacity used classically to define the state. There are no European gaols, nor is there a distinct European police force or army. As a consequence the European system relies on its persuasive power and its ability to draw on the normative authority and coercive apparatus associated with national legal systems, particularly through the preliminary reference procedure which was examined above. While the European legal system has been much more successful than conventional international law in ensuring that its rules are implemented and enforced, the 'implementation gap', which is often significant in national contexts, poses even more of a problem in the EU.

The boundaries of 'European' law – or the European Union/ Community legal system – are not easy to define, for at least two reasons. First, the internal structure of the EU is differentiated and extremely complex. Second, the boundary of 'the European' within the law may be difficult to establish, because, to an extent, national courts have become 'European' courts, as we have seen. On the first point, the relationship between the European Union and the European Community (or Communities) is a source of potential difficulties, especially within the law, as we shall see in more detail below. Moreover, this relationship changes (sometimes very rapidly) over time.

The ECJ does not have direct jurisdiction over the whole of the EU. The TEU specifically places certain parts of the Treaty beyond the domain of the Court. We have seen that the ECJ's jurisdiction is mainly within the EC, rather than the broader EU which includes the second and third pillars. While the parts of the TEU over which the Court has jurisdiction could be understood as a new form of law – Community law is neither conventional international law nor state law – other parts of the TEU are, in effect, a form of international law. As the Court has responsibility to police the boundaries of Community law, it may face difficult decisions about the relationship between the Communities and other facets of the Union.

Even if we could define the scope of the EC and the EU at a European level, there are conceptual problems in defining the boundary of 'the European' within the law. The interplay of European and national law has made an enormous contribution to the implementation and enforcement of European law. Equally it has resulted in a partial mixing of 'the European' with each of the various ~~national~~ national legal systems. Thus, while it may be heuristically useful, the notion of 'legal integration' in Europe is also problematic. While these developments clearly involve some 'integration' of the law, this integration is not necessarily or wholly on the terms of 'European law'. Moreover, because the national legal systems vary, a variegated pattern of 'legal integration' may have developed across the different member states. As we have seen, then, European law can be understood only in its relationship with the legal systems of the member states, so too the behaviour of the Court of Justice makes sense only in context – with the challenge for commentators being to specify the relevant contextual factors.

The Court and EC Policy-Making

A large number of legal decisions could be cited in which the Court apparently made a striking and innovative contribution to the development of an important sector of Community policy. Moreover, in public debate, especially in the UK, the Court is often depicted as if it had a substantive policy agenda, particularly in relation to environmental and social policies. These factors, and others, have led to an overestimation of the influence of the Court on particular policies. While the Court can have an important impact on the policy process, the circumstances within which it can have such an impact are crucial and need to be specified in each case. Moreover, a view of the ECJ as concerned first to protect and perhaps expand its own prerogatives *as a Court* and, secondly, to specify, shield and extend the competences of the Community is more likely to be fruitful than an image of the Court having substantive policy preferences in, say, social policy.

Nevertheless, the appearance that the Court has substantive preferences in particular policies prevails in individual national debates. For example, in the UK between 1979 and 1997 the hostility of the government to anything that implied the expansion of social policy or trade union rights meant that ECJ judgements on such issues as the rights acquired by individuals during a period of employment appeared as a political challenge to the UK government. European legislation adopted in 1977 meant that when a business was sold (its ownership 'transferred') employees remained employed on the same terms and conditions they had originally enjoyed (Directive 77/187). During the 1980s a significant number of UK state-owned businesses were privatized and services previously provided directly by public bodies were 'contracted out', often to the same groups of people after the public sector managers had set up as private sector contractors. An important source of the 'efficiency gains' achieved by these privatizations was the worsening of terms and conditions of employees. In the early 1990s the Court made it clear that the contracting-out of services was a form of 'legal transfer' which fell within the scope of Directive 77/187, a decision which was unsurprising in terms of the earlier case-law on the Directive, but which nevertheless produced a large amount of litigation within the UK, much of it supported by

UK trade unions. There was a clear political dimension to the UK litigation – it represented a confrontation between the UK government, committed to privatization and facing the prospect of an expensive bill for compensation, and the unions, which had been cut out of their traditional position in the circuits of policy-making. However, the ECJ was applying its conventional methods of interpretation in a relatively straightforward way to a law passed unanimously by the member states, albeit much earlier and by governments of a rather different political complexion (see More, 1995 for a discussion of the Acquired Rights Directive; for a brief description of the impact of the Court in some other policy areas see Wincott, 1996, pp. 176–80).

To place the substantive policy-making role of the Court in an appropriate perspective it is important to remember that, as a general rule, it is not able to create a fully fledged policy on its own. The Court usually requires some sort of Treaty basis, or other legislation, on which to act. In other words, the Court generally changes the meaning of policies that already have some sort of existence. Yet if a legislative or Treaty basis is a necessary condition, it is not a sufficient one. Some policy sectors with a strong legal basis nevertheless have had 'dead letter' status for long stretches of the Community's history. Crucially, the Court needs to have a case to consider before it can come to judgement and there is nothing to guarantee that it will be supplied with the cases it requires. If the Court is to have a significant direct impact on policy, it is likely to require not one particular case, but a stream of related cases. In other words, it is likely that a 'repeat player' of some sort, rather than a one-shot litigant, will need to exist – unless the legal situation is sufficiently uncertain and concerns a significant enough area of policy to generate multiple cases on a single issue, independently of one another. Indeed, even to have an impact on the legislative process, the existence or threat of a stream of cases is usually necessary (in this context it is worth noting that areas where the Court has had an impact – such as, gender equality, competition policy, the free movement of goods – strategic litigants have either existed or been on the point of coming into existence). Although strategic litigation has usually furthered the cause of integration in the past, there is no reason to suppose that anti-integrationists are precluded from strategic litigation.

Even where the Court has made a striking contribution to the character of a particular policy, usually its contribution has been to unsettle an established policy regime or to break up a gridlock in the process of legislation, rather than to create a policy itself. Some of the Court's most famous 'pathbreaking' cases have been in core areas of Community policy (*Cassis de Dijon* – free movement of goods; *Philip Morris* – the regulation of competition), in which an established body of policy existed. The most important impact of these cases has been the provocation of further legislation, not their direct impact on policy (on *Cassis*, see Alter and Meunier-Aitsahalia 1994).

Historically, where the Court has had a significant impact on substantive policy, this impact has sometimes been associated with aspects of the 'constitutional' development of the Community. For example, litigation in the 1970s raised the profile of European Community gender equality policy. Although the Court undoubtedly had a major impact on these policies, its interest in these policies was probably more concerned with the constitutional implications of these cases than their policy substance. Court decisions have continued to have an impact on gender equality policy, but these have been more a consequence of the interest and attention generated by the early cases, which have generated a flow of litigation (not least from the UK's Equal Opportunities Commission – see Barnard, 1995 for a discussion), than of any deep, independent commitment to gender equality on the part of the Court.

It is important to remember that this chapter deals more with substantive policy than with judicial policy or procedure. At the margin between judicial and substantive policy, an argument might be made that the Court has, for example, generated a 'human rights policy' for the Community. Even if it is taken as a substantive policy, however, to the extent that human rights protection exists at the Community level, its development has been crucially influenced by the political institutions. In other words, although its main dynamic has been in the interplay of Courts, it has been crucially influenced by the endorsement of the political institutions of the Community (Wincott, 1994a).

Maastricht and Amsterdam – Reining in the Court?

Just as political scientists and international relations scholars have begun to pay serious attention to the role of the Court of Justice in the process of European integration, a number of commentators have noted that the Court's position has become increasingly difficult. This difficulty is hardly a product of an increased radicalism on the part of the Court itself – if anything, the ECJ has been less, rather than more, bold since the TEU, if not the SEA. Instead, it is a change in the Court's environment, rather than its underlying preferences, which is important here (see Weiler, 1993, 1994; Wincott, 1994b). As the member states have found themselves increasingly (and perhaps unexpectedly) constrained by the Community legal system, they have become more alert to the tactics of the Court in strengthening its role and increasing the scope of its competence. As well as moves by the member states which are specifically concerned with the jurisprudence of the Court, the member states have also sought to find ways of cooperating in Europe which escape the relatively tight constraints of the Community legal system. Ironically, to the extent that the member states made it difficult to pass legislation in the Community, in order to protect their sovereign prerogatives, they also made it difficult to regain control over legal decisions which they disliked. Where a unanimity decision rule was required, the states would be prevented from revising legislation if only one state supported the position of the Court *after* it had come to a decision.

At Maastricht the member states did act in certain areas specifically to rein the Court in. The most notable of these was the 'Barber' Protocol, which dealt with the subject-matter of a particular Court judgement (on gender equality in pensions provision – for a discussion, see Hervey, 1994). In principle, difficulties were also posed for the Court by more general provisions which amount to particular exceptions to the general rules of the Community in core areas of policy. One example of this was the 'Danish Second Homes' Protocol, which allowed the restriction of ownership of property in parts of Denmark to be restricted to Danes, thus exempting this sphere of activity from the general principle of free movement.

More generally still, it is clear that the complex pillared structure of the TEU, described above, has also caused the Court problems, although these should not be overstated. The Treaty did not retrench the scope of the ECJ in areas it already controlled. Instead, the CFSP and JHA pillars represented another stage of partial formalization in the gradual development of areas of European cooperation which had initially emerged informally around the edges of the European Community. Indeed, there were provisions which would allow some policies initially placed in the new intergovernmental pillars to be moved within the Community itself. Nevertheless, the motivation for the states in specifically excluding the Court from jurisdiction over these pillars was a 'rebellion' against a 'mono-centred, vertically integrated' 'classical European constitutional vision' of the European Community/Union (Weiler, 1998, p. 171). The main potential difficulty for the ECJ is in judging the boundaries between those areas over which it has jurisdiction, and others over which it has none. More particularly, the Court has to guard against the states using parts of the Union over which it has no control to encroach on areas of Community competence, perhaps precisely in order to escape the discipline of the Court.

The ratification process for the Maastricht Treaty further complicated the position of the Court. The general sense of ambivalence about the integration process, reflected in many of the national referendums, may have had an impact on the Court (see Alter, 1998, p. 142). More specifically, during the ratification process the German Constitutional Court, the *Bundesverfassungsgericht* was asked whether the Treaty on European Union was constitutionally acceptable in Germany. The Court decided that the Treaty could be ratified but in its judgement it placed considerable emphasis on the fact that the Treaty was a union of the *peoples* (rather than a people) of Europe, and thus that the member states remain the 'masters of the Treaty'. The German Court was particularly concerned to establish that the ECJ alone did not have the competence to decide where its own competence ends.

The Amsterdam Treaty illustrates many of the issues about the scope and limits of ECJ autonomy from the member states. Perhaps most importantly, the IGC negotiations, leading up to the Treaty, illustrate the difficulties that a member state faces if it attempts to rein in the Court. As the IGC began the UK Government had a strong intention to unpick some of the structure of the European legal system. Despite some indications that the German Government might support proposals to alter the preliminary reference procedure, perhaps limiting it to high courts, in the planning and negotiation of the IGC no other government was prepared to renegotiate the Community's legal order. The UK Government tempered its proposals, suggesting an appeal procedure according to which the ECJ could be asked to reconsider a decision as well as proposals to limit retrospective application of Court judgements and the liability of states which had acted in good faith. Despite this tempering of its position, all the UK Government's proposals were rejected by other member states (see Alter, 1998b, pp. 140–2).

The Amsterdam Treaty retained the pillar structure, with its associated legal problems, for the European Union. However, important aspects of the JHA pillar, as well as aspects of the Schengen system which is concerned with border controls and police cooperation, have been moved into the European Community. As a consequence the jurisdiction of the ECJ was extended. However, even here the member states appear to have learnt lessons about the Court. First, the provisions on justice and home affairs matters will not grant individuals rights under Community law within national courts. They will not create direct effects – individuals will be able to challenge the European law itself, rather than its national implementation. In addition, lower courts – the most important source of preliminary references in Community law – are not allowed to make references to the ECJ in the areas of Schengen or in respect of the maintenance of law and order and the safeguarding of internal security. In respect of police and judicial cooperation, each individual state will be able to decide whether its courts will be able to make preliminary references. In other words, within the domain of Community law itself, a complex and differentiated legal structure has been created, which may further aggravate the political difficulties that the Court might have at the boundaries of various forms of its jurisdiction (see Alter, 1998b). Second, the Amsterdam Treaty has increased the possibility that the Court will face difficulties in monitoring the perimeters of (different forms of) its authority in another way. If the Maastricht Treaty introduced various forms of differentiated integration and a new vocabulary – of variable geometry, multi-speed and *à la carte* integration – was spawned, the IGC leading up to the Amsterdam Treaty generated an extensive debate on the general notion of 'flexible' integration, covering all three forms mentioned parenthetically above. Stubb (1998, p. 3) has identified elements of the Amsterdam Treaty which take each of these three forms. Perhaps most importantly the notion of flexibility was institutionalised to some extent in the Treaty itself in a title concerned with 'Provisions on closer co-operation' (Langrish, 1998; Shaw, 1998).

Is There a Legitimate European Constitution?

The idea that the European Community has a constitution is more or less conventional wisdom among EC lawyers (but see Eleftheriadis, 1996). Since the 1960s the Court itself has deployed various constitutionalist discourses, although often somewhat tremulously. In conventional EC legal language, the claim that a European constitution exists appears to mix two distinct notions. The first is a relatively uncontroversial claim that organizations or institutions are constituted by – operate according to – a fairly clear set of grounding rules. The second is a more directly statist discourse, which implies that the existence of a European constitution suggests a vocation for the EU as a federal state. However, for most of the existence of the Community there has been relatively little debate about the normative significance of the integration process. Although there has been a strongly normative element in many accounts of integration, most of these accounts have been presented as positive analyses: their normative agenda has usually been left implicit.

In the last few years the normative debate about integration has taken off dramatically, mostly in the context of interdisciplinary political and legal analysis. Two themes have been particularly important in this debate – one concerns the relationship between political and legal constitutionalism and the other considers constitutionalism after the demise of the sovereign state. The first theme is the question of the legitimacy of the integration process, and has been centrally concerned with the relationship between political and legal constitutionalism. There is a question about whether a legal system can legitimately make itself supreme, and in that sense create a 'constitution' by 'pulling itself up by its own bootstraps' (compare Eleftheriadis, 1996 with the perspective of systems theory). Several political theorists have suggested that the Union needs a moment of political constitutionalism – perhaps in the form of a 'democratic baptism' – before it can become legitimate (Weale, 1995; and see the contributions in Bellamy and Castiglione (eds), 1996).

The second theme suggests that European constitutionalism has developed in the context of, and has further encouraged, the development of politics beyond sovereignty. Particularly associated with the work of Neil MacCormick (1990, 1997), this perspective focuses on freeing the legal imagination from the assumption that state law is the paradigmatic form for law. Viewed in this way, questions of supremacy become less central to the understanding of the development of European law. Instead the complex pattern of interaction and co-evolution of European and national law is treated more on its own terms. In this context, the relationship between, say, the *Bundesverfassungsgericht* and the ECJ appears less problematic – some sort of notion of partnership and cooperation is an accurate way to describe the relationship. The possibility of a conflict which determines the 'ultimate' source of legal authority seems to fade into the background.

This view has also been associated with an emphasis on civic conceptions of political community, rather than ethnic ones. However, if the general implication of theorizing post-sovereign law is to undercut the potential conflict between the German and European legal orders, the *Bundesverfassungsgericht* has been sharply criticized for its apparently ethnic conception of European political communities, and its disinterested, if not actually hostile, attitude towards civic alternatives (Weiler, 1996).

Conclusion: A Changing Court or a Transformed Environment?

Two key themes have run through this chapter. The first concerned the interplay of structure and agency, and suggested that these issues are crucial to understanding the significance of European law and the role of the Court of Justice. Recently political scientists have gone some way towards developing such an analysis, usually cast in terms of principal–agent theory (see Pollack, 1997; Alter, 1998b; Mattli and Slaughter, 1998 – a similar approach, developed in a different vocabulary is found in Wincott, 1995a). Principal–agent theory describes the structure of the relationship between principals (actors presumed to hold initial power or authority) and agents (delegated by the principals to meet objectives which the latter might otherwise find difficult or impossible to achieve). This analysis addresses the issue of the potential autonomy of the Court and has produced interesting conclusions, albeit at the risk of concentrating too much on the role of the Court (Moravcsik, 1995; Pollack, 1997; see also Alter, 1998b). A focus on the contribution of the Court was understandable – even acceptable – as the political analysis of legal aspects of European integration began. However, such a focus runs the risk of downplaying the role of the law. Increasingly attention should be focused on the character of the law and the location and significance of the law and the Court(s) within wider European structures and processes (see Mattli and Slaughter, 1998 for a similar view).

Some current political analysis begins to place the ECJ in context by broadening the research agenda to cover the interplay of a variety of courts within European law. Thus it avoids the risk of focusing exclusively on the ECJ (Alter, 1998a; Weiler, 1998; Mattli and Slaughter, 1998). Indeed, some such work calls for the Court and the law to be placed in the context of general processes of integration (and disintegration) in Europe (Mattli and Slaughter, 1998) and indeed wider trends and tendencies in political economy (see Wincott, 1995b). The importance of paying attention to 'context' was the second theme of this chapter, both for the impact of contextual factors on the Court and law, but also for the 'external' influence of the legal sphere. Here the impact of developments which were primarily initiated within the legal sphere on normative debates concerning the current character and future evolution of the EU may become particularly important.

Understandably the Court of Justice has been the focus of considerable attention, particularly as far as as the question of judicial activism is concerned. Recently the Court has come in for strong political criticism for this supposed activism. However, if it is important to place the Court (and law) in context, if structure is emphasized alongside agency, then the explanation of the increased intensity of criticism may be found in changes in the Court's environment, rather than an increase in activism on the part of the Court itself (Weiler, 1994; Wincott, 1994b).

Further Reading

The development of European law and the role of the Court of Justice are discussed from a political science perspective in Wincott (1995a) and Alter (1996) and from a more legal viewpoint in Weiler (1994). The influential paper by Burley and Mattli (1993) considers these issues from the perspective of neo-functionalist theory. A good, politically informed, legal text on these issues is Shaw (1996). Weiler (1991) provides a wide-ranging interpretation of the history of the Community from a contextually sensitive legal perspective and a number of aspects of integration are considered from a similarly sensitive point of view in Shaw and More (1995) and Snyder (1990). Due consideration is given to the role of law in analyses of European policy-making by Armstrong and Bulmer (1998) and Cram (1997). The current preoccupations of political science in the area of 'legal integration' are well represented in Alter (1998) and Mattli and Slaughter (1998), the latter of which suggests that the agenda for political research is on the point of broadening dramatically. Good examples of the new normative theory of European integration can be found in Bellamy and Castiglione (eds) (1996) and MacCormick (1997).

References

Alter, K. (1996) 'The European Court's Political Power: The Emergence of an Authoritative International Court in the European Union', *West European Politics*, vol. 19, pp. 458–87.

Alter, K. (1998a) 'Explaining National Court Acceptance of European Court Jursiprudence: A Critical Evaluation of Theories of Legal Integration', in A.-M. Slaughter, A. Stone Sweet and J. H. H. Weiler (eds), *The European Courts and National Courts: Doctrine and Jurisprudence*. Oxford: Hart Publishing, pp. 227–52.

Alter, K. (1998b) 'Who Are the "Masters of the Treaty"?: European Governments and the European Court of Justice', *International Organization*, vol. 52, pp. 121–47.

Alter, K. and Meunier-Aitsahalia, S. (1994) 'Judicial Politics in the European Community: European Integration and the Pathbreaking Cassis de Dijon Decision', *Comparative Political Studies*, vol. 24, pp. 535–61.

Armstrong, K. and Bulmer, S. (1998) *The Governance of the Single European Market*. Manchester: Manchester University Press.

Armstrong, K. and Shaw, J. (eds) (1998) 'Integrating Law', special edition of *Journal of Common Market Studies*, vol. 36, no. 2, pp. 147–54.

Barnard, C. (1995) 'A European Litigation Strategy: The Case of the Equal Opportunities Commission', in J. Shaw and G. More (eds), *New Legal Dynamics of European Union*. Oxford: Clarendon Press, pp. 253–72.

Bellamy, R. and Castiglione, D. (eds) (1996) 'Constitutionalism in Transformation: European and Theoretical Perspectives', special edition of *Political Studies*, vol. 44, no. 3

Burley, A.-M. and Mattli, W. (1993) 'European before the Court: A Political Theory of Legal Integration', *International Organization*, vol. 47, pp. 41–76.

Cram, L. (1993) 'Calling the Tune without Paying the Piper? Social Policy Regulation: the Role of the Commission in European Community Social Policy', *Policy and Politics*, vol. 26, pp. 135–46.

Cram, L. (1997) *Policy-making in the EU: Conceptual Lenses and the Integration Process*. London: Routledge.

Eleftheriadis, P. (1996) 'Aspects of European Constitutionalism', *European Law Review*, vol. 21, pp. 32–42.

Garrett, G. (1992) 'The European Community's Internal Market', *International Organization*, vol. 46, pp. 533–600.

Garrett, G and Weingast, B. (1993) 'Ideas, Interests and Institutions: Constructing the European Community's Internal Market', in J. Goldstein and R. Keohane (eds), *Ideas and Foreign Policy: Beliefs, Institutions and Political Change*. Ithaca: Cornell University Press, pp. 173–206.

Golub, J. (1996) 'The Politics of Judicial Discretion: Rethinking the Interaction between National Courts and the European Court of Justice', *West European Politics*, vol. 19, pp. 360–85.

Hervey, T. K. (1994) 'Legal Issues Concerning the Barber Protocol', in D. O'Keeffe and P. M. Twomey (eds), *Legal Issues of the Maastricht Treaty*. London: Chancery, pp. 329–37.

Langrish, S. (1998) 'The Treaty of Amsterdam: Selected Highlights', *European Law Review*, vol. 23, pp. 3–19.

Maher, I (1994) 'National Courts as European Community Courts', *Legal Studies*, vol. 14, pp. 226–43.

MacCormick, N. (1990) 'Beyond the Sovereign State', *Modern Law Review*, vol. 56, pp. 1–18.

MacCormick, N. (1997) 'Democracy, Subsidiaitry, and Citizenship in the "European Commonwealth"', *Law and Philosophy*, vol. 16, pp. 331–56.
Mattli, W. and Slaughter, A.-M. (1998) 'Revisiting the European Court of Justice', *International Organization*, vol. 52, pp. 177–209.
Moravcsik, A. (1995) 'Liberal Intergovernmentalism and Integration: A Rejoinder', *Journal of Common Market Studies,* vol. 33, pp. 611–28.
More, G. (1995) 'The Acquired Rights Directive: Frustrating or Facilitating Labour Market Flexibility', in J. Shaw and G. More (eds), *New Legal Dynamics of European Union*. Oxford: Clarendon Press, pp. 129–45.
Pollack, M. (1997) 'Delegation, Agency and Agenda Setting in the EC', *International Organization*, vol. 29, pp. 99–134.
Shaw, J. (1996) *European Community Law*, 2nd edn. London: Macmillan.
Shaw, J. (1998) 'The Treaty of Amsterdam: Challenges of Flexibility and Legitimacy', *European Law Journal*, vol. 4, pp. 63–86.
Shaw, J. and More, G. (eds), (1995) *New Legal Dynamics of European Union*. Oxford: Clarendon Press
Snyder, F. (1990) *New Directions in European Community Law*. London: Weidenfeld and Nicolson.
Stein, E. (1981) 'Lawyers, Judges and the Making of a Transnational Constitution' *American Journal of International Law*, vol. 75, pp. 1–27.
Stubb, A. (1998) 'The Amsterdam Treaty and Flexible Integration', *ECSA Review*, vol. 9, pp. 1–5.
Weale, A. (1995) 'Democratic Legitimacy and the Constitution of Europe'. in R. Bellamy, V. Bufacchi and D. Castiglione (eds), *Democracy and Constitutonal Culture in the Union of Europe* London: Lothian Foundation Press.
Weiler, J.H.H. (1991) 'The Transformation of Europe', *Yale Law Journal*, vol. 100, pp. 2403–83.
Weiler, J.H.H. (1993) 'Journey to an Unknown Destination: A Reterospective and Prospective of the European Court of Justice in the Arena of Political Integration' *Journal of Common Market Studies*, vol. 31, pp. 417–46.
Weiler, J.H.H. (1994) 'A Quiet Revolution: The European Court of Justice and its Interlocutors', *Comparative Political Studies*, vol. 26, pp. 510–34.
Weiler, J.H.H. (1996) 'European Neo-Constitutionalism – In Search of Foundations for the European Constitutional Order', *Political Studies*, vol. 44, pp. 517–33.
Weiler, J.H.H. (1998) 'Epilogue: The European Courts of Justice: Beyond 'Beyond Doctrine; or the Legitimacy Crisis of European Constitutionalism' in A.-M. Slaughter, A. Stone Sweet and J.H.H. Weiler (eds), *The European Courts and National Courts: Doctrine and Jurisprudence*. Oxford: Hart Publishing, pp. 365–91.
Wincott, D. (1994a) 'Human Rights, Democratization and the Role of the Court of Justice in European Integration', *Democratization*, vol. 1, pp. 251–71.
Wincott, D. (1994b) ' Is the Treaty of Maastricht an Adequate "Constitution" for the European Union?', *Public Administration*, vol. 72, pp. 573–90.

Wincott, D. (1995a) 'The Role of Law or the Rule of the Court of Justice?: An Institutional Account of Judicial Politics in the European Community, *Journal of European Public Policy*, vol. 2, pp. 583–602.

Wincott, D. (1995b) 'Political Theory, Law and European Union', in J. Shaw and G. More (eds), *New Legal Dynamics of European Union*. Oxford: Clarendon Press, pp. 293–311.

Wincott, D. (1996) 'The Court of Justice and the European Policy Process', in J.J. Richardson (ed.) *European Union: Power and Policymaking*. London: Routledge, pp. 170–84.

6

Interests

SONIA MAZEY AND JEREMY RICHARDSON

Lipsky defined a political opportunity structure as 'the degree to which groups are likely to be able to gain access to power and to manipulate the political system' (Lipsky, quoted by McAdam, 1996, p. 23). The story which follows in this chapter is simple enough: it is of the emergence and development of the EU as a set of opportunity structures or venues which have generally been very favourable towards interest groups of all kinds, and which have played a key role in stimulating the emergence of a fully fledged EU interest group intermediation system. Our account is, therefore, consistent with most research on opportunity structures which 'has sought to show how *changes* in some aspect of a political system create new possibilities for collective action' (McAdam *et al.*, 1996, p. 17). In practice, a dense European lobbying system has emerged over time, which now exhibits many of the features of interest group intermediation systems long familiar in Western Europe.

Origins and Growth of Interest Intermediation in the European Union: Discovering New Opportunity Structures or Venues

The Logic of Group Involvement at the European Union Level

At the very outset of what is now known as the European Union (EU), the founding fathers recognised the 'logic' of interest group involvement in the European public policy-making process. For example, what was then called the 'High Authority' (the executive

Jeremy Richardson wishes to acknowledge the Nuffield Foundation's support for his contribution to this chapter.

of the European Coal and Steel Community – ECSC) very quickly began to exhibit the traditional characteristics of public bureaucracies, especially functional specialization. By 1955 the High Authority had begun to resemble a traditionally structured bureaucracy. Thus, along with increased bureaucratic specialization came the emergence and creation of various types of policy networks (see Peterson, 1995) involving state actors, policy professionals and experts (what we now term epistemic communities [see Haas, 1992]) and, of course, interest groups of different kinds (Mazey, 1992, pp. 31–48). That interest groups should have been involved in these very early stages of European integration is entirely unsurprising. There is no bureaucracy invented which did not, sooner or later, develop some kind of relationship with groups – a process of interest group intermediation – in order to function effectively as a Weberian bureaucracy. Thus, the demands of efficiency – both in the formulation of public policy and its implementation – have an associated 'logic of group consultation'. This is not to say that the structure and organization of the European interest group 'system' might not exhibit some unique features (see below), but that *some* kind of interest group system would emerge was, surely, inevitable.

Why should this be so? As we have suggested, public bureaucracies habitually involve interest groups in the policy process on grounds of efficiency. Put simply, it is very difficult to make effective public policy without the *specialized expertise* which interest groups possess. Moreover, their cooperation in the *implementation* of public policy is a prime condition for implementation success. Finally, from the bureaucratic perspective, the mobilization of a constituency of *support* is vital to the long-term survival of bureaucracies. In times of trouble, it is always helpful to bureaucracies to have a constellation of interest groups 'out there' who can be mobilized in their defence. Hence, bureaucracies generally devise strategies of 'lock-in' so that groups develop some kind of dependency relationship over time. Bureaucracies, including the European Commission, generally make themselves attractive as opportunity structures to interest groups. The process of interest group intermediation is, however, a two-sided game.

So far, we have outlined the attractions to the European Commission of creating a stable process of interest group intermediation. Equally, groups themselves have natural tendencies to look for and exploit new *opportunity structures* (Kitschelt, 1986) which offer them additional scope for influencing public policies. This is not to suggest that these opportunity structures are neutral as between different types of interest group. Indeed, as group theorists stress, the structural opportunities for groups can exhibit an almost permanent bias (Lindblom, 1977; Dahl, 1982; McAdam, 1996). However, as neo-functionalist theory predicted (Haas, 1958), a dense and mature *European* interest group system has, indeed, emerged.

As Sidjanski noted, some of the groups were formed at the same time as the European institutions were created. Many others were created when it became clear that the European regulations emanating from these new institutions, would directly affect a wide range of societal interests (Sidjanski, 1970, p. 402). The incentive structure was twofold. First, European regulations could have an adverse effect on interests. Secondly, as always, the introduction of new regulations was also an *opportunity* to be exploited to the disadvantage of others. Rules of the game (regulations being formalized and state-sanctioned rules of the game) distribute costs and benefits between interests unevenly. If one set of interests can 'rig' the rules in their favour, they secure all sorts of direct benefits.

Rather like bees around a honeypot, interest groups are attached to regulatory institutions in swarms. Once one set of groups begins to exploit incentive and opportunity structures at the European-level, others are bound to follow; they cannot afford to be left out, whatever the cost. In practice, business groups were generally the earliest to recognise the benefits of participating in European level policy-making and, therefore, to devote the necessary (and increasing amounts of) resources required to create win situations in the Euro-policy game. However, they were inevitably followed by their opponents. As Kirchner (1977, p. 28) found from his study of trade union lobbying in the European Community, European trade union interest group organizations emerged because of a perceived threat from already organised business groups. He also notes that there were also positive incentives for trade unions, as well as for firms and their associations. Thus, one reason for increased trade union mobilization at the European level was that they could 'promote, at the European level, the interests which become increasingly difficult to promote at the national level' (Kirchner, 1980a, p. 132). Reflecting neo-functional theory, his broad conclusion was that there was a linkage between the extent to which Community policies exist in a given sector and the degree of cooperation and integration reached by European interest groups in that sector (Kirchner, 1980b, p. 115). Deciding which phenomenon comes first – the creation of European regulation or the creation of European-level interest intermediation – is a difficult empirical question. Kirchner seems to imply that European policy precedes interest group formations. Whatever the empirical truth might be, we are at least sure that an interest group system is now highly developed at the European level. Organizations involved in lobbying processes at the European level can be classified under at least seven headings as follows:

1. European associations, e.g. Association of Petrochemicals Producers of Europe, Greenpeace International-European Unit.
2. National associations, e.g. Confederation of British Industry, Federation of Swedish Industry.
3. Individual firms, e.g. Imperial Chemical Industries, Ford Motor Company.
4. Lobbying consultancy firms, e.g. Hill and Knowlton, Government Policy Consultants.
5. Public bodies such as regional governments and local authorities, e.g. province of Salzburg Liaison Office, Birmingham City Council European Office.
6. Ad hoc coalitions for a single issue, e.g. European Campaign on Biotechnology Patents , Software Action Group for Europe.
7. Organisations of experts and epistemic communities, e.g. European Heart Network, Federation of Veterinarians of Europe.

Each of these categories of Euro-lobbyist has seen a dramatic increase in the past two decades. By 1992 the Commission estimated that there were 3,000 special interest groups in Brussels with up to 10,000 employees working in the lobbying sector (Commission, 1992, p. 4). The most *European* of the interest organizations are, of course, the European associations. These are associations created at the European level who purport to represent a European-wide (often beyond the European Union) constituency to European-level policy-makers. In a sense, the Commission admits to an institutional bias as an opportunity structure by stating a preference for consulting Euro-associations. Alan Butt Philip (1985, p. 1) estimated that there were approximately 500 such associations in 1985, but this figure has risen to nearer 700 today (Commission, 1996). Recently, however, the formation of Euro-associations appears to have slowed considerably, probably for two main reasons. Firstly, most significant interests in Europe have now formed a Euro-association, no doubt partly reflecting the fact that there are few areas of public policy still unaffected by European legislation of various types. Secondly, as knowledge of the European policy process spreads, interests multiply their lobbying strategies and spread the available lobbying resources across a wider range of organizations. Recognising that Euro-associations are often rather sluggish policy actors, due to their often complex and slow processes of consensus-building, member organizations (such as national associations of firms) increasingly spread their lobbying resources in a risk avoidance strategy. For example, there appears to be a proliferation of ad hoc coalitions focusing on single issue politics (Coen, 1997; Pjinenburg, 1998), a trend quite familiar in Western democracies generally. The more complex the Euro policy game becomes, the greater the need for flexibility and manoeuvrability by interest groups if they are to create policy win situations. Creating ad hoc coalitions (often between groups which might oppose each other on different issues) is a sensible strategy, particularly when multiple opportunity structures (each having a different instiutional bias) present themselves

Explaining the Growth of Lobbying at the European Union Level

How can this proliferation of lobbying and its increasing institutionalisation at the EU level be explained? One obvious explanation (as suggested above) is that more European policy means more European interest groups. In effect, interests are happy to ignore Europe until something from Europe hits their wallet! This is undoubtedly true. Once one group is seen to 'win' something at the European level, others will see opportunities for themselves and copy the behaviour of the first movers. Even if allocating resources to Brussels is irrational, groups are as subject to fashion as the rest of us. Hence, there is probably an element of 'lobbying fashion' at work in driving the EU-level intermediation system forward.

Another, more recent, theory has been developed by Alec Stone Sweet and Wayne Sandholtz – the so-called 'theory of supranational governance'. A central feature of the emergence of supranational governance in the EU is the generation of *demand* for European-level regulation as a result of increased cross-border transactions and communications, which supranational organizations such as the Commission and European Court of Justice (ECJ) work to supply. In this transaction-based theory of European integration (rather similar to that proposed by Deutsch, 1957) a process of institutionalization takes place in which *transnational society* plays an important role (Stone Sweet and Sandholtz, 1997). This society consists of transnational actors – interest groups, business, knowledge-based elites etc. These transnational actors '*have a choice of fora in which to exert their influence*. They may target national governmental structures – executive, legislative or judicial – as well as supranational bodies, and they may play one level off against the other' (Stone Sweet and Sandholtz 1997, p. 305, emphasis added). Transnational society (in which interest groups are key players) and the expansion of tasks or the autonomy of supranational organizations feed on each other. Thus 'an expansion of the tasks or autonomy of supranational organisations creates opportunities for political action, which actors and groups will seek to exploit, thus expanding transnational society' (Stone Sweet and Sandholtz, 1997, p. 305). It is to the interplay between the supranational organizations of the EU and the current, highly developed European interest group system that we now turn. This sometimes symbiotic relationship is a classic example of interest groups seeking to exploit new opportunity structures, or *venues* (Baumgartner and Jones, 1993) and of the *institutionalization* of interest group intermediation.

Exploiting Opportunity Structures and Alternative 'Venues'

The creation of the European Coal and Steel Community in 1951 – and its subsequent development into the European Community, and later the European Union – was bound to be seen by existing interests in European society as a set of new opportunity structures in which they could participate. As these new European institutions produced more *European* public policy, this merely reinforced the natural tendencies of groups to seek out new arenas, sites or 'venues' where they might secure policy pay-offs for their members. Thus, each 'wave' of European integration, but especially the 1986 Single European Act (SEA), the Treaty of European Union (TEU) at Maastricht in 1992 and the 1997 Amsterdam Treaty, has given a further boost to European-level interest group activity. Paradoxically, European integration has also reinforced *national*-level interest group activity as groups fight hard to influence the preference formation of national governments. Indeed, some authors claim that the national level remains the most important channel for lobbying aimed at influencing European level policy (see below). Whether European-level lobbying is more important than national lobbying as a means of influencing European policy-making is difficult to determine empirically. More accurately, perhaps, Euro-lobbying usually involves indirect lobbying via the national route and direct pressure on the EU institutions. In short, Euro-lobbying is, essentially, a multi-strategy, multi-level and multi-venue process. As Baumgartner and Jones (1991, p. 1045) have suggested in the US context, interest groups not only try to control the prevailing image of a policy problem, they also 'try to alter the roster of participants who are involved in the issue by seeking out the most favourable venue for consideration of their issues'. It is easy to translate this analysis of US politics to the European level where groups seek to exploit the many and competing venues where European policy is decided – from lobbying national governments to seeking favourable ECJ rulings, often against national governments. Thus institutions really *do* matter. They encompass institutional biases which privilege certain interests against others. Groups recognise this and are capable of learning and adapting accordingly. In addition, the system as a whole may have an inbuilt bias in favour of resource rich interests, not least because it demands multi-level, multi-arena lobbying strategies which are inherently costly. For example, multinational corporations have both resources and locational features (that is, they operate in several if not all of the member states) which facilitate effective Euro-lobbying. However, it can also be argued that multiple structures can favour groups which are not particularly resource-rich (see below).

Even resource-rich lobbying organizations, however, have to make rational calculations as to how to target those resources to the best effect. Hence, in terms of lobbying venues, some kind of institutional hierarchy has emerged. Following our earlier argument that we should expect European bureaucracies and European interest groups to develop similar behavioural patterns to those observed in national policy-making systems, the institutional hierarchy or ranking of opportunity structures in Euro-lobbying looks rather familiar. Thus, most research findings support the view that interests exhibit a strong preference for the bureaucratic venue – the European Commission.

The European Commission

The Commission is charged, under the EC Treaty, with the key policy formulation role in the European Union. Despite its protestations (especially vociferous in the 1990s, in response to an increasingly hostile climate of opinion), that it is really the Council of Ministers and national governments which initiate the bulk of EU policies, the Commission remains the 'engine' of the European policy process. This basic fact has been unchanged by the Maastricht and Amsterdam Treaties – even though they have shifted the balance of power between EU institutions somewhat. As we have argued elsewhere (Mazey and Richardson, 1997a, p. 180), the Commission is at the centre of a complex and varied network of relationships and can act as a '*bourse*' (or garbage can) where problems, policies and interests are traded. Thus, although the EU policy process is decidedly 'messy' (multi-level and multi-arena), all policy proposals invariably have to pass through the Commission gateway and are subject to detailed *processing* at that institutional site. Moreover, much of the substance of European integration is about technical detail – standards, parameters, procedural rules, etc. – which can only be handled effectively in a bureaucratic/technical setting. It leads to routine (and increasingly routinized) day-to-day policy-making of the type familiar in national policy settings. Most debates are not about high politics – or what Peterson terms 'history-making decisions' (Peterson, 1995) and do not prompt life-and-death fights between member states. Periodically, the Union goes through what may appear to be history-making phases – the SEA and the TEU being obvious examples. However, the process of European integration in between these 'big bang' policy occasions is more about politics at the margins than about changing the shape and direction of European integration as a whole. This is not to say that groups are not concerned with these history-making events or that those events do not shape subsequent lobbying strategies via changes in institutional arrangments (see Mazey and Richardson, 1997b). However, the classic interest group focus is on detail – one group's detail being another group's poison, as it were. For groups, the devil is usually in the detail. In consequence, the Commission is an especially attractive opportunity structure or venue, for lobbying as this is where much of the detail is decided.

As a maturing bureaucracy, the Commission is a receptive institution to interest groups. Thus, *pressure* group would be quite the wrong term to describe most EU interest groups; they rarely need to apply pressure on the Commission. It is an eager consumer of knowledge and advice, which is willing to nurture and support groups which it feels need help, in its attempt to create a balanced and pluralistic interest group system of the EU. Thus, it exhibits the usual behavioural traits of a public bureaucracy and has developed intimate, sometimes symbiotic, relationships with groups. In practice, this means a very heavy emphasis on *consultation* with groups (and individual firms). This is achieved in formal consulation exercises where policy proposals are sent out to all relevant groups for their comments; in conferences and workshops which bring the affected interests together; in specialised advisory committees (both permanent and ad hoc); in daily meetings, often at the request of groups, between Commission officials and interest group representatives permanently based in, or visiting, Brussels; and, of course, via correspondence and telephone conversations between groups and Commission officials. Thus, group lobbying is about maximizing contact with Commission officials at every stage of the policy process and via as many channels as possible.

The European Parliament

It has been conventional wisdom to argue that the European Parliament is an inherently weak institution and therefore a relatively unattractive opportunity structure for interest groups Yet important qualifications to this analysis are needed. One qualification is that the EP has, for a very long time, (and long before the recent increases in its powers) attracted a great deal of lobbying activity – so much so, in fact, that the question of regulating lobbying has been a key issue within the EP for several years (see below). There are three obvious explanations for this apparent inconsistency. Most groups, as rational actors, recognise that the EU policy process demands a multi-track lobbying strategy – a 'belt and braces' approach to lobbying. Expressing a preference for one opportunity structure over another does not preclude some lobbying of less favoured structures. Secondly, it seems likely that the EP attracts a disproportionate amount of lobbying from certain types of groups (environmentalists, women, consumers, animal rights), which may not enjoy such easy access to the Commission and/or national governments. Thirdly, the EP's power in the EU policy process varies across policy sectors. Where there are effective EP committees, such as in the environmental field, lobbying of the EP is likely to be more intense. Thus, as we suggested earlier, institutions are not neutral opportunity structures – they filter out certain types of interest and favour others.

Another, and more important qualification is that the SEA, TEU and the Amsterdam Treaty have changed the institutional balance between EU institutions, strengthening the EP's role in the policy process. Put simply, 'the co-decision' procedure (see Chapter 7 of this volume) has significantly (some would say dramatically) improved the attractiveness of the EP as an opportunity structure for interest groups of all types – including business groups which, hitherto, probably relied rather heavily on contacts with the Commission and national governments. As the EP's legislative role has expanded over time, this has changed the calculation of the logic of influence by groups. Institutional change has also changed the relative attractiveness of opportunity structures. It was quite predictable that, if the EP's powers were increased, then the EP would attract more lobbying and from a wider range of groups, on the 'venue shopping' principle. One needs to look no further than the influential role of the EP in the fields of bio-technology policy (the patenting of new genetic material) and the so-called 'Auto Oil Programme' (designed to control pollution from motor vehicles) to see that the EP can be, on occasions, a very real threat to business groups and provide an important opportunity structure for their opponents. A key development in recent years has thus been the elevation of the EP's importance as a lobbying target (for data see Kohler-Koch, 1997). As Kohler-Koch suggests, 'according to the new role of the EP as an important institution in the European decison-making process, the Parliamentarians are becoming a decisive target group for lobbyists, and lobbyists have to cope with the institutional structure, the procedures, and the policy style within the Parliament' (Kohler-Koch, 1997, p. 10). Indeed, her research suggests that interest groups and the Parliament can sometimes be effective 'advocacy coalitions' in the EU policy process, albeit sometimes coalitions of the weak. As she argues, changes in the Parliament's role, and in its relationship with groups, seem to be shifting the EP in the direction of a US Congress-type legislature. For example, there has been a proliferation of EP 'intergroups' (of which there are now approximately 60). These 'intergroups' are informal meetings of MEPs which offer an opportunity to discuss policy issues. As one lobbyist has reported, intergroups (such as the Pharmaceutical Intergroup), are often the target of interest groups (Porter, 1998, p. 4). Two lobbyists have argued that the increased role for the EP has 'arrested power from the other institutions of the EU, and especially from closed negotiations between governments and officials in Brussels' and that this is 'good for commercial and other interests' (Earnshaw and Wood, 1998, p. 10). Thus, though much more needs to be known about the relationship between lobbies and the EP, we can conclude that it is now established as an important opportunity structure which has further increased the complexity of the Brussels lobbying game.

The European Court of Justice

Here, again, we see the EU interest intermediation system exhibiting some familiar features. In those political systems which accord the judiciary a major role in the interpretation of legal and constitutional arrangements, recourse to the courts has long been a standard 'lobbying' strategy. For example, much of the progress gained by black groups in the US (and by newer 'movements' such as the anti-nuclear energy movement) has been achieved through the Supreme Court and other courts in the US political system. This is in great contrast to the UK, for example, where judicial institutions have, traditionally, not been seen as a major opportunity structure by interest groups. In the EU, however, once the ECJ had acquired for itself a major role in the EU policy process it was inevitable that interest groups would pay it a lot of attention and allocate resources to influencing Court rulings. In practice, the ECJ has emerged as a perfect example of the working of the 'venue shopping' theory of Baumgartner and Jones, cited earlier. When groups have failed to gain satisfaction at the national venue, the Commission, EP or Council of Ministers, they have the option of bringing cases (usually in the name of individuals) before the Court, or of persuading the Commission to bring a case before the Court.

Women's and environmental groups (and also trade unions) have been adept in securing favourable ECJ decisions which have been just as, if not more, effective than bringing about change in EU policy via other means. For example, Mazey (1998, p. 136) argues that the EU generally has been an important venue for women's groups and that the ECJ, in particular, has been a very important opportunity structure or venue in supporting the plight of working women and forcing national policy change. The ECJ (in conjunction with the Commission) has been an important institution in the campaign by womens' groups to secure policy expansion in the EU (Mazey, 1998, p. 148). In the environmental field, Cichowski (1998) has reached similar conclusions. She argues that the ECJ has played an important role in the creation of supranational norms which fuel the integration process, often in opposition to the preferences of member states. Private litigants (individuals and interest groups) have played an integral role in this process. As a result, Cichowski argues, interest groups will use the Court to challenge national environment laws that hinder transnational activity and to attack national environmental norms which enshrine lowest common denominator European environmental norms or least integrative norms. These interest groups are, of course, not exclusively environmental groups; they also include business groups who seek to prevent national environmental laws from being used to undermine the principles of free and unrestricted trade enshrined in the SEA. At a more general level, Stone Sweet and Brunell have portrayed the Court as a 'supplying' institution – supplying integrative decisions in response to the demands of transnational actors such as businesses and individuals 'who need European rules, and those who are advantaged by European law and practices compared with national law and practices' (Stone Sweet and Brunell, 1998, p. 72). Their analysis is broadly consistent with a neofunctionalist view of European integration as they found 'broad support for theories of European legal integration that emphasise the reciprocal impact of litigants and transnational exchange, EC law, and judicial rule-making' (Stone Sweet and Brunell, 1998, p. 95). In practice, the Court is part of an integrative and self-sustaining system in which groups play an important role.

The Council of Ministers and National Governments

In theory, the Council of Ministers should be the main opportunity structure to be targeted by interest groups. Whether or not one accepts the intergovernmentalist stance (namely, that the most important EU policies are the result of bargains struck between national governments), the Council is the most authoritative single EU policy making institution in that all EU policies (except for specified policy areas in which legislative power is delegated to the Commission) must, ultimately, be approved by it. Yet, it is the least *directly* accessible of all EU institutions. As with Cabinets in Western democracies, lobbying has to be rather indirect. However, as Hayes-Renshaw and Wallace suggest, although groups 'have no formalised relationship with the Council, their influencing efforts pervade the atmosphere in which the Council works' (Hayes-Renshaw and Wallace, 1997, p. 22).

There are three main channels of indirect lobbying of the Council. First, interest groups routinely lobby the national delegations in Brussels, that is those national officials who are members of the so-called Permanent Representations based in Brussels. These representatives meet together in the Committee of Permanent Representatives (COREPER). As with Cabinet Secretariats, these national bureaucrats do much of the preparatory work for each Council meeting.

Where possible, they try to reach consensus and compromise between their respective national governments, leaving only the most contentious points to be resolved when the ministers meet in the respective Councils (see Chapter 2).

As each national representative in COREPER plays such a key role in the Council process, national groups (either based in or visiting Brussels) make sure that they lobby 'their' national officials, who (the interest groups hope) will then lobby on their behalf in COREPER meetings – hence the description of members of COREPER as the 'lobbied lobbyists' (Spence, 1993, p. 48). Euro-groups and those national associations and firms who really understand the importance of intergovernmentalism in EU policy making will also lobby a range of national delegations in COREPER – particularly of those member states who are known to hold strong positions on any given policy issue. In addition, it appears that 'explanatory material' from lobbyists is sometimes circulated within the Council Secretariat (Hayes-Renshaw and Wallace, 1997, p. 22).

A second indirect means of lobbying Council is for interest groups to lobby members of the many Council working groups (see Chapter 2). Rather like COREPER, this form of institutionalized 'issue processing' presents opportunities for detailed, technical arguments to be presented and for national representatives to be won over. The working groups are a sort of boiler-house of European integration. Composed of national officials

> 'congregating in their thousands every working day in Brussels, they (constitute) the backbone of the European system of integration . . . they are performing the vital and frequently time-consuming technical groundwork for what will eventually become a piece of European legislation or policy (Hayes-Renshaw and Wallace, 1997, p. 98).

Thus, for example, if a Council working group on vehicle pollution is meeting and contains a civil servant from the Swedish government, the civil servant will certainly be lobbied by Volvo and Saab and will be fully aware of the ways in which the Swedish motor vehicle industry will be affected by any proposed EU legislation. Occasionally, interest groups may secure representation on Council working groups if one of their officials is 'deemed' by a national government to be a civil servant for those purposes.

The third and most obvious means of influencing the Council is directly, via national governments. Several authors see national governments as, in fact, the *main* opportunity structure for interest groups, not just as a means of influencing Council but as the key opportunity structure through which groups can influence the EU policy process as a whole. For example, Grant has long been sceptical of the thesis that Brussels is the most effective lobbying arena (Grant, 1993). Similarly, Greenwood describes the 'national route' as the 'tried and tested ground for many organised interests' (Greenwood, 1997, p. 32). The national level 'is where established policy networks operate which can equally well be used for the purposes of EU representation as they can for the governance of domestic affairs' (Greenwood, 1997, p. 32). Bennett's survey data on the lobbying strategies of British business associations confirms this view of interest group behaviour. He found that the national route was the preferred Euro-lobbying strategy of the majority of associations (except federations). He, too, argues that this is perfectly-rational: '[T]he preference for this route can be explained by its relative cheapness and its continuity of use of traditional channels of information and exchange that have developed from the period before European economic integration' (Bennett, 1997, p. 85).

Clearly, the importance of national governments as an opportunity structure varies according to the policy issue, type of interest group, time, and the nature of the national government itself. On the latter, Aspinwall and Greenwood (1998, p. 22) suggest that 'in hierarchical, state dominated systems, interests tend not to develop transnational (EU level) strategies as readily as in more open, liberal polities'. This analysis is confirmed by Josselin's study of the behaviour (and differing success) of French and British financial interests in the EU. She concluded that British sectoral actors, who are 'less tied to a strict policy structure than the French are better able to exploit the multi-access lobbying system of the EU' (Josselin, 1996, p. 314). Also in the French case, Kassim has argued, more generally, that French interest groups are having to loosen their ties and dependency on the French state in order to increase their own influence in the EU (Kassim, 1997, p. 179). He sees this as a consequence of the weakening (in the EU arena) of even the traditionally strong EU states such as France – what he calls the 'dissipation of the national'. Elsewhere, we have argued that the extension of qualified majority voting (qmv) in the Council is bound to erode still further the traditional ties between interest groups and national governments and force interests to develop strategies independent of 'their' governments. Even when an interest group and a national government are on the same side (often not a reasonable assumption), the group cannot rely on a national government to be able to deliver under qmv (Mazey and Richardson, 1996, p. 212). Moreover, as cross-sectoral trade-offs between member states are not uncommon in last minute bargaining, national governments may choose to 'dump' an interest group in favour of some other policy goal. This is exactly what happened to the French farmers at a key stage in the Uruguay Round of the GATT negotiations (1986–93), when the French government shifted its original position because of more important policy needs. As Epstein argues, at a certain point in the GATT negotiations, 'the exclusivity and stability that normally characterise (French) agricultural policy were absent, as decisions were taken by different sets of high-level government actors in alternative arenas' (Epstein, 1997, p. 366). He sees the case as contradicting the basic tenets of policy community theory. One need not go this far to recognise that groups who do rely on the 'tried and tested' channels run very great risks. The EU policy game is quite different in character to many national systems, contains a much more diverse and numerous roster of parcipants, and demands new modes of lobbying behaviour. Thus, it is one thing to argue that the majority of groups still rely on the national opportunity structures, but quite another to conclude that this is an efficacious form of behaviour. It is no accident that large firms appear to show a growing preference for Euro-level lobbying. For example, Coen's study of 94 of Europe's largest firms found that these firms were gradually shifting the location of their lobbying resources to the European level and away from the national level (Coen, 1997, pp. 99–105). Groups will seek out those structures that work for them, and will shift lobbying resources to those structures, as Coen suggests. Rarely will they totally abandon structures, however (hence, lobbying of national governments will always be important), even though they will seek to find new ones. It is to a newly emerging European-level opportunity structure that we now turn.

'Newshole' Lobbying

Traditional lobbying strategies in domestic politics have always included an element of what we might call 'newshole lobbying'. The term 'newshole' lobbying, refers to attempts to influence the news content of newspapers, television and radio, both to ensure that a group's views do not go unreported and to try to structure the way in which a particular policy issue is 'framed'. By influencing the structure of policy discourse in the media, a group can hope to influence policy outcomes. The European level is generally lacking in the media opportunity structures familiar at the national level. However, there are now a few genuinely European-level media outlets and there are signs that some of these are perceived by groups as worthwhile channels for communicating to European policy-makers. The best example of such an outlet is an *Economist* publication, *European Voice*. Rather similar to *Roll Call* in the US (published in Washington and also owned by *The Economist*), it is published weekly and has a circulation of 18,000. It is read widely by European (35 per cent of the circulation is accounted for by Brussels subscribers) and national-level policy-makers and other policy stakeholders such as interest group leaders and firms. The policy positions of groups are reported regularly (indeed, the newspaper, in seeking advertising copy for forthcoming special features, specifically claimed that companies could place their advertising message 'in the hands of Europe's policy makers' – see *European Voice*, 23–9 July 1998, p. 16). Of course, this might have been poetic licence on the part of the advertising section of the paper. However, groups and individual companies do take out full-page advertisements (at a cost of £3,500 per page), often over a period of months when controversial issues – such as control of genetically engineered products, are passing through a key phase of the legislative cycle (particulary in the EP). For example, one interest group recently spent approximately £40,000 over a six-month period as part of its lobbying strategy on an issue central to its concerns. This suggests that under certain circumstances, some interests are prepared to allocate significant resources to the media as an opportunity structure. The beginnings of a Euro-level media read by policy-making elites is part of a more general trend for the expansion of policy information, debate, and advice – again illustrating the *maturation* of the EU as a polity. (This expansion includes numerous Euro-think-tanks, such as the Centre for European Policy Studies and the Trans-European Policy Studies Association, and many think tanks at the national level which play a significant role in influencing domestic preference formation on European issues. Some of these think-tanks have links with interest groups of various kinds and can be seen a subtle means of massaging Euro policy agendas.)

Similarly, groups see the reporting of European policy issues at the national level as a means of influencing the behaviour of national governments and structuring public perceptions of European issues. As Bulmer suggests, the intergovernmentalist thesis needs to be tempered by a recognition that 'national governments are in many cases prisoners of domestic and international circumstances' (Bulmer, 1983, p. 360). These 'domestic circumstances' are in part conditioned by public and elite perceptions of what the national interest is on a given European issue. Groups recognise this and hence try to condition debate via the media. (For example, bigger firms in Britain have been running a loosely coordinated campaign to secure a more favourable reporting of the possibility of Britain joining the single currency.) Domestic and European politics are inextricably linked and it is, therefore, a sensible strategy to try to shape domestic politics via media coverage.

Again, we see Euro-lobbying following familiar patterns. As students of social movements have noted, the media is often a key opportunity structure for such organistations. For example, McCarthy *et al.* (1996, p. 291) argue that social movements 'often lack the political and/or material resources necessary for routine access to political decision-makers and must therefore rely primarily on "outsider" strategies to draw the attention of publics and policy-makers to the problems they wish to have resolved'. Hence, the media are certainly a major target for social movement framing efforts. Much of the success of the environmental movement in securing European-level action to protect the environment can be attributed to their success in attracting media coverage, across the EU, to their 'environmental frame'. Via this process, they have often been more effective Euro-agenda-setters than their wealthier industrial opponents. The latter, for example the European chemical and fertilizer industries, have commissioned opinion research in an attempt to find ways of counteracting the framing successes of the environmentalists. They have devised media campaigns of their own, only to find their 'ratings' doggedly stuck in the mire of hostile public opinion.

Bias or Balance in European Opportunity Structures: Ruling Business or Business Rules?

Any policy problem, as it reaches the political agenda, brings with it a whole constellation of interests, institutions and ideas. Public policy emerges from the *melange* of actors and ideas and can be said to reflect the balance of forces in society at any given time. For example, the EU has often been characterized as reflecting a business agenda in the 1990s, by which is meant that business interests decided the pace and direction of European integration and secured for themselves many policy benefits to the disadvantage of others. Thus, the SEA might be seen as a useful indicator of business power, instituting the whole complex process of creating a single competitive market. Indeed, Maria Green Cowles has argued that 'the agenda for the single market programme was set by economic interests' (Green Cowles, 1995, p. 552).

More recent developments might be said to lend support to this general thesis. For example, much of the 'policy framing' which characterizes policy debates across a wide range of Directorates-General in the European Commission is consistent with pressure from the business community in Europe. Thus, in terms of Rein and Schön's definition of a policy frame (a perspective from which an amorphous ill-defined situation can be made sense and acted upon (Rein and Schön, 1991, p. 262)), business interests seem to have 'captured' many sectoral policy debates in the so-called 'competitiveness' frame. This frame structures policy debates – such as over the rights of women, the need for environmental protection or the need for increased product safety legislation – in terms of a claimed *overriding* need not to adversely effect the competitiveness of European industry in world markets. Most EU (and national) policy problems must be passed through this 'intellectual filter' before they can progress through the highly complex EU policy process. Linked to this broad policy frame are subsidiary (but crucial in terms of business interests) questions regarding deregulation, privatization, and labour market flexibility. Pressure has also been exerted by business interests for processual and institutional changes within the EU. These demands include greater flexibility in the implementation process; a simplified EU legislative procedure; the use of more framework (i.e. general) laws; introduction of a whole range of new policy instruments, such as voluntary agreements; and the strengthening of certain institutions (particularly the Commission) at the expense of others. The period since the SEA has, therefore, seen a growing intensity of business lobbying, especially in terms of attempts to structure and shape the EU's broad agenda. This has put other interests on the defensive.

Classic group theorists – and the modern pluralist writers – would be sceptical of a conclusion which suggested total business dominance. The group struggle is rarely so simple or stable. One does not have to be a pluralist (arguing that the group struggle is more or less equal) to claim that the EU group process, particularly following

SEA and TEU, is much more competitive, fluid and unpredictable than the 'business rules OK' thesis might imply. As we suggested earlier, the EU group system is no longer an adolescent system. It has been developing since the formation of the Coal and Steel Community (and was recognised by the founding fathers of the EU such as Jean Monnet at the very outset as being essential to the creation of the European ideal – see Mazey, 1992). As the data cited earlier suggests, the density and comprehensiveness of the group system at the European level is now rather similar to the familiar group–state interactions that have emerged in all post-war Western European societies. Any notion that any one set of interests can *dominate* the EU policy process over a long period of time is unfounded. The marketplace for lobbying is overcrowded, the degree of competition between EU institutions themselves, and between EU institutions and member states, so intense that it is impossible for any actor (public or private) to consistently control the trajectory of the policy game. A system of policy-making characterized by multi-level, multi-arena and nested games, with a proliferation of stakeholders, is unlikely to produce a stable set of winners and losers.

Thus, the Single European Market project and the subsequent policy fashion for deregulation and increased competitiveness have not prevented advances by, for example, women's and environmental groups. Both the TEU and Amsterdam Treaties resulted in the policy demands of these groups becoming further entrenched in terms of their Treaty basis (Mazey and Richardson, 1998). Moreover, these groups have themselves become embedded in EU institutions, especially inside the Commission and the EP, both of which have an institutional interest in issue expansion. For example, both DG XI (Environment) and the Equal Opportunities Unit within DGV (Employment and Social Affairs) have a strong institutional self-interest in resisting any policy erosion in their own policy sectors as a result of business pressure. They are finding ways of 'legislating in hard times' (Mazey and Richardson, 1998). It would also be mistaken to see the business lobby as unsophisticated – simply pushing for more and more policy gains, irrespective of the impact of such gains on opposing interests. The whole European project is a 'high politics' issue of great importance to the business community (particularly to large multi-national companies), which, generally speaking, acknowledges the need for side-payments (policy concessions) to opposing groups such as trade unions, as a means of maintaining broad support for further Europeanization. In truth, the bias system in the EU is not dissimilar to that in the US. Thus, we would echo the view of the US system presented by Baumgartner and Leech, namely that 'whatever the biases stemming from differences in public involvement and the occupational bases of many interest groups in America, these biases are not the same at all times, for all issues, and in all areas of political life. The set of interest groups active in Washington is anything but stable: it has undergone dramatic transformations over time; it differs from areas to area; and it varies from issue to issue (Baumgartner and Leech, 1998, p. 100). The very fact that the EU system is characterized by multiple venues and opportunity structures, that there is often intense institutional competition (for example between the EP and the Commission), and that the basic decision rules are still fluid and subject to a rolling reform programme guarantees instability of bias. This instability, combined with massive interest group mobilization (surely an appropriate label for the current level of EU lobbying), prevents domination by any one set of groups over time. As Pollack suggests, whilst the EU opportunity structures present real risks to what he terms diffuse interests such as consumers, women and environmentalists, the facts are that such interests have been quite adept in exploiting these opportunity structures. They have also prevented the rollback of earlier gains which has sometimes occurred at the national level (Pollack, 1997, p. 587).

Conclusion: Lobbies as Transmission Belts

One of the signs that the EU lobbying system is no longer adolescent and has reached a level of 'maturity' akin to national interest group systems in Western Europe is that the *regulation* of EU lobbying has emerged as a key issue in recent years. The EU interest intermediation system now exhibits the costs and benefits with which interest group theorists have long been familiar. Clearly, groups serve the interests of democracy in providing what McKenzie (1958) called the 'transmission belt' between citizens and their rulers. In coining this term, McKenzie was expressing doubts about the efficacy of British political parties in performing the traditional functions attributed to them by modern democratic theorists. Bearing in mind the fact that the European polity has yet to develop a *European* party system, it seems reasonable to argue that interest groups may play a potentially important role in the democratisation of the EU. Without the high degree of interest mobilization and the array of welcoming opportunity structures and venues available to these groups, the EU governing elites would have much less contact with their peoples. In practice, national governments are usually acutely aware of the EU preference structures of domestic interest groups, and EU institutions are able to obtain a fairly broad overview of how interests across the EU (and beyond) are likely to be affected by policy change.

The problem is not that decision-makers at the national and EU levels are unaware of citizen demands. The situation is quite the opposite – they are often overloaded with demands from interest groups. There is not an under-supply, but an over-supply of lobbying to the multiple opportunity structures available in the EU. Predictably, therefore, the old issue of the regulation of lobbying has emerged. The familiar debates have been held with the familiar outcome – namely a recognition that it is virtually impossible to regulate lobbying effectively. Greenwood's comprehensive analysis of the regulatory issue concludes by suggesting that at least the agenda has been set and initatives have been taken by the EP, the Commission and some commercial lobbying organizations themselves which 'may signal the start of a restructuring of the relationship between outside interests and the European institutions' (Greenwood, 1997, p. 100). The danger of regulation, as Greenwood suggests, is that regulatory rules themselves may constitute a form of bias. Thus, he argues that the Commission's tentative approach to regulation has emphasized the broadening of consultation, whereas the EP's initiatives might 'further privilege the already privileged' (Greenwood, 1997, p. 98), because they might lead to some form of official (and therefore, exclusive) 'recognition' of certain groups at the expense of others.

In terms of the changes in the nature of the interest group intermediation system in the EU, the Comission's attempts to broaden and institutionalise interest group participation in the EU policy process are likely to prove the most important. For example, the Commission has an entrenched organisational culture which emphasises access and consultation. To limit access would run counter to this culture (itself an important strategy in mobilizing support for the European project as a whole). Hence, the Commission seems intent on a process of *institutionalization* as a means of creating stability and predictability in the policy process. What does this mean in practice? In essence, it means a growing number of permanent consultative structures – often in the form of fora bringing together the range of interest group (and other) stakeholders in a given policy area. Typical examples include the Forum on Sustainable Development run by DGXI, the European Social Policy Forum, organized by the Commission in 1996 (over 1,000 delegates attended this meeting), and the Energy Forum, designed to bring together power firms, consumer organizations and environmental groups to discuss the implications of deregulation in the EU's electricity and gas markets. This form of institutional innovation is being grafted onto the long-standing system of advisory committees, widely used by the Commission, in which interest groups participate alongside other stakeholders. Each phase of EU reform and institutional change has merely reinforced and expanded the historical pattern of EU interest intermediation. This trend is likely to continue. We conclude, therefore by predicting the emergence of more and better organized groups, and the further proliferation of EU opportunity structures accompanied by institutionalization, which will further bind interest organizations into the European project.

Guide to Further Reading

For a range of chapters dealing with the role of interest groups in different policy sectors at EU level, see the edited books by Greenwood, Grote and Ronit (1992) and Mazey and Richardson (1993). For a general overview of the activities of interest groups in the context of the European Union, see Greenwood (1997) and for a discussion of the new forms of collective action which may be emerging at EU level see the various contributions to Greenwood and Aspinwall (eds) (1998). For a discussion of the emergence of a form of corporatist interest intermediation in the area of EU social policy, see Falkner (1998).

References

Aspinwall, M. and Greenwood, J. (1998) 'Conceptualising collective action in the European Union: An Introduction', in J. Greenwood and M. Aspinwall (eds), *Collective Action in the European Union: Interests and the New Politics of Associability*. London: Routledge, pp. 1–30.

Baumgartner, F. and Jones, B. (1991) 'Agenda Dynamics and Instability in American Politics', *Journal of Politics*, vol. 53, no. 4, pp. 1044–73.

Baumgartner, F. and Jones, B. (1993) *Agendas and Instability in American Politics*, Chicago: Chicago University Press.

Baumgartner, F. and Leech, B. (1998) *Basic Interests. The Importance of Groups in Politics and Political Science*. Princeton: Princeton University Press.

Bennett, R. (1997) 'The Impact of European Integration on Business Associations: The UK Case', *West European Politics*, vol. 20, no. 3, pp. 6–90.

Bulmer, S. (1983) 'Domestic Politics and European Community Policy-making', *Journal of Common Market Studies*, vol. 21, no. 4, pp. 349–63.

Butt Philip, A. (1985) *Pressure Groups in the European Community*. London: University Association for Contemporary European Studies (UACES).

Coen, D. (1997) 'The Evolution of the Large Firm as a Political Actor in the European Union', *Journal of European Public Policy*, vol. 4, no. 1, pp. 91–108.

Commission (1992) *An Open and Structured Dialogue Between the Commission and Interest Groups* (SEC (92) 2272 final) Brussels: European Commission.

Commission (1996) *Directory of Interest Groups*. Brussels: European Commission.

Cichowski, R. (1998) 'Constrained Court or Autonomous Policy-maker? The European Court of Justice and Integration', *Journal of European Public Policy*, vol. 5, no. 3, pp. 387–405.

Dahl, R. (1982) *Dilemmas of Pluralist Democracy*. London: Yale University Press.

Deutsch, K. (1957) *Political Community at the International Level: Problems of Definition and Management*. New York: Doubleday & Co.

Earnshaw D. and Wood, J. (1998) 'Winning in Brussels', *The Public Affairs Newsletter*, July.

Epstein, P. (1997) 'Beyond Policy Community: French Agriculture and the GATT', *Journal of European Public Policy*. vol. 4, no. 3, pp. 355–72.

Falkner, Gerda (1998) *EU Social Policy in the 1990s: Towards a Corporatist Policy Community*. London: Routledge.

Grant, W. (1993) 'Pressure Groups and the European Community: An Overview', in S. Mazey and J. Richardson (eds), *Lobbying in the European Community*. London: Routledge, pp. 27–46.

Grant, W. (1995) *The Political Economy of Corporatism*. London: Macmillan.

Green Cowles, M. (1995) 'Setting the Agenda for the New Europe: The ERT and EC 1992', *Journal of Common Market Studies*, vol. 33, no. 4, pp. 501–26.

Greenwood, J. (1997) *Representing Interests in the European Union*. London: Macmillan.

Greenwood, J. and Aspinwall, M. (eds) (1998) *Collective Action in the European Union: Interests and the New Politics of Associability*. London: Routledge.

Greenwood, J., Grote, J. and Ronit, K. (1992) *Organised Interests in the European Community*. London: Sage.

Haas, E. B. (1958) *The Uniting of Europe: Political, Social and Economic Forces 1950–57,* London: Stevens.

Haas, P. (1992) 'Introduction: Epistemic Communities and International Policy Co-ordination', *International Organization*, vol. 46, no. 1, pp. 1–35.

Hayes-Renshaw, F. and Wallace, H. (1997) *The Council of Ministers*. London: Macmillan.

Josselin, D. (1996) 'Domestic Policy Networks and European Negotiations: Evidence from British and French Financial Services' *Journal of European Public Policy*, vol. 3, no. 3, pp. 297–317.

Kassim, H. (1997) 'French Autonomy and the European Union', *Modern and Contemporary France*, vol. 5, no. 2, pp. 167–80.

Kirchner, E. (1977) *Trade Unions as Pressure Groups in the European Community*. Farnborough: Saxon House.

Kirchner, E. (1980a) 'International Trade Union Collaboration and the Prospect for European Industrial Relations', *West European Politics*, vol. 3, no. 1, pp. 124–37.

Kirchner, E. (1980b) 'Interest Group Behavior at the Community level', in L. Hurwitz (ed.), *Contemporary Perspectives on European Integration*. London: Aldwich pp. 95–119.

Kitschelt, H.P (1986) 'Political Opportunity Structures and Political Protest: Anti-nuclear Movements in Four Democracies', *British Journal of Political Science*, vol. 16, no. 1, pp. 57–85.

Kohler-Koch, B. (1997) 'Organised Interests in the EU and the European Parliament', Paper presented to International Political Science Association XV111 Congress, Seoul, 17–21 August 1997.

Lindblom, C. (1977) *Politics and Markets*. New York: Basic Books.

McAdam, D. (1996) 'Conceptual Origins, Current Problems, Future Directions', in D. McAdam, J. McCarthy and M. Zald, (eds), *Comparative Perspectives on Social Movemenmts: Political Opportunities, Mobilizing Structures, and Cultural Framings*, Cambridge: Cambridge University Press, pp. 23–40.

McCarthy, J., Smith, J. and Zald, M. (1996) 'Accessing Public, Media, Electoral, and Governmental Agendas', in D. McAdam, J. McCarthy, and M. Zald, (eds), *Comparative Perspectives on Social Movements*. Cambridge: Cambridge University Press, pp. 291–311.

McKenzie, R. (1958) 'Parties, Pressure Groups and the British Political Process', *Political Quarterly*, vol. 29, no. 1, pp. 1–16.

Mazey, S. (1992) 'Conception and Evolution of the High Authority's Administrative Services (1952–56): From Supranational Principles to Multilateral Practices', *Yearbook of European Administrative History*. Baden-Baden: Nomos, pp. 31–48.

Mazey, S. (1998) 'The European Union and Women's Rights: From The Europeanization of National Agendas to the Nationalization of a European agenda?', *Journal of European Public Policy*, vol. 5, no. 1, pp. 131–52.

Mazey, S. and Richardson, J. (eds) (1993) *Lobbying in the European Community*. London: Routledge.

Mazey, S. and Richardson, J. (1996) 'The Logic of Organisation: Interest groups', in J. Richardson (ed.), *Power and Policy-Making in the European Union*. London: Routledge, pp. 200–15.

Mazey, S. and Richardson, J. (1997a) 'The Commission and the Lobby', in G. Edwards and D. Spence (eds), *The European Commission*. London: Cartermill, pp. 178–98.

Mazey, S. and Richardson, J. (1997b) 'Policy Framing: Interest Groups and the Lead Up to the 1996 Inter-Governmental Conference', *West European Politics*, vol. 20, no. 3, pp. 111–33.

Mazey, S. and Richardson, J. (1998) 'Framing and Re-framing Public Policy in the EU: Ideas, Interests and Institutions in Sex Equality and Environmental Policies' Paper presented to the Joint Sessions of Workshops, ECPR, Warwick 23–8 March 1998.

Peterson, J. (1995) 'Decision-making in the European Union: Towards a Framework for Analysis', *Journal of European Public Policy*, vol. 2, no. 1, pp. 69–94.

Pijnenburg, B. (1998) 'EC lobbying by Ad Hoc Coalitions: An Exploratory Case Study', *Journal of European Public Policy*, vol. 5, no. 2, pp. 303–21.

Pollack, M. (1997) 'Representing Diffuse Interests in EC Policy-making', *Journal of European Public Policy*, vol. 4, no. 4, pp. 572–90.

Porter, M. (1998) 'Intergroups and Interest Representation in the EP', *ELIR Newsletter,* vol. 4, no. 1, pp. 4–5.

Rein, M. and Schön, D. (1991) 'Frame-reflective Policy Discourse', in P. Wagner, C.H. Weiss, B. Wittrock and H. Wollman (eds), *Social Sciences and Modern States: National Experiences and Theoretical Crossroads.* Cambridge: Cambridge University Press, pp. 262–89.

Sidjanski, D. (1970) 'Pressure Groups and the European Economic Community', in C. Cosgrove and K. Twitchett (eds), *The New International Actors: The United Nations and the European Economic Community*. London: Macmillan pp. 222–36.

Spence, D. (1993) 'The Rôle of the National Civil Service in European Lobbying: The British Case', in S. Mazey and J. Richardson (eds), *Lobbying in the European Community*. Oxford: Oxford University Press, pp. 47–73.

Stone Sweet, A. and Brunell, T. (1998) 'The European Court and the National Courts: A Statistical Analysis of Preliminary References, 1961–95', *Journal of European Public Policy* vol. 5, no. 1, pp. 69–97.

Stone Sweet, A. and Sandholtz, W. (1997) 'European Integration and Supranational Governance', *Journal of European Public Policy*, vol. 4, no. 3, pp. 297–317.

7

Decision-Making

NEILL NUGENT

This chapter examines the varied, complex, and highly distinctive nature of decision-making in the EU. The chapter is structured around two main parts. In the first part, key characteristics of EU decision-making are described and considered. In the second part, the EU's principal decision-making procedures are outlined and analysed.

Key Characteristics of EU Decision-Making

EU decision-making displays many distinctive characteristics, the most important of which are now examined.

Diffusion of Leadership

The EU does not have the base for the exercise of leadership that is found in its member states. The precise nature of these national bases varies both in terms of character and effectiveness, but in broad terms they can be said to rest on two main pillars. On the one hand, there is an *institutional* pillar. The customary pattern here is that governments, supported by majorities in parliaments, provide a lead on the basis of the authority that has been invested in them by the citizenry in national elections. On the other hand there is what might be called an *identificational* pillar. This consists of a bond of shared identity between members of the government who are united, to at least some degree, by ideological affinity and/or political understanding.

In the EU there is no comparable body that can provide the institutional location for leadership in the manner of a national government. Rather there are several possible locations, each of which is limited in the leadership it can provide by internal weaknesses of various kinds. One of these weaknesses, especially in the more intergovernmental locations, is a poorly developed sense of shared identity.

There are three main institutional locations which, it may be thought, could potentially provide the EU with leadership:

The Commission The potential of the Commission to provide leadership rests on such factors as its power of initiative, its knowledge of EU policies and policy needs, its permanence, and the widely-held perceptions and expectations of it as the motor force and facilitator of integration. The Commission's leadership potential is weakened, however, by its lack of a democratic base and its reliance on other institutions for final decision-making. Circumstances, therefore, have to be favourable for the Commission to be able both to offer and give effect to strong and clear leadership. In very general terms it can be said that such circumstances – which include, above all, the Commission being given broad support from the member states when it pioneers and champions new proposals – have not applied as much in recent years as they did between the mid-1980s and the early 1990s, when a highly activist Commission under the leadership of Jacques Delors was promoting the 're-launch' of the European Community. A consequence of these less favourable circumstances has been that the Commission has become more cautious about launching bold initiatives – as witnessed, for example, by the rather modest proposals that were contained in its long-heralded and much-trumpeted growth and employment initiative in 1994, and by its decision not to call for an increase in medium-term EU expenditure in its 1997 *Agenda 2000* proposals.

The European Council The leadership potential of the European Council stems primarily from the fact that, as the forum in which heads of government meet, it has the highest political status, and arguably the greatest political legitimacy (although the EP would contest that), of any EU institution. It is weakened, however, by the breadth of the political and national affinities of its members, the short duration and conference style of its meetings, and its unwillingness (apart from only very occasionally) to take decisions other than by unanimity. These weaknesses have tended to result in the European Council being more of a reactive and legitimizing body than an innovating one in its own right. Whilst virtually all of the EU's major decisions of recent times – most notably on treaty reform, enlargement, and EMU – have been channelled through and approved by the European Council, the development and drafting of the proposals on which the decisions have been taken has usually taken place elsewhere: most commonly in the Commission.

The Council of Ministers Within their various formations, meetings of the Council of Ministers have similar strengths and weaknesses to the European Council, albeit at a less elevated political level. Ministers can press the Commission to bring proposals before them and they do, of course, take decisions on important matters within their spheres of responsibility. They are, however, even more than the European Council, highly dependent on the Commission working with it in a cooperative manner. Within the Council of Ministers, and indeed within the European Council, too, there is some limited scope for the Presidency to offer leadership through the prioritization of objectives and effective management, but the short period of office of the Presidency – six months – inevitably means that little can actually be started and finished in one term.

The potential for leadership in the EU is thus divided or, it might be said, is shared, between several locations. How this affects decision-making can be illustrated by examining developments leading up to the launch of a single currency in 1999:

- Jacques Delors, Commission President from January 1985 to January 1995, was very prominent in pressing the case for Economic and Monetary Union (EMU) throughout his period of office, and chaired the 1988–9 committee of central bankers which produced the extremely influential 'Delors Report' that recommended a three stage progression to EMU;
- during the transition to the single currency, Commissioners consistently advocated EMU and the Commission as an institution regularly produced reports and documentation that facilitated the transition process;

- several member states, and most crucially France and Germany given their centrality to the EMU project, worked consistently in EU forums and also on a direct basis with each other, to ensure the single currency would be achieved;
- the Economic and Finance Council of Ministers (Ecofin) was concerned with EMU throughout the transition process, and all relevant matters – from providing guidelines to assist the member states to meet the convergence criteria to the design of euro notes and coins – came before it for consideration;
- and all major decisions – including the conditions and timetable set out in the Treaty on European Union (TEU) for progressing to EMU, the rules of the Stability and Growth Pact that would apply to single currency members, and the designation of the countries qualifying for membership of the single currency – were formally taken at European Council Meetings, albeit largely on the basis of preparatory work undertaken by, and recommendations of, the Commission and Ecofin.

Leadership in the EU thus emanates from several sources. The Commission is the most favourably placed to launch ideas, initiatives, and policies, but the prospects for such leadership as it offers being effective very much depends on it being supported by the member states, or at least by a sufficient number of them.

A Profusion of Actors

The EU is very much a multi-actor system, with an enormous number and a very great variety of actors involved in its decision-making processes. These actors can be grouped in various ways. A broad three-fold classification is used here:

The EU Institutions. The involvement of the EU's main institutions in decision-making processes is explored in earlier chapters of this book, and is also considered in other sections of this chapter. The adage ascribed to the relations between these institutions used to be that 'The Commission proposes, the Council decides, the Parliament advises, and the Court interprets'. This was always somewhat simplistic, not least insofar as the Commission was usually sensitive to

Council wishes when it proposed, and Court rulings sometimes had the effect of making new laws. Over the years the adage has become even more inappropriate as treaty reforms and political practice have resulted in the European Council, the Council of Ministers and the European Parliament (EP) becoming strong influences on what the Commission proposes, and with the EP becoming a co-decision-maker with the Council in respect of most EU legislation (see below).

National authorities. The most important national authorities to be involved in EU decision-making are, of course, national governments, which make up the membership of the European Council and of the Council of Ministers. This national governmental involvement is most obvious at the political level, with governmental leaders meeting in the European Council at least twice a year and with governmental ministers meeting as and when their spheres of responsibility require it – which in the case, for example, of Foreign Ministers usually means at least once a month and in the case of Education Ministers normally means just once per Council Presidency. Beneath this political level, national government officials – some of whom are based in Brussels in the Permanent Representations (embassies) to the EU, but most of whom are based in national capitals – handle much of the more routine and day-to-day business associated with national involvement in the EU.

A developing feature of the involvement of national authorities in EU decision-making has been the growing role of subnational authorities. This has partly been a consequence of the development of regionalism and localism in the member states, and partly a consequence of encouragement by the Commission – which sometimes wishes to by-pass the national governmental 'gatekeepers' and which, with subsidiarity becoming a guiding principle for decision-making in the 1990s, has been able to do so with greater authority. This growing importance of subnational governmental involvement in EU affairs – which is seen, for example, in the establishment of many regional government offices in Brussels – has led some commentators to conceptualize the EU as a system of multi-level governance (see, for example, Marks *et al.*, 1996). By this they mean not just that the EU is multi-layered in character, but also that the different layers – supranational, national and subnational – often deal directly with one another rather than being confined to operating within a rigid hierarchy of relationships.

Interests. A wide range of nongovernmental interests focus attention on the EU. Their purposes in so doing are many and varied, but the main aims are to influence the thinking of decision-makers, to shape outcomes, and to affect how EU policies are applied.

There are estimated to be about 10,000 lobbyists in Brussels, ranging in nature from full-time employees of single interests to private consultants working for several interests at the same time. The interests are of three main types. First, private and public companies, of which the most influential tend to be large multinational or national companies which have large numbers of employees and/or are located in what are deemed to be key sectors. Second, national interest groups, of which the more important are industrial and agricultural groups. Third, Euro-groups – that is groups which are of an umbrella type in that their membership is not usually direct but is made up of affiliations from national groups. There are around 550 Euro-groups, of which about 50 per cent represent industry and commerce, about 25 per cent agriculture and food, about 20 per cent services, and about 5 per cent other interests. (A fuller analysis of the nature of interests at the EU level is given in Chapter 6.)

Within the context of what is known as the social dialogue, the EU's three 'social partners' – the European Trade Union Confederation (ETUC), the Union of Industrial and Employers Confederations of Europe (UNICE) and the European Centre of Enterprises with Public Participation (CEEP) – have, since the TEU, become quasi-decision-makers themselves. This is because the Commission can invite them to contract draft labour law agreements that may then be turned directly into legislative proposals. A number of such invitations from the Commission have been unsuccessful, with one or more of the partners being unwilling to reach agreement on such matters as consultations with workers, procedures to deal with sexual harassment, and the burden of proof in sex discrimination cases. Two invitations have, however, produced agreements and legislation: on parental leave and on the rights of part-time workers.

Many Procedures

The EU has many decision-making procedures. Precisely how many depends on just what is counted: all procedures or just legislative procedures?; if only legislative procedures are considered, are all variations to be included or not?; and what about the many informal procedures that are woven into formal procedures? Most estimates put the number of clearly distinctive procedures at between 20 and 30. For example, in a report it prepared for the 1995 Reflection Group (see Chapter 15), the Commission listed a total of 29 'main decision-making procedures provided for in the Treaty on European Union': 22 under the European Community pillar; four under the Common Foreign and Security Policy (CFSP) pillar; and three under the Justice and Home Affairs (JHA) pillar (*Commission Report for the Reflection Group*, Annex 8, pp. 80–4). Despite hopes that the number of procedures would be reduced by the Amsterdam Treaty, little progress was made.

The main reason why there are so many procedures is, quite simply, that national political elites, who decide on the EU's 'constitution' in intergovernmental conferences (IGCs), have taken different views on such key questions as which policy areas should be located within the framework of the founding treaties and which outside, when qualified majority voting (qmv) should be available in the Council of Ministers and when unanimity should be required, and what powers should be 'granted' to the EP. These and related questions have been answered by different states, in different ways, at different times, with the consequence that the 'deals' that have been necessary at IGCs to produce agreements have cumulatively produced an almost bewildering patchwork of decision-making procedures.

Creeping Supranationalism

The objection that 'Eurosceptics' most commonly lodge against the EU is that it is moving progressively in an ever more centralist – what some critics label a 'federalist' – direction. The evidence that is usually cited to support this view is, on the one hand, the seeming steady expansion in the EU's policy portfolio and, on the other hand, the apparent remorseless increase in the supranational character of the EU's decision-making processes. The extent to which the first of these two alleged developments is occurring can be judged from other chapters of this book. The extent to which the second is occurring will be considered briefly here.

That EU decision-making displays supranational characteristics is clear. There are five main dimensions to this supranationalism, three of which are directly concerned with decision-making processes and two of which are concerned more with the outcome of those processes. These dimensions, and the extent to which they are becoming increasingly supranational, are as follows:

- The *Commission* – an appointed, non governmental body – is a major player in the making of EU law. In respect of 'political' law it is the formulator of legislative proposals and it exercises great influence over the progress of proposals as they make their way through the Council and the EP (see below). In respect of 'administrative' law the Commission is itself the main decision-maker, though its actions are monitored by, and can indeed usually be controlled by, committees of national government representatives. The policy sphere in which the Commission has greatest discretion is competition policy: it can take direct action against such practices as abuse of dominant market positions and illegal state aids, and it exercises a key role in respect of granting or withholding permission for proposed large company mergers.
- The *Council of Ministers* can take many decisions on proposals for EU law by qualified majority vote (qmv). That is to say, many EU laws can be made against the wishes of one member state or a minority of member states. After years of being unwilling to use qmv because of the impact of the 1966 Luxembourg Compromise (which implied that member states could veto proposals to which they strongly objected), qmv gradually came to be accepted in the early to mid 1980s as a necessary way of proceeding in some circumstances. The three rounds of treaty reform which have occurred since then – via the Single European Act (SEA), the TEU, and the Treaty of Amsterdam – have all increased the policy spheres in which qmv is permissible, to the point that, as is shown in the second part of this chapter, there is now only a relatively small number of sensitive policy spheres in which qmv cannot be used.
- The *European Parliament* is supranational by virtue of being composed of directly elected Members of the European Parliament (MEPs) rather than governmental representatives, by virtue of taking its decisions by majority – or, in some cases, by an absolute majority – vote, and by virtue of having real decision-making powers. These powers have been greatly increased by the SEA, the TEU, and the Amsterdam Treaty, to the extent that the institution which used to be dismissed as little more than a rather special sort of advisory body now has veto powers over most significant decisions that are made under the EC pillar of the EU.
- *EU law* takes precedence over national law should the two conflict. This long-established principle has inevitably become of ever-greater significance as EU law has steadily expanded in scope. There are now virtually no areas of public policy in which EU law

does not have at least a foothold, and there are many in which it is either the main provider of law (notably external trade, agriculture, and various aspects of market regulation), or is a major provider of law (such as in the regional, social, and environmental policy spheres).

- The *European Court of Justice (ECJ)* is the final authority on the interpretation of EU law and on 'boundary disputes' between EU law and national law. As EU law has broadened in scope so have the demands on the Court inevitably increased. In Chapter 5 above, Daniel Wincott gives some examples of the political impact Court rulings can have.

The Importance of Tiers and of Hierarchy

In three of the EU's four main decision-making institutions, internal decision-making is very much based on multi-tiered hierarchical structures. Ideas and proposals are channelled up the tiers and as they proceed they are subject to extensive scrutiny and, normally, revision.

The two clearest hierarchies are those that exist in the Commission and the Council of Ministers, simplified diagrams of which are shown in Figure 7.1. The nature of the tiers in these hierarchies is explained by Fiona Hayes-Renshaw in Chapter 2 and by Laura Cram in Chapter 3. (For more detailed information on the Council see Hayes-Renshaw and Wallace, 1997, and on the Commission see Edwards and Spence, 1997, and Cini, 1996).

Generally speaking, the lower levels of the hierarchies concentrate on the more technical aspects of proposals and the upper levels concentrate on the more political and sensitive aspects.

The tiered structure of the European Council is much less formal and rigid than those of the Commission and the Council of Ministers. Such a structure can none the less be said to exist insofar as summits are extensively prepared by ministerial meetings – in particular by General Affairs (Foreign Ministers) and Ecofin Councils – which are, in their turn, prepared in the normal Council of Ministers manner (see Figure 7.1).

The fourth decision-making institution, the EP, cannot really be said to operate on the basis of a tiered or hierarchical structure. Rather, it operates more on a delegated structure, with its detailed work being undertaken by committees which report their findings to full plenary sessions for approval, rejection, or amendment.

Commission

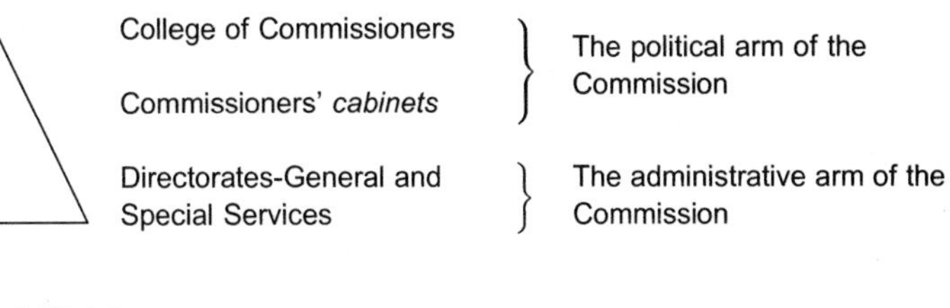

Council of Ministers

Ministerial meetings
Composed of national politicians
Committee of Permanent Representatives (COREPER)
Working groups
Composed of national officials

FIGURE 7.1 *The hierarchical structures of the Commission and the Council of Ministers*

The Importance of Efficiency and of Time

The EU used to be notorious for the protracted nature of its decision-making processes. Proposals would often be advanced by the Commission and then make little or no progress for years as they become bogged down in the Council of Ministers. However, a number of factors have combined in recent years to impart much greater senses of efficiency and timeliness into EU decision-making.

First, EU decision-makers have come to appreciate the benefits of attaching timetables to initiatives, plans and proposals. The two most obvious instances of timetabled commitments are the Single European Market (SEM) and EMU schedules, both of which were given treaty status – by the SEA and TEU respectively. On a regular working basis, examples of timetabling that have reaped decisional benefits have been the increased use of multi-annual programming (such as those in the research and development and environmental policy spheres), the importance that has come to be attached to the Commission's annual legislative programme, and the cooperation that now exists between the Commission, Council and EP on legislative planning.

Second, the increased availability and use of qmv means that there are now few decisions that single member states can veto. Member states which find themselves in a minority of one can always attempt to find allies with a view to constructing a blocking minority, but if this fails they have little option but to negotiate the best concessions they can and then accept – perhaps after having formally voted against or abstaining – whatever decision is taken. Qmv has done much to speed up EU decision-making: whereas in the early 1980s, when decision-making by unanimity was the norm, the average length of time taken to adopt Council directives (that is, the average time between Commission transmission and adoption) was about 36 months, it is now around 18 months.

Third, the cooperation and co-decision legislative procedures (see below) have timetables attached to their later stages. Delay is still possible up to the point that the Council has issued what is known as its common position, but thereafter decisional deadlines apply.

Fourth, for reasons of national status and prestige member states have become increasingly concerned that their period in office as Council President is, and is seen to be, successful. Since the most important indicators of success are bringing proposals through to final decision and having a well-managed and productive 'rounding-off' European Council meeting, there is invariably a sense of matters moving increasingly quickly as presidencies draw to an end. This is seen in a bunching of decision-making Council of Ministers meetings in June and December (the closing months of Council Presidencies), and in often near-feverish preparations by the Presidency as summits loom.

Fifth, and finally, there has been a considerable reduction in the legislative workload of the Commission, the Council, and the EP since the completion of most of the SEM programme and the importance that has come to be attached to the subsidiarity principle. Whereas the Commission's 1990 legislative programme contained 185 proposed directives, the 1998 programme contained only 31. Naturally, this lighter legislative load has resulted in a greater focus of attention on what is presented, and has made it less likely that proposals will – as they sometimes did in the past – 'disappear' in Council recesses.

High Sectoralization

All modern political systems have to try to find a balance in their decision-making systems between policy sectoralization and policy coordination. The structural response of national governments to this problem is normally, in broad terms, to divide responsibility for the main policy sectors into separate and specialized ministries and to overlay these ministries with authoritative coordinating mechanisms – most commonly a head of government working in close association with senior ministers through both formal (a cabinet or council of ministers) and informal channels.

EU decision-making processes are strong on sectoralization but rather weak on coordination. This is most apparent in the Commission and the Council of Ministers.

The Commission has long been criticised for being too hierarchical in its structural arrangements, with both Directorates General (DGs) and Commissioners being over-protective of their 'turf'. Coordinating arrangements exist at all levels within the Commission, but they tend to be focused on specific issues rather than on overall direction and strategy. Aware of this problem – which relates to the leadership deficit that was discussed earlier – the Commission's submission to the 1996–7 IGC (Commission, 1996) stressed the need for key actors within the Commission, especially the President, to be given greater leadership capacity. The Amsterdam Treaty acknowledged this need, notably via amendments to the Treaty Establishing the European Community (TEC) designed to increase the authority of the President within the College: the nominee of the national governments for President must now be approved by the EP (this institutionalizes what happened with Santer in 1994); the other nominations for Commission must now be made 'by common accord with the nominee for President' (Article 214, TEC); and the Commission shall henceforth 'work under the political guidance of its President' (Article 219, TEC).

Sectoralization in the Council takes the form of ministers meeting in over 20 formations – 21 in 1997 – with Foreign Ministers holding most meetings (15) and Tourism and Youth Ministers holding the least (one each). Foreign Ministers (meeting in what is known as the General Council) and Ecofin Ministers constitute the two most important Councils, but they do not stand in a hierarchical relationship to, or have the authority to issue instructions or impose direction on, other formations of the Council. Symptomatic of the sectoralization of the Council is the fact that although much of Council decision-making is oiled and smoothed by deals and trade-offs, these are almost exclusively negotiated within single Council formations: deals and trade-offs between Council formations are rare, not least because they are organizationally difficult to arrange. It can, therefore, be difficult, especially during a weakly managed Council Presidency, for the Council as an institution to be functioning in a wholly coordinated fashion.

Beyond the functioning of the Commission and the Council, a more general feature of sectoralization is the existence of sector-focused policy networks. People working in particular sectors – be they based in the Commission, in the permanent representations, in the EP, or in interest lobbies – usually get to know one another and can become well acquainted. Understandings and trust build, so that information and ideas flow in mutually beneficial ways. Those who are excluded from such networks can be disadvantaged. (There is a growing literature on policy networks in the EU. See, for example, Peterson, 1995, and Peterson and Bomberg, 1999.)

The Importance of Informal Processes

The point just made about policy networks illustrates a more general feature of EU decision-making, namely the importance of informal processes. Brussels is sometimes described as being 'an insiders' town', and is so because the formal structures and procedures of the EU are interwoven and supplemented by a myriad of informal relationships and working methods.

Apart from policy networks, there are countless other examples of ways in which informal processes are extremely important features of EU decision-making. To take, for example, the functioning of the Council of Ministers, the formal treaty voting rules give only a very partial picture of what happens in practice. The fact is that whether qmv is available or not, members of the Council prefer to take decisions by consensus whenever possible and generally feel uncomfortable if there is a vote, regardless of who is in the minority. Member states in the minority often prefer to 'trade' rather than be outvoted, with the consequence that negotiators in working groups and in COREPER may be instructed 'not to overdo it on the details – find an agreement'. Those states in the majority are usually willing to see if a general agreement can be found when it is felt that the member state(s) in the minority has (have) genuine difficulties with the issue in question. Because of this preference for consensual decision-making, votes are held in only about one quarter of the instances in which they are possible, and even then opposition is usually marginal (Hayes-Renshaw and Wallace, 1997, p. 53). In 1997 the Council acted by qualified majority on 47 occasions (Corbett, 1998).

Constant Evolution

A central feature of EU decision-making is that it is constantly evolving. In institutional terms the major changes of recent years have been the expanded provisions for qmv in the Council of Ministers and the increased powers of the EP. The changes in the qmv provisions have been designed to increase the efficiency of the EU – by making it easier for decisions to be made through reducing the use of national vetoes. The increased powers of the EP have been designed to enhance the democratic base of the EU – by strengthening the position of the only body that is directly elected as an EU institution.

The main way in which changes to decision-making occurs is, of course, through treaty reform. As Desmond Dinan shows in Chapter 15, this involves long and difficult negotiations in IGCs, the formal signing of a treaty, and ratification of the treaty in all member states. This is not, however, the only means of change: other, less formal, often more gradualistic, means are also commonly utilized. Two very different examples can be taken to illustrate this.

The first example concerns the decision of the December 1997 Luxembourg European Council meeting to establish the Euro-X committee (later to become known as the Euro-11 committee, when it was formally constituted in May 1998 with 11 founding members). The background to this was a strong feeling by most of the countries that were ready and willing to participate in the single currency phase of EMU that they should be able to meet to discuss matters of mutual interest without non members of the single currency being present. For their part, the potential non-members, led by the UK, objected to this, fearing that they would be excluded from a potentially important decision-making forum. After protracted intergovernmental exchanges in the run up to and at the summit, a fudged compromise was agreed in which the 'defining position of the Ecofin Council at the centre of the economic coordination and decision-making process' was affirmed, but in which also it was recognised that '(t)he Ministers of the States participating in the euro area may meet informally among themselves to discuss issues connected with their shared responsibilities for the single currency' (European Council, 1997, p. 16). A new body was thus added to the EU's institutional framework, but with precisely what role and powers remained to be determined by custom, practice, and possibly considerable argumentation: would it, as UK ministers privately hoped and predicted, be little more than a high-level discussion forum, or would it, as several ministers from euro-participating states anticipated, be taking decisions on economic and monetary policy?

The second example concerns the establishment of a number of mechanisms designed to promote effective working relationships between the Commission, the Council and the EP. That such mechanisms have become increasingly necessary is largely a consequence of the treaty reforms that have assigned greater powers to the EP, and in the particular context of EU legislation have established decision-making processes that now rest on an institutional triangle. However, the precise nature of these mechanisms are not laid down in the treaties, but rather emerge from (largely) informal discussions and negotiations. Amongst mechanisms to have been established in this way are regular trialogue meetings between the Presidents of the three institutions and inter-institutional agreements covering various aspects of how the institutions are to work with one another.

Decision-Making Procedures

Different Types

As has already been noted, the EU has many decision-making procedures. These procedures can be classified in various ways. To draw on points made above, procedures can, for instance, be classified in terms of their intergovernmental/supranational balance, their formality/informality, and the respective roles and powers exercised by the EU's main institutions.

A basis of classification that is especially useful in helping to draw out the sheer number and variety of procedures that exist is the type of decisions that procedures produce. Taking this as the basis for classification, the main categories of decision-making procedures are those leading to: decisions on the contents of the treaties; broad directional decisions – that is, decisions laying down a framework for EU policy development; legislative decisions; common commercial policy (external trade) decisions; pillar two and pillar three decisions (arguably two separate categories, especially since the Amsterdam Treaty); budgetary decisions; and administrative decisions. Each of these categories of procedures is distinctive, not least in terms of their institutional mix and balance. So, for example: direction determining procedures see the European Council centre stage, but with its deliberations and decisions heavily influenced and conditioned by inputs from other institutional actors – most particularly the Commission and the General Affairs and Ecofin Councils; external trade procedures rest essentially on a close working relationship between the Commission and the Council of Ministers; budgetary decisions are very much shaped by Commission preparatory work, but are taken by the Council and the EP acting as joint budgetary authorities; and administrative decisions are largely the provenance of the Commission, though in making decisions it is often subject to Council control via a complex network of committees staffed by national governmental representatives.

Most of these categories of decision-making procedures are considered at some length in other chapters of this book. One important category that is not considered in sufficient depth elsewhere, however, is legislative decision-making.

Legislative Procedures

The EU has three main legislative procedures: consultation, co-decision and assent. There used to be a fourth such procedure – the cooperation procedure – but this was virtually abolished by the Amsterdam Treaty, which reduced its application to four aspects of EMU.

An outline now follows of the principal features of the three main procedures and of the different types of decisions to which they apply.

Consultation. This is a single reading procedure in which the Council is the sole final decision-maker. However, it cannot take final decisions until it has received the opinion of the EP. On some proposals it must also await the opinions of the Economic and Social Committee (ESC) and the Committee of the Regions (CoR).

The consultation procedure was the only legislative procedure until the SEA came into effect in 1987. However, the creation by the SEA and then the TEU of other procedures, and the 'transfer' of policy spheres from consultation to these other procedures, has necessarily reduced the number of policy areas to which the consultation procedure applies. Following the Amsterdam Treaty, it is now largely confined to agriculture and to those justice and home affairs issues that are located within the EC Treaty.

Co-decision. The co-decision procedure, which was created by the TEU, is a one-, two-, or three-stage procedure. Proposals only advance to the third stage if the Council and the EP cannot reach agreement at the first or second stage.

The provision for only one stage was not included in the Maastricht Treaty but was created by the Amsterdam Treaty in an attempt to streamline what was generally agreed to be a somewhat cumbersome procedure. Under the Amsterdam revision, a text can be adopted at first reading providing the Council and the EP agree on its contents, and providing also, of course, that other 'standard' legislative requirements are met – notably, the ESC and the CoR are consulted when appropriate, and amendments with which the Commission does not agree receive unanimous support in the Council.

If the Council and the EP do not reach agreement at first reading, the Council, on receipt of the EP's opinion, adopts a common position – with qmv usually, although not always, being available for this purpose. The Council must provide the EP with an explanation of its common position, and the Commission also must explain its position and intentions to the EP – especially in regard to whether or not it accepts EP amendments.

At second reading the EP can approve, amend, reject, or take no action on a common position. If the first or last of these options are exercised, the Council can adopt its common position as a legislative act. If, however, a common position is rejected or amended by an absolute majority of all MEPs, and the Council at its second reading is unable to accept the EP's position, a third legislative stage then occurs, with the proposal referred to a conciliation committee composed of an equal number of representatives of the Council and the EP. About 40 per cent of legislative proposals subject to the co-decision procedure – in 1996 there were 30 co-decision proposals and in 1997 there were 28 – require the convening of a conciliation committee. At these committees, the Council is normally represented by senior officials from the national permanent representations to the EU and the EP is represented by a mix of semi-permanent conciliation committee members and members of relevant Parliamentary committees. If the conciliation committee agrees on a joint text, the proposal is referred back to the Council and the EP for final adoption, with the former acting by qmv and the latter by a majority of the votes cast. Under the original procedure, as outlined in the Maastricht Treaty, the Council could attempt to impose the common position in the event of non-agreement in the conciliation committee, but this possibility was removed by the Amsterdam Treaty, with the consequence that failure by the Council and the EP to agree on a text means the proposal cannot be adopted.

Up to early 1999, there had been only three outright failures under the co-decision procedure: in 1994 the EP rejected the Council's confirmed common position on a directive concerning the application of open network provision to voice telephony; in 1995 the EP rejected an agreement reached in the conciliation committee on a biotechnology directive; and in 1998 the conciliation committee failed to reach agreement on a directive on investment services and the Council decide not to confirm its common position. Significantly, both the voice telephony and biotechnology directives were subsequently re-presented by the Commission in a form that enabled them to be approved by the Council and EP.

The conduct of conciliation committee proceedings illustrates the frequently informal and flexible nature of EU decision-making. Much of the business in conciliation is not conducted in formal, across-the-table, Council–EP bargaining sessions, but elsewhere. Most particularly, trialogue meetings between representatives of the Council, EP and Commission are often important in preparing the ground for conciliation committee meetings. Instances of such meetings occurred in May–June 1998 in respect of legislation on the EU's Fifth Environmental Action Programme and on the establishment of a network for the epidemiological surveillance and control of communicable diseases. The key players at these meetings were the UK's Deputy Permanent Representative to the EU (the UK held the Council Presidency at the time), the chairman of the EP's Environment Committee, and the EP *rapporteurs* on the two pieces of legislation in question. Other players were kept informed of the outcomes of these pre-meetings, progress at which was such that when the conciliation meetings formally met they had little to do other than to rubber-stamp what had been agreed in the trialogues (*European Voice*, 18–24 June 1998).

The co-decision procedure thus encourages the EP, the Council and the Commission to engage in extensive inter-institutional liaising and bargaining. In so doing, the procedure boosts the shift in inter-institutional perceptions and relationships that was initiated by the cooperation procedure (see Karlheinz Neunreither's discussion on the impact of the cooperation procedure in Chapter 4). The most important of these shifts has been an obligation on the Council to take the legislative role of the EP very seriously, for under co-decision the EU can be said to have a bicameral legislature.

The Amsterdam Treaty more than doubled the number of treaty articles subject to co-decision – from 15 to 37. Eleven of these new articles were previously subject to cooperation, two to consultation, one to assent, and eight were additional articles. This means that most EU legislation – apart from agricultural, justice and home affairs, trade, fiscal harmonization, and EMU issues – is subject to the co-decision procedure.

Assent. This is the simplest of the four procedures in that it is a single-stage procedure and there is no provision for the EP to amend Commission proposals. Assent requires unanimity in the Council, whilst in the EP a simple majority suffices for some measures but an absolute majority is required for others.

The assent procedure is not used for what may be thought of as 'normal' legislation, but rather is reserved for special circumstances. These include international agreements of certain kinds, EU enlargements, the framework of the Structural Funds and – a provision introduced by the Amsterdam Treaty – sanctions in the event of a serious and persistent breach of fundamental rights by a member state.

Future Prospects

A recurring theme of this chapter has been that the EU's decision-making arrangements have been subject to considerable changes in recent times. More changes can be expected in the next few years. One reason for anticipating further changes is that the long-standing demands from many quarters that EU decision-making should be more efficient and more democratic were not fully satisfied by the Maastricht and Amsterdam Treaties, even though they each contained significant advances in respect of both efficiency and democracy. Another reason for anticipating further changes is that it is generally agreed by EU elites that present mechanisms will be quite unsuitable when, as is anticipated, the EU increases in size to over 20 members sometime around 2004–5.

Such is the widespread acceptance of the need for changes to accommodate enlargement that a protocol on this very matter was attached to the Amsterdam Treaty. Under Article 2 of the *Protocol on the Institutions with the Prospect of Enlargement of the European Union* (Treaty of Amsterdam 1997):

> At least one year before the membership of the European Union exceeds twenty, a conference of representatives of the governments of the Member States shall be convened in order to carry out a comprehensive review of the provisions of the Treaties on the composition and functioning of the institutions.

In other words, another IGC is likely be convened before too long.

Guide to Further Reading

There is a wealth of literature on EU decision-making. Books dealing with the general character of decision-making include Andersen and Eliassen (1993), Peterson and Bomberg (1999), and Wallace and Wallace (1996). Books dealing with decision-making in particular sectors include Armstrong and Bulmer (1998), Grant (1997), and Matlary (1997). And texts that include extensive considerations of decision-making include Dinan (1999), McCormick (1999), Nugent (1999), and Richardson (1996).

Many studies of particular aspects of EU decision-making and of the making of particular decisions can be found in the relevant academic journals. See, in particular, *Journal of Common Market Studies*, *Journal of European Public Policy* and *Journal of European Integration.*

References

Anderson, S.S. and Eliassen, K. A. (1993) *Making Policy in Europe: The Europeification of National Policy-Making*. London: Sage.

Armstrong, K. and Bulmer, S. (1998) *The Governance of the Single European Market*. Manchester: Manchester University Press.

Cini, M. (1996) *The European Commission: Leadership Organisation and Culture in the EU Administration*. Manchester: Manchester University Press.

Commission (1996) *Intergovernmental Conference 1996. Commission Opinion: Reinforcing Political Union and Preparing for Enlargement*. Luxembourg: Office for Official Publications of the European Communities.

Corbett, R. (1998) 'Governance and Institutions', in G. Edwards and G. Wiessela (eds), *The European Union 1998: Annual Review of Activities*. Oxford: Blackwell, pp. 39–49.

Dinan, D. (1999) *Ever Closer Union*, 2nd edn. Basingstoke: Macmillan.

Edwards, G. and Spence, D. (1997) *The European Commission*, 2nd edn. Harlow: Longman.

European Council (1997) *Presidency Conclusions*, Luxembourg 12–13 December. Brussels: General Secretariat of the Council.

European Voice, Brussels: Economist Group (weekly).

Grant, W. (1997) *The Common Agricultural Policy*. Basingstoke: Macmillan.

Hayes-Renshaw, F. and Wallace, W. (1997) *The Council of Ministers*. Basingstoke: Macmillan.

Marks, G., Hooghe, L. and Blank, K. (1996) 'European Integration From the 1980s: State-Centric v Multi-Level Governance', *Journal of Common Market Studies,* vol. 34, pp. 341–78.

Matlary, J. (1997) *Energy Policy in the European Union*. Basingstoke: Macmillan.

McCormick, J. (1999) *Understanding the European Union*. Basingstoke: Macmillan

Nugent, N. (1999) *The Government and Politics of the European Union,* 4th edn. Basingstoke: Macmillan.

Peterson, J. (1995) 'Policy Networks and European Union Policy Making', *West European Politics,* vol. 18, pp. 389–407.

Peterson, J. and Bomberg, E. (1999) *Decision Making in the European Union*. Basingstoke: Macmillan.

Richardson, J. (ed.) (1996) *European Union: Power and Policy-Making*. London: Routledge.

Treaty Establishing the European Community (1997) in *European Union Consolidated Treaties*. Luxembourg: Office for Official Publications of the European Communities; also in *Official Journal of the European Communities,* C 340, 10 November 1997.

Treaty on European Union (1997) in *European Union Consolidated Treaties*. Luxembourg: Office for Official Publications of the European Communities; also in *Official Journal of the European Communities,* C 340, 10 November 1997.

Treaty of Amsterdam (1997) in *Official Journal of the European Communities,* C 340, 10 November 1997.

Wallace, H. and Wallace, W. (1996) *Policy-Making in the European Union*. Oxford: Oxford University Press.

PART 3

Policies and Policy Objectives

8

Creating a European Market

MICHAEL CALINGAERT

Although the philosophical basis and impetus for what has evolved into the European Union (EU) was largely political, the history of European integration has been largely economic. The founding fathers concluded that the most effective way of achieving their goal of political union was through the progressive reduction and elimination of barriers to the movement of economic forces among member states. This, they believed, would produce clear and identifiable economic benefits, leading to support for political integration.

The initial steps were the establishment of a Common Agricultural Policy (CAP) and the elimination of all customs duties on trade between member states combined with the erection of a common external tariff. Assisted by a period of economic prosperity, the member states were able to conclude this customs union in 1968, two years ahead of schedule. However, that was only the beginning of a long, tedious and often-contentious process of enabling factors of production to move freely between the member states. Progress came slowly during the 1970s, in part because of the oil-shock-induced economic downturn and an accompanying spirit of malaise – widely called 'Euro-sclerosis' – among the member states. By the mid-1980s it was clear that further progress would be limited unless a way could be found to relaunch the effort to remove the Community's internal economic barriers.

Such a way was found with a programme to 'complete the single market' by removing the remaining barriers to the free movement of goods, services, capital and people within the Community, undertaken at the initiative of Jacques Delors, when he assumed the Presidency of the European Commission in 1985. This '1992 programme' – so termed because it was to be completed by the end of 1992 – identified about 300 measures to be taken or areas to be addressed by Community legislation. Under the energetic leadership of Delors, ably assisted by Commissioner Lord Cockfield, the 1992 programme became the focus of much of the EU's activity during the 1990s.

The programme could not have succeeded, however, had it not been for the first significant revision of the Treaty of Rome, the 1986 Single European Act (SEA). The SEA provided that an extensive number of issues relating to the internal market would be decided in the Council on the basis of qualified majority voting (a system of weighted voting) rather than by unanimity, thereby overcoming the blockage that had developed in the Community's legislative process.

Thus, the recent story of market integration consists of three main strands: evolution of the CAP; efforts to complete the legislative agenda of the 1992 programme and, increasingly important, to implement it; and progress in integration of other key areas not covered by the 1992 programme. These developments have taken place in the context of a trend toward greater assertiveness by the member states *vis-a-vis* the EU institutions, initial steps of introducing a single currency, and impending enlargement of the EU to the east.

The Common Agricultural Policy

The CAP was designed to achieve a number of economic, political and social objectives enumerated in the Treaty of Rome, notably ensuring the availability of agricultural supplies at reasonable prices to the consumers, while providing a 'fair' standard of living for the Community's agricultural community. Although the contents of the CAP were not spelt out in the Treaty, it was clear that achievement of the political and social objectives could not be achieved through market liberalization. Thus, political reality – including the strength of agricultural interests throughout the Community – dictated a protectionist approach to market unification rather than market-opening, which characterized the other phases of economic integration in the EU. The system that evolved combined strong production incentives with a high level of protection from outside competition through guaranteed prices for major agricultural commodities, variable levies to keep import prices higher than domestic ones, and export subsidies to enable excess production to be sold abroad. Under the CAP, agricultural production has soared and, in many sectors, become more efficient.

However, by maintaining prices above world levels and creating a supply imbalance, the CAP proved to be enormously expensive, both in subsidies paid to farmers and costs of holding and disposing of chronic surplus production. CAP outlays traditionally accounted for as much as two-thirds of the EU's budget. None the less, the member states were willing to bear this burden through the 1980s. Periodically, efforts were made to reduce EU outlays for agriculture, usually through lower support prices, but these met with only limited success. However, by the early 1990s financial pressures for change had become irresistible.

Budgetary pressure was not the only factor leading the EC to reform of the CAP. Multilateral trade negotiations were taking place in the Uruguay Round of the GATT, at which the United States and other agricultural exporting countries insisted that the comprehensive package to be agreed at the end of the Round would have to include a substantial reduction in agricultural protection – a requirement aimed directly at the EU. Thus, concurrently with deliberations inside the EU over changes in the CAP, the EU's trade negotiators were participating in the development of a radically different form of international agreement on agriculture, which promised to constrain the EU's ability to maintain the existing CAP by placing limits not only on export subsidies but also domestic support policies.

These two sets of pressures, internal and external, resulted in a reform of the CAP. Proposed in 1991, it was approved the following year, though only after long and contentious discussions among the member states. The reform package represented the beginning of a fundamental policy shift away from supporting farm income, especially through high product prices for the cereals sector. It did so by sharply reducing the level of support for cereals and introducing two new elements: acreage controls and direct income support payments to farmers.

Although the share of agriculture in the EU's budget declined to about one-half the total in succeeding years, both because of the 1992 reform and world price trends, pressure for further reductions in agricultural supports continued. This pressure was exacerbated by prospective EU enlargement. Agriculture accounts for a considerably larger share of economic activity in the ten applicant countries of Central and Eastern Europe. Whereas agriculture accounts for 6 per cent of the working population and 2.5 per cent of GDP in the EU, the comparable figures average 27 per cent and 8 per cent respectively among the applicants. Thus, the extension of the benefits of the CAP on existing terms and conditions would create a massive claim on the EU's budget and likely result in even greater production in the applicant countries, as happened after previous accessions.

Partly in response to this prospect, the Commission, upon the request of the European Council, issued *Agenda 2000* in 1997 (Commission, 1997d), a set of policy recommendations for the EU as it heads into the twenty-first century. A major component was further CAP reform, deemed essential not only because of prospective enlargement but also because of market imbalances and anticipation of further agricultural liberalization in a new round of international trade negotiations under the auspices of the WTO. The CAP proposals were more far-reaching than the 1992 reform in that they advocated the most significant change in the CAP since its inception, exposing agriculture to further competition, both internal and external. Support would be based increasingly on direct income payments to farmers by broadening the product coverage beyond cereals to include beef, dairy and, potentially, Mediterranean products; by sharply reducing price supports for cereals, beef and dairy; by setting acreage controls at zero; and by providing direct payments to compensate in part for the decrease in the level of price supports.

Not surprisingly, the reaction of the EU agricultural community to the Commission's proposals was largely negative. Most member states voiced strong opposition to the proposals, as did many farmers' organizations. Criticisms were directed at the principle of reducing levels of support and protection, at alleged imbalances in the treatment accorded different sectors, and at certain specific proposals. At the same time, counter-pressures existed. With increasing pressure on the EU's budgetary resources, non-agricultural interests forcefully supported measures to reduce agricultural spending, and some agricultural sectors supported the proposals, either because they used agricultural inputs (notably, beef cattle consume cereals) or because, as efficient producers, they preferred freedom to compete on the world market.

At the March 1999 Berlin European Council meeting agreement was reached on the *Agenda 2000* reform programme, but the CAP element was somewhat diluted. Accordingly, reform of the CAP will remain a contentious issue. However, as was the case with the previous reform effort, when the dust settles European agricultural policy will have again moved closer to the market economy.

The Single Market

The Legislative Programme

The 1992 programme for achieving a single market, contained in the 1985 Commission White Paper *Completing the Internal Market* (Commission, 1985), was unique on two counts: it consisted of a comprehensive set of actions to be taken without exceptions, and it set deadlines for each stage of the legislative process (proposals by the Commission, approval by the European Parliament (EP), adoption by the Council, and implementation by the member states), thereby creating pressures for action and a bench-mark for success. These features contributed to focusing public attention on the 1992 programme. For a combination of reasons, the programme generated a high degree of enthusiasm and became the centerpiece for the EU's 'Euro-phoria' of the first half of the 1990s.

The 31 December 1992 deadline for completion of the single market did not mark the end of the process – indeed, it had never been expected that all actions would be completed by that date, or that completion of the legislative process would in itself bring about the elimination of all barriers. Nevertheless, by the end of 1992 a substantial portion of the legislative programme had been completed. In 1993 the Commission reported that over 95 per cent of the legislative measures called for by the White Paper had been adopted, as regulations or directives, by the Council (Commission, 1993, p. 5). The figure has crept upwards since then, leaving only a small number of legislative proposals – the most contentious ones – outstanding as of 1999.

However, following approval by the Council, it was necessary for the members states, in most cases, to take legislative or administrative action to 'transpose' the legislation, that is, to put it into effect at national level. Here, progress has been slower. By late 1992, 75 per cent of the member state transpositions had taken place, but transposition by all member states had taken place for less than 25 per cent of the legislation (Commission, 1992, p. 4); these figures had improved to 93 per cent and 58 per cent respectively by 1996 (Commission, 1996a, p. 2), and in 1998 the European Commission reported that over 80 per cent of single market rules were in effect in all member states (Commission, 1998a, p. 5). However, despite the relatively high overall rate of accomplishment, transposition has lagged in a number of important sectors: as of 1998, less than 50 per cent of the single market directives had been fully transposed in intellectual and industrial property, public procurement, and transport (Commission, 1998a, p. 6).

Qualitative Assessment

Although the numbers indicate the general degree of success of the 1992 programme, a qualitative assessment is more relevant and revealing. In most areas significant progress in laying the legislative basis for the single market has been achieved. However, unfinished business remains in a few areas.

First, the relatively successful areas:

- *Movement of goods.* Goods now cross the borders between member states with minimal physical controls, the number of forms required has been reduced drastically, and documentation is normally submitted electronically to government authorities. The result has been considerable savings in the time and cost of moving goods from one member state to another.
- *Movement of capital.* Controls over capital movements were eliminated in the early 1990s.
- *Financial services.* Legislation has established a liberal regime under which companies in the banking, insurance and financial services sectors can operate in the single market under the principles of 'single license' and 'home country control': once a firm is duly licensed in one member state, it can operate in all the member states, subject to supervision by the authorities of the state in which it is licensed.
- *Transport.* National quotas on road haulage, limiting firms' ability to carry goods out of countries other than their own and prohibiting *cabotage* (carrying goods between two other countries), were phased out in the mid-1990s. National controls on air transport, extending from market access to routing, frequencies, and prices, were phased-out in 1997. Although airlines can now fly between any two points in the EU and at any price, some residual elements of national control, such as ground handling services, continue to hamper competition.
- *Regulations and technical standards.* The critical element of the single market programme was the replacement of earlier efforts to harmonize standards by taking a 'new approach' that now covers a large number of industrial sectors. Its main features are that EU

legislation will be limited to (i) establishing the 'essential requirements' to which products must conform, while leaving scope for variations in national legislation and awaiting the development of detailed standards by the private Europe-wide standards bodies; and (ii) the principle of 'mutual recognition', under which products meeting the essential requirements and conforming to national standards are accepted in the other member states. Less progress has been achieved with the second stage in the standards process – harmonizing and extending mutual recognition to national testing and certification systems.

- *Intellectual and industrial property protection.* An EU trademark and a European Trademark Office have been established, and a number of measures adopted in the copyright field. Two major pieces of legislation were approved in 1998 after long debate: a legal protection regime for industrial designs and models (provisions for automobile spare parts being the main subject of controversy) and a similar regime for biotechnological inventions (the most difficult issue being the patentability of genetically modified organisms).
- *Public procurement.* The potential to open the market for purchases by governmental entities and governmentally-regulated monopolies (about 12 per cent of the EU's GDP) is contained in comprehensive legislation, which requires transparency and nondiscriminatory treatment for purchases above specified threshold amounts and provides remedies in cases of violation.

Despite this progress, 'unfinished business' remains in two major areas. In both cases the requirement that the Council vote by unanimity has been an important factor in blocking progress.

- *Company law.* Although some harmonization of company law has taken place, the establishment of a homogeneous legal environment has been impeded by the impasse on a number of issues, including corporate governance, cross-border mergers and takeovers, and – most notably – a European company statute creating a new legal entity, a 'European company', which could operate throughout the EU under a uniform legal regime. Its adoption has been blocked since 1989 by a deadlock over provisions mandating worker participation in the firms' decision-making process (in essence, pitting pro-participation Germany against anti-participation United Kingdom), although recent UK flexibility may bring about an agreement in the not-too-distant future.

- *Taxation.* Bowing to the political reality that member states will continue to exercise sovereignty in the field of taxation, the Commission has limited its ambitions to seeking approximation, as opposed to harmonization, of indirect taxes, but with only limited success. Agreement was reached only on setting the minimum level for member states' value-added tax (the rate of tax ranges from 15 to 25 per cent) and on an 'interim' regime (constituting administrative improvements). Agreement has been reached – but only in principle – to adopt a 'definitive' regime, under which the tax would be levied at the point of purchase rather than, as at present, at the point of production (the latter runs counter to the concept of the single market). Similarly, wide differences remain in tax and withholding rates on savings, reflecting a conscious (and largely successful) effort by certain member states to attract capital. In 1998 the Commission revived and revised an earlier proposal for a common minimum tax on interest paid to savers; proponents are guardedly optimistic about eventual approval this time. Also in 1998, member states committed themselves, under a 'code of conduct', to impose some self-discipline over tax incentives for inward investment.

Other Areas of Market Integration

Although the 1992 programme covered a wide range of issues and sectors, telecommunications and energy were excluded. However, the Commission recognized that developments in these sectors were significant determinants of growth and competition in the EU, and thus it undertook efforts at liberalization in parallel to the 1992 programme.

Telecommunications

When discussions over creating a single market began in the 1980s, with the exception of the UK national monopolies operated the telecommunications system and exercised tight control over the purchase of equipment in every member state. The result was a sector characterized by high costs, inflexibility and a resistance to innovation.

In 1987 the Commission issued a green paper (discussion document) on telecommunications (Commission, 1987), which called for broad deregulation of both equipment and services. The following year a Council resolution established policy goals for creating an EC-wide market for telecommunications equipment and services, with full inter-connectivity between all public networks. From these flowed, in the succeeding years, a series of proposals and actions that progressively abolished the tight regulatory hand of national governments and authorities. The first step was a 1988 directive terminating member states' exclusive rights to import, market and install terminal equipment, such as telephone sets, private branch exchanges, data transmission terminals and mobile telephones. Such quick action was possible only because the Commission, over the objections of some member states, used an anti-monopoly provision of Article 90 TEC (now Article 86) to issue this directive on its own authority, rather than following the normal legislative procedure that requires approval by the Parliament and Council.

Under two 1990 directives, member states were required to end their monopolies over telecommunications services except basic telephone services, and telecommunications operators were required to grant equal access to their network infrastructure and services (the so-called 'open network' provision). That was followed by provision for mutual recognition of member states' conformity requirements for terminal equipment and the separation of national authorities' regulatory functions from operating activities.

But the most visible step affected voice telephony, which accounted for about 90 per cent (though a decreasing share) of telecommunications revenue. Under a 1993 agreement, basic business and residential telephone services were opened to competition throughout the EU as of the beginning of 1998 (though with a phase-in period for some countries). In parallel, a number of measures were taken to instill competition in the growing field of cellular telephony. Finally, in 1997, two important directives furthered the liberalization process: one set conditions of access by carriers to the dominant network; the other ensured consistency of member state guidelines in licensing new telecommunications companies.

Thus, a sea-change has taken place in the EU's telecommunications sector: in considerable measure through the single-mindedness and persistence of the Commission, monopoly control in the telecommunications sector has been largely replaced by competition.

Energy

The production, transmission and distribution of electricity and gas have historically been regulated by European governments, usually under a monopoly system. As a result, energy costs in Europe have been considerably higher than those in countries where competition among energy suppliers exists, notably the United States. The argument for maintenance of the status quo was largely that of the 'public service' requirement – the government's responsibility to ensure availability of electricity and gas at a reasonable price to all citizens. In the absence of government regulation, it was argued, competition would result in a diminution of service and/or higher prices to customers in outlying areas. On the other hand, major energy consumers, particularly industry, looked forward to deregulation, which would offer them greater flexibility of supply and lower prices.

The debate proceeded throughout the 1990s with the member states lining up on the issue – France as leader of the states seeking to preserve the status quo and the United Kingdom, already in the throes of deregulation, leading the 'liberalizers'. The debate centred on the degree to which national monopoly transmitters of energy should be required to open their system to others wanting to supply the market and the terms under which such supplies would become available.

After long debate the issue was resolved in favour of liberalization – first for electricity and then for gas. The electricity directive, adopted in 1996, provides that a part of the national electricity markets, i.e. the largest energy users, will be gradually opened, initially covering 22 per cent of the market, but rising to 32 per cent by 2003. The directive also provides for reciprocity and, on a hotly debated point, permits member states to choose between establishing a single-buyer system or allowing electricity producers, suppliers and eligible customers to negotiate access to the market. Interestingly, despite the difficulty in obtaining agreement even on this limited measure, early indications are that market liberalization is proceeding faster than the minima established in the directive.

With the principle established on electricity, the gas sector followed, with a directive in 1998 providing for a phased liberalization of the almost 100 billion euro gas market in the EU. Within two years of entering into effect, 20 per cent of consumption is to be liberalized, rising to at least one-third after ten years. However, as in the case of electricity, the market may force a more rapid degree of de facto liberalization.

Next Steps

Adoption of the 1992 legislative programme – or at least the major part of it – and of legislation in related areas was only the first step in the effort to create a European market. As the Commission stated just after the 1992 deadline: '. . . the establishment of a single market is not simply a question of adopting Community-level legislation. It is a more complex, long-term process of gradually changing legal structures and administrative practice at the national level and of encouraging new attitudes and behaviour from economic operators in the market' (Commission, 1994). Many issues had to be addressed in pursuit of the single market goal: *legislation*, both the 'unfinished business' described above and 'new measures' deemed necessary subsequent to the 1992 programme; the *transposition* of the single market legislation by the member states; *enforcement* of the single market through judicial action and competition policy; and *facilitating and promoting* the operation of the single market by influencing the attitudes and actions of private citizens, economic operators and government officials.

In these areas, the Commission has played a leading role. From the outset it has been the driving force behind the efforts at integration. It has provided ideas and recommendations, taken actions, and pressed the member states to play their part in making the single market a reality. In particular, the Commission has long been conscious of the need to move beyond the legislative programme.

With the legislative basis now laid for the intended changes, the Commission sponsored a study in 1992, the so-called Sutherland Report (High Level Group) on problems in the operation of the single market. The report emphasized the need for enforcement of EC law and for greater mutual confidence and cooperation among EC and member state institutions and administrations. That was followed the next year by the Commission's *Strategic Programme* (Commission, 1993), which was intended as a guide for 'completing, managing and the further development' of the single market. Addressed both to the Community and the member states, the Plan looked beyond the legislative framework and transposition to ensuring the quality of enforcement and increasing tangible benefits to individuals and enterprises.

Finally, and most ambitiously, the Commission issued, and the European Council endorsed, an 'Action Plan' in 1997 (Commission, 1997c). Building on the Commission's 1996 communication on the impact and effectiveness of the single market (Commission, 1996b), the Action Plan defined four strategic targets: making the rules more effective, dealing with key market distortions; removing obstacles to market integration; and delivering a single market for the benefit of all citizens. Under each target it listed a number of specific, detailed actions, 19 in all, with deadlines for action. The Plan divided these actions into three phases: short-term actions not requiring legislation (for example, transposition of outstanding legislation); measures proposed but awaiting approval by the EP and Council (for example, the European company statute); and measures requiring Commission proposals (for example, changes in value-added tax) or where further efforts were required to achieve a legislative consensus (for example, taxation of energy products). Combining breadth with specificity, plus the discipline of deadlines and the endorsement of the member states' heads of government, the Action Plan has become the focal point of the effort to achieve the single market goal.

In order to maintain pressure on the member states and EU institutions to produce results and meet the deadlines, the Plan provides that each meeting of the Internal Market Council and the European Council review progress on carrying out the actions called for in the Plan. As the centrepiece for these reviews, the Commission devised a 'Single Market Scoreboard' (Commission, 1997e), which has been issued twice-yearly since late 1997 and which catalogues in detail the extent of progress. Contrary to its earlier practice, the Commission has increasingly adopted a 'name and shame' policy, specifying publicly how badly (or well) the individual member states have performed.

Legislative Action

Turning to the first area of post-1992-programme action, the outstanding legislative proposals, few in number but major in content, remain subjects of discussion and controversy. Not surprisingly, certain issues have proven difficult to resolve because of sharply conflicting – and strongly held – views among the member states and the requirement for unanimity in voting. There has been a certain ebb and flow in efforts by the Commission and, at times, the Council Presidency to unblock the legislation, usually by seeking to inject greater flexibility (that is, less harmonization) into the provisions. However, with the new focus on 'action' to make the single market a reality, a more sustained effort will likely be made to obtain the necessary political consensus for Council approval, even if the results fall short of the original intentions.

Although the 1992 programme consisted of about 300 legislative proposals, in fact the corpus of legislation affecting the single market is considerably larger. The Commission has broadened its interpretation of single market legislation to include approximately 1,300 measures. For the most part, this addition represents 'recategorizing' legislation, proposed and adopted, particularly in the fields of regulations and standards and telecommunications. Very little has consisted of new legislation and by the mid-1990s, the Commission had sharply reduced its volume of legislative proposals.

None the less, additional legislation was deemed necessary in some areas of existing single market activity – for example, harmonization of conditions for 'distance advertising' and classification of medicinal products – and certain new areas were added to the list. Notable among the 'new areas' was electronic commerce, which had barely existed at the time of the 1985 White Paper. By the 1990s it had become a 'front-line' topic, the subject of a Commission communication on an European initiative in electronic commerce (Commission, 1997a). Relevant legislation under consideration in early 1999 relates to encryption, electronic-signatures, and data protection.

Transposition

Transposition of Council directives remains a focus of attention. Since the early 1990s the Commission has published updates on the extent of member state transpositions, coupled with urgings for faster action. With the Action Plan, however, it increased the pressure. Member states were required to submit a timetable specifying the quarter of the year during which each outstanding transposition would take place, with the entire process to be competed by 1 January 1999, to coincide with Stage 3 of Economic and Monetary Union (EMU). The Scoreboards issued in follow-up to the Action Plan then measured actual transpositions against member state timetables. Although the initial results were unsatisfactory – during the first two quarters of the exercise only 54 per cent of the promised transpositions had taken place – the existence of the timetables and the attendant publicity should contribute to faster member state action.

Also of note was the shift from reporting the percentage of transpositions taken (and only incidentally indicating the percentage of directives fully transposed) to focusing on the extent to which action has not been completed. Thus, as of the spring of 1998, transposition of 18 per cent of directives remained incomplete (the figure dropped to 11 per cent for those transposed by 14 of the 15 member states). Rates of transposition still outstanding in the member states varied, but none was higher than 7 per cent, in many cases a significant decline over the previous six months.

Enforcement

An important element in creating the single market is the enforcement of compliance with the EU treaty and legislation. This takes two forms: infringement proceedings against member states and administrative and judicial actions against enterprises and governments. In both areas the Commission plays a key role.

Insofar as the single market is concerned, infringement proceedings are undertaken when a member state has not notified the Commission that legislation has been transposed or when the Commission (on its own initiative or on the basis of a complaint) deems that legislation has not been properly transposed or that a member state has taken an action contrary to legislation – for example, by imposing conditions on citizens of another member state for exercising a profession. In such cases, the Commission first sends the member state an 'infringement letter', requesting remedial action. If the issue is not resolved at that stage, the Commission follows up with a more formal 'reasoned opinion'. If that does not produce the desired result, the Commission takes the case to the European Court of Justice (ECJ). Adding to the pressure, the Treaty on European Union (TEU) empowered the Court to levy fines, upon the recommendation of the Commission, on member states for failure to comply with a Court judgment. Although none has been levied thus far, the Commission has spelt out the criteria it will use in recommending fines (seriousness of the infringement, duration, and need to establish a deterrent to further infringements) (Commission, 1997b, pp. 19–20).

The Commission has actively pursued single market violations. From 218 infringement letters in 1995, the number rose to 283 in 1996, and 392 between March 1997 and March 1998 (Commission, 1997e, 1998a). The Commission has used publicity to increase pressure on the member states. The Commission issues a press release each time a case is referred to the Court. The semi-annual Scoreboards contain a section on infringement, which includes statistics – broken down by member state – on the percentage of infringement letters not answered, length of time for member state responses, numbers of letters of infringement, reasoned opinions, cases referred to the Court, and judgments of the Court.

EU competition policy plays a crucial role in promoting the effective operation of the single market. The TEC gives extensive powers to the Commission, and ultimately to the Court, to take action against market-restrictive or distorting agreements and abuses of dominant positions. All Commissioners responsible for competition policy since the 1985 White Paper have wielded their power aggressively. The vast majority of cases are disposed of informally, but often on the basis of a settlement negotiated between the firm and the Commission's competition authorities. However, the number of formal decisions has risen sharply from one decade to the next. Some have involved high-profile cases, such as price-fixing and market-sharing by steel tube manufacturers and market restrictions imposed on its dealers by Volkswagen. The Commission has used its authority to fine violators (up to 10 per cent of annual turnover) – in the cases just cited, over 100 million ECU.

Under the provisions of a 1989 regulation, the Commission has been increasingly active in determining whether mergers and acquisitions 'with a Community dimension' represent a dominant position. Although most cases are disposed of under an expedited procedure, an increasing number have been subjected to a more detailed examination. Frequently, the examination entails a negotiation between the Commission and the firm(s) in question over the terms of the transaction, with the Commission giving its approval only if certain changes (usually divestments) are made – for example, Nestle's acquisition of Perrier. Occasionally, the Commission has refused to give approval to a merger or acquisition, as in the proposed Bertelsmann–Kirch digital pay-television joint venture in 1998. Such instances, though increasingly frequent, are still relatively rare.

One particularly sensitive aspect of competition policy is state aids. Assistance by member states to groups and individuals can, and often does, distort competition, thereby impinging on the effective functioning of the single market. While the TEC permits state aids, it also sets conditions. In an effort to address the issue in a balanced manner, the Commission has issued a series of studies, beginning in 1989, on the nature and extent of such aids, the most recent of which reports that state aids range from 0.4 to 2.0 per cent of member states' GDP, averaging 1.4 per cent in the EU as a whole (Commission, 1998b, p. 42).

In adjudicating on state aids, the Commission frequently finds itself involved in a highly politicized conflict with the member state in question. Discussions and negotiations are often lengthy, public and acrimonious, such as with large (and recurring) bail-outs of several national airlines and with the French government's rescue of Credit Lyonnais. None the less, the Commission has achieved reasonable success, often with backing from the Court, in setting limits on the amount and conditions of aid and, on occasion, forcing the refund of aid – for example, Saxony's incentive package for the construction of a Volkswagen factory.

Facilitation and Promotion

From the very outset of the development of the 1992 programme, it was realized that creation of a single market depended not only on putting in place appropriate legislation and rules, but on changing attitudes and actions of individuals and organizations throughout the EU. The extent to which they understood, accepted, and took advantage of the new circumstances would significantly contribute to the success of the effort. This thought was central to the Sutherland Report of 1992, which emphasized the need to create greater understanding of and confidence in the single market. The effort to do so has been aimed at three groups: government institutions and officials, enterprises, and individuals.

By its nature, market integration necessitated changing government officials' attitudes and methods of operation at the national and subnational level. Apart from officials whose livelihood was directly threatened, such as customs officials in a border-less Union, others found increasingly that – like it or not – they had to interact with officials in other jurisdictions (for example, in the regulatory area). Thus, the Council established the Karolus Programme in 1992 to improve cooperation and promote mutual confidence between national officials engaged in implementation of EU legislation by arranging exchanges, seminars, and other joint training exercises.

To a considerable extent, the business sector was thrust into the single market, in that market opening changed the conditions under which firms operated. However, not all barrier-removing legislation produced or led immediately to actions by the private sector taking advantage of the opportunities afforded. This was the case, for example, in the financial services and air transport sectors, at least in the early stages, and it was particularly true for public procurement. Despite legislation that opened tendering on an EU-wide basis, compliance by tendering authorities has been patchy, and bidding has remained largely local. To counter the latter factor, the Commission is actively encouraging suppliers to participate more actively in the public procurement market – an effort it believes will be significantly enhanced as electronic commerce becomes more common in the information and tendering process.

The Commission has also developed a number of programmes to spread information about the single market to enterprises and individuals, including the establishment of information centres in all member states, a vast programme of publications, and the organization of conferences and seminars. In addition, particularly since the TEU ratification, the Commission has emphasized the need to develop a closer dialogue with the citizens of the EU. For example, in the Action Plan it undertook to establish a 'permanent mechanism for dialogue with citizens' (Commission, 1997c, p. 10) with two purposes: (i) providing information about single market developments and the opportunities they afford; and (ii) soliciting the concerns of the citizens and advising on remedies.

None the less, these efforts can only contribute marginally to the creation of a real single market. More important will be the increasing interaction that takes place on a day-to-day basis – in other words, the habit of interaction and the cooperation that stems from it.

Measurements of Success

Assessing the results of the effort to create a single market is complicated by the difficulty of separating single market phenomena from other factors. None the less, at least intuitively and anecdotally, much progress has been achieved. It is undeniable that the economic attitudes and actions of governments, companies, and individuals have an EU perspective to a far greater degree than prior to the 1992 programme.

However, beyond the anecdotes, several economic indicators also contain evidence of a trend toward integration. Trade flows between member states have risen more rapidly than trade with third countries or than GDP (the ratio of intra-EU trade to GDP rose from 12 per cent in 1993 to 15 per cent in 1997); the EU's share as a recipient of global foreign direct investment has risen sharply (from 28 per cent in 1982–7 to 44 per cent in 1991–3), as has the share of such investment sourced from other member states (57 per cent in 1986–91 to 65 per cent in 1992–6); merger and acquisition activity has soared (trebling between 1986 and 1996); and price divergences between member states have declined (by three points on consumer goods and five points on services between 1985 and 1993) (Commission, 1998a, pp. 17–19).

In 1996 the Commission published the first comprehensive study of the results of the single market programme. This consisted of 38 analyses conducted by independent experts on the impact on manufacturing, services, trade and investment, competition and economies of scale, and the aggregate and regional impact; it also included the results of a business survey (Commission, 1996b). On the basis of its analyses, the Commission reported 'clear signs of significant change in the European economy' and identified 'positive, albeit preliminary, effects of the single market', including the creation of between 300,000 and 900,000 jobs, an increase of 1.1–1.5 percentage points in income over the period 1987–93, an increase in investment of 1–3 per cent, a decrease in inflation of 1.0–1.5 percentage points, and a convergence in levels of GDP between different EU regions. On a sectoral basis, it concluded, *inter alia*, that the single market was responsible for annual savings of ECU 5 billion in the cost of transporting goods across member state borders, an increase of 20–30 per cent in trade in manufactured products, and a 7 per cent reduction in the price of telecommunications equipment.

A Look to the Future

It is impossible to give a definitive or single-dimensional judgement on the single market. The process of integration is on-going – with no specific end-point – and the results have been uneven. None the less, what can be termed a 'European market' has been created, although it is far from 'perfect' (it would be illusory to expect it could ever be such, even assuming agreement on the definition of 'perfect'). The list of accomplishments is impressive, as is the momentum that has developed among governments, firms and individuals for achieving continued economic integration.

Yet, it would be foolhardy to assume a straight-line progression to ever-greater integration. As was indicated at the beginning of the chapter, the course of integration is being affected in significant measure by three important realities: the tendency of member states to oppose further erosion of the intergovernmental, as opposed to supranational, nature of decision-making; the impending enlargement of the EU; and the creation of EMU.

The trend toward supranationalism, epitomized in the SEA and reflected in much of the single market legislation, was slowed down by the adverse public reaction, largely unexpected, in several member states to the TEU. Since the ratification process, voters have expressed fears that national identities and differences are not being sufficiently protected in the face of increasing 'encroachment' by the Union. This will inevitably hamper efforts to move the integration process forward, in particular in the two main areas where EU legislation has been blocked. As long as unanimity is required in Council voting, it is difficult to envisage that significant progress will be made.

The process of enlargement of the EU has begun. Negotiations are under way for accession by five Central and Eastern European countries plus Cyprus; five more countries are waiting in the wings; and Malta and Turkey remain candidates for membership. During these negotiations the applicant countries will have to adapt – within agreed time limits – to the single market, a difficult and complex process spelt out in a Commission White Paper (Commission, 1995). At the same time, they will have some influence, at least implicitly, over the outcome of discussion of possible further measures. When these countries join the EU and become part of its decision-making process, it is likely that, as a consequence of their being considerably less advanced economically than the present members, they will tend to oppose measures furthering economic integration. On the other hand, their accession will force the EU to change its decision-making procedures, presumably involving a reduction in the extent of unanimous voting, and that should help overcome some of the present impasse.

Finally, a positive development: introduction of the single currency. EMU would not have been possible had the single market not been created – a single currency could not have operated in a segmented market. That condition having been met, however, EMU has been launched, a step that will further the process of economic integration. EMU will, by definition, remove yet another – and critical – barrier to the conduct of business across member state borders. By reducing costs, lightening the administrative burden, and increasing the transparency of transactions, it will increase the efficiency of markets, thereby leading to increased competition, lower prices, and, presumably, an increased level of economic activity. In particular, it is expected that introduction of the single currency will result in a sharp growth and development of financial markets. And pressures will be created to harmonize tax policies, one area where, as described above, progress has been limited. In sum, the single currency will consolidate, if not complete, the process of creating a European market.

Guide to Further Reading

An official historical review of developments since issuance of the White Paper on the 1992 programme is contained in a series of Commission reports (1986–92, 1993–5, 1994–5). The results of the Commission's analysis of the single market are summarized in readable form (1996c). Relatively few books are devoted solely to the single market. The basics are set forth in Calingaert (1988), with a more recent overview in Calingaert (1996). Other books include Cockfield, and Jacquemin and Wright. A good overview is the chapter by Helen Wallace and Alasdair Young on the single market in Wallace and Wallace (1996). Mayes concentrates on rule-making in the single market; and a more detailed analysis is contained in the single market chapter of Neal and Barbezat. Books, articles and Commission reports abound on more specific aspects of the single market. It is best to look under the individual listings. On the CAP, recent works include Fennell and the CAP chapter in Neal and Barbezat.

References

Calingaert, M. (1988) *The 1992 Challenge from Europe: Development of the European Community's Internal Market*. Washington: National Planning Association.

Calingaert, M. (1996) *European Integration Revisited: Progress, Prospects and U.S. Interests*. Boulder, CO: Westview Press.

Cockfield, A. (1994) *The European Union: Creating the Single Market*. London: Wiley Chancery Law.

Commission (1985) *Completing the Internal Market*, White Paper COM(85) 238, 15 June.

Commission (1986–92) *Implementation of the White Paper*. Brussels: Commission.

Commission (1987) *Summary Report Concerning the Green Paper on the Development of the Common Market for Telecommunications Services and Equipment*, XIII/197(87), 26 May. Brussels: Commission.

Commission (1992) *Seventh Report of the Commission to the Council and the European Parliament Concerning the Implementation of the White Paper on the Completion of the Internal Market*, COM(92)383, 2 September. Brussels: Commission.

Commission (1993) *Making the Most of the Internal Market: Strategic Programme*, COM(93)632, 22 December. Brussels: Commission.

Commission (1993–5) *The Single Market*. Brussels: Commission.

Commission (1994) *The Community Internal Market – 1993 Report*, COM(94)55, 14 March. Brussels: Commission.

Commission (1994–5) *The State of Community Law Concerning the Internal Market*. Brussels: Commission.

Commission (1995) *Preparation of the Associated Countries of Central and Eastern Europe for Integration into the Internal Market of the Union*, White Paper, COM(95)163, 3 May. Brussels: Commission.

Commission Spokesman's Service (1996a) *Single Market Cannot Deliver Full Benefits Without Better Implementation*, MEMO/96/100, 24 October. Brussels: Commission.

Commission Communication (1996b) *The Impact and Effectiveness of the Single Market*, COM(96)520, 30 October. Brussels: Commission.

Commission Staff Working Paper (1996c) *The 1996 Single Market Review*, SEC(96)2378, 16 December. Brussels: Commission.

Commission (1996d) *The Single Market and Tomorrow's Europe*. London: Kogan Page.

Commission (1997a) *A European Initiative in Electronic Commerce*, COM(97)157, 16 April. Brussels: Commission.

Commission (1997b) *Fourteenth Annual Report on Monitoring the Application of Community Law (1996)*, COM(97)299, 29 May. Brussels: Commission.

Commission (1997c) *Action Plan for the Single Market*, CSE(97)1, 4 June. Brussels: Commission.

Commission (1997d) *Agenda 2000: For a Stronger and Wider Europe*, DCO/97/6–7, 15 July. Brussels: Commission.

Commission (1997e) *The Single Market Scoreboard*, No. 1, November. Brussels: Commission.

Commission (1998a) *The Single Market Scoreboard*, No. 2, May. Brussels: Commission.

Commission (1998b) *Sixth Survey on State Aid in the European Union in the Manufacturing and Certain Other Sectors*, COM(98)417, 1 July. Brussels: Commission.

Fennell, R. (1997) *The Common Agricultural Policy: Continuity and Change*. Oxford: Clarendon Press.

High Level Group (1992) *The Internal Market after 1992: Meeting the Challenge*, Report to the Commission, October.

Jacquemin, A. and Wright, D. (eds) (1993) *The European Challenges Post-1992: Shaping Factors, Shaping Actors*. Aldershot: Edward Elgar.

Mayes, D. (ed.) (1997) *The Evolution of the European Single Market*. Lyme, NH: Edward Elgar.

Neal, L. and Barbezat, D. (1998) *The Economics of the European Union and the Economies of Europe*. New York and Oxford: Oxford University Press.

Wallace, H. and Wallace, W. (eds) (1996) *Policy-Making in the European Union*. Oxford: Oxford University Press.

9

Promoting Solidarity and Cohesion

JAMES MITCHELL AND PAUL McALEAVEY

This chapter starts by considering the variation in regional government across the European Union. The absence of uniformity in the Union is striking and has implications for the development of solidarity and cohesion, especially for the implementation of EU policies. The differential impact of European integration is then discussed, followed by an account of the evolution of EU cohesion policies. The tensions in EU policies are noted and the manner in which attempts have been made to create a genuinely European policy are considered. Institutional changes are also examined. The post-Maastricht situation and the implications of the enlargement of the Union are set in this context. The prospects for future developments are viewed against the background of proposed changes in the Structural Funds, *Agenda 2000* and the ever-changing context of European integration.

Centre–Periphery Relations in Member States and the EU

No two member states have exactly the same structure of government, nor cater for regional diversity in the same way. This variety ranges from centralized states such as the United Kingdom (though changes are impending following positive endorsement of change in devolution referendums in Scotland, Wales and Northern Ireland), Ireland and Greece, through regionalized states such as Italy and France, to federal states such as Germany and Austria – not to mention the highly decentralized Belgian state (see Table 9.1). This pattern of territorial diversity within member states is combined with

TABLE 9.1 *Typology of regional government in European Union states*

Classic Unitary	*Devolving Unitary*	*Regionalized*	*Federal*
Denmark	France	(Belgium)	Germany
Finland	The Netherlands	Italy	Austria
Greece	Portugal	Spain	Belgium
Ireland	(Finland)		
Luxembourg			
Sweden			
United Kingdom*			

Note: * The UK is moving into a 'devolving unitary' according to this typology (Stoker, Hogwood and Bullman, 1996, p. 52).

a considerable degree of diversity in how regional questions and issues manifest themselves and how governments respond through domestic public policies. In some cases, notably Spain and Belgium, linguistic and cultural communities have historically provided pressure from below for institutional reform and for financial and other support. In addition to these pressures from below, the needs of the centre will often lead it to devolve responsibilities. Only the smallest state with a developed range of public policies could operate without some regional or local structures of government. Pressures from above and pressures from below combine to create the varied mosaic of regional government across the EU.

The integration of Europe has had an impact on regional structures and policies in member states, but only indirectly. The EU has avoided interfering directly in the domestic arrangements of its member states. None the less, the development of EU policies in areas traditionally the preserve of regions within member states (though there are vast differences in the competences of regional government across Europe) has affected domestic centre-periphery relations. This has been most notable in the case of Germany where the *Länder* were given exclusive competence under the Basic Law (the German constitution) for policy areas such as education and training, transport and environmental policy, but the Bund (Federal level) had exclusive competence over foreign affairs and the right to 'transfer sovereign powers to international institutions' (Hrbek, 1991). *Länder* competences were transferred to Brussels without their consent, thus affecting the domestic balance between the *Bund* and the *Länder*

(Jeffrey, 1996, pp. 254–5). This became a pressing issue at the time of the Single European Act (SEA). One *Land* Minister expressed fears that the *Länder* might simply 'degenerate into administrative units, dependent on Bonn and Brussels' (quoted in Jeffrey, 1997, p. 58). This led to pressure from regions, led by the *Länder*, for changes in the position of regions within the EU.

The impact of EU policies on subnational levels of government has been considerable. In 1991, the Audit Commission in the UK published a report in which it identified three main ways in which the EU affected local authorities in the UK. These conclusions can also be applied to sub levels of national government throughout the EU:

- *Euro-regulation* imposes unavoidable obligations to implement, enforce and monitor EC legislation (such as directives in the environmental field);
- *European economic integration* creates new opportunities for – and pressures on – the local economic base (through the Single European Market for instance); and
- *Euro-funds* – most notably the Structural Funds (see below) - offer potential support for the local economy and for a range of local authority projects. (Audit Commission, 1991, p. 7)

Emphasis has tended to focus on the Euro-funds, but the first two ways in which local and regional governments are affected are at least as significant. In addition, policies which are thought to be territorially neutral in their impact often have a differential impact, affecting one region more or less than another, whether positively or negatively. The most significant set of policies affecting regions have been those designed to create a Single European Market and bring about Economic and Monetary Union. As Tsoukalis (1993, p. 28) has noted, the distributional impact of integration has been 'paramount in the minds of national politicians and representatives of various pressure groups' and 'strongly influenced negotiations' from the start.

A Europe of Regions?

A 'Europe of Regions' has been an objective of regionalist idealists for many years (Loughlin 1997, p. 147). It has recently been given support by some of those concerned with the position of regions and who are critical of the EU's 'democratic deficit'. In 1991, for example, David Martin, a Vice President of the European Parliament, argued that regional devolution complements European integration and advocated the creation of a second chamber of the Nations and Regions, consisting of representatives from national and regional parliaments, which could eventually replace the Council of Ministers (Martin 1991, p. 19). However, such hopes for a radical overhaul in the structures of member states and the EU are unlikely, at least in the foreseeable future. None the less, changes in the relations of regions, member states and the EU have been evident.

As mentioned above, the SEA provoked fears amongst regions, notably the German *Länder*, that they would lose out in the integration process. Reforms were demanded which would give official voice to Europe's regions within the European Community decision-making structures. These demands focused on the arrangements within member states and Europe as a whole. The SEA made reference to the principle of subsidiarity, citing environmental policy as an area in which the Community should take action only when objectives could be 'attained better at Community level than at the level of individual member states' (SEA Article 130 R). This became a rallying cry for regions across Europe, not least in the debates leading up to the Maastricht Treaty. Four specific demands were articulated by the *Länder*:

- entrenching subsidiarity in any treaty amendment;
- opening up the Council of Ministers in matters of exclusive subnational responsibility to ministers from that level;
- establishing a 'regional organ' at the European level; and
- establishing a right of appeal from the subnational level to the European Court of Justice against infringements of rights by the Council or Commission. (Jeffrey, 1996, p. 256)

These demands had limited success. The Maasticht Treaty formalized the position of regions as never before: the formulation of mainstream policy would henceforth have to take account of cohesion; provision was made for reform of the Structural Funds; and cultural policy would also have to respect the national and regional diversity of member states. The main focus of the debate on subsidiarity at the time of Maastricht was, however, on the relationship between the EU and the member states' governments rather than on the position of regions. The primary aim of the subsidiarity principle in the Treaty was to regulate the use made of the Commission's non-exclusive competences (Dehousse, 1994, pp. 110–11). Entrenching subsidiarity in the Treaty occurred, but not to the advantage of the regions. No right of appeal for regions to the European Court was agreed.

The EC Treaty was revised by the Maastricht Treaty to enable regions to represent member states in Council meetings. Spain, Germany, Belgium and Austria have taken advantage of this change and permit subnational levels to participate directly in Council of Ministers meetings. In Belgium, reflecting domestic constitutional change there, Council of Ministers meetings are classified into four different types: those dealing with matters which are the exclusive competence of the federal government; those dealing with competences which are mostly federal matters; those dealing with matters which are mostly regional competences; and those dealing with the exclusive competences of regions. The level of participation by federal or regional ministers reflects the degree of responsibility of each level (De Rynck and Maes, 1996). However, most member states, including the United Kingdom, have not taken advantage of this provision and regional governments from these countries generally do not participate directly in Council meetings.

The most significant victory for regions in the Maastricht Treaty, symbolically at least, was the establishment of the Committee of the Regions (CoR). As a new institution representing the interests of regions and local authorities, CoR was given an advisory role. However, its limited resources, divisions between local and regional representatives, the emergence of political and geographical groupings, its consultative nature and its tendency to offer opinions on a very wide range of issues have limited its ability to affect outcomes (Van der Knaap, 1994; Christiansen, 1996). The symbolic significance of the CoR has been considerable, though perhaps more for member states wishing to demonstrate their willingness to accommodate regions than for the regions themselves in gaining formal status within the EU. Of the *Länder's* four specific demands, they failed with respect to the entrenchment of subsidiarity in the Treaty and with respect to the right of appeal to the Court, but they were successful in creating a 'regional organ' and, at least for some regions, in gaining direct access to the Council of Ministers.

The TEU reforms reflected the fact that regions had been asserting themselves ever more loudly at the European level from around the mid-1980s. An increasing number established 'lobbying' offices in Brussels which essentially gathered information on EC/EU initiatives to send back to the region. By 1988 there were 15 such offices, but this number had tripled five years later (Marks *et al.*, 1996, p. 40). In addition, regions across Europe have worked together where they can identify a common interest, as in the case of some peripheral maritime regions or traditional industrial regions – now called regions of technological innovation to provide a more positive image (McAleavey and Mitchell, 1994; Weyand, 1997). By 1998, the Regional Policy Directorate-General of the European Commission estimated that there were over 120 offices in Brussels with a regional interest. The lobbying aspect of their work is often exaggerated in an effort to legitimize the offices' existence back in the regions where the costs of maintaining a Brussels presence requires justification. The motivations behind establishing offices in Brussels are both symbolic and functional. As some regions begin to establish a presence in Brussels, there is a symbolic value to other regions in having a Brussels office. While the lobbying aspect of their activities may have been exaggerated, these offices do offer opportunities to gather information and intelligence on forthcoming initiatives.

More significant is the role that regions play in the European policy process back home. With a small staff and limited resources, the Commission relies heavily on officials working on the ground in regions across Europe for information to tailor the implementation of policy. Viewed from the perspective of models of policy-making, regions have become part of policy networks in which there is a high degree of 'resource dependence' between the several affected public and private institutions, including regions, especially at the implementation stage, though the national government in most member states has 'clung to its "gatekeeping" role' (Rhodes *et al.*, 1996, p. 385). In other words, in some cases regions have cut out a role for themselves as an indispensable part of the policy process.

All of this suggests that regions are beginning to establish a significant role for themselves in the EU policy-making process. Some observers have suggested that a system of 'multi-level governance' (another metaphor refers to a 'third level') has emerged in Europe, with regions playing an increasing role in European decision-making (Marks, 1993). The notion that the EU is a single, multi-level polity has not gone unchallenged. Some critics place greater emphasis on 'intergovernmental' explanations, which stress the relationship between member states' governments in developing policies. Such critics often view the EU's Structural Funds as mere 'side payments extended in exchange for other policies' (Moravcsik, 1993, p. 496). This sees such funds as mere bargaining chips used by the member states. None the less, it cannot be disputed that the role of regions in policy implementation has increased as a result of the growing significance of regional funds.

The Emergence of the European Regional Development Fund

There have been three stages in the development of EU regional policy since the establishment of the EEC in 1958:

1. 1958–75: characterized by the absence of any common regional policy;
2. 1975–88: the creation of new regional policy instruments and strengthening of the regional dimension of other instruments already available, as well as a steady increase in funds available;
3. 1988–: reform of the Structural Funds and the search for more effective regional policy, accompanied by substantial increase in funds. (Tsoukalis, 1993, pp. 232–3)

One of the Structural Funds is the European Regional Development Fund (ERDF), which finances infrastructure and business development schemes. The other main Structural Funds are the European Social Fund (ESF), which finances employment and training initiatives, and the Guidance Section of the European agricultural funds (known as EAGGF). Grants from these funds are often accompanied by loans from the European Investment Bank (EIB) or the European Coal and Steel Community (ECSC). The ERDF is the largest of the Structural Funds in financial terms and was established in 1975, two years after the UK joined the Community and 18 years after the Treaty of Rome. Less than 5 per cent of the Community's budget was initially devoted to this fund and fixed quotas were set aside for each member state. In effect, this severely limited the discretion of the Commission and regional and local bodies in the policy-making process. Member states determined the total amount to be spent and how this would be allocated. A small non-quota section was introduced in 1979 (raised in 1984) and this gave the Commission a small but important opportunity to build a genuine European policy into the existing arrangements.

The ERDF has had an ambiguous role from the outset. It has both attempted to promote regional development and to provide a channel for rebates to certain member states for contributions to the Community's budget which were considered excessive (Buck, 1982, pp. 25–6). The conflict between the *development* and the *compensatory* functions has been at the heart of the Fund's evolution. It was a variation on a common theme: the tension between genuinely supranational European policies and policies designed to meet the coincident interests of member states. The development vs. compensatory tension was a reflection of the supranational vs. intergovernmental debate. Fifty years ago, when the ECSC was being established, the negotiating process which set it up established a pattern comparable to that associated with the ERDF. Jean Monnet's original conception of a supranational High Authority (precursor of the Commission) with considerable scope for action and capable of developing genuine common policies had been severely circumscribed. Member states attempted to 'control and distribute the gains and losses which might arise in the particular sectors involved in such a way as to determine beforehand the extent to which the national interest of each party to the agreement would be satisfied' (Milward, 1984, p. 498).

An alternative interpretation was articulated by Haas (1958). He saw the High Authority, albeit within limits, developing distinct European policies. This old debate and the same issues have been replicated in recent and contemporary discussions of regional and other policies. Compensatory, as opposed to development, considerations explain the 'complicated and perhaps economically "irrational" nature' of some decisions (Tsoukalis, 1993, p. 236). Some descriptions of the ERDF at its inception are remarkably similar to Milward's on the ECSC: 'the establishment of a Regional Development Fund is not so much an instrument to deal with regional disparities as a means to cope with national disparities regarding contributions from and payments to the Community budget' (Van Doorn, 1975, p. 400).

Against this backdrop, the Commission's attempts to create a genuine European regional policy, with an emphasis on its developmental function, have been constrained by the member states. Especially latterly, regions have attempted to join in the decision-making process. A major reform of the Structural Funds in the late 1980s increased the scope for the involvement of regional actors in the design and implementation of regional policy programmes.

From ERDF to European Regional Policy

Successive reforms have altered the nature of the Fund and a genuine European regional policy began to emerge in the late 1980s. The ERDF was given Treaty status with the passage of the SEA, which included a new title on 'Economic and Social Cohesion' stating that the Union 'shall aim at reducing disparities between the levels of development of the various regions and the backwardness of the least favoured regions' (Article 130a). The accession of Spain and Portugal in 1986 had widened the gap between the richest and poorest regions and this gap was officially the rationale behind incorporating the new regional emphasis. However, as McCrone (1969, p.13) had noted in his study of regional policy in Britain, disparities usually exist long before they are officially recognised as a political problem. As had happened when the ERDF had been established, the SEA's title dealing with cohesion reflected inter-state bargaining. Five member states – Spain, Portugal, Ireland, Greece and Italy – would have been unwilling to sign up to provisions in the SEA without the inclusion of this new title and these countries were important subsequently in ensuring that the budget for the Structural Funds was doubled. By 1992, Community structural spending would reach 27 per cent of the Community budget compared with 17 per cent in 1987.

Major reforms in the way that Structural Funds were spent occurred following the SEA. While the initial pressure for change had come as a result of inter-state bargaining, this had some unintended consequences marking a move towards a genuine European regional policy. In 1998 four basic principles were set out in the new regulations governing the Structural Funds and remain the key principles today: concentration; programming; partnership; additionality.

Concentration

The principle of concentration meant that funds would be concentrated in the most disadvantaged regions. This took the form of the elaboration of five priority 'Objectives'. The ERDF addressed three of the Objectives (1, 2 and 5b), but not in isolation – the ESF and the EAGGF were also used. With the exception of some specially designed projects, such as the Integrated Development Operations and Integrated Mediterranean Programmes, these instruments had previously operated separately.

Objective 1 regions were the poorest parts of the Community and would receive around 65 per cent of funds. The whole of Greece, Ireland and Portugal as well as substantial parts of Spain and Italy were eligible under this Objective. In addition, Corsica and Northern Ireland were classified as Objective 1 regions even though they had not met the statistical criteria. France and the UK had argued for their inclusion given the special political conditions in these regions. Sixty regions were classified eligible under Objective 2, regions suffering industrial decline, with the UK being the main beneficiary and receiving 39.7 per cent of available funds. Objective 5b was concerned with developing rural areas. A new Objective 6 was later added, after the accession of Austria, Sweden and Finland. Objective 6, which focuses on sparsely populated areas, only covers regions in these three new member states.

In addition, special Community Initiatives were given support over which the Commission had greater power. Member states would be invited to submit proposals for consideration under these initiatives with each targeted at resolving serious problems associated with implementation of Community policies or resolving problems in certain types of region. These included RECHAR (designed to assist areas affected by the closure of coal-mining), INTERREG (promoting cross-border co-operation), ENVIREG (addressing environmental problems). In total, 13 such Initiatives were created.

Programming

This principle referred to the abandonment of a short-term project-by-project approach and its replacement by multi-annual programmes of three or five years. The aim was to move towards more effective and coherent policy-making. This involved a three-stage planning procedure with a plan submitted to the Commission from the appropriate member state which would be responded to as 'Community Support Frameworks' before being implemented as 'Operational Programmes' (OPs).

Partnership

This principle referred to the involvement in the preparation, financing, monitoring and assessment of OPs by different levels of government – the Commission, member states and the relevant authority at local, regional or national level. The hope was that the outcome would be greater than the sum of each level involved. It was inevitable that, as the Structural Funds grew, greater involvement would be required by 'street level bureaucrats' (Lipsky, 1980) – those involved in the implementation of the policy. It made sense to involve them at all stages in order to maximize the impact of projects. Through the creation of Monitoring Committees in the eligible regions – bodies bringing together all the national, regional and local partners with the European Commission to implement the agreed policy priorities – the partnership principle increased the scope for regional and local involvement in the process.

Additionality

This proved to be one of the most contentious issues in the European Structural Funds and battles over the application of this principle centred around the degree to which they represented a genuinely European regional policy. Additionality meant that Structural Funds should be additional to, and not simply a substitute for, existing or planned domestic investment. That is, member state governments should not use European funds to replace national funds that they would have spent anyway. One commentator (Mény, 1982, p. 377) had described this practice of governments pocketing resources to replace their own expenditure in the early years of the ERDF as the 'extreme nationalisation' of regional development policy. The Commission and local/regional authorities found themselves in common cause against the central governments of member states. One problem was verifying additionality. Member states would deny that Community funds replaced what had been planned. In 1992, the Commission concluded that Ireland, Portugal, Greece, Germany and Belgium applied the principle but were dissatisfied with what happened elsewhere. This proved a highly controversial matter in the UK, especially with regard to the RECHAR Community Initiative (McAleavey, 1992, 1993).

After Maastricht

As noted above, the Maastricht Treaty promoted economic and social cohesion as one of the Union's 'tasks'. However, in the context of an economic recession and some backlash within member states against the process of integration, there was resistance to major changes in the Structural Funds – and particularly to the Commission increasing its power in the process. This had adverse consequences for the development of a European regional policy. A second tranche of Structural Funds was agreed in 1993 to operate from 1994–9. Minor changes were made, but the basic structure created in 1988 was maintained. The number of regions covered by Objective 1 increased to cover over a quarter of the Union's population – only Denmark and Luxembourg had no Objective 1 areas under the new classification. There was some degree of 're-nationalizing' regional policies, with member states gaining greater control of aspects of the policy. On the other hand, there was also an increase in resources made available to the Structural Funds. Furthermore, it was decided that regional policy should be more fully integrated with the Union's environmental policies, though the degree of success in this respect has been questioned (Wishlade, 1996, p. 53). As the period covered by the post-Maastricht regulations was drawing to a close, the next stage was prepared and discussed. The Amsterdam Treaty restated the importance of cohesion and gave priority to tackling unemployment with a new title on employment.

The 1993 reform of the Structural Funds consolidated the major amendments which had been made in 1988. In line with the multi-annual financial programming adopted by the EU, the 1993 revised Structural Funds regulations covered the period 1994 to 1999. In this six year-period, around 51 per cent of the EU population lived in a region eligible for European regional support (whether under Objectives 1, 2, 5b or 6). Their regional and local governments, in line with the partnership principle set out above, were involved in the design and implementation of the regional policy programmes supported by around 200 billion ECU of Structural Fund support across the lifetime of the programme.

Another reform of the Structural Funds was soon on the horizon, with the prospect this time of an overhaul in the way the European regional policy operates. The European Council meeting in Madrid in December 1995 requested that the Commission should prepare a comprehensive proposal concerning the finances and policy tools which the EU would need to move into the new millennium. In response, the Commission adopted a Communication entitled *Agenda 2000: For a Stronger and Wider Europe* on 16 July 1997. *Agenda 2000*, which was published after a long process of internal reflection within the Commission, set out the Commission's proposals for the new financial programme period 2000 to 2006. It constituted an ambitious, single framework for the development of European policies into the new millennium, including preparations for the accession of the countries of Central and Eastern Europe, reform of agricultural policy, reform of the Structural Funds, and specification of the finances necessary over this medium term (Commission, 1997).

Agenda 2000 reaffirmed the priority policy goal of economic and social cohesion. However, it did not propose a dramatic increase in the share of EU resources allocated to the Structural Funds, as had been the case at the time of the last two reforms. Rather, it proposed that the ceiling of 0.46 per cent of Gross Domestic Product (GDP), which had been set for economic and social cohesion expenditure at the European Council in Edinburgh in December 1992, should be maintained for the period 2000 to 2006. Assuming a sustained growth in EU GDP, then the resources available should total around 275 billion ECU. As 45 billion ECU was set aside for enlargement preparations in candidate countries, and the period covered seven years as opposed to six in the past (1994 to 1999), it is clear that the Commission was not proposing an increase in Structural Fund resources.

In March 1998, the Commission published its proposals for the reform of the Structural Fund regulations. These regulations became the subject of intensive negotiations in Council of Ministers' working groups, negotiations in which regions themselves did not participate directly. The principles underpinning the previous reforms of the Structural Funds – concentration, programming, partnership and additionality – remained central in the draft regulations. However, among these principles, *concentration* assumed a particular political importance. The political imperative to concentrate resources in advance of enlargement, alongside the twin political imperatives to *simplify the system* and *redefine the Commission's role* in implementing programmes, pointed in the direction of a significant overhaul of the regulations and thus of the way in which European regional policy operates.

The Commission clearly signalled its intention to concentrate eligibility for European regional policy resources in the 2000–6 period upon the most needy regions. The fact that around 51 per cent of the EU's citizens were living in regions eligible for ERDF support is testimony to the continuing compensatory role of the Fund. The Commission proposed that a number of regions should see their eligibility phased out, so that by 2006 the ERDF would cover only between 35 and 40 per cent of the EU population. This was seen to be necessary not just to focus resources on the regions in greatest need, but also to prepare the ground for further enlargement, as the candidate countries of Central and Eastern Europe will most likely draw heavily on Objective 1 funds. The proposal to concentrate proved to be the most controversial of the Commission's reform proposals.

In addition to the proposal to concentrate resources, the Commission proposed a radical simplification of the Structural Funds. It proposed that the number of Objectives be reduced to just three: regions whose development is lagging behind (new Objective 1); areas undergoing economic and social conversion (new Objective 2); and the development of human resources (new Objective 3). Old Objectives 1 and 6 would be merged into the new Objective 1, under which the eligibility criteria would be strictly applied; Objectives 2 and 5b would be reformed as a revised Objective 2, for which member states would have a greater role in determining eligibility; and, in addition to these regional Objectives, present Objectives 3 and 4 would be merged into a horizontal Objective 3 to provide continuing ESF support outside eligible regions. Moreover, the Commission proposed that there should be just three Community Initiatives, as opposed to the thirteen at present: transnational, cross-border and inter-regional. Other simplifications proposed included a radical revision of the way in which finances would be paid to member states and regions, and a reduction in the level of detail to be included in the formal regional policy 'contracts' between the Commission, member states and regional partnerships.

Linked to the proposal for simplification was a proposed redefinition of the role of the Commission in the regional policy process. The former President of the Commission, Jacques Santer, famously suggested in 1995 that the Commission should 'do less, but do it better'. In short, the Commission must face a period of 'zero growth' in its budget and staff resources, in which it must focus on what is essential and prioritize areas where it can bring real added value. Under the 1988 reform proposals once the subsidiarity test had been passed, all policies would be subject to the test of *proportionality*: even if there was a case for EU-level action (the subsidiarity test), the

Commission should only act if it was convinced that the resources required to achieve a task were in reasonable proportion to the impact expected (the proportionality test). In the area of regional policy, this meant that the Commission would be less involved in detailed implementation issues on a day-to-day basis. For example, the Commission proposed that it should no longer be a full member of the regional Monitoring Committees (see above), but should attend in an observer capacity only.

The Commission's proposals for reform received a mixed reception. Member state governments welcomed the proposed simplification of the regional policy system, but many were cautious of the proposals for greater concentration. The European Parliament (EP) warned that simplification and a redefinition of the role of the Commission should not lead to a 'renationalization' of European regional policy. Some regional actors feared the redefinition of the role of the Commission, worrying that they may lose a useful ally in battles against central government. At the March 1999 Berlin European Council, heads of government reached agreement on the *Agenda 2000* reform programme. As part of the agreement it was decided that, with some modest adjustments, the Commission's proposals for the reform of the Structural Funds would be accepted. This therefore means that, subject to the EP giving its approval and the necessary implementing regulations being passed, total Structural Fund spending will be reduced (from 29.4 billion euro in 2000 to 26.7 billion euro in 2006 at 1999 prices) and EU regional policy and funding will become more concentrated, simplified and decentralised.

The Future of Cohesion Policy

Cohesion policy does not operate in a vacuum. Policies designed to tackle inequalities in wealth across the regions of the EU depend on perceptions of need and expectations of public policy success. Inequalities had long existed before member states decided to tackle them. Indeed, the motive for creating the ERDF had more to do with perceived unfairness in budgetary matters between member states. This motive affected the nature of the policy which emerged in the mid-1970s which was the base for all that followed thereafter. The challenge in creating a genuine European regional policy focused on the relative power of the Commission, member states and regions. The member states have retained the upper hand, but the other two have cut out roles for themselves in the process. The ERDF emerged at a time when a backlash against interventionist economic policies was developing in reaction to recession. This was a time when member states, and most notably the UK, were redefining the role of the state *vis-à-vis* the market. The perception that old-style interventionist regional policies did not work played a part in the evolution of European regional policy and made some states even more reluctant to see it as anything other than a transfer payment.

The context in which the policy emerged was therefore important. The buoyancy of Europe's increasingly integrated economy affects the prospects for cohesion and the prospects for regional policy success. During recessions, the resources available are likely to be more limited and therefore the chances of poorer regions catching up are decreased. Other public policies, at European, member state, regional or local level, will have an impact on cohesion and the prospect of success. In addition, external policies – notably external trade policies – have implications for cohesion. Almost all public policies have implicit regional effects. In a sense, then, all policies are regional policies. The impact of economic integration, monetary union and the creation of the single currency will differ across the Union's regions. Impending changes in the Common Agricultural Policy will have regional consequences and, of course, the enlargement of the Union raises important issues for cohesion policy.

Much progress has been made, not least in demonstrating to Europe's citizens that the EU is close to their concerns as witnessed by the numerous EU signposts celebrating job creation projects funded by the Structural Funds across the Union. This symbolic aspect should not be underestimated. However, success in achieving social and economic cohesion across Europe will require it to have a central place informing the range of mainstream EU policies. In much the same way that an attempt has been made to incorporate environmental concerns into regional prescriptions, cohesion will have to be more fully incorporated into the central concerns of economic integration to begin to tackle regional disparities. However, as has been witnessed with the regional environmental relationship, meshing different policies with potentially divergent objectives is not easy.

More significant, however, remains the tension between the development and compensatory functions of the policy. Unless the EU is able to reconcile these two functions, further cohesion may prove elusive – especially in light of the anticipated expansion of the EU to Central and Eastern European countries.

Guide to Further Reading

Keating (1998) discusses the challenges Western Europe is facing from above in the form of globalization and European integration and from below from new regionalist movements. The book also offers an account of the structures of regional government operating in different European states. The edited volume by Le Galès and Lequesne (1998) has two parts: one is thematic and the other considers the experience of individual states in Europe. Hooghe (ed.) (1996) is wide-ranging. The first section considers the making of EU cohesion policy, the second discusses the 'role of territory', and how regions operate in individual member states regarding cohesion policy, and the third section describes and explains variation across Europe.

Different perspectives on cohesion policy are available in the literature. For a 'multi-level governance' perspective, see Marks (1992). For an intergovernmentalist perspective, see Pollack (1995). *Regional and Federal Studies* is a journal which carries relevant articles and has occasional special issues devoted to EU matters, including vol. 7, no. 1, Spring 1997, which was devoted to the EU Committee of the Regions. The EU Web site on economic and social cohesion is found at: http://europa.eu.int/pol/reg/en/reg.htm

References

Audit Commission (1991) *A Rough Guide To Europe: Local Authorities and the EC*. London: HMSO.

Buck, T. (1982) 'New Proposals for the European Regional Development Fund', Memorandum submitted to the House of Lords Select Committee on the European Communities, *Regional Policy*, Session 1981–82, 12th Report, HL Paper 126, London: HMSO, pp. 25–9.

Christiansen, T. (1996) 'Second Thoughts on Europe's "Third Level": The European Union's Committee of the Regions', *Publius: The Journal of Federalism*, vol. 26, pp. 93–116.

Commission (1997) *Agenda 2000 – For a Stronger and Wider Union*, Com (97) final. Brussels: Commission.

Dehousse, R. (1994) 'Community Competences: Are there Limits to Growth?', in R. Dehousse (ed.), *Europe After Maastricht: An Ever Closer Union?* Munich: Beck, pp. 103–25.

De Rynck, S. and Maes, R. (1996) 'Belgium: Regions, Communities and Subregional Authorities in the European Integration Process', in J.J. Hesse (ed.), *Regions in Europe*. Baden-Baden: Nomos, pp. 101–28.

Haas, E.B. (1958) *The Uniting of Europe. Political, Social and Economic Forces, 1950–57*. Stanford: Stanford University Press.

Hooghe, L. (ed.) (1996) *Cohesion Policy and European Integration*. Oxford: Oxford University Press.

House of Lords (1977) *EEC Regional Policy*, Report of Select Committee on the European Communities, Session 1976–77, 13th Report, HL Paper 75, London: HMSO.

Hrbek, R. (1991) 'German Federalism and the Challenge of European Integration', in C. Jeffrey and P. Savigear (eds), *German Federalism Today*. Leicester: Leicester University Press, pp. 84–102.

Jeffrey, C. (1996) 'Towards a "Third Level" in Europe? The German *Länder* in the European Union', *Political Studies*, vol. 44, no. 2, pp. 253–66.

Jeffrey, C. (1997) 'Farewell the Third Level? The German *Länder* and the European Policy Process', in C. Jeffrey (ed.), *The Regional Dimension of the European Union: Towards a Third Level in Europe?* London: Frank Cass, pp. 56–75.

Keating, M. (1998) *The New Regionalism in Western Europe*, Cheltenham: Edward Elgar.

Le Galès, P. and Lequesne, C. (eds) (1998) *Regions in Europe*. London: Routledge.

Lipsky, M. (1980) *Street-Level Bureaucracy: Dilemmas of the Individual in Public Services*. New York: Russell Sage Foundation.

Loughlin, J. (1997) 'Representing Regions in Europe: The Committee of the Regions', in C. Jeffrey (ed.), *The Regional Dimension of the European Union: Towards a Third Level in Europe?* London: Frank Cass, pp. 147–65.

McAleavey, P. (1992) 'The Politics of European Regional Development Policy: The European Commission's RECHAR Initiative and the Concept of Additionality', *Strathclyde Papers on Government and Politics*, no. 88.

McAleavey, P. (1993) 'The Politics of European Regional Development Policy: Additionality in the Scottish Coalfields', *Regional Politics and Policy*, vol. 3, no. 2, pp. 88–107.

McAleavey, P. and Mitchell, J. (1994) 'Industrial Regions and Lobbying in the Structural Funds Reform Process', *Journal of Common Market Studies*, vol. 32, no. 2, June 1994, pp. 239–48.

McCrone, G. (1969) *Regional Policy in Britain*. London: George Allen and Unwin.

Marks, G. (1992) 'Structural Policy in the European Community', in A. Sbragia (ed.), *Europolitics: Institutions and Policymaking in the 'New' European Community*. Washington, DC: The Brookings Institution, pp. 191–224.

Marks, G. (1993) 'Structural Policy and Multilevel Governance in the European Community', in A. Calfruny and G. Rosenthal (eds), *The State of the European Community*. New York: Lynne Rienner, pp. 391–410.

Marks, G., Nielsen, F., Ray, L., Salk, J. (1996) 'Competencies, Cracks and Conflicts: Regional Mobilization in the European Union', in G. Marks, F.W. Scharpf, P.C. Schmitter, and W. Streeck (eds), *Governance in the European Union*. London: Sage, pp. 40–63.

Martin, D. (1991) *Europe: An Ever Closer Union*. Nottingham: Spokesman.

Mény, Y. (1982) 'Should the Community Regional Policy Be Scrapped?', *Common Market Law Review*, vol. 19, pp. 87–108.

Milward, A. (1984) *The Reconstruction of Western Europe, 1945–51.*, London: Methuen.

Moravcsik, A. (1993) 'Preferences and Power in the European Community: A Liberal Intergovernmentalist Approach', *Journal of Common Market Studies*, vol. 31, no. 4, pp. 473–524.

Pollack, M. (1995) 'Regional Actors in an Intergovernmental Play: The Making and Implementation of EC Structural Policy', in S. Mazey and C. Rhodes (eds), *The State of the European Union III*, Boulder, C: Lynne Rienner, pp. 361–90.

Rhodes, R.A.W., Bache, I. and George, S. (1996) 'Policy Networks and Policy-Making in the European Union: A Critical Appraisal', in L. Hooghe (ed.), *Cohesion and European Integration: Building Multi-Level Governance*. Oxford: Oxford University Press, pp. 367–87.

Tsoukalis, L. (1993) *The New European Economy: The Politics and Economics of Integration*. rev. 2nd edn, Oxford: Oxford University Press.

Van der Knaap, P. (1994) 'The Committee of the Regions: The Outset of the Europe of the Regions?', *Regional Politics and Policy*, vol. 4, no. 2, pp. 86–100.

Van Doorn, J. (1975) 'European Regional Policy: An Evaluation of Recent Developments', *Journal of Common Market Studies*, vol. 13, no. 4, pp. 391–401.

Weyand, S. (1997) 'Inter-Regional Associations and the European Integration Process' in C. Jeffrey (ed.), *The Regional Dimension of the European Union: Towards a Third Level in Europe?* London: Frank Cass, pp. 165–82.

Wishlade, F. (1996) 'EU Cohesion Policy: Facts, Figures, and Issues', in L. Hooghe (ed.), *Cohesion Policy and European Integration: Building Multi-Level Governance*. Oxford: Oxford University Press, pp. 27–58.

10

Environmental Policy

JOHN McCORMICK

After being overlooked for many years, the environmental policy of the European Union is slowly drawing more public and media attention. While opinions remain divided about the merits of the single currency, the Common Agricultural Policy (CAP), and some of the consequences of the single market, there is a growing consensus that European integration has been good for the environment. A regional response to environmental issues has advantages over separate national responses because many environmental issues cross national boundaries, differences in environmental standards may create trade distortions, and individual states are more likely to tighten their environmental laws if they know their neighbours are moving in the same direction. There is also wide public support for EU environmental activity: recent *Eurobarometer* polls reveal that more than two-thirds of Europeans believe that decisions on the environment should be taken at the EU level rather than at the national level.

Although environmental problems were largely ignored by European policy-makers until the early 1970s, much lost ground has been made up in recent years, notably since the Single European Act (SEA) and the Maastricht Treaty on European Union (TEU) formalized the place of environmental policy on the European agenda. The EU has published five action programmes since 1973; run several continent-wide research programmes and created a data-processing European Environment Agency; been a forceful actor in international negotiations on environmental protection; established several programmes to finance environmental management projects; published many green and white papers on environmental issues; and – by early 1999 – had agreed more than 700 laws on matters as varied as air and water quality, waste disposal, noise pollution and habitat protection. Environmental policy in the EU is now arguably driven more by the needs and effects of regional integration than by the priorities of the individual member states.

This chapter assesses the European record on environmental law and policy. It describes the emergence of the environmental dimension in EU activities, outlines the problems that still need addressing, attempts to understand the European definition of 'the environment', and identifies emerging trends that may lead to changes in the way the EU approaches environmental management.

The Evolution of the Environmental Dimension

The environment was a latecomer to the European policy agenda. The Treaty of Rome contained no direct references to environmental policy, and the issue drew little political attention during the 1950s and 1960s. Euratom paid passing attention to the dangers of radiation, and a few measures were agreed based on Article 2 of the EEC Treaty (with its general references to the quality of life, the 'harmonious' development of economic activities, and 'balanced' expansion), and on Article 100 (providing for harmonization of the laws of the member states 'as directly affect the establishment or functioning of the common market'). Article 235 – which allowed the Council of Ministers to take action to achieve the goals of the Community where the Treaty had not explicitly provided powers – was also occasionally used as a justification for new laws.

Political views began to change following the 1972 UN Conference on the Human Environment, held in Stockholm. Widespread political and public attention was drawn to transboundary and global environmental problems for the first time, prompting the creation of national environmental ministries and a growth in the volume of national environmental law (McCormick, 1995, chapter 5). It also became clear to Community leaders that the strengthening of domestic law in member states such as West Germany and the Netherlands was causing trade distortions that undermined the common market (Garner, 1996, pp. 120–1). A meeting of the heads of government of the member states in Paris in October 1972 resulted in agreement on the need for action. The following year, a small Environment and Consumer Protection Service was set up and attached to DGIII (the Directorate-General of the Commission responsible for Industrial

Policy), a standing Committee on the Environment was created in the European Parliament (EP), and the Community adopted its first Environmental Action Programme (EAP).

There was still no clear legal basis for Community action, however, and while environmental laws were developed and adopted, most were still based on creative readings of Articles 100 and/or 235. Whichever article was used, decision-making in the Council demanded unanimity, so proposals were often watered down, and their final content usually imposed only minimal obligations on member states.

Three significant changes came in the 1980s. In 1981, a reorganization of the Commission resulted in environmental responsibilities being transferred from DGIII to a reformulated DGXI, which is now responsible for environment, nuclear safety and civil protection. In 1982, the third EAP (1982–6) emphasized the need to take preventive action to protect the environment, and argued that environmental concerns should be integrated into all Community policies. Finally, a 1985 Court of Justice decision (*Procureur de la République* v. *ADBHU*) argued that environmental protection was 'one of the Community's essential objectives', a notion that was confirmed when the 1986 SEA gave the Community legal competence in environmental matters by introducing a new Title VII (Environment). Community goals were to include the preservation and protection of the environment, and qualified majority voting was introduced for environmental measures relating to the single market.

The Maastricht Treaty further refined EU powers by making 'sustainable and non- inflationary growth respecting the environment' a fundamental goal of the EU (Article 2), reiterating the importance of the 'precautionary principle' (the EU should take action if there is a suspicion that an activity might cause environmental harm, rather than waiting until the scientific evidence is clear), and giving legal force to the application of subsidiarity to all EU policy sectors. Voting by qualified majority became standard procedure for most environmental measures, and the co-decision procedure gave Parliament more powers to amend draft legislation (Haigh, 1992, 2.3). The Amsterdam Treaty built on these changes by confirming that sustainable development (economic development that takes place within the carrying capacity of the environment) would be one of the general goals of European integration.

Concerns about the quality of the data upon which Community policy was based led to the creation in 1985 of CORINE (Coordinating Information on the Environment), and to the foundation in 1994 of the European Environment Agency (EEA), based in Copenhagen. The Agency is not a policy-making or implementing body, but generates and provides data to the Commission, and helps identify new ideas for law and policy.

One of the EEA's first major projects was the preparation and publication in 1995 of a lengthy survey of Europe's environment (the Dobris Assessment), which provided the most comprehensive picture to date of the state of a regional environment anywhere in the world (Stanners and Bourdeau, 1995). The findings of the Dobris Assessment, and of a follow-up assessment published in 1998 (EEA, 1998), have painted a picture of mixed progress:

- Europe's water and air is cleaner, there is more public awareness of the threats posed by chemicals to food and water, fish stocks are better managed, the EU is quieter (45 pieces of legislation have been adopted on noise pollution), and differences in environmental standards pose less of a handicap than before to trade among the member states.
- In the case of poorer states such as Greece, Spain and Portugal, with little in the way of pre-existing laws and policies, almost all their environmental activities have been driven by the obligations of EU membership.
- While levels of sulphur dioxide, lead and particulates have declined in the EU, many European cities still have dirty air, mainly because of heavy (and growing) concentrations of road vehicles. Goods vehicle traffic increased by 54 per cent between 1980 and 1994, passenger vehicle traffic increased by 46 per cent between 1985 and 1995, and the volume of road traffic in Western Europe is expected to almost double by 2010 (from 1990 levels). As a result, the benefits of vehicle emission controls could be cancelled out.
- The EU is making little progress in responding to concerns about global climate change. The EEA believes that a reduction in emissions of greenhouse gases of between 30 and 55 per cent is required in industrialized countries by 2010 (from 1990 levels) if global temperature increases are to be controlled. However, it predicts that EU emissions will increase by 5 per cent by 2000 (from 1990 levels).
- Energy consumption in the EU continues to grow, particularly in the transport sector, and while the production and consumption of ozone-depleting chlorofluorocarbons (CFCs) and halons has fallen

almost to zero, the ozone layer over Europe thinned by 5 per cent between 1979 and 1995.

- Intensive agriculture continues to exert pressure on natural habitats, helping threaten 45 per cent of Europe's reptiles and 42 per cent of its mammals with extinction, introducing nitrogen and phosphorus into surface waters, and emitting acidifying ammonia into the atmosphere. Meanwhile, groundwater concentrations of some pesticides frequently exceed maximum admissible levels.
- There has been little progress in the development of waste disposal policies, and total waste production in OECD Europe grew by nearly 10 per cent between 1990 and 1995, although the proportion going into landfill has fallen as the use of incinerators has grown.
- While fresh water is overexploited, and polluted by sewage, pesticides, and industrial waste, over-fishing and pollution continue to be problems in many coastal zones and marine water (EEA, 1995, chapter 4).

Defining Environmental Policy

Despite growing public and policy interest in 'the environment', it is a term that is seldom defined in the literature. Scholars routinely list issues which they regard as 'environmental' (such as air and water pollution, threats to animals and plants, and the problem of waste disposal), but rarely try to define the boundaries of those issues. One suggests that the environment 'is the milieu within which we survive as biological creatures' and that environmental policy 'has to do with sustaining the ecological basis of life' (Wells, 1996, p. 1). Another suggests that 'the raw material of the environmental debate is the deleterious effects of human activity on the planet' (Garner, 1996, p. 5), while others argue that global environmental issues are those 'involving threats to the integrity of the biosphere on which all human life depends' (Porter and Brown, 1991, p. 16).

Of course, it could be argued that 'the environment' is boundless in the sense that almost every human activity has some kind of environmental impact, but without a clear sense of where administrative responsibilities begin and end, the policy process would be confused. In theory, the best point of departure for understanding the European definition of environmental policy should be official EU sources, but these are of surprisingly little help. At no point in the treaties is 'the environment' or 'environmental policy' defined, and while the annual

Directory of Environmental Legislation in Force should be an authoritative source, it deals mainly with laws generated by DGXI, excludes laws developed in related areas by other Directorates-General, and – because DGXI is also responsible for consumer issues and public health protection – includes laws on consumer credit, cancer prevention, and the control of narcotics.

The official Web site of the European Union (Europa Homepage, 1998) offers contradictory advice. At one point it suggests that EU environmental law and policy is limited to waste management, noise, air and water pollution, nature conservation, and industrial risks, but expands the list elsewhere to include the control of chemicals and genetically modified organisms, nuclear safety, and radiation protection. The site also suggests that the environmental *acquis* (the body of environmental law adopted by the EU) consists of 280 legal acts. However, its list includes two laws restricting the use of leghold traps, and one law relating to experiments on animals.

For present purposes, 'the environment' is defined as the natural and man-made surroundings in which humans exist, 'environmental issues' as matters arising out of the two-way relationship between humans and those surroundings, and 'environmental policy' as any actions taken – or not taken – by government that are aimed either at managing human activities with a view to preventing harmful effects on nature and natural resources, or at ensuring that man-made changes to the environment do not have a harmful effect on humans. Given the history of the relationship, environmental issues commonly take the form of problems created by human activity, and policy is commonly a response to such problems. More recently, however, as understanding has grown about the nature and implications of the relationship, policy has become increasingly proactive and preventive.

Using this definition, and setting aside the EU's own definition of environmental policy, a more thorough study of the environmental *acquis* reveals that the EU has agreed a substantially larger body of law – and has been involved in a broader range of environmental issues – than it gives itself credit for. The total number of laws passed by the end of 1997 was 706 – just over half of these were new laws, with the remainder being amendments to these laws. As Figure 10.1 indicates, the output of environmental legislation as measured by adoptions grew steadily to a peak in 1994. The emphasis of the Santer Commission on consolidation rather than the development of new legislation subsequently led to the passage of fewer new laws, and an emphasis on amendments to existing laws. In terms of legislative

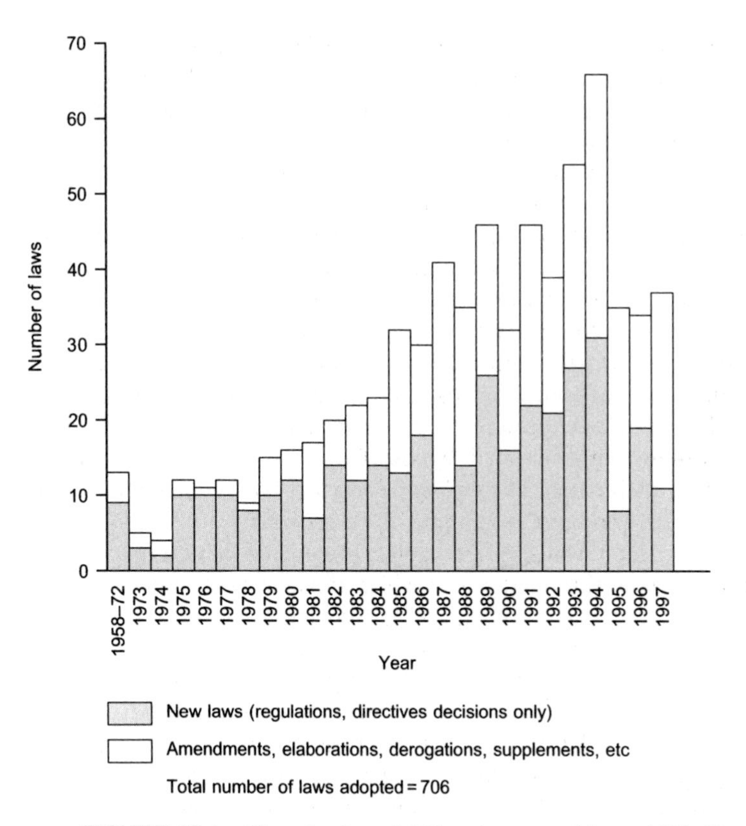

FIGURE 10.1 *The adoption of EU environmental laws, 1958–97*

tools, directives have been the most popular, accounting for 54 per cent of environmental laws, with regulations accounting for 25 per cent and decisions the remainder. The EU has also adopted a variety of non-binding opinions, recommendations, conclusions, declarations, and resolutions on the environment, and has relied increasingly since the early 1990s on the development of green and white papers.

An analysis of the subjects of EU environmental laws (McCormick, 1999) reveals the following:

- The control of chemicals in the environment has been the major priority. Nearly 110 laws (or 15 per cent of the total) focus on such issues as the packaging and distribution of chemicals. (Of course, it could be argued that most or all laws relating to air and water pollution, the control of pesticides, and hazardous waste management have the control of chemicals as their major objective, in which case nearly 340 EU laws (or 47 per cent of the total) are focused on chemicals.)

- The control of air pollution has also been a priority, being the subject of 80 laws (or 11 per cent of the total); freshwater pollution has been given less attention, being the focus of 28 laws (4 per cent).
- The management of fisheries and the marine environment have been given priority (100 laws, or 14 per cent of the total), as have issues relating to wildlife and biodiversity (52 laws, 7 per cent), but the management of forests has only been the subject of 18 laws (2.4 per cent of the total).
- The EU has also been active in areas that are not conventionally defined as being part of 'environmental' policy at the national level, notably the control of noise pollution (45 laws, 6 per cent) and of genetically-modified organisms (19 laws, nearly 3 per cent).
- Among the lower priorities: the impact of agriculture on the environment (22 laws, 3 per cent), and the promotion of energy conservation and alternative sources of energy (16 laws, 2 per cent).

Two important conclusions can be drawn from this analysis. First, the evolution and the content of European environmental law and policy makes it clear that the EU has so far had a somewhat idiosyncratic view of what constitutes an environmental issue. The EU definition of 'the environment' has been heavily influenced by the rather ad hoc manner in which EU policy and legislative priorities have evolved since the Treaty of Rome. This record is a consequence of: (i) the administrative history of Community institutions (for example, the early focus on chemicals is a result of the fact that environmental laws were initially developed in the directorate-general of the Commission responsible for industrial affairs); and (ii) the legal basis of the development of environmental policy (most early laws were driven by a desire to remove the barriers to free trade, of which differences in the management of natural habitats, for example, was not one).

Secondly, while amendments to the treaties have provided more focus to the goals and underlying principles of EU environmental policy, the EU lacks a comprehensive environmental policy. Until recently, it limited itself to issues that were transnational in scope, related to the functioning of the single market, and/or were the subject of international treaties. An attempt was made by the

Commission during the negotiations leading up to the SEA to provide Community policy with more clarity and focus. It proposed a list of the issues that ought to be addressed in the development of policy, among which were air and water quality protection, combating noise, protecting soil and landscapes, conserving fauna and flora, the re-use, recycling and destruction of waste, the prevention of damage caused by dangerous industrial activities or by the use/handling of dangerous or toxic substances, and environmental research. In the event, several member states argued that such a detailed outline was unnecessary, and that general goals would suffice (Vandermeersch, 1987).

Combining the objectives listed in Article 130r of the SEA (as amended by the TEU) with those listed in the fifth EAP and the mission statement of DGXI produces the following list of broad goals:

- preserving, protecting and improving the quality of the environment (130r);
- protecting human health (130r);
- prudent and rational (or equitable (DGXI)) utilization of resources (130r), or the maintenance of continued access to natural resources (5th EAP);
- promoting measures at the international level to deal with regional or worldwide environmental problems (130r);
- improvement (or maintenance (5th EAP)) of the overall quality of life (DGXI);
- increased environmental efficiency (DGXI);
- preservation of the rights of future generations to a viable environment (DGXI), or development which meets the needs of the present without compromising the ability of future generations to meet their own needs (5th EAP).

Current Developments

If measured by the output of laws and policy statements alone, the EU has established an impressive record in the field of environmental policy. However, a number of problems have emerged in recent years which need to be addressed if the EU is to ensure that its efforts are directed as effectively as possible. Some of these problems are structural, and some relate to the difficulties of addressing an issue as broad and as all-encompassing as the environment.

The Complexities of Policy Integration

Given the broad-ranging nature of environmental problems, and the growing complexity of EU decision-making processes, the time taken to develop new environmental laws and policies has lengthened. DGXI officials complain that while it once took between 2 and 3 years to develop a new piece of legislation, the process may now take as long as 6 or 7 years. This allows more interests to have their say, and – theoretically – helps ensure that the implications of EU actions are thoroughly considered, but it also makes it difficult for the EU to respond quickly to worsening problems. DGXI is further handicapped by its small size: with about 500 staff and a budget of 140.5 million ECU in 1998, it is only a middle- ranking DG in terms of its size and powers, and is both understaffed and underbudgeted given the scale of its responsibilities.

The challenge faced by the Commission is heightened by the ambitious goals that the leaders of the member states have set for the EU. Most notably, the SEA (Article 130r(2)) introduced the principle that 'environmental protection requirements shall be a component of the Community's other policies'. This was strengthened by Article 6 of the Amsterdam Treaty, which requires that they '*must be integrated* into the definition and implementation' of Community policies (my emphasis). In few other EU policy areas does this principle apply, and its effect has been to oblige the Commission to ensure that legislative proposals are widely distributed and discussed before being sent to the Council and Parliament. This has meant often lengthy interactions involving DGXI, the *cabinets* of interested Commissioners, officials from other interested DGs, COREPER, representatives of the member states in Council working groups, Parliament and its committees, the Economic and Social Committee, national bureaucrats, representatives of non-EU governments where necessary, and representatives of industry and non-governmental organizations (NGOs).

To complicate matters, Jans (1996) points out that it is unclear what is meant by 'environmental protection requirements', that questions have been raised as to whether or not the principle implies that environmental policy has priority over all other EU policy areas, and that nothing is said in the treaties about how conflicts between environmental protection and the goals of other policy areas should be resolved. It also raises the legal question of whether or not the legitimacy of an action of the Council or the Commission in the fields of transport or agriculture, for example, could be challenged on the basis that it infringed or did not fully take into account the environmental implications. In an attempt to improve policy integration, in 1996 DGXI launched an internal reorganization aimed at improving its internal coordination and helping it keep up with developments in other units of the Commission.

Unbalanced Interests

Like most units of the Commission, DGXI has become adept at identifying and working with outside parties – in its case the parties being those with an interest in environmental law. However, those interests are unbalanced, and industry has considerably more influence over the legislative process than environmental NGOs. The result is that EU environmental law and policy reflects more fully the priorities of corporate Europe than it does of NGOs and European consumers.

The development of legislative proposals involves DGXI in discussions not only with the member states and other interested DGs, but with corporate interests and with Brussels-based industrial federations such as the European Chemical Industry Council, Eurelectric (representing public and private electricity generators), and the European Crop Protection Association (representing pesticide manufacturers). These bodies represent communities with specific interests, are well organized and funded, employ technical experts who can respond persuasively to the often-detailed technical content of DGXI proposals, and have a vested interest in the negotiations given that they are centrally involved in the implementation of subsequent legislation. The result is that they have developed a symbiotic relationship with the Commission, and are actively involved in the development of new laws and policies from the earliest stages.

By contrast, two other sets of interests are relatively poorly represented in the DGXI policy-making process: the EP and environmental NGOs such as Greenpeace and Friends of the Earth. The Environment Committee is one of the biggest and most influential of the EP's committees and has often prompted or strengthened new environmental laws and policies, but the influence of Parliament is compromised by the workload of MEPs and their support staff, who have little in the way of the kind of specialist technical knowledge and background that is often required of participants in the development of environmental law. The result is that they are rarely involved in the critical early stages of the development of new laws in the Commission, and their role in initiating or influencing the development of proposals is marginal (Williams, 1991, p. 160).

For their part, environmental NGOs have become more active and more professional in recent years, and have expanded their presence in Brussels, but they have only limited resources and represent a constituency that is both broad and sometimes difficult to define. NGOs are invited to the Commission's advisory committees where new laws and policies are developed, but they are often too short-staffed to make an effective contribution. Another problem for environmental NGOs is that they often find themselves facing the formidable resources of industry. For example, during the debate over the EU climate change policy in 1990–2, they had to compete with such powerful industrial lobbies as the Union of Industrial and Employers Confederations of Europe (Skjaerseth, 1996, p. 31). Similarly, while NGOs in 1993 had only one full-time expert on biotechnology among them, industry had a Senior Advisory Board sponsored by 31 corporations, including such giants as Bayer, Ciba-Geigy, Hoechst and Unilever, whose resources were at the disposal of the Board (Rucht, 1993).

The Commission has long been aware of the problem, and has provided considerable assistance to NGOs. For example, it has funded the European Environmental Bureau, an umbrella body founded in 1974 to represent the interests of local, national and regional NGOs in Brussels. With Commission prompting, the General Consultative Forum on the Environment was created in 1993, providing representatives of NGOs, industry, business, local authorities, trade unions and academia with a channel through which they could advise the Commission on policy development. In 1997, it was renamed the European Consultative Forum on the Environment and Sustainable Development (or the European Green Forum, for short), its membership was expanded to non-EU states, and it was given increased independence. Also in 1997, an EU decision (97/872) set aside nearly 3 million ECU in annual funding for European-level NGOs.

The Implementation Deficit

While the Commission has been productive in terms of the development of new laws and policies, its record on implementation has not been so strong. Annual Commission reports have revealed in recent years that there are more suspected breaches of environmental law than of law in any other area except the internal market (*Official*

Journal, 29 September 1995). Levels of transposition have ranged from between 76 and 82 per cent in Italy, Britain and Portugal, to 98–100 per cent in the Netherlands and Denmark, and even where laws have been transposed there are doubts about the efficacy of practical application.

The reasons for poor implementation are many and varied. Haigh (1996) notes the complications arising out of the large volume of EU law, the difficulties of assessing the many different goals and time-frames of environmental law, the many different national, regional and local authorities that may be involved in implementation, the large number of projects subject to broad-ranging laws such as the 1985 directive on environmental impact assessment, and ambiguities in reporting requirements. Other problems include the costs involved, the variable quality of information provided by the member states to the Commission, the ambiguity of the wording in many environmental directives (for example, the 'safe disposal' of waste), and the Commission's lack of powers of enforcement.

Attempts have been made to improve the record with the creation of the EU Network for the Implementation and Enforcement of Environmental Law (IMPEL). This brings national enforcement authorities together informally at biannual meetings chaired jointly by DGXI and the member state holding the Council presidency. Its goal is to improve implementation by encouraging the exchange of information and experience and improving communication among the Commission and the member states. IMPEL has encouraged the Commission to draw up fewer new laws and to concentrate instead on improving the efficacy of existing laws. However, until the Commission has more power to oblige national governments to transpose EU law into national law, to closely monitor the application of EU law, and to compel relevant national and local authorities to apply the law and report on its application, problems with implementation will remain.

The Changing Balance of Member States

There has always been a multi-speed approach to environmental protection in the EU, with some member states (notably the Netherlands and Germany) being in favour of tighter regulation and others (notably Britain) not. The political balance shifted in favour of a more aggressive approach with the accession in 1995 of Austria, Finland and Sweden, but it will shift in favour of a less aggressive approach when poorer Central and Eastern European countries

(CEECs) join the EU. It is already clear that countries such as Poland, Hungary and the Czech Republic have much to do to meet the environmental policy conditions required for entry; for example, they lack national strategies and have a poor record on monitoring and enforcing national law (*Environmental Liability Report*, January 1996, pp. 7–8).

The process of adjustment has been anticipated to some extent in cooperative programmes aimed at helping poorer EU member states and CEECs make the transition. For example, the PHARE programme was created in 1989 to provide economic assistance to Poland and Hungary, but it has since been expanded to include almost all CEECs. Its environmental element was initially reactive in the sense that it focused on providing equipment, studying specific problems, and helping establish standards and regulations, but it now supports activities linked to national environmental policy implementation. In its first five years of operation (1990–5) it spent about 430 million ECU on environmental and nuclear safety projects. Meanwhile, the Cohesion Fund – set up in 1994 – has helped compensate Greece, Portugal, Spain and Ireland for the costs of tightening environmental regulations.

The environment is a key element in the *Agenda 2000* programme. Proposed by the Commission in 1997, the programme is aimed at promoting growth and competition while strengthening and reforming EU policies to deal with enlargement, and it emphasizes the need to help aspirant members adopt key pieces of EU environmental law. The environment has been slipping down the policy agenda in Eastern Europe as governments have put more effort into economic growth, and there are concerns that approximating the environmental laws of the CEECs to those of the EU will be expensive – current plans are to spend at least 1 billion ECU per year over the period 2000–6. In May 1998, an informal network called AC-IMPEL was launched to bring together officials from CEEC governments and those from EU member states to discuss implementation issues in the period leading up to accession.

New Instruments for Environmental Policy

Following the model of the member states, EU policy on the environment has so far emphasized a 'command and control' approach that sets uniform standards, mandates the methods required to meet such standards, and tries to assure compliance through monitoring the activities of member states (Golub, 1998a, p. 2). Thus the EU has limited emissions from road vehicles and combustion plants, set limit values for discharges of dangerous substances into water, and placed limits on noise levels from machinery. In recent years, there has been a shift away from this approach at the level both of the EU and of the member states. Inherent problems with command and control – such as the economic inefficiencies that tend to arise from the imposition of uniform standards and targets – have combined with concerns about worsening economic problems such as unemployment, and the need for the EU to become more competitive in the global market, to encourage a new focus on more flexible and cost-effective solutions to environmental problems, tailored to different environmental needs and conditions. Among the more notable examples has been a reconsideration of the EU approach to acidification. The EU has so far focused on limiting motor vehicle emissions, reducing the sulphur content of fuel, and encouraging a sliding scale of percentage reductions in emissions of SO_2 and NOx. While these measures have contributed to a halving of SO_2 emissions in the EU, some of the progress is being undone by the growth in road traffic, and there are concerns about the ability of CEECs to reduce their emissions without compromising their economic development goals. The result has been an inclination to move away from imposing reduction targets on member states and industry (the source-based approach) towards basing those targets instead on differences in the sensitivity of different environments to acidifying pollutants (the effect-based approach).

Consolidation Rather than Expansion

There has been a new emphasis in the Commission since the mid 1990s on consolidating existing activities rather than launching new initiatives. This has been due mainly to the legal force given by Maastricht to subsidiarity, which has led to the tabling of fewer new proposals and the withdrawal of some (Haigh, 1992, 2.3). Figure 10.1 shows clearly that the relative volume of new legislation and amendments has changed significantly. While 65–90 per cent of the environmental laws adopted by the Council of Ministers in the late 1970s were new, this proportion had fallen to 45–55 per cent by the 1990s (falling as low as 23 per cent in 1995). Of the 106 pieces of legislation adopted in 1995–7, nearly two-thirds were amendments of existing laws (McCormick, 1999).

The trend was no more clearly seen than in the Commission's work programme for 1996, which was notable for its emphasis on discussion rather than legislation. The theme of the programme was 'stimulating more and legislating less' (*ENDS Report*, November 1995, pp. 35–6), and while only 19 entirely new pieces of legislation were proposed that year, the Commission promised nearly 50 action plans and 35 measures aimed at stimulating public debate. In the environmental field, only two new legislative initiatives were proposed, while the Commission proposed stimulating public debate on voluntary agreements with industry, green levies and charges, improvements in implementation, and future policy on noise, waste, and recycling (Commission, 1996). The 1997 and 1998 programmes focused on the environmental implications of other policies, and the latter put a particular emphasis on the problems of enforcement.

The Future

There is little question that much has already been achieved as a result of EU initiatives on the environment, but equally little question that new approaches are needed to address the many problems that remain, and the new problems that will arise out of eastward expansion. Weaknesses in the 'command and control' approach offered by regulation have combined with weaknesses in the enforcement of EU law to encourage the Commission to shift increasingly towards solutions based on economic incentives, voluntary agreements with industry (which, in a sense, confirm the already close association that exists between the Commission and industry), strategic approaches to problems, and more flexible solutions tailored to fit the different needs of different environments and member states.

Thanks in large part to pressure from the more environmentally progressive Scandinavian member states, the EU has given new emphasis to the importance of making environmental protection more effective and coherent with a view to promoting sustainable development. There has also been a greater emphasis on ensuring the integration of environmental policy with other policy areas – notably agriculture, transport, industry, and European transport and energy networks. Other priorities for the near future include the improvement of enforcement and implementation, clarification of the implications of subsidiarity in relation to environmental law, greater public access to EU documents and to Council discussions on legislation, the extension of majority voting to all environmental decisions, and renewed attempts to have the right to a healthy environment included in the treaty provisions.

Guide to Further Reading

Most published work on EU environmental policy currently takes the form either of journal articles, book chapters, or edited book-length studies. Examples of the latter include Liefferink *et al.* (1993), Judge (1993), Baker (1997), Golub (1998b), and Lowe and Ward (1998). Among the very few book-length monographs on the environmental policy of the European Union are Johnson and Corcelle (1995) and McCormick (1999). There are also a number of studies of EU environmental law which provide useful commentaries on policy; these include Winter (1996) and Krämer (1998). The standard source on the effect of EU law on Britain is Haigh (1992, updated twice annually). For the state of the European environment, see Stanners and Bourdeau (1995) and European Environment Agency (1998). Studies of particular environmental issues in the EU include Whitby (1996) and O'Riordan and Jaeger (1996). In addition to these publications, the Institute for European Environmental Policy in London publishes its own reports on various aspects of EU policy – see its Web site at <http://www.greenchannel.com/ieep/>. For official EU information, see the Web sites for DGXI at <http://europa.eu.int/eu/ comm/dg11/dg11home.html> and the European Environment Agency at <http://www.ea. eu.int/>.

References

Baker, R. (ed.) (1997) *Environmental Law and Policy in the European Union and the United States*. Westport, CT: Praeger.

Commission of the European Communities (1996) *The Commission's Programme for 1996*, Supplement to the *Bulletin of the European Union* (COM(95) 512 final).

Directorate General XI, Environment, Nuclear Safety and Civil Protection (1996) *Management Plan 1996*. Brussels: DGXI.

Europa Homepage, World Wide Web <http://europa.eu.int/>

European Environment Agency (1995) *Environment in the European Union 1995*. Luxembourg: Office for Official Publications of the European Communities.

European Environment Agency (1998) *Europe's Environment: The Second Assessment*. Copenhagen: EEA.

Garner, R. (1996) *Environmental Politics*. London: Prentice-Hall.

Golub, J. (ed.) (1998a) *New Instruments for Environmental Policy in the EU*. London: Routledge.

Golub, J. (ed.) (1998b) *Global Competition and EU Environmental Policy*. London: Routledge.

Haigh, N. (1992) *Manual of Environmental Policy: the EC and Britain.* Harlow: Cartermill.
Haigh, N. (1996) 'Effective Environment Protection – Challenges for the Implementation of EC Law'. Background paper presented to a Joint Public Hearing on Implementation and Enforcement of EC Environmental Law, European Parliament, Brussels.
Jans, J. (1996) 'Objectives and Principles of EC Environmental Law', in G. Winter (ed.), *European Environmental Law: A Comparative Perspective.* Aldershot: Dartmouth Publishing.
Johnson, S.P. and Corcelle, G. (1995) *The Environmental Policy of the European Communities*, 2nd edn., London: Kluwer Law International.
Judge, D. (ed.) (1993) *A Green Dimension for the European Community: Political Issues and Processes.* London: Frank Cass.
Krämer, L. (1998) *EC Treaty and Environmental Law*, 3rd edn. London: Sweet and Maxwell.
Liefferink J.D., Lowe, P.D. and Mol, A.P.J. (eds) (1993) *European Integration and Environmental Policy.* London: Belhaven.
Lowe, P. and Ward, S. (eds) (1998) *British Environmental Policy and Europe: Politics and Policy in Transition.* London: Routledge.
McCormick, J. (1995) *The Global Environmental Movement*, 2nd edn. London: John Wiley.
McCormick, J. (1999) *Environmental Policy and the European Union.* Basingstoke: Macmillan.
O'Riordan, T. and Jaeger, J. (eds) (1996) *The Politics of Climate Change: A European Perspective.* London: Routledge.
Porter, G. and Brown, J.W. (1991) *Global Environmental Politics.* Boulder, Co: Westview Press.
Rucht, Dieter (1993) '"Think Globally, Act Locally"? Needs, Forms and Problems of Cross-national Cooperation Among Environmental Groups', in J.D. Liefferink, Lowe, P.D. and Mol, A.P.J. (eds), *European Integration and Environmental Policy.* London: Belhaven pp. 75–95.
Skjaerseth, Jon Birger (1994), 'The Climate Policy of the EC: Too Hot to Handle?', in *Journal of Common Market Studies*, vol. 32, no. 1, pp. 25–45.
Stanners, D. and Bourdeau, P. (eds) (1995) *Europe's Environment: The Dobris* Assessment. Luxembourg: Office for Official Publications of the European Communities.
Vandermeersch, D. (1987) 'The Single European Act and the Environmental Policy of the European Economic Community', *European Law Review*, vol. 12, no. 5, pp. 407–29.
Wells, D.T. (1996) *Environmental Policy: A Global Perspective for the Twenty-First Century.* Upper Saddle River, NJ: Prentice-Hall.
Whitby, M. (ed.) (1996) *The European Environment and CAP Reform: Policies and Prospects for Conservation.* London: CAB International.
Williams, S. (1991) 'Sovereignty and Accountability in the European Community', in R.O. Keohane and S. Hoffmann (eds), *The New European Communty: Decisionmaking and International Change*, Boulder, Co: Westview Press pp. 155–76.
Winter, G. (ed.) (1996) *European Environmental Law: A Comparative Perspective.* Aldershot: Dartmouth.

11

Trade and Aid: The European Union in the Global System

FINN LAURSEN

The EU is the world's largest trading group as well as the most important donor of development and humanitarian aid. From an economic perspective, the EU is thus a major international actor, its trade and aid policies having turned it into a leading global 'civilian' power. By contrast, the EU's efforts to develop a Common Foreign and Security Policy (CFSP), and ultimately a defence policy, have not so far been successful (see Chapter 12). As the term is generally understood, therefore, the EU is not a 'superpower'. Simply put, it cannot project power in the way that the United States can, since it lacks the military means to do so. Nevertheless, trade and aid can be used to influence developments in other parts of the world, not least by linking trade and aid policy with issues of human rights and democracy. The EU is increasingly establishing such links, thereby leveraging political advantage from its undisputed economic weight.

The Common Commercial Policy (CCP) is the cornerstone of the EU's trade policy. Based on the Customs Union and Common External Tariff (CET) established at the end of the 1960s, the CCP enables the EU to speak with one voice in multilateral forums such as the World Trade Organization (WTO) – successor to the General Agreement on Tariffs and Trade (GATT) – and to conclude trade agreements with third countries. Other EU common policies, especially the Common Agricultural Policy (CAP), also have important external economic implications.

As regards relations with the developing world, former colonies of the member states have always been associated with the EU, first through the Yaoundé Convention and later the Lomé Convention. These have provided privileged access to the European market and have also included various aid programmes. Lomé IV, covering the period 1990–2000, embraces 70 African, Caribbean and Pacific (ACP) states. The EU grants special treatment to a larger group of developing countries through the General System of Preferences (GSP).

The EU's external economic relations are in a state of transition. EMU entails both a boost in the EU's international profile and a possible change in the orientation of its international trade, with euroland members likely to increase their trade with each other, possibly at the expense of trade with non-euroland UK and with key third country partners. At the same time, the transformation of the EU's relations with Central and Eastern Europe, culminating in enlargement, has opened up important trade and investment opportunities. The EU continues to upgrade its economic relations with Asia and Latin America, despite the long shadow cast by the international financial crisis of 1997 and 1998. Economic relations with the United States – the EU's biggest trading partner – are generally sound, but are buffeted by disputes in traditional areas (such as bananas) and in regulatory areas concerning new technologies and services. Given the importance of both players in the multilateral system, disputes between the US and the EU assume a significance beyond their immediate economic importance, especially within the WTO. Finally, prospects for a renegotiating of the Lomé Convention are far from promising, reflecting long-standing disillusionment on both sides.

The Policy-Making Process

EU policy-making in the field of external economic relations is multilayered, with EU institutions, national governments and interest groups all playing a part. At the same time, policy-making is constrained by global multilateral regimes and the expectations of other international economic actors, especially the two biggest: the US and Japan.

As responsibility for trade and aid is located within the EC pillar of the European Union, their decision-making procedures are based on the Community method, which none the less varies according to the subject-matter concerned. In respect of trade, the rules by which the CCP is conducted are set out in Article 133 (formerly Article 113) of the European Community Treaty (TEC). According to Article 133(1), commercial policy includes 'tariff rates, the conclusion of tariff and trade agreements, the achievement of uniformity in measures of liberalization, export policy and measures to protect trade as those to be taken in case of dumping or subsidies'. The Commission may launch a trade policy initiative and then, on the basis of a negotiating mandate given to it by the Council, conduct negotiations 'in consultation with a special committee appointed by the Council to assist the Commission in this task and within the framework of such directives as the Council may issue to it' (Article 133(3)). The outcome of negotiations requires Council approval, which can be given by qualified majority vote (qmv). The EP has no formal powers, although in practice it is usually consulted and kept informed about trade issues by the Commission. The European Court of Justice (ECJ) is sometimes called upon to make key decisions about which institution is competent to do what in the conduct of trade policy.

Trade policy is considered to be an exclusive competence of the EC. The member states, therefore, cannot have their own autonomous trade policies. Until completion of the single market programme at the end of 1992, many of them retained national quotas for sensitive products, in accordance with Article 134 TEC (formerly Article 115). Most of these were phased-out as part of the single market programme, but some were turned into EC quotas (the banana quota being the best known).

Article 300 (formerly Article 228) deals with international agreements other than pure trade agreements. Negotiating and decision-making procedures are similar to those that apply under Article 133, but unanimity is sometimes required in the Council and for agreements 'establishing a specific institutional framework . . . having important budgetary implications' or amending acts adopted under the co-decison procedure, the assent of the EP must be obtained.

Wide-ranging association agreements, which involve 'reciprocal rights and obligations, common action and special procedures' (Article 310, formerly Article 238) also require unanimity in the Council, and the EP must give its assent (see Article 300(3)).

As soon as agreements with third countries include matters that go beyond commercial policy and touch on issues where the member states have retained some competence, they become 'mixed agreements' that need to be ratified by the member states. For political or procedural reasons, ratification can be time-consuming at the national level. Accordingly, when the EU negotiated Europe Agreements with the Central and Eastern European countries (CEECs) in the early to mid 1990s, it was decided to let the commercial parts of the agreements – areas of exclusive EC competence – enter into force immediately, as so-called interim agreements. The full agreements only entered into force after being given the assent of the EP (because they were association agreements) and being ratified by the member states.

The question of EC versus member state competence became a major political issue when the Uruguay Round of the GATT was completed in 1993. Specifically, the Council disputed the Commission's right to conclude those parts of the agreement relating to services and to Trade-Related Aspects of Intellectual Property Rights (TRIPs). The Commission asked the Court for an opinion, which it gave in November 1994. To the Commission's surprise, the Court ruled that the Community and the member states shared competence to conclude the new General Agreement on Trade in Services (GATS), and were jointly competent to conclude the TRIPs Agreement.

In order to extend its competence over new services and intellectual property rights, during the 1996–7 IGC the Commission attempted to change Article 133. Member states indeed agreed to reword the article, but not in the way that the Commission hoped: 'The Council, acting unanimously on a proposal from the Commission and after consulting the European Parliament, may extend the application of paragraphs 1 to 4 to international negotiations and agreements on services and intellectual property insofar as they are not covered by these paragraphs.' As the unanimity requirement is a formidable obstacle to the extension of Community competence, the outcome of the IGC's discussion of trade policy represented a setback for the Commission. It remains to be seen whether or not the de facto maintenance of the status quo will impair the EU's effectiveness in subsequent TRIPS and GATS negotiations, as the Commission claims that it will.

Concerning development cooperation, the Maastricht Treaty added a new title to the TEC according to which development cooperation is 'complementary to the policies pursued by the Member States'. Apart from fostering sustainable economic and social development in the beneficiary countries, development policy should also contribute to 'the smooth and gradual integration of the developing countries into the world economy.' The main obligation is for member states to coordinate their policies, although they may also undertake joint action (Articles 177–81). Because most member states jealously guard their right to pursue their own development policies, coordination of national and European development policies remains elusive.

In the Commission, responsibility for external relations is currently divided between at least four directorates-general (DGs). DG I is responsible for commercial policy and relations with North America, the Far East, Australia and New Zealand; DG IA covers relations with Europe and the newly independent states, the CFSP, and external missions; DG IB covers Southern Mediterranean, Middle East, Latin America, South and South East Asia and North–South Cooperation; and DG VIII is responsible for development cooperation with Africa, the Caribbean and the Pacific, including the Lomé Convention. There are corresponding Commissioners for each of these policy areas. Coordination is supposed to take place through the College of Commissioners and a number of mechanisms at DG level. Nevertheless, the proliferation of external relations portfolios and Commissioners is highly unsatisfactory, and is likely to be curtailed under the Prodi Commission (see Chapter 3).

Policy Instruments

Tariffs are the best known – and have traditionally been the most important – instrument of trade policy. The CET has gradually been reduced over the years through successive trade negotiation rounds within the GATT. The EU reduced tariffs by an average of 37 per cent following the Uruguay Round. Nearly 40 per cent of the EU's industrial imports are now free of customs duty (Commission, 1997a, pp. 87–8).

As international tariffs have been reduced, non-tariff barriers (NTBs) to trade have become more important, though the GATT/WTO has also attempted to curtail their use. GATT/WTO has also sought to minimize resort to quantitative restrictions, which remained in place for some sensitive products in some member states until completion of the single market programme. In some sectors quantitative restrictions still exist in the form of Voluntary Export Restraints (VERs). In 1992, for instance, the EC obliged Japan to accept a VER agreement for automobiles, which is subject to renegotiation in 1999.

Anti-dumping measures – the imposition of tariffs on imports that are deemed to benefit from unfair trading advantages – are an increasingly important, and highly controversial, instrument of EU trade policy. Anti-dumping has long been partly regulated through GATT, and the Uruguay Round further tightened the international rules. None the less, between 1992 and 1996 the Commission initiated 161 anti-dumping investigations, mainly in the Far East (28 cases involved China, 12 Thailand, 10 South Korea, and nine involved India, Indonesia and Malaysia) (Commission, 1997b, Annex E). In terms of products, 32 cases involved textiles, 30 electronics, 22 chemicals and 21 iron and steel, all of which are politically sensitive for some member states (*ibid.*, Annex F).

Most Favoured Nation (MFN) treatment – a key principle of the international trade regime – implies that a reduced tariff between countries A and B must be extended to other Contracting Parties (CPs) to the WTO. There is no obligation to apply MFN treatment to WTO non-members, such as Russia, China and Taiwan, but the EU has usually done so anyway, at least in recent years. MFN treatment is an integral part of the partnership and cooperation agreements (PCAs) with Russia and other former Soviet Republics. It was also the main element of the first generation of trade and cooperation agreements negotiated with the CEECs as the Cold War came to a close in 1988–9.

In the EU hierarchy of trade preferences, MFN treatment is at the bottom. Today it mainly applies to a few industrialized countries – the United States, Canada, Japan, Australia and New Zealand – as well as to the newly independent republics of the former Soviet Union through the PCAs, with the exception of the Baltic countries which have free trade for industrial products granted first through Free Trade Agreements (FTAs) that entered into force in 1995 and more recently through Europe Agreements that entered into force at the beginning of 1998. Relations with the few remaining state-trading economies, for instance Cuba, are also mostly based on MFN treatment (World Trade Organisation, 1995, vol. 1, p. 19).

Moving up the trade preferences hierarchy, the EU applies the General System of Preferences (GSP) to a large group of developing countries. The GSP is a non-contractual preferential scheme in which benefits are autonomous and non-binding. Non-sensitive products are given duty-free treatment, while tariffs for other products are reduced according to different degrees of sensitivity.

Next comes the Lomé Convention, which gives the ACP countries free access to the EU market for almost all their industrial products. The Convention provides for preferential reductions for agricultural products. A number of Mediterranean countries also have non-reciprocal, Lomé-like free access to the EU market for various products. The EU is thus extending preferential access to its market without requiring the same in return.

Reciprocal free trade – the next highest form of EU trade preference – applies to the trading relationship with Israel and Turkey and also with the CEECs. However, the Europe Agreements with the CEECs go beyond free trade for industrial products to include certain freedoms in respect to services and capital movements and various other kinds of cooperation. There is also a political dialogue component to the Europe Agreements, aimed as they are at facilitating the CEECs' accession to the EU.

The highest form of trade agreement is the European Economic Area (EEA), which links the EU with three of the remaining four EFTA states – Norway, Iceland and Liechtenstein. The EEA is not a customs union, but rather an improved free trade area that extends the so-called 'four freedoms' of the single market – free movement of goods, services, capital and people – to the three EFTA states. The fourth remaining EFTA state – Switzerland – participated in the EEA negotiations, but rejected the agreement in a referendum in December 1992. In consequence, Switzerland is left with its free trade agreement from 1972, plus a number of sectoral bilateral agreements (Laursen, 1997).

EU Trade Patterns

Inevitably, after the fall of the Berlin Wall, EC trade with former communist countries in Central and Eastern Europe increased substantially in the 1990s. For instance, exports increased by 508.3 per cent to Poland and by 580.7 per cent to the former Czechoslovakia (now the Czech Republic and Slovakia) between 1988 and 1996. On the import side, the increases were 199.5 and 366.7 per cent respectively. Although such growth cannot continue in the future, the CEECs will remain important EU trading partners pending their accession in the coming decade.

EU trade with the industrialized countries – including the US and Japan – accounted for 46 per cent of exports and 40.9 per cent of imports in 1996. Despite occasional disputes, trade relations with the US remain the most important for the EU. EU trade with developing countries varies from 7 per cent of imports and 8.6 per cent of exports in the case of the four leading Asian newly industrializing countries (Hong Kong, Singapore, South Korea, and Taiwan); to 5.2 and 5.7 per cent respectively in the case of Latin America; to 3.8 and 3.0 per cent respectively in the case of the ACP countries (Commission, 1997a, table 37).

Relations with the Central and Eastern European Countries

The end of the Cold War started the process of improved relations between the EC and the CEECs. The EC soon concluded trade and cooperation agreements – later called first generation agreements – with most of the CEECs. Under the terms of these agreements, the two sides accorded each other MFN treatment, and the EC abolished some quantitative restrictions. In August 1990, the Commission proposed extending and broadening the trade and cooperation agreements with the CEECs and negotiating association agreements, called Europe Agreements. At the time of writing ten CEECs have Europe Agreements with the EU. The Agreements have established a political dialogue at the highest level, and will realise a free trade area over a ten-year period. For industrial products many tariffs were abolished when the agreements entered into force. Asymmetry was foreseen: the EC was to abolish all customs duties for industrial products over five years; the CEECs would take more time, with variations between the countries and products, but there should be total elimination within ten years.

There were special protocols in spheres that were especially sensitive for some member states notably agricultural products, textiles, and coal and steel. Given the CAP, the EC could not offer free trade for agricultural products, but some concessions were made. The agreements did foresee free trade in textiles and steel, but after longer transition periods than for other products. The CEECs' were highly critical of the EC's position in these product areas, since they included some of the CEECs most productive products. The inclusion in the agreements of safeguard measures, anti-dumping rules, and rules of origin were also criticized by the CEECs, since these could be used as NTBs.

The agreements also contained rules on 'movement of workers, establishment, and supply of services'. However, the agreements granted only national treatment to workers from the associated countries legally established in the EC as regards working conditions, remuneration, or dismissal. Social security was not included in the same way (Maresceau, 1993, p. 228). In the area of services national treatment was to be granted, but there could be some problems of recognition of qualifications. There was to be progressive liberalization, 'taking into account the development of the service sectors' in the EC and associated countries. Capital movements relating to the movement of goods, services and persons were to be liberalized. There would also be free movement of investment-related capital.

Competition policy is an important aspect of the Europe Agreements. Indeed, the agreements incorporated the basic principles of Articles 81, 82 and 87 (formerly Articles 85, 86 and 92) TEC. In effect, the associated countries committed themselves to apply the EC's competition policy regime in their domestic laws and practice. Lastly, the agreements included provisions for economic, financial and cultural cooperation.

Following the Europe Agreements, the next step in the evolution of EU–CEEC trade relations was the adoption of the pre-accession strategy for EU membership at the Essen summit in December 1994. It was based on the association agreements but supplemented by multilateral structural relations and by the Commission's White Paper, Preparation of the Associated Countries of Central and Eastern Europe for Integration into the Internal Market of the Union (Commission, 1995a). The White Paper gives the CEECs a guide to the process of preparing for integration in the internal market, listing the most important EC legislative acts relating to it and providing suggestions concerning the order in which they might be adopted.

Relations With Other European States

As already noted, the EU has very close relations with the EFTA states of Norway, Iceland and Liechtenstein, through the EEA. The special nature of the EEA has obliged these countries to introduce the relevant parts of the EU's *acquis communautaire*, which apart from internal market legislation includes legislation in flanking policy areas, such as competition policy, environmental policy and social policy. By including competition policy, it has been possible to rule out the use of anti-dumping measures within the EEA, which makes the EEA member states the only group of states with which the EU has agreed not to use this instrument of trade policy.

In the mid-1990s the EU concluded PCAs with most of the former Soviet republics (except the Baltic states). There are variations in content between the individual agreements, although all rather modestly grant MFN treatment to the partner countries. The agreements with Russia, Ukraine, Belarus and Moldova mention the possibility of free trade at a later stage, and contain a 'rendez-vous' clause that provided for consideration as to whether negotiations on an FTA should be initiated. All PCAs establish a political dialogue and refer to respect for democratic principles and human rights as an essential element of the agreements (Commission, 1998a). The Russian PCA was the first to enter into force, on 1 December 1997; the PCA with Ukraine entered into force on 1 May 1998; and that with Moldova on 1 July 1998. On 15 September 1997 the EU Council decided not to conclude the PCA with Belarus because of the political situation in the country.

In the Balkan area, Albania has had a trade and cooperation agreement with the EU in force since December 1992 and has also received aid through the PHARE programme of assistance to the CEECs. Apart from Slovenia, a candidate for EU accession, the former Yugoslav republics have a number of economic and political problems that must be solved before they can hope to conclude trade and cooperation agreements, not to mention Europe Agreements, with the EU. Relations with the Federal Republic of Yugoslavia (Serbia and Montenegro), having been strained because of the lack of democracy and respect for human rights, broke down in 1999 following the outbreak of war over Kosovo. Relations with Croatia are also strained, with the EU seeing insufficient respect for human rights and basic rules of democracy. In Bosnia-Hercegovina the EU is now the biggest international donor in connection with the rebuilding process. The former Yugoslav Republic of Macedonia signed a cooperation agreement and a financial protocol with the EU in April 1997.

Elsewhere in Europe, Cyprus is negotiating membership in the EU and Malta has reactivated its membership application following a change of government in 1998. Turkey has had an association agreement with the EU since 1963 and a customs union agreement since 1995. Despite a membership application dating back to 1987, however, Turkey is not yet in the group of countries negotiating membership. The EU's clear lack of enthusiasm for Turkish membership has upset the Turkish leadership and greatly strained EU–Turkey relations, with damaging consequences for trade and investment.

The EU also has association or cooperation agreements with Southern and Eastern Mediterranean countries on the borders of

Europe. These agreements, which give duty-free access to the EU for all or most industrial products, concessions for some agricultural products, and financial aid, have been 'relaunched' on the basis of a Partnership Declaration adopted in Barcelona in November 1995. The declaration foresees closer political cooperation and increased EU efforts to promote development in the Mediterranean region. The ambitious target is a free trade zone by 2010 between the EU and the countries represented at Barcelona: Algeria, Morocco, Tunisia, Egypt, Israel, Jordan, Lebanon, the Palestinian autonomous territories, Syria, Turkey, Cyprus and Malta (Hakura, 1997). However, the variable levels of political and economic development in these countries, and the EU's more pressing obligations elsewhere in the world, make it unlikely that the objectives of the Barcelona Declaration will be fully realized.

Relations with Other Industrialized States

The US is the EU's largest trading partner and there are important flows of Foreign Direct Investments (FDI) in both directions. This has created a high degree of interdependence between the world's two economic giants. Together the EU and the US account for about 40 per cent of world trade.

US–EU trade relations have endured a number of disputes since the early 1960s. Some have been resolved promptly – with the assistance sometimes of GATT/WTO panels – whilst others have dragged on for years. A particularly intractable dispute has concerned growth-promoting hormones in US beef, which has been running since 1987. At the time of writing, there is a particularly fierce dispute over bananas, with the US threatening to impose prohibitive tariffs on a range of European products in retaliation against what it sees to be preferential access to the EU market for Caribbean, as opposed to Latin American, bananas. (US firms largely control Latin American production and distribution). Much to the irritation of the EU, the US has sometimes threatened to use Section 301 of the US Trade Act, which allows the US to use unilateral action outside the WTO against countries engaging in unfair trading practices and trading with regimes of which it disapproves.

Although the US, Canada and most EU member states are members of a common security organization – the North Atlantic Treaty Organization (NATO) – there is no similar organization covering transatlantic trade. In 1990 the EU and the US agreed on a Transatlantic Declaration, which was complemented by a New Transatlantic Agenda (NTA) signed in Madrid in December 1995. The NTA was formulated in very general terms, mentioning four areas of cooperation: peace and democracy; global challenges; world trade; and bridges across the Atlantic. The section on 'contributing to the expansion of world trade and closer economic relations' referred to strengthening the multilateral trading system, implementing the Uruguay Round results, and completing unfinished business – concentrating, in particular, on the areas of telecommunications and maritime services (Piening, 1997, pp. 108–12).

Follow-on discussions about a more formalized transatlantic trade relationship have had only limited results. Proposals for transatlantic free trade have come up against protectionist forces on both sides, as well as a feeling that a strengthened bilateral relationship should not undermine the multilateral trading system. A Commission proposal for a New Transatlantic Marketplace (NTM), which would create free trade in services and abolish industrial tariffs by 2010, ran into stiff French opposition, because the US wanted NTM talks to include agricultural subsidies and audio-visual trade, both very sensitive issues in France. Nevertheless the US and EU announced a Transatlantic Economic Partnership in November 1998.

The main issue in EU–Japan relations over the years has been the growing and persistent Japanese trade surplus with the EU. This has created protectionist pressures in the EU, leading to the negotiation of VERs in a number of areas and to anti-dumping duties against some Japanese goods entering the EU market. At the same time, the European side has tried to get alleged Japanese protectionism reduced, first through the reduction of tariffs and the abolition of quotas, and more recently through the elimination of various NTBs.

There have been regular official consultations between the EU and Japan for nearly 30 years, and in 1991 the two parties agreed on a 'Joint Declaration between the European Community and its Member States and Japan' which established general principles, objectives and a framework for dialogue and consultations. In March 1995 the Commission issued an important communication to the Council concerning EC–Japan relations which welcomed Japan's efforts to play a greater role on the world stage as well as Japan's impending five-year deregulation programme. Although the communication was relatively optimistic about EU–Japan relations, the Commission remained concerned about obvious imbalances:

> Since the completion of the Internal Market, Japanese exports face almost no structural barriers in the world's largest unfragmented market, which is subject to powerful rules enforcing competition, Japanese inward investment is welcomed and sometimes even subsidised and Japanese companies established in the EU benefit fully from national treatment. In contrast, as has been well documented, EU and other non Japanese companies face a range of administrative and structural barriers when exporting to Japan and also meet obstacles if they attempt to invest directly in Japan (Commission, 1995b, p. 5).

The Council largely accepts the Commission's analysis, having confirmed 'the soundness of the constructive policy followed since 1992, combining dialogue and cooperation on matters of mutual interest with a pro-active approach to resolving clearly identified problems regarding market access and Community business presence' (General Council Affairs Conclusions, 29 May 1995). Japan's serious economic crisis from the late 1990s presents both an opportunity to restructure EU–Japan trade relations and a danger that Japan will intensify its resistance to pressure from the EU to open its market.

Relations with Canada, Australia and New Zealand are also based on MFN treatment, but these relations have been less conflictual than those with Japan. A Transatlantic Declaration with Canada was issued in 1990, and a Joint Political Declaration on Canada–EU relations was signed in 1996. Negotiations with Australia and New Zealand about a framework agreement ran into problems in 1997 because of EU insistence on the inclusion of a human rights clause, now routine in EU agreements with third states (Piening, 1997, p. 163). So far no agreements have been concluded.

Relations with China and the Asian Newly Industrialized Countries

During the 1990s the EU's relations with China, which stretch back to the mid-1970s, were gradually upgraded, although questions of human rights complicated the agenda. In 1995 the Commission issued a communication on 'A Long-Term Policy for China-Europe Relations', in which it argued that Europe and China share a number of interests in global issues and regional security – for instance, non-proliferation of nuclear weapons and protection of the environment. Global economic stability was also seen as being a shared interest: 'China's size and influence on world trade gives its economic policy global significance. It is in the world's interest, as well as China's, that the Chinese economy continues to grow and to open up, and that China takes its place as a major player in the world system of economic rules and policies. It is also essential to help China to participate fully in the rules-based system of the World Trade Organisation' (Commission, 1995c, p. 3). It was also argued that 'An active role for EU business in China, where U.S. and Japanese competition is already fierce, is essential.'

Clearly the EU has important commercial interests in China, the world's most populous country. A communication from the Commission in March 1998 referred to the ambitious economic and social reforms adopted by the XVth Chinese Communist Party Congress in 1997 and the successful handover of Hong Kong to Chinese rule in July 1997 as expressions of China's more mature and responsible approach to its changing role. It was proposed to upgrade the political dialogue with China and provide support for China's transition to an open society based upon the rule of law and respect for human rights as well as China's further integration in the world economy (Commission, 1998b).

As trade has increased very quickly with China in recent years, questions of market access have also become more important. The EU has a huge trade deficit with China which has promoted a demand for easier access to the Chinese market, both for goods and increasingly also for services. Along with other international traders, the EU has made it clear that China's accession to the WTO is dependent on it cutting tariffs and removing many NTBs. At the same time, however, the Commission has argued that 'China's WTO accession should not be seen as a new constraint imposed by the outside world on China, but rather as a supportive process which will strengthen its own internal reform programme' (Commission, 1998b, p. 14).

Market access issues have also been important in relations with other fast-growing East Asian countries, including Hong Kong, Singapore, South Korea and Taiwan. Because these countries have adopted strategies of export-led growth like Japan, they have become involved in disputes with the EU, most notably over anti-dumping measures and restrictive textile quotas.

The EU has had a cooperation agreement with the Association of Southeast Asian Nations (ASEAN) since 1980. This group, which now includes Brunei, Indonesia, Laos, Malaysia, Myanmar, Philippines, Singapore, Thailand and Vietnam, has plans to become an

FTA, but so far the achievements of the group have mainly been political. The EU takes part in meetings of the ASEAN Regional Forum (ARF), where political and security issues in the Asia-Pacific region are discussed.

In April 1998 the second Asia–Europe (ASEM) summit took place in London, bringing together the leaders of ten Asian countries and the 15 EU member states, as well as the President of the Commission. The ASEM process also includes meetings of foreign ministers, finance ministers and economics ministers. ASEM agendas include political dialogue, economic cooperation (such as trade facilitation), and cooperation in social and cultural fields (Commission, 1998c). ASEM has proved a useful forum for the EU to involve itself in a possible solution to the Asian economic crisis.

Relations with Latin America

Latin America is becoming increasingly integrated into the international economic system: throughout much of the 1990s, the region enjoyed strong economic growth; many Latin American countries have turned away from trade policies based on import-substitution to more open trade policies that seek export-led growth; and regional integration is being intensified.

Since 1990 numerous cooperation agreements have been contracted between the EU and Latin American countries. According to the Commission, these agreements mark a new stage in EU–Latin American relations, not least by including a 'democratic principles' clause as well as a 'future developments' clause, enabling the parties to expand and step up cooperation (Commission, 1995d).

Two recent developments in EU–Latin American relations are especially noteworthy. First, in December 1995 the EU and Mercosur (the Southern Cone Common Market) signed an inter-regional framework agreement, the first agreement between two customs unions (*Official Journal*, L 66, 19 March 1996). Mercosur has a total population of about 200 million, includes two of Latin America's largest economies (Argentina and Brazil), and is the EU's fastest-growing export market. The EU–Mercosur agreement aims for free trade between the two groups and also institutionalizes a political dialogue. Second, in 1996 the EU started negotiating a far-reaching political, commercial and economic agreement with Mexico. This has now been signed and is in the process of being ratified. The agreement involves reciprocal trade liberalization and increased economic cooperation. Mexico is the EU's second largest trading partner in Latin America, after Brazil (Piening, 1997, p. 136). Talks on a future EU–Mexico free trade accord – the first between the EU and a Latin American country – opened in July 1998.

The Lomé Convention

Relations between the EU and the ACP countries fall under the Lomé Convention, which has gone through various changes over the years since it was first signed in 1975. The current Lomé IV (1990–2000) went through a mid-term review in 1995 which reinforced the Convention's political elements – including a human rights suspension clause. The financial protocol signed in Mauritius in 1995 allocated 14.6 billion ECU for the period 1995–2000, which accounts for around 55 per cent of all EU aid.

Preparations for a new Lomé agreement began in late 1998, with much of the analysis and debate focusing on the inability of many ACP countries to participate in global economic growth. Accordingly, some interested parties – including the Commission – have suggested that a successor agreement should devote greater attention to poverty alleviation and stimulation of enterprise from the bottom up. Although there is support for keeping the ACP together as a group, many experts feel that there should be more differentiation among ACP regions. The Commission has proposed a series of free trade agreements with ACP countries by 2005, complemented by EU support for ACP efforts to integrate into world markets (*European Dialogue*, May–June 1998).

Conclusion

The future of EU external economic relations will depend on various factors, both internal and external. Important issues on the EU agenda at the moment, notably enlargement and the consolidation of the single currency and negotiations for enlargement, will affect the EU's capacity as an international economic actor.

Exactly how enlargement will affect external relations is difficult to predict. Will it make the EU more inward looking? Certainly, there will be more internal problems to deal with, as the EU grapples with a greater diversity of interests and perspectives than exist among the current member states. The EU will need to upgrade its institutions to make decision-making sufficiently effective – in the realm of external economic relations as elsewhere – to deal with such a new situation.

In monetary matters euroland will become a leading international player, on a par with the US and Japan. The euro can be expected to become an international reserve currency, with Europe consequently increasing its influence inside global financial institutions. The trade-related impact of EMU will not be as marked, but could none the less be significant.

The international trade regime will depend much on the future work of the WTO, whose agenda includes a review of the still unsatisfactory dispute settlement rules and procedures, the operation of the TRIMs agreement, discussions on competition policy and government procurement, and further liberalization of trade in agricultural products and services. The ability of the EU's member states to reach agreed positions on these issues will determine how proactively the EU can respond to this challenging new international trade agenda.

Guide to Further Reading

Heidensohn (1995), Paemen and Bensch (1995), and Piening (1997) provide good reviews of the EU and world trade. Bildt *et al.* (1997) raise and consider important questions about the EU in the international system. Useful studies of the EU's relations with other international actors include Grant (1995), Guggenbühl (1995), Heuser (1996), and Laursen and Riishøj (1996).

References

Bildt, C. *et al.* (1997) *What Global Role for the EU?* Brussels: The Phillip Morris Institute.

Commission (1995a) *Preparation of the Associated Countries of Central and Eastern Europe for Integration into the Internal Market of the Union*, White Paper, COM(95) 163 final, 2 vols., 3 and 10 May. Brussels: Commission.

Commission (1995b) *Europe and Japan: The Next Steps*, COM(95) 73 final, 8 March. Brussels: Commission.

Commission (1995c) *Communication from the Commission: A Long Term Policy for China–Europe Relations*, COM(95) 279 final, 5 July. Brussels: Commission.

Commission (1995d) *The European Union and Latin America. The Present Situation and Prospects for Closer Partnership 1996–2000*, COM(95) 495 final, Brussels 23 October.

Commission (1997a) Directorate-General for Economic and Financial Affairs, 'The European Union as a World Trade Partner', *European Economy*, No. 3.

Commission (1997b) *Fifteenth Annual Report from the Commission to the European Parliament on the Community's Anti-Dumping and Anti-Subsidy Activities*, COM(97) 428 final, Brussels, 16 September.

Commission (1998a) DGIA, *Partnership and Cooperation Agreements (PCAs) with the New Independent States*, Http://europa.eu.int/en/eupol/pcag.html.

Commission (1998b) *Building a Comprehensive Partnership with China*, COM(1998) 181 final, Brussels, 25 March.

Commission (1998c) *Reinforcing the partnership of Equals between Asia and Europa: The Second Asia–Europe Meeting in London (ASEM 2). Background Note*, Http://europa.eu.int/en/comm/dg01/asem21.htm.

Grant, R. L. (1995) *The European Union and China: A European Strategy for the Twenty-First Century*. London: Royal Institute of International Affairs.

Guggenbühl, A. (1995) 'The Political Economy of Association with Eastern Europe', in F. Laursen (ed) *The Political Economy of European Integration*. The Hague: Kluwer.

Hakura, F. S. (1997) 'The Euro-Mediterranean Policy: The Implications of the Barcelona Declaration', *Common Market Law Review*, vol. 34, pp. 337–66.

Heindensohn, K. (1995) *Europe and World Trade*, London: Pinter.

Heuser, B. (1996) *Transatlantic Relations: Sharing Ideals and Costs*, London: Chatman House.

Laursen, F. (1991) 'The EC in the World Context: Civilian Power or Superpower?', *Futures*, vol. 23, no. 7 (September), pp. 747–59.

Laursen, F. (1996) 'The European Union (EU) and Japan: The Drama of the Persistent Trade Imbalance', in *Report of Special Research Project on the New International System*. Tsukuba: The University of Tsukuba, pp. 433–91.

Laursen, F. (1997), 'European Integration and Trade Regimes: From the European Economic Area to the "Europe" Agreements', in M.O. Hosli and A. Saether (eds), *Free Trade Agreements and Customs Union: Experiences, Challenges and Constraints*. Maastricht: European Institute of Public Administration, pp. 267–91.

McGoldrick, D. (1997) *International Relations Law of the European Union*. London: Longman.

Maresceau, M. (1993) "Europe Agreements": A New Form of Cooperation between the European Community and Central and Eastern Europe', in P.-Ch. Müller-Graff (ed.), *East Central European States and the European Communities: Legal Adaptation to the Market Economy*. Baden-Baden: Nomos, pp. 209–33.

Paemen, H. and Bensch, A. (1995) *From the GATT to the WTO: The European Community in the Uruguay Round*. Leuven: University of Leuven Press.

Peers, S., 'From Cold War to Luke Warm Embrace: The European Union's Agreements with the CIS States', *International and Comparative Law Quarterly*, vol. 44 (October 1995), pp. 829–47.

Piening, C. (1997) *Global Europe: The European Union in World Affairs*. Boulder, Co: Lynne Rienner.
Wolf, M. (1994) *The Resistible Appeal of Fortress Europe*. London: Centre for Policy Studies.
World Trade Organization (1995) *Trade Policy Review: European Union*, 2 vol. Geneva: WTO.
World Trade Organization (1997) *Trade Policy Review: European Union*. Geneva: WTO.

12

The Common Foreign and Security Policy

MARTIN HOLLAND

Traditional analyses of the Common Foreign and Security Policy (CFSP) fall into three distinct groups: institutional and historically descriptive accounts; theoretical approaches; and specific case studies. The organizing principle behind this chapter avoids this compartmentalization. Seven key CFSP questions are presented that link both empirical and theoretical issues and provide a basis for further analysis. These questions are: Who makes EU foreign policy? Why is there an EU foreign policy? How is it expressed? What are the constraints? What is the record? What are the prospects? Does foreign policy matter?

Europe first began coordinating its foreign policy in 1970 under the somewhat obtuse label of European Political Cooperation (EPC). Formally, CFSP has only been in operation since November 1993 when the provisions of the Treaty on European Union (TEU) became effective. However, under both EPC and CFSP one of the most significant and pervasive EU developments has been the erosion of national autonomy in external relations: in trade agreements, development and in foreign policy. While the principal focus of this chapter is CFSP, the more inclusive notion of external relations should not be ignored as it constitutes an important element in assessing Europe's capacity to be an 'international actor'. Member states still conduct bilateral foreign policies across a range of issues, but CFSP has progressively expanded its scope. It is essential to understand that CFSP and national foreign policies exist in tandem.

Although foreign policy is essentially political in nature, CFSP operates within a precise legal context. The three revisions of the Treaty of Rome – the Single European Act (SEA) and the Maastricht and Amsterdam Treaties – each advanced Europe's common foreign policy conceptually and practically. Perhaps the most significant reform has been the 'pillarization' of Maastricht confirming (to the dismay of federalists) the CFSP's intergovernmental nature. The introduction of the three-pillar structure in 1993 complicated the legal basis on which foreign policy rested. While the TEU promoted the trinity of the three 'C's' – coherence, complementarity and coordination – the mixed intergovernmental and *communautaire* nature of Europe's external relations makes these criteria difficult to apply and implement consistently. A fundamental question underpins these constitutional debates over CFSP. Simply put, what is the relationship between foreign policy and the integration process: is it an optional extra or a necessary prerequisite? With this question in mind, this chapter now addresses each of the seven CFSP questions in turn.

Who Makes EU Foreign Policy?

In the early 1970s, the US Secretary of State, Henry Kissinger, frustrated by the pluralistic nature of Europe's foreign policy process, quizzically and contemptuously asked 'who' spoke for Europe in foreign affairs. Almost three decades later only marginal improvement can be detected. Despite the appearance of intergovernmentalism, typically multiple actors within the EU have been involved in foreign policy formation and policy execution. These include the member states themselves (acting either in the European Council or in the Council of Foreign Ministers), the Council Presidency assisted by the 'Troika', the Commission, the European Parliament (EP), and may involve domestic lobbies and other external actors as well.

Under Article 18 (formerly Article J.8) TEU, the Council Presidency represents the collective CFSP position and is 'responsible for the implementation' of CFSP decisions. However, the role of the Presidency is to seek consensus and in no sense can it be seen as independently defining EU foreign policy. Indeed any presidencies that have tried to be more than *primus inter pares* have found the authority of their presidencies seriously compromised. During the 1970s, third parties often questioned whether the smaller member states (specifically Luxembourg) could speak authoritatively in foreign affairs when holding the Presidency. While this view is no longer widely held, individual member states – particularly the UK, France and Germany – tend to be the more important actors. Despite the appeal of simplicity, an analysis based on the foreign policy preferences of member states may provide a better explanation of the EU's common approach than an analysis focused purely on the Presidency.

The participation of the Commission in CFSP underlines both the implausibility and impossibility of confining CFSP to an exclusively intergovernmental process. First, when the EU meets – either as the 15 or the 'Troika' –the Commission is also present. Second, certain CFSP instruments, such as sanctions, require Community-level (pillar one) authority. Here the Commission's implementation as well as legal role is fundamental. Third, since Maastricht the Commission has had a 'shared right of initiative' in CFSP, something it did not enjoy under the EPC framework. Fourth, several Directorate-Generals (DGs) are involved in the general area of external relations and CFSP specifically. The most important of these are DG IA (external political relations); DG I (external economic relations); and DG VIII (development). While strictly speaking CFSP decisions are taken by the states acting collectively, the Commission's input into the policy process and its agenda management ability confirms its status as a CFSP actor. Lastly, Article 20 (formerly Article J.10) TEU recognises the pivotal role of EC Delegations in third countries and provides a legal basis for Commission involvement in the diplomatic and operational aspects of CFSP. Paradoxically, although the Maastricht and Amsterdam Treaties specify CFSP as an intergovernmental, second pillar, process, both contain procedures that have extended Commission involvement.

To compound matters, the EP's involvement in foreign policy has also grown under the CFSP provisions. Prior to the TEU the Parliament had exercised a moral influence, but lacked control of either the content of the EU's foreign policies or their funding. Article 21 (formerly Article J.11) TEU modifies this partially: the presidency is required to 'consult' Parliament 'on the main aspects and basic choices' of the CFSP, as well as ensure that Parliament's views 'are duly taken into consideration'. Of greater potential importance, however, has been Parliament's energetic insistence on fully exercising its budgetary powers regarding Community CFSP expenditure. Article 28(4) TEU and an inter-institutional agreement between the Parliament, Commission and Council on provisions regarding the financing of CFSP confirm this role. Experience suggests that Parliament's authority can only increase as the Community's non-compulsory budget expands.

This interplay of different actors highlights a core problem: the lack of a single authoritative CFSP decision-making focus. An Amsterdam Treaty initiative has gone some way to resolving this, if imperfectly. While the position of a CFSP High Representative was finally established, the exact status and profile of this new position was a matter of considerable debate. A Franco-German proposal that the post be high-profile and political in nature failed to gain sufficient support at Amsterdam. Consequently, Article 18(3) states that the Presidency 'shall be assisted by the Secretary-General of the Council who shall exercise the function of the High Representative'. The High Representative is assisted by a new planning and early warning unit that will help to formulate, prepare and implement CFSP decisions. The High Representative will also represent the EU externally providing, hopefully, a partial remedy to Kissinger's complaint. However, up to the time of writing (early 1999), debate continued among the member states on the status and autonomy of both the High Representative and of the planning unit. Clearly scope exists within this seemingly modest reform for a powerful new CFSP actor to develop: however, the potential for this development will largely depend on who is chosen as the first CFSP High Representative.

Despite this recent reform and the coordinating role played by the Presidency, any theoretically meaningful analysis of EU foreign policy must adopt a variety of conceptual lenses. To focus on a single actor or to disregard all frameworks other than intergovernmentalism can only provide partial explanations. Even though CFSP is a pillar two activity, many of the instruments and actors involved derive their competences from pillar one authority. While the phrase has become commonplace, it is necessary to acknowledge the *sui generis* nature of CFSP. Its legal context, limited obligations and essentially consensual nature set it apart from traditional nation-state foreign policy processes. Consequently, we should not be surprised to find that the EU does not typically behave like a state in its foreign relations.

Why is there an EU Foreign Policy?

A variety of conceptual approaches have been used to understand European integration in general and CFSP in particular (for example, see Hill, 1993; Hix, 1994; Holland, 1991, 1997; Rummel, 1992). One, neo-functionalism, provides a framework for answering the question of why there is an EU foreign policy. In its most simple form, neo-functionalism argues that the integration process cannot be confined to a limited number of policy areas. Consequently, the progressive integration of domestic intra-EU policy sectors will 'spill-over', almost inevitably, to common approaches being extended to external policy areas. For neo-functional purists it is inconceivable that the EU could operate a common monetary policy, a single market and common external tariffs whilst the member states conduct independent foreign policies. If we accept neo-functional theory, foreign policy is no different to any other policy sphere and cannot be isolated from the consequences of spill-over.

A further conceptual rationale highlights the synergies and mutual dependence between political and economic aspects of integration theory. The political–economic dichotomy is appealing, but misleading. While exact parity should not be expected, successful integration does demand a balance between economic and political integration. A fully integrated single market with a common currency, for example, requires a commensurate level of political agreement both within the EU and in the conduct of foreign affairs. Where such a synergy is missing, the foundations of internal integration may be seriously compromised. Furthermore, the EU's dominant position in global trade demands the exercise of a coherent foreign policy. An economically powerful EU without a common foreign policy would constitute no more than a customs union and as such would, arguably, be destabilizing globally, economically and politically.

Political will, as much as legal competences and obligations, lie at the heart of the development of the EU's international persona. National leaders, particular those of the larger member states, can promote or retard the development of Europe's foreign policy (French President Charles de Gaulle comes immediately to mind). Despite concerted pressure from some member states and their leaders, the collective political will of most member states has typically favoured incremental change over radical innovation in the development of EU foreign policy.

From a legal perspective the original Treaty of Rome created an international role for the then Community. Although any direct mention of foreign policy was avoided a number of provisions suggested that integration was not confined to purely domestic political issues. The Treaty provided for five areas in which an international role could develop: a common trade policy; association with Overseas Territories; association agreements with third countries; the authority to conclude international treaties; and, the ability of the Community to receive and establish diplomatic missions

(Holland, 1994, p. 118). Consequently, a simple answer to why an EU foreign policy exists is that the founding treaty permitted and encouraged such a development.

The treaty reforms of the 1980s and 1990s built on these foundations and further communautairised Europe's foreign relations. The SEA formalized what had become the informal EPC status quo as well as extending foreign policy coordination. The necessary involvement of the Commission finally provided legal recognition as did the 'associated' role for the Parliament. It introduced EC involvement in 'the economic aspects of security' and established a small Secretariat, thereby creating the first beginnings of an independent European foreign policy expertise. The Maastricht Treaty built on these procedures and further formalized the policy-making process and replaced EPC with the CFSP. Notable innovations were the creation of 'joint actions'; the partial introduction of the Western European Union into an EU security structure; and the extension of the shared right to initiate policy to include the Commission as well as the member states. In keeping with this incremental style, the Amsterdam Treaty modified existing procedures. As noted above, it upgraded the bureaucratic support by introducing a policy and planning unit and strengthened the base for the provision of leadership by creating a CFSP High Representative. More importantly, however, Amsterdam provided for the possibility of making foreign policy decisions that challenged the long-held principle of consensus.

Finally, an explanation as to why the EU has a foreign policy can be traced to the 'idea of Europe' espoused by the Community's founding advocate, Jean Monnet. For Monnet, Europe was 'a moral idea' (1978, p. 392) which would eventually lead to 'political union which is the goal of our Community and to establish the United States of Europe' (p. 431). From the very beginning the European idea was viewed as a complex, unique and expanding concept. As Monnet argued: 'We can never sufficiently emphasise that the six Community countries are the forerunners of a broader united Europe whose bounds are set only by those who have not yet joined. Our Community is not a coal and steel producer's association: it is the beginning of Europe.' (1978, p. 16, 392).

Such a comprehensive conceptualization of Europe encapsulated both internal and external integration in which foreign policy was an essential element. While the EU has yet to realize all of Monnet's ambitions, the underlying motivations are still central to the current integration process.

How is EU Foreign Policy Expressed?

Conceptually, foreign policy is a more inclusive term than Europe's narrowly defined CFSP. In particular, a variety of treaty-based agreements are a significant aspect of the EU's external relations and international profile. These cover association, commercial and trade agreements and external economic relations in general. As is argued later, the EU's civil power nature means that economic external relations often constitute the EU's foreign policy instruments – both within and outside the CFSP framework. The difficulties that this poses are addressed, in part, in Article 3 of the consolidated TEU, which is devoted to effective and coherent external policy and discusses both CFSP and external economic relations (albeit under separate chapters). However, despite acknowledging the importance of coherence and implementing minor changes, most commentators agree that the reforms have failed to adequately clarify or consolidate this linkage.

Similarly, the Lomé Convention is clearly part of Europe's foreign relations, but not within the parameters of the CFSP (see Chapter 11). Lomé's origins can be traced to the colonial histories of the member states – most importantly, but not exclusively, France and the UK. The Lomé framework was intended to create a 'partnership' between Europe and the developing world. It provided preferential access for specified ACP exports to the European market and instigated a coordinated collective aid programme. Conditionality (both political and economic) was progressively introduced into the Convention, making Lomé tantamount to the EU's common foreign policy towards the developing world. For example, continued relations became dependent on the maintenance of good governance, human rights and democracy and structural adjustment programmes became part of the EU's aid vocabulary (Lister, 1997). We have no problem in identifying such behaviour as 'foreign policy' when conducted by the USA: why should it be so problematic when applied to the EU?

The explanation again lies in the intergovernmental–*communautaire* integration debate. Consensus has never existed to move beyond intergovernmentalism as the basis for foreign policy. Consequently, from a strictly treaty-based interpretation foreign policy can only exist as a first-pillar activity; where such action occurs under pillar two it is defined automatically as external relations, and not as foreign policy, no matter how illogical or selective that is. Working within this narrow definition, then, formally EU foreign policy has only ever been expressed through EPC and latterly the CFSP.

As discussed in the previous section, the principle of consensus underpinned EPC and only minor modifications to this have been introduced under CFSP. Consequently, unanimity remains the prerequisite for the expression of EU foreign policy. The TEU was the first attempt to define CFSP objectives. These were later modified in the Amsterdam Treaty which stipulates that the EU and the member states 'shall define and implement a common foreign and security policy covering all areas of foreign and security policy'. Specifically, its objectives are:

- to safeguard the common values, fundamental interests, independence and integrity of the Union in conformity with the principles of the United Nations Charter;
- to strengthen the security of the Union in all ways;
- to preserve peace and strengthen international security, in accordance with the principles of the United Nations Charter, as well as the principles of the Helsinki Final Act and the objectives of the Paris Charter, including those on external borders;
- to promote international cooperation;
- to develop and consolidate democracy and the rule of law, and respect for human rights and fundamental freedoms (Article 11.1 TEU)

The Amsterdam Treaty extended the TEU's objectives by incorporating provisions safeguarding the integrity of the Union in accordance with the UN Charter and by introducing international security objectives in relation to external borders. A 'political solidarity' clause was also included which committed member states actively and unreservedly to support the CFSP 'in a spirit of loyalty and mutual solidarity' and to refrain from any action that may impair the effectiveness of the EU as an international actor. The Amsterdam Treaty also clarified and specified five CFSP instruments in new Title V, Articles 12–15. Three of these (principles and guidelines, common positions and joint actions) already existed under the TEU, whereas the other two (common strategies and systematic cooperation) were innovations. The European Council determines what common Union strategies are adopted, the respective objectives, means of implementation and the duration of the action. Similar criteria were set for common positions and joint actions. For all three, qualified majority voting (qmv) decisions are now possible, if under limited circumstances, including the use of a veto to defend a 'vital' national interest.

Finally, the security and defence aspects of CFSP have typically been expressed through cooperation with the WEU. This tradition was extended at Amsterdam and the status quo left largely intact. The Treaty refers to the 'progressive framing of a common defence' policy 'which *might* lead to a common defence' (my emphasis) and while closer links between the EU and the WEU are foreshadowed, no timetable or mechanism for the eventual integration of the WEU is proposed. Although member state cooperation in armaments was suggested, the only substantive development was the incorporation of the so-called 'Petersberg missions' within the CFSP (Article 17(2)) which provide for humanitarian and rescue tasks, peacekeeping missions and tasks of combat forces in crisis management.

What are the Constraints?

The consensual nature of CFSP described above is often cited as a major constraint on the effectiveness of EU foreign policy. The Amsterdam Treaty requires unanimity for the adoption of common strategies. Theoretically, joint actions and common positions may be determined by qualified majority; in practice, formal voting is avoided and consensus is sought wherever possible. Unanimity in the European Council can be required where vital national interests are at risk. While consensus building can be protracted – with the convoy moving as fast as the slowest ship (Wallace, 1983, p. 14) – any foreign policy decision that lacked the full support of the Union would be precariously placed. If consensus is a limitation, it appears to be a necessary one for effective action.

Constitutional requirements imposed on foreign policy in some member states can provide a further constraint. For example Austria, Ireland and Sweden (although each in different ways) are bound by policies of 'neutrality'. Consequently, the EU has been compelled to act as a civilian power and lacks a significant independent military capacity, relying instead on the WEU structures already discussed.

Typically, EU foreign policy has been described as reactive in nature. This was undeniably the case under EPC and even these responses were often too belated to be effective. To be fair, very few international actors have the capacity to be proactive and the Maastricht and Amsterdam reforms have provided at least the infrastructure for a more proactive CFSP. Here, the new policy planning and early warning unit and role of the High Representative will be crucial and, if successful, will build on the existing CFSP reputation in areas such as peace-keeping, election monitoring and negotiations. Funding is central to a more proactive EU presence in international affairs; as noted already, the questions of budgetary contributions and expenditure oversight remain contentious areas. Without a clear and sizeable budget, CFSP will find it difficult to move beyond a reactive policy-making style.

CFSP is frequently characterized by its inadequacies rather than its abilities. While the record warrants critical review, it is important to recognise that CFSP operates under specific constraints, especially if erroneous comparisons with national foreign policies are to be avoided. CFSP is not an exclusive activity. It has always been quite legitimate for member states to conduct bilateral national foreign policies independently provided that these do not conflict with, or compromise, the EU's common policies. Clearly, there are areas where the member states have such divergent foreign policies that any collective approach is prohibited. Agenda management theories are particularly useful conceptual tools here: a foreign policy issue can be defined in such a way to exclude it from discussion. Consequently, currently the CFSP can only constitute a partial and not a comprehensive foreign policy for Europe.

A final problem when assessing CFSP is that expectations are too high given the constraints within which CFSP operates. Often the tasks expected of the EU do not match its capabilities (Hill, 1993). Here, the problem is perhaps less one of having a scarcity of instruments and policies and one more of setting unrealistic demands or equating the EU with an international actor such as the US. Clearly, the EU is not a global superpower and no one should be surprised when it fails to act as one. Interestingly, it is often third countries who demand that the EU play a more active global role – a paradoxical situation for a foreign policy that is supposedly so ineffective.

Indeed, with the exception of direct military action, the EU presents an impressive array of foreign policy instruments. Sanctions have been widely employed under EPC and CFSP utilizing the pillar one external trade competences of the EU. While the effectiveness of sanctions may be questioned, practically speaking they may only be used at the EU level. With the creation of the single market the possibilities for individual member states to operate bilateral sanctions has been removed: only collective sanctions can have any real effect (and even here the chosen legal basis for adoption is crucial). Diplomatic statements have also been used extensively as a CFSP instrument as has the suspension of diplomatic ties by the member states acting in concert. Mixing the intergovernmentalism of CFSP with treaty-based external relations, the EU invokes a wide range of activities that can be applied as foreign policy instruments, including codes of conduct; aid programmes; conditionality; the European Community Humanitarian Office (ECHO); and preferential trade regimes (see Chapter 11). If there is a capabilities-expectations gap, it is not because of a lack of policy options.

What is the Record?

Under EPC, common positions were increasingly achieved although effective action was less easily obtained. During the 1980s, there was a collective European response to issues as diverse as the Falklands War, Iran, Poland, Afghanistan and South Africa – Europe's anti-apartheid policy and subsequent involvement in monitoring South Africa's first democratic elections in 1994 displayed all the hallmarks of an effective international actor (Holland, 1998). In contrast, the 1990s saw the EU largely fail to meet the challenge posed by the Gulf War, Yugoslavia or Rwanda.

Cumulatively these disappointments have led some to conclude that a common foreign policy is impossible; others, including the former Commission President Jacques Delors, have seen in these same events an absolute necessity for the EU to act collectively in the future. The failures make the CFSP even more essential. No matter how flawed EU policy on Yugoslavia may appear, it has never been argued that 15 separate bilateral national foreign policies towards the region would have produced a better outcome. While holding a common line simply for the sake of staying together may not be a sufficient rationale for foreign policy, the positive contribution of collective action for regional security should not be overlooked. Critics may have lamented the absence of direct EU military intervention in the former Yugoslavia, but other options have been used by the EU: a series of peace conferences have been convened, sanctions imposed, peacekeepers deployed and administrations supervised, albeit to little effect.

While the EU has struggled when confronted with foreign policy aggression, there have been a significant number of achievements in less dramatic policy spheres. The promotion of human rights as a foreign policy issue has been a dominant and successful EU theme since 1989. Europe's general response both to German reunification as well as the democratic transition in Central and Eastern Europe are clear foreign policy successes, albeit ones strictly outside the ambit of CFSP. During the first three years of CFSP (1993–6) some 68 joint actions and common positions were adopted, on 23 separate foreign policy issues (see *European Foreign Affairs Review*, 1997). These ranged, for example, from Yugoslavia, Nigeria and the Middle East peace process to policies on anti-personnel mines, biological weapons and the Stability Pact.

Not even the most ardent Euro-federalist would deny that the EU's foreign policy record is blemished: the new expectation is that monetary union and the single market will jointly promote a more cohesive foreign policy based increasingly on shared interests and assumptions. As CFSP matures, the 'natural' area of common policies is set to expand at the expense of the more disparate aspects of bilateral foreign policies: only then will collective action become the norm rather than the exception.

What are the Prospects?

CFSP faces a significant number of crucial issues – both practical and theoretical – that will determine its future direction and effectiveness. First, at the conceptual level, perceptions of sovereignty need to be modified if the CFSP is to develop. Sovereignty is not zero-sum. Rather than member states losing sovereignty to some undefined centre called 'Brussels', national sovereignty needs to be seen as compatible with, even tantamount to, EU sovereignty – and not in conflict with it. If sovereignty means controlling what happens to the state, then arguably the collective sovereignty of the 15 is far more effective than the individual sovereignties of the member states – France, Germany and the UK included.

Second, a 'common' foreign and security policy is not the same as a 'single' foreign and security policy. However, clearly where independent bilateral foreign policies are the norm and CFSP policies the exception, the EU's credibility as a collective international actor is minimized. Consequently, for CFSP to grow in stature its scope must become inclusive and progressively expand while national foreign policies become marginalized.

Third, if the CFSP is to move beyond the intergovernmentalism of Maastricht and Amsterdam, the so-called 'pillar' structure separating EU competences has to be revised. Of course, this inventive architecture was the result of an uneasy compromise between the *communautaire* and the intergovernmental member states and any changes to the status quo will require a political realignment. Despite the persuasive arguments of integration theories, European integration has been above all an elite-driven process and the prospects for CFSP will principally be determined at this level.

A number of practical issues will also influence the prospects for CFSP, not least the Amsterdam Treaty reforms. Many proponents of CFSP have equated qmv with better decision-making and look to the extensions of qmv at Amsterdam to enhance this possibility. Perversely, others argue that qmv may work against the effective implementation of decisions. The tyranny of unanimity may remain an essential prerequisite. Similarly, while a High Representative was established any decision not to give political legitimacy to this role might compromise its potential effectiveness. In both these regards the caution of the Amsterdam reforms (combined with the pre-accession requirements associated with the next enlargement) will inevitably necessitate another Intergovernmental Conference in the near future.

Enlargement poses a further challenge to CFSP, just as it does to the EU's entire institutional and policy-making structures. Consensus may become increasingly difficult to achieve in a Union of more than 20 member states, especially one with such diverse geopolitical interests. Qmv, however, runs the risk of dividing the EU on either a North–South or an East–West axis. Security concerns may also be compounded with the accession of the Central and Eastern European countries and Cyprus. At the time of writing, the CFSP has had the luxury of accommodating security and defence through the WEU and the NATO structures. With a rapidly changing European security situation, however, the question of EU security architecture can no longer be avoided if the 'Security' aspect of CFSP is to be credible.

The prospects for CFSP also depend on an enhanced capacity to act. As noted already, the expectations for the EU to play an international role are overwhelming. Sufficient instruments already exist – what has been generally missing is a concerted political will to exercise these instruments effectively. Too often differences between the member states have resulted in policy compromises that only serve to reinforce the EU's ineffectual image – and public perceptions and support are fundamental to the successful exercise of foreign policy.

Finally, in a general rather than legal sense, subsidiarity and flexibility may indirectly influence the development of CFSP. Can it be shown that foreign policy is better expressed and conducted at the EU and not the member state level? In what aspects of foreign policy is the EU superior to the 15 acting independently? While common economic relations, the single market and EMU define a clear EU external relations role, does this necessarily establish the EU as the appropriate guardian of the political and security aspects of foreign policy? The pervasive philosophy of subsidiarity could see a re-nationalization of Europe's foreign affairs. Alternatively, flexibility may also pose a threat to the CFSP. The Community method is no longer uniform: variable geometry, multi-speed Europe or a Europe of concentric circles have all been used to explain recent intra-EU developments. Similar ideas can be applied to CFSP: indeed, as noted above, Amsterdam makes provision for the possibility of member states absenting themselves from common positions. If qmv becomes institutionalized behaviour, a CFSP core and periphery could well develop. 'All for one and one for all' has lost its resonance as a policy metaphor.

Does Foreign Policy Matter?

Why has it been relatively easy to establish monetary union and not a common foreign policy? Both impinge upon traditional notions of sovereignty – and arguably monetary union has the greater immediate and direct effect for individuals. The inclusion of foreign policy within the integration process is a necessary requirement for political union. And political union is essential if economic integration is to be sustained and accepted. Popular support, whether for foreign policy or economic policy, is the fundamental condition on which integration is based. Just as successful economic policies will generate popular support, so must CFSP. So far the modest successes have failed to provide the level of popular legitimacy needed. CFSP is undeniably part of the theoretical debate on European integration and how it can be achieved. A central dilemma, however, remains. Should CFSP lead the integration process or should it follow public opinion and elites? Such a dilemma, of course, has been at the heart of the integration process since the beginning.

The thrust of this chapter has been to locate CFSP within the broader EU context: as such, it is argued that the integration process and CFSP are inseparable. Theoretically neo-functionalism posits such a link and in an ever-increasing practical sense foreign policy reflects deeper internal integration. CFSP certainly does matter then – for both internal and external reasons. Without a CFSP the EU is tantamount to an economic common market; with it, perhaps, a federal Union as suggested by Monnet could eventually be realised. Even the current imperfect CFSP has contributed to both regional and global stability and security, Yugoslavia and the Gulf War notwithstanding. In the evolving post-Cold War environment, it is important that the EU helps to fill the political vacuum created by the collapse of the Soviet Union, particularly in Central and Eastern Europe. The question was asked in the introduction to this chapter whether the CFSP was central to, or an optional extra, in the integration process. The answer given here is that it is very much a necessary and essential prerequisite.

Conclusion

The challenge for the EU is to break from a tradition of intergovernmental behaviour and re-conceptualize CFSP. The CFSP has illustrated the complexities of mixed-pillar competences. The Amsterdam Treaty has contributed to achieving coherence, complementarity and coordination between CFSP and external relations, but so long as these EU activities are artificially dichotomized between intergovernmental and *communautaire* pillars European integration will remain incomplete.

This chapter has also illustrated how different integration theories posit different forms of European integration. While a neo-functional approach has been advanced here, alternative conceptual frameworks can be explored as mechanisms for locating CFSP within the integration process that may lead to different conclusions. Paradigmatic dogma is only rarely justified analytically. Implicit throughout this discussion has been the importance of elites in shaping the CFSP and in the changing power relationship both between the EU institutions and with the member states themselves. Despite its second-pillar designation, both the EP and the Commission have increased their involvement in foreign policy under the Maastricht and Amsterdam reforms.

Finally, as a method for conducting foreign relations CFSP has evolved more through incremental adaptation and ad hoc compromises than through systematic planning or rational thought. Perhaps the most surprising feature is not that CFSP works so imperfectly, but that it works at all.

Guide to Further Reading

Most general texts on integration provide a reasonable overview of CFSP. For more detailed analyses from institutional or historical perspectives, see Foster and Wallace (1996), Holland (1994, 1995a), Nuttall (1992), Pijpers *et al.*, (1988), Regelsberger and Wessels (1996), and Rummel (1992). For theoretical approaches, see Allen and Smith (1990), Carlsnaes and Smith (1994), Hill (1993), Holland (1987, 1991, 1995b, 1997) and Ifestos (1988). There is a surprising lack of either EPC or CFSP case studies. The notable exceptions are Edwards (1982, 1992), Edwards and Regelsberger (1990), Ginsberg (1989), Holland (1995a, 1998), Salmon (1992) and Smith (1995). The *Journal of Common Market Studies* and the *European Foreign Affairs Review* should be regularly consulted for new CFSP articles. *Agence Europe* and the *EPC Documentation Bulletin* are good sources for the factual reporting of CFSP.

References

Allen, D. and M. Smith (1990) 'Western Europe's Presence in the Contemporary International Arena', *Review of International Studies*, vol. 16, pp. 19–39.

Carlsnaes, W. and S. Smith (eds) (1994) *European Foreign Policy: the EC and Changing Perspectives in Europe*. London: Sage.

Edwards, G. (1984) 'Europe and the Falkland Islands Crisis 1982' *Journal of Common Market Studies*, vol. XXII, pp. 295–313.

Edwards, G. (1992) 'European Responses to the Yugoslav Crisis: an Interim Assessment', in R. Rummel, *Toward Political Union*. Baden-Baden: Nomar.

Edwards, G. and E. Regelsberger (eds) (1990) *Europe's Global Links: the European Community and Inter-Regional Cooperation*. New York: St. Martin's Press.

European Foreign Affairs Review (1997) vol 2–1, pp. 143–56.

Foster, A. and W. Wallace (1996) 'Common Foreign and Security Policy', in H. Wallace and W. Wallace (eds), *Policy-Making in the European Union*. Oxford: Oxford University Press, pp. 411–35.

Ginsberg, R. (1989) *Foreign Policy Actions of the European Community: The Politics of Scale*. Boulder, CO: Lynne Reinner.

Hill, C. (1993) 'The Capabilities–Expectations Gap or Conceptualising Europe's International Role', *Journal of Common Market Studies*, vol. 31, pp. 305–28.

Hill, C. (ed.) (1996) *The Actors in Europe's Foreign Policy*. London: Routledge.
Hix, S. (1994) 'The Study of the European Community: The Challenge to Comparative Politics', *West European Politics*, vol. 17, pp. 1–30.
Holland, M. (1987) 'Three Approaches for Understanding European Political Co-operation: A Case-Study of EC–South African Policy', *Journal of Common Market Studies*, vol. 25, pp. 295–314.
Holland, M. (ed.) (1991) *The Future of European Political Cooperation: Essays on Theory and Practice*. London: Macmillan.
Holland, M. (1994) *European Integration: From Community to Union*. London: Pinter.
Holland, M. (1995a) *European Union Common Foreign Policy: From EPC to CFSP Joint Action and South Africa*. London: Macmillan.
Holland, M. (1995b) 'Bridging the Capabilities–Expectations Gap: a Case Study of the CFSP Joint Action on South Africa', *Journal of Common Market Studies*, vol. 33, pp. 555–72.
Holland, M. (ed.) (1997) *Common Foreign and Security Policy: The Record and Reforms*. London: Pinter.
Holland, M. (1998) 'Vices and Virtues: Europe's Foreign Policy and South Africa, 1977–1997', *European Foreign Affairs Review*, vol 3, pp. 215–32.
Ifestos, P. (1988) *European Political Cooperation: Towards a Framework of Supranational Diplomacy*. Aldershot: Avebury.
Lister, M. (1997) *The European Union and the South: Relations with Developing Countries*. London: Routledge/UACES.
Luxembourg Report (1970) 'Report by the Foreign Ministers of the member states on the Problems of Political Unification', *Bulletin of the EC*, vol. 6–11.
Monnet, J. (1978) *Memoirs*. New York: Doubleday.
Nuttall, S. (1992) *European Political Cooperation*. Oxford: Clarendon Press.
Pijpers, A., Regelsberger, E., Wessels, W. and Edwards, G. (eds) (1988) *European Political Cooperation in the 1980s: a Common Foreign Policy for Western Europe?* The Hague: Martinus Nijhoff.
Regelsberger, E. and Wessels, W. (1996) 'The CFSP Institutions and Procedures: A Third Way for the Second Pillar', *European Foreign Affairs Review*, vol. 1, pp. 29–54.
Rummel, R. (ed.) (1992) *Toward Political Union: Planning a Common Foreign and Security Policy in the European Community*. Baden-Baden: Nomos.
Salmon, T. (1992) 'Testing Times for European Political Cooperation: the Gulf and Yugoslavia, 1990–1992', *International Affairs*, vol. 68, pp. 233–53.
Smith, H. (1995) *European Union Foreign Policy and Central America*. London: Macmillan.
Wallace, W. (1983) 'Introduction: Cooperation and Convergence in European Foreign Policy', in C. Hill (ed.), *National Foreign Policies and European Political Cooperation*. London: George Allen and Unwin/RIIA pp. 1–16.

13

Cooperation on Justice and Home Affairs Matters

EMEK UÇARER

When the 1957 Treaty of Rome set Europe on the path to 'an ever closer union', the free movement of individuals within its territory was named as one of four objectives that the European integration process was intended to achieve. Though the Treaty's goal of achieving a customs union was completed ahead of schedule, the goal of eliminating borders for the free movement of persons remains unachieved after 40 years and has only been put back on the integration agenda since the mid-1980s.

During the negotiations leading up to the Single European Act (SEA) of 1986 and the Treaty on European Union (TEU, or Maastricht Treaty) of 1992, it became apparent that the ultimate objective of doing away with *internal* border controls within the European Union was inextricably intertwined with generating common policies to apply to its *external* borders. In order to assure the safety and security of the peoples of the European Union (EU), it was argued, members had to have comparable screening and security mechanisms at the external borders. While this was a logical conclusion, its implementation was fraught with difficulty. In a shrinking and interdependent globe, the ability to determine who is allowed into one's territory was understandably protected as one of the last bastions of sovereignty. Because embarking on a path to formulate *common* rules to apply to the Union's external borders implied a potential challenge to the individual sovereign prerogatives of the member states, cooperation around issues that involved transborder phenomena got off to a relatively belated start in the EC/EU. The dilemma faced was this: members were initially trying to relinquish as little sovereignty to Brussels as possible while attempting to do away with internal borders and reinforce external ones.

This chapter will briefly review the context and content of Justice and Home Affairs (JHA) cooperation in the EU, which became the institutional context within which these efforts were launched after Maastricht. While the importance of the efforts leading up to Maastricht cannot be understated, the chapter will focus on the post-Maastricht developments and will review the most recent substantive developments in the field as well as the newest institutional developments contained in the Amsterdam Treaty.

Why Cooperate?

The first incentive to cooperate on border-crossing matters came with the political commitment to a border-free Europe contained in the Treaty of Rome, which founded the European Communities (EC), and the Maastricht Treaty, which created the European Union (EU). Economic issues, where participants had economic and financial incentives to cooperate lent themselves better to enhanced cooperation. Border-crossing matters, on the other hand, were considered strictly a sovereign prerogative and thus did not work their way into the integration process until the mid-1980s. It was no coincidence that the surfacing of border issues on the European agenda also coincided with a period of changing demographic realities in Western Europe. In the mid-1980s, most Western European countries were trying to come to grips with growing minorities in their polities and increasing migratory pressures into their territory. The asylum crisis at the end of the 1980s, which resulted in unprecedented numbers of applicants, and increasing transborder organized crime, lent an urgency to cooperation efforts (Koslowski, 1997; Uçarer, 1997). Regardless of the implications for eroding sovereignty, it was agreed that unilateral responses were insufficient under the changing circumstances.

Another catalyst that placed border issues irreversibly on the collective European agenda was the SEA. In signing the SEA, member states agreed to create an area 'without internal frontiers in which . . . goods, services, *persons*, and capital' (my emphasis) would flow freely. While this was set as a political goal, Article 18(2) of the SEA excluded policies relating to most border-crossing matters from the supranational EC decision-making process (European Communities, 1987). The political impetus given to the issue with the SEA created a flurry of multilateral activities between member states on border-crossing issues. Numerous groups dealing either tangentially or exclusively with JHA matters sprung into existence. The result was a complicated network of *ad hoc* consultation fora which often duplicated each others' work and produced little by way of concrete policy output.

These efforts are intriguing for two reasons. In theoretical terms, cooperation on JHA matters represented an opportunity to test the willingness of member states to allow supranational decision-making in a new policy domain that was previously dealt with in the sole sovereign domain of member states. Supranational and intergovernmental interests came to a head during the formative phases of JHA cooperation, and the debate was temporarily won by the latter. Yet, the post-Maastricht period highlighted the weaknesses of the intergovernmental method and relaunched the debate on a gradual shift to supranationality. In practical terms, the cooperation efforts are creating the blueprint for the movement of individuals *into* the Union territory, as well as *within* it. As a result, in addition to formulating the inclusion and exclusion rules for entry, the efforts are taking on uncharted territory in terms of multilateral public policy. But let's first look at the development, institutionalization and current state of JHA cooperation.

Maastricht and the Creation of the Third Pillar

JHA cooperation was formally institutionalized by the Maastricht Treaty. In January 1991 the Luxembourg Council Presidency submitted a working paper proposing four alternatives for extending the EC's competence to JHA issues to the IGC that prepared the Treaty. The first alternative was to continue cooperation on these issues outside the Community framework. The second was to cursorily refer to cooperation in this area in the Treaty, but leave it to the Council to agree on the procedural details at a later date. The third was to draft a series of specific treaty provisions defining the issues to be covered and precisely the decision-making apparata to be employed. And finally, the fourth alternative was to bring these issue areas wholly into the ambit of the Community and engage the EC decision-making apparata, a concept that was later referred to as *communautarization*. None of these four alternatives found wholehearted approval from all member states: the Netherlands, Belgium, Italy, and Spain preferred the fourth alternative; France and Germany supported the third in the short term with a possibility to move towards the fourth in the long run; Portugal favoured the third alternative; the United Kingdom, Ireland, and Greece preferred the second option; and Denmark could only support alternatives one or two (Hix, 1995, pp. 9–10).

Luxembourg responded to these divergent opinions by crafting a draft treaty that tried to accommodate the greatest number of member states. It was apparent that there was general consensus among the member states that no member was determined to keep these issues completely out of the Community's competence. Creating a hybrid between the second and third alternatives described above, the Luxembourg document envisioned a European Union based on a 'three-pillared' edifice that some enthusiasts imagined to be a new European temple. The first pillar was the Treaty of Rome, the second was Common Foreign and Security Policy (CFSP), and the third was JHA. This was clearly an effort to compromise the two extremes on the architecture of the EU and find common ground between Germany, Italy and the Netherlands on the one hand and the UK and Denmark on the other. The resulting Title VI of the TEU embodied the institutional arrangement that allowed intergovernmental negotiations to take place within this 'European Temple', although the influence of the temple's custodians in the European Commission was considerably constrained. Accordingly, measures associated with any programme for a frontier-free EU would have to be drawn up by intergovernmental bodies so that, in the short run, the Community institutions would be marginalized in policy-making. The new set-up afforded the negotiating parties the opportunity to maintain regular contact and begin working on a variety of dossiers in the new competence area. Title VI of the TEU spelled out nine areas of 'common interest' which were to fall under the newly institutionalized JHA cooperation:

- Asylum policy;
- Rules governing the crossing of the Community's external borders;
- Immigration policy and policy regarding third country nationals;
- Combating drug addiction;
- Combating international fraud;
- Judicial cooperation in civil matters;
- Judicial cooperation in criminal matters;
- Customs cooperation; and
- Police cooperation for the purposes of preventing and combating terrorism, unlawful drug trafficking, and other serious forms of international crime.

The Treaty established a five-tiered negotiation framework, summarized in Figure 13.1. These five levels of negotiations marked a substantial change from traditional three-tiered EC decision-making, adding two new negotiation levels to the already time-consuming mechanism. As part of the JHA decision process, the Treaty also specified the roles to be played by the existing EC institutions in JHA matters.

- The dominant actor in the third pillar was to be the *JHA Council*, comprising the JHA ministers of the member states. It was to be the supreme intergovernmental actor, acting as the final arbiter after negotiations on issues worked their way up to the top of the five-tiered framework (Lobkowicz, 1995).
- The *Commission* found itself playing the role of a somewhat awkward junior partner. None the less, mandated by Article K3 of the TEU, it became officially – and somewhat more authoritatively – involved in negotiations. Perhaps the most important setback to the Commission's work was the absence of an exclusive right of initiative which it continued to enjoy in the first pillar. Though an improvement from its previous position in intergovernmental discussions relating to JHA matters, a *shared* right of initiative was clearly an indication that the Commission was envisioned as one of 16 actors in the third pillar to take initiative in JHA matters (ibid.).
- The *European Parliament (EP)*, the sole elected body representing the citizens of Europe, was even more constrained under the new arrangements, although it wanted to be fully associated with the work in this area. Although the Treaty stated that the Parliament should be consulted by the Council on all matters at hand, the EP soon found itself in a situation where it was often bypassed and poorly informed. Even so, the Parliament has made use of whatever institutional influence it could wield, and being the institution that most probably had the least to lose became the most vociferous critic of the Maastricht institutional framework.
- Under Article L of the TEU, the *European Court of Justice (ECJ)* was left without a mandate in JHA matters, raising eyebrows about the lack of judicial review.

The institutional dynamic put in place by the TEU was considerably different and far more confusing than the already complicated decision-making apparatus of the Community. This was no surprise since the Treaty itself was the result of a hasty move to appease the

Council of Ministers for Justice and Home Affairs
Responsible Ministers from Member States
Final decision-making body

COREPER
Committee of Permanent Representatives (Ambassadors)
Oversees cooperation
Prepares Council meetings

K.4 Committee
Highest ranking officials from Member States and European Commission
Coordinates activities
Contributes to Council discussions

Steering Group I
Asylum and Immigration
High officials from Member States and Commission
Develops policy on asylum and immigration

Working Groups
Delegations and Experts
Prepare policy positions
- Asylum
- Migration
- Visa
- External borders
- False documents
- EURODAC
- CIREFI
- CIREA

Steering Group II
Police and Customs Cooperation
High officials from Member States and Commission
Develops policy on police and customs cooperation

Working Groups
Delegations and Experts
Prepare policy positions
- Terrorism
- Police cooperation
- Europol
- Drugs and organized crime
- Customs cooperation
- EURODAC
- CIREFI
- CIREA

Steering Group III
Judicial Cooperation
High officials from Member States and Commission
Develops policy on civil and criminal judicial cooperation

Working Groups
Delegations and Experts
Prepare policy positions
- Extradition
- Criminal and community law
- Brussels Convention
- Transmission of acts
- Driving bans
- International organized crime

FIGURE 13.1 *Third pillar decision-making bodies*

parties involved and therefore had numerous shortcomings. Confounding matters still further was the Maastricht provision that would allow the decision-making arena to be shifted from the third pillar to the first pillar as specified in Article K9 of Title VI. This article provided for a bridge (*passerelle*) between the Community proper and the intergovernmental set-up within it, leaving an open door for the eventual transfer (*communautarization*) of some of Title VI by creating a distinction between transferable and nontransferable issues in the third pillar. The transferable issues were items the *communautarization* of which could be agreed upon in the not-too-distant future. The nontransferable issues, on the other hand, were those that were considered non-negotiable in terms of a short-term transfer of sovereignty to Brussels.

Post-Maastricht JHA Cooperation

Transferable Issues: Asylum, Immigration and External Borders

Cooperation on these matters dates back to the mid-1980s when member states became engaged in multilateral talks about how to respond to increasing migration pressures into the EC territory. Yet, differences of opinion over precisely what policies to develop soon divided the members and made it impossible for Community-wide policies to be adopted at that stage. As a result, a subset of member states – the Benelux countries, France, Germany and Italy – embarked on a project to progressively do away with controls at their mutual borders and cooperate on measures to be applied to the external borders. This conscious decision to start a 'two-track' process on these matters resulted in the signing of the two Schengen conventions in 1985 and 1990 (Meijers, 1990).

The Schengen intergovernmental framework, which did not include the UK, Ireland and Denmark, soon became the blueprint on which post-Maastricht JHA cooperation was modelled. Accordingly, initial work in JHA concentrated on adopting common policies for the handling of asylum applications, and agreeing on common guidelines to apply to the movement of non-Union nationals into and within the Union territory. The most notable developments with respect to asylum was the conclusion of the 1990 Dublin Convention in which the signatories agreed to the rules designating one member state for the handling of an asylum claim. In 1992 member states also adopted the non-binding, yet politically significant, London resolutions on common criteria to be used to determine the validity of an asylum claim. Later on, subsequent JHA Councils adopted a resolution on the harmonized application of a refugee definition (March 1995), a resolution on minimum guarantees for asylum procedures (June 1995) (Council of JHA Ministers, 1996a), and a common format to be used for determining the state responsible with reviewing an asylum application (Council of JHA Ministers, 1996b). Finally, on 25 September 1995, the Council adopted a resolution on burden-sharing with regard to the admission and residence of displaced persons on a temporary basis. The other matters under negotiation, such as the creation of the EURODAC fingerprinting system to determine the identity of asylum-seekers, and agreeing on comparable measures to apply to individuals who were seeking temporary protection status in the EU, have not yet yielded concrete results.

On the immigration front, member states negotiated various restrictions on the entry of third country nationals (TCNs) into the Union territory. On 30 November 1994, three Council resolutions were adopted that set common rules for the admission of TCNs for employment and study purposes. On the same date, two recommendations were adopted, one on a standard travel document for the expulsion of TCNs and the other on a specimen bilateral readmission agreement between member states and third countries. On 26 May 1997, the convention relating to the extradition between the member states of the EU was adopted. These are the only tangible result of the cooperation on immigration matters, regarded by many as minor achievements in the face of the work that is yet to be done.

Cooperation on the rules to apply to the external borders has likewise not borne much fruit. In fact, the only concrete development, which was the agreement on a uniform format for visas and the list of countries whose nationals must possess a visa to enter the Union territory, was achieved not in the third pillar but in the first. The External Borders Convention, which was proposed by the Commission in December 1993 and was to form the blueprint of EU immigration policies, remains deadlocked as a result of a dispute between Spain and the UK over the status of Gibraltar.

Nontransferable Issues: Customs, Police, and Judicial Cooperation

There was a reasonably long history of cooperation between the national bureaucracies of the member states on customs, police and judicial matters, but before Maastricht these cooperative efforts were not brought under a single roof. The third pillar provisions in these fields were manifestations of the belief that combating transborder crime went beyond the ability of individual states and required joint and coordinated multilateral efforts. Yet, these issues were seen as even more closely linked to national sovereignty. Therefore, while member states agreed to cooperate through information exchange, police, customs, and judicial cooperation in criminal matters, they were excluded from the *passerelle* provided for in the TEU.

Post-Maastricht efforts on customs cooperation have centred on the drafting of the *Convention on the Use of Information Technology for Customs Purposes*, known as the CIS Convention because it led to the establishment of the Customs Information System. In 1995, the JHA Council finally reached agreement on CIS but its implementation continued to be fraught with difficulty because it was unclear what the role of the ECJ would be.

Cooperation on police matters dates back to the initiation of the Trevi Group in 1975, which was formed to combat terrorism and organized crime. The second major effort to cooperate on police matters can be attributed to the Schengen Group. The 1990 Schengen Implementation Convention provided for hot pursuit and cross-border surveillance between the signatories. Following Maastricht, member states initiated an even more ambitious agenda as they began to develop Europol, the European Police Office. This project begin with a German proposal to the Luxembourg European Council in 1991 which envisaged the creation of a European Central Criminal Investigation Office by the end of 1993 (Boschi Orlandini, 1995, p. 209).

Europol was seen as an information exchange mechanism to prevent and fight against transborder crimes such as terrorism, illicit drug trafficking, and trafficking in human beings. While the political decision to create Europol was taken at Maastricht, the conclusion of the negotiation of the Europol Convention which legally created the organization came as a result of a compromise reached at the Cannes European Council in July 1995, after three years of drawn out negotiations. Unable to resolve the deadlock on the role of the ECJ with respect to the Europol Convention, member states agreed to meet the deadline and leave the legal jurisdiction questions aside. For the time being, Europol works strictly as an information exchange mechanism which does not have operational powers (Monar, 1997, p. 333).

In the drugs portfolio, EU members signed a ministerial agreement creating the Europol Drugs Unit (EDU) in June 1993. Similar to the role of Europol, EDU's task is to assist national police units with criminal investigations by providing case-relevant information. After the Unit started its work in 1994, member states agreed to a five-year plan in 1995. In an effort to strike at the supply of drugs smuggled into the Union, member states also initiated bilateral cooperation efforts between the EU and the US, Caribbean, and Latin America.

Institutional developments

From the early days of the intergovernmental system that was institutionalized by the TEU, it became apparent that the apparatus created was unable to deal efficiently with the existing workload. The overview of the policy output outlined above demonstrates the gap between the ambitious agenda and the meagre results. This was generally attributed to the deficiencies of the Maastricht Treaty and the institutional defects of the intergovernmental third pillar. EU institutions – most notably the Parliament (Bourlanges and Martin, 1995) and the Commission – as well as most of the member states were quick to point to these and call for reform. For many politicians and practitioners alike, this new model of intergovernmental negotiations was not only not particularly efficient, but also posed significant problems with respect to transparency (O'Keefe, 1995, 1996; Collinson, 1994) and the democratic deficit (Curtin and Meijers, 1995).

The most frustrating aspects for the participants were the policy instruments available to officials and the decision-making structure within which they had to operate. Soon after Maastricht, it became clear that the premier policy tool provided for in Title VI – International Conventions – would in fact stifle the policy-making process by turning into an extremely drawn-out negotiation process. To make matters worse, ratification by national parliaments took years, delaying the conventions' entry into force. The other policy instruments were not appreciably better. The joint positions and joint actions – policy tools created with the Maastricht Treaty which included resolutions, recommendations and declarations – were even more problematic because it was not clear in the Treaty whether these instruments were binding or not. Most importantly, the unanimity requirement in decision-making often deadlocked negotiations, preventing the adoption of some of the most important instruments that were developed over the years. Furthermore, the unanimity rule all but guaranteed a lowest common denominator outcome, a criticism often levelled against the developments in the asylum dossier.

Among the policy domains of the EU, the third pillar was the least transparent and most secretive. Meetings generally took place behind closed doors and debates were not made public on account of the 'sensitive nature' of the issues at hand. In addition, third-pillar affairs began to look singularly undemocratic in an era when the Union was trying very hard to appeal to the general European public and to establish clear guidelines on accountability. The upshot of these shortcomings was that, in the words of the 1996 Irish Presidency, 'cooperation on matters such as asylum, visas and immigration . . . in the view of many, lacked sufficient coherence, consistency and impetus' (Council of the European Union, 1996).

The 1996–7 IGC and the Amsterdam Treaty

After the TEU came into effect, a near-unanimous agreement quickly developed on the need to reform the third pillar to allow for greater transparency and accountability. There was, however, no consensus on just what reforms were required. Fortunately, the TEU had provided for a review of the functioning of the new architecture by calling for a further IGC in 1996. Accordingly, from 1995, member states and EU institutions began to prepare for the next round of reform.

The Reflection Group, consisting of one representative from each member state, one from the Commission and two from the EP was appointed in 1995 to take stock of the achievements and shortcomings of the Maastricht Treaty with a view towards reforming these shortcomings when the IGC convened. The Group, chaired by Carlos Westendorp, issued its final report in December 1995 (Reflection Group, 1995). In its report, the Reflection Group acknowledged the different standpoints on reform of the third pillar and cautiously called for improved cooperation between the member states. In order not to alienate any member state, the report made various vague references to 'flexible' arrangements that could be created. In fact, until very late in the Group's deliberations, member states even entertained France's idea of an intermediate pillar between the first and the third, between the supranational and the intergovernmental.

In the IGC itself, the disagreements challenging the reform process were twofold: on the substantive side was the question of how far the harmonization process was to go and what it was ultimately to cover; on the institutional side was the question of decision-making. This latter issue was a particularly divisive one, pitting those who favoured supranational decision-making against those who had more intergovernmental aspirations.

The Commission was among the first to register its discontent with the functioning of the Treaty in two reports on the reform of the Maastricht Treaty. The first was a report on the functioning of the Treaty, submitted to the Reflection Group in 1995 (Commission, 1995). The second portrayed the Commission's stance on political union and enlargement, delivered to the IGC in February 1996 (Commission, 1996). The two reports, which both sought to promote the supranational agenda, proposed reforming the third pillar along the following lines (Hix and Niessen, 1996, p. 32):

- summarizing third pillar objectives into main themes, including common rules of entry and residence of third-country nationals and mutually recognizing the judgements of national courts;
- replacement of the unanimity rule in all areas by qualified majority voting;
- extending to the Commission the right of initiative in all areas;
- developing more effective legal instruments, such as directives instead of joint actions or common positions; and
- submitting decisions to review by the European Court of Justice. (ibid. pp. 11–12).

The Commission was not alone in pushing the *communautarization* of at least some of the JHA issues: the Parliament and several member states supported the Commission's position. The draft revision that was produced by the Irish Presidency in December 1996 appeared to have taken the Commission suggestions into account, and even though it was by no means the authoritative text showed some signs of moving in a favourable direction for the Commission. The Presidency's draft – which read less like a treaty and more like general guidelines – addressed the five major aims of the IGC as these were set by the Florence European Council of June 1996. The first of these aims, geared towards making 'the Union more relevant to its citizens and more responsive to their concerns', was of direct relevance to the third pillar of the Union (Council of the European Union, 1996, p. 6).

Appropriately, the first section of the draft concerned the creation of 'an area of freedom, security and justice' for which the Irish

Presidency proposed a target deadline of 1 January 2001. In the areas of free movement of persons, asylum, and immigration, the Presidency proposed setting target dates for adopting clear procedures governing the crossing of external borders, establishing provisions for common visa regulations, and tackling the issue of asylum and illegal drugs collectively. In order to achieve these goals, the Presidency 'considered' the drafting of a new title and the incorporation of this title in the Treaty of Rome which would mean a transfer of these issues to the first pillar. Arguing that the role of the institutions remained to be considered in the conference – and hinting at the lack of consensus – the Presidency suggested the initiation of a process during which the shared right of initiative for the Commission would move along an automatic and previously decided upon schedule towards an exclusive right of initiative. The Presidency suggested that the conference could consider retaining the unanimity rule but by setting the schedule for a move towards qualified majority decision-making.

The Dutch Presidency, which took over the helm in January 1997, produced a similar draft which was debated until the Amsterdam European Council where, on 17 June 1997, a final text was agreed. The text of the Amsterdam Treaty represents less of a compromise than the Maastricht Treaty. It transferred issues concerning internal and external borders, visa, asylum, and immigration policies and judicial cooperation in civil matters to a new Title IV in the EC pillar, leaving only police cooperation and judicial cooperation on criminal matters in the revised third pillar. Table 13.1 compares the post-Maastricht and post-Amsterdam institutional frameworks.

The comparison set out in Table 13.1 reveals a fundamental institutional change in JHA cooperation, especially for those issues that are now housed in the first pillar. For the *communautarized* issues, there is now potentially a greater role for the Commission, Parliament, and Court, something generally associated with increased supranationality. The intergovernmental third pillar is also streamlined, its objectives are spelled out more explicitly and the Commission is given a right of initiative in police and criminal justice cooperation, which constitutes an improvement on its Maastricht position.

Yet, perhaps the biggest shortcoming of the 1996-7 IGC was the failure to agree on an automatic transition from unanimity to qualified majority decision-making, which is the cornerstone of supranational decision-making. The Irish and Dutch draft treaties

TABLE 13.1 *The post-Maastricht and post-Amsterdam institutional frameworks*

	Post-Maastricht	*Post-Amsterdam*	
		First Pillar	*Third Pillar*
Asylum Immigration External Borders	Third Pillar, Title VI, Article K of TEU.	Articles 61–64 of TEC.	N.A.
Police cooperation	Third Pillar, Title VI, Article K of TEU.	N.A.	Revised Title VI of TEU, Article 30.
Judicial cooperation	Third Pillar, Title VI, Article K of TEU.	*Civil* Matters: Article 65 of TEC.	*Criminal* Matters: Revised Title VI of TEU, Article 31.
European Parliament (EP)	Limited role.	Consultation for the first five years after Amsterdam Treaty takes effect, co-decision afterwards.	Consultation.
European Court of Justice (ECJ)	No jurisdiction.	Referral for an obligatory first ruling for national last-instance courts.	Limited jurisdiction. ECJ may review the legality of decisions taken in the Third Pillar. ECJ may settle disputes between member states on the application of Third Pillar acts.
Decision-making	*Unanimity* rule on all issues.	Council acts *unanimously* on proposals from Commission and member states for the first five years. After five years, Council will act unanimously on a move towards *qualified majority voting*.	*Unanimity* rule continues in revised Third Pillar.
Right of initiative	*Shared* right of initiative for the Commission and Member States. Commission has *no right of initiative* in judicial and police cooperation.	Commission has *exclusive* right of initiative in Title IV of TEC five years after the entry into force of treaty.	Commission has *shared* right of initiative in all issue areas in revised Title VI.

both foresaw such an automatic transition after a five-year period following the entry into force of the new Treaty. Yet, during the final days of negotiation, this idea was struck down by Germany's Chancellor Kohl. Feeling pressured by Germany's *Länder* governments, which adopted an increasingly unfriendly stance to the transfer of decision-making capacity to Brussels on immigration and asylum matters, Kohl eventually insisted on unanimity in decision-making, at least for the first five years following the implementation of the Treaty. The final text of the Treaty reflects this compromise: while member states agreed to transfer some of the Maastricht third pillar issues to the first, they did so by retaining the unanimity rule for five years. After this time, the Council will decide 'unanimously, but without the need for national ratification' whether qualified majority voting should become the rule for some or all of the new first-pillar issues (Petit, 1998).

Those countries that were even less sympathetic to bringing third-pillar issues into the supranational domain – namely, the UK, Ireland and Denmark – received further concessions at the IGC. Instead of the opt-outs which were secured for the 'Eurosceptics' on other occasions during the European integration process, the new Treaty provided for opt-ins: while the new Title IV of the amended Treaty of Rome does not apply to the UK or Ireland, both countries are allowed to participate in issues of their own choosing. Denmark, on the other hand, secured a general opt-out from the new Community framework, a stance to which it became committed during the ratification process of the Maastricht Treaty.

Where to after Amsterdam?

Some tentative conclusions can be drawn from the experience of the last decade. There is no longer any doubt that JHA matters can be dealt with at the European level. A novel idea only 15 years ago, cooperation on sensitive issues such as immigration, drug trafficking and criminal justice is now firmly rooted in the European discourse, both substantively and institutionally. While the cooperation process has not always been smooth and did not initially produce significant policy output, the post-Maastricht experience has slowly but surely locked member states into an institutionalized dialogue that continues to unfold.

It appears that the routine consultation process has raised expectations about the level of cooperation in the EU. While most member states were initially unwilling to consider *communautarizing* some of the JHA matters, the resistance waned considerably over time, culminating in the institutional restructuring in the Amsterdam Treaty. While this is by no means a definite victory for those who wish to engage in supranational policy-making, it can be considered an encouraging step forward. Considering the trajectory of JHA cooperation, which was initiated outside the Community framework and was later brought into the intergovernmental structure created with the Maastricht Treaty, the latest institutional developments represent an important step in anchoring JHA issues firmly in the European policy domain.

Yet, the opt-ins, opt-outs and exceptions granted with the protocols annexed to the Amsterdam Treaty also allow for a less optimistic interpretation of the achievements of JHA cooperation: is 'Europe of the free movement of persons, as in many other fields, several-speed Europe?' (MEP Brigitte Ernst of the EP Greens, quoted in *Agence Europe*, 1993, p. 12). Are the unusual decision-making provisions and right of initiative for member states which are incorporated into the new Title IV the result of an effort to buy five more years of negotiations, or are they, in fact, tantamount to the sneaking of intergovernmentalism and unanimity into the first pillar (Devuyst, 1997, p. 13)? There is undoubtedly some truth to these arguments. Until the effect of the new Treaty provisions has been felt, it is premature to speculate on the success or failure of the Treaty. It is also too early to predict the extent to which the countries with opt-outs will cooperate. However, one thing is certain: JHA cooperation will further establish itself as a permanent feature in European discussions.

Guide to Further Reading

The most comprehensive accounts of the developments in Justice and Home Affairs (JHA) are available in Bieber and Monar (1995) and Monar and Morgan (1995). These edited books deal with the many facets of JHA cooperation from both historical and substantive perspectives. This is an area that is developing rapidly, and the literature that exists is still sketchy but growing. Immigration-related issues are covered in Collinson (1994) and Joly (1996). For police cooperation, see Marenin (1996). For institutional developments, see Lipsius (1995) and Monar (1997). For the 1996 Intergovernmental Conference in general, see Edwards and Pijpers (1997), which not only covers JHA but is also an excellent collection of essays dealing with events leading up to the 1996 IGCs. Despite the slow increase in publications that deal with JHA issues, the best sources of information are still the European Union's own documents. Many of these are available from the Europa Web site at <http://europa.eu.int/>. Further information can be obtained from the monthly newsletters such as *Migration News Sheet* and *Migration News* (http://migration.ucdavis.edu/mn/mntxt.htm) that cover JHA developments in the EU. Finally, *Agence Europe* also provides timely information on JHA matters.

References

Agenda Europe (1993) 'The "Greens" in the European Parliament explain the opposition to Schengen's Implementing Convention: The Intergovernmental procedure does not offer guarantees, in their opinion', 14 January, p. 12.

Agence Europe (1995) *Report of the Council on the Functioning of the Treaty on European Union*. Brussels: Council of the European Communities.

Agence Europe (1998) 'Viel Lärm – und ein Ja', *Süddeutsche Zeitung,* 30 May.

Bieber, R. and Monar, J. (eds) (1995) *Justice and Home Affairs in the European Union: The Development of the Third Pillar*. Brussels: European Interuniversity Press.

Boschi Orlandini, F. (1995) 'Europol and the Europol Drugs Unit: A cooperation structure in the making', in J. Monar and R. Morgan (eds), *The Third Pillar of the European Union*. Brussels: European Interuniversity Press, pp. 209–16.

Bourlanges, J. L. and Martin, D. (1995) *Report on the Functioning of the Treaty on European Union with a View to the 1996 Intergovernmental Conference – Implementation and Development of the Union: Explanatory Statement*. Brussels: European Parliament Committee on Institutional Affairs.

Collinson, S. (1994) 'Toward further harmonization? Migration policy in the European Union', *Studi Emigrazione,* vol. 31, pp. 210–37.

Commission (1994) *Communication from the Commission to the Council and the European Parliament on Immigration and Asylum Policies*. Brussels: Commission of the European Communities.

Commission (1995) *Bericht über die Funktionsweise des Vertrags über die Europäische Union*. Brussels: Commission of the European Communities.

Commission (1996) *Reinforcing Political Union and Preparing for Enlargement: Commission Opinion for the Intergovernmental Conference 1996*. Luxembourg: Office for the Official Publications of the European Communities.

Council of JHA Ministers (1996a) *Council Resolution of 20 June 1995 on Minimum Guarantees for Asylum Procedures*, Official Journal of the European Communities, Brussels, C 274 96 274/01, 19 September.

Council of JHA Ministers (1996b) *Standard form for determining the state responsible for examining an application for asylum*, Official Journal of the European Communities, Brussels, C 274 96 274/01, 19 September.

Council of the European Union (1996) *The European Union Today and Tomorrow, Adapting the European Union for the Benefit of Its Peoples and Preparing It for the Future: A General Outline for a Draft Revision of the Treaties*. Brussels: Council.

Curtin, D. and Meijers, H. (1995) 'The principle of Open Government in Schengen and the European Union: Democratic retrogression?', *Common Market Law Review*, vol. 32, pp. 391–442.

Devuyst, Y. (1997) 'The Treaty of Amsterdam: An introductory analysis', *ECSA Review*, vol. 10, pp. 6–14.

Edwards, G. and Pijpers, A. (eds) (1997) *The Politics of European Treaty Reform: The 1996 Intergovernmental Conference and Beyond*. London: Pinter.

European Communities (1987) *Single European Act*. Luxembourg: Office for the Official Publications of the European Communities.

Hix, S. (1995) *The 1996 Intergovernmental Conference and the Future of the Third Pillar*. Brussels: Churches Commission for Migrants in Europe.

Hix, S. and Niessen, J. (1996) *Reconsidering European Migration Policies: The 1996 Intergovernmental Conference and the Reform of the Maastricht Treaty*. Brussels: Churches Commission for Migrants in Europe.

Joly, D. (1996) *Haven or Hell? Asylum Policies and Refugees in Europe*. New York: St Martin's Press.

Koslowski, R. (1997) 'Migration and the democratic context of European political institutions', in E. M. Uçarer and D. J. Puchala (eds), *Immigration into Western Societies: Problems and Policies*. London: Pinter, pp. 70–94.

Lipsius, J. (1995) 'The 1996 Intergovernmental Conference', *European Law Review*, vol. 20, pp. 235–67.

Lobkowicz, W. de (1995) 'Intergovernmental cooperation in the field of migration – From the Single European Act to Maastricht', in J. Monar and R. Morgan (eds), *The Third Pillar of the European Union: Cooperation in the Fields of Justice and Home Affairs*. Brussels: European Interuniversity Press, pp. 99–122.

Marenin, O. (ed.) (1996) *Policing Change, Changing Police: International Perspectives*. New York: Garland Publishing.

Meijers, H. (1990) 'Refugees in Western Europe: 'Schengen' affects the entire Refugee Law', *International Journal of Refugee Law*, vol. 2, pp. 428–41.

Monar, J. and Morgan, R. (eds) (1995) *The Third Pillar of the European Union: Cooperation in the Fields of Justice and Home Affairs*. Brussels: European Interuniversity Press.

Monar, J. (1997) 'European Union – Justice and Home Affairs: A Balance Sheet and an Agenda for Reform', in G. Edwards and A. Pijpers (eds), *The Politics of European Treaty Reform: The 1996 Intergovernmental Conference and Beyond*. London: Pinter, pp. 326–39.

O'Keefe, D. (1995) 'Recasting the third pillar', *Common Market Law Review*, vol. 32, pp. 893–920.

O'Keefe, D. (1996) 'A critical view of the third pillar', in A. Pauly (ed.), *De Schengen à Maastricht: voie royale et course d'obstacles*. Maastricht: European Institute of Public Administration.

Petit, Michel (1998) 'The Treaty of Amsterdam', *Harvard Jean Monnet Chair Working Paper Series, no. 2*, Harvard Law School.

Plender, R. (1995) 'Asylum policy: Deficits of intergovernmental cooperation', in R. Bieber, and J. Monar (eds), *Justice and Home Affairs in the European Union: The Development of the Third Pillar*. Brussels: European Interuniversity Press, pp. 141–65.

Reflection Group (1995) *Progress Report on the 1996 Intergovernmental Conference*. Brussels: Reflection Group.

Uçarer, E. M. (1997) 'Europe's search for policy: The harmonization of asylum policy and European integration', In E. M. Uçarer and D. J. Puchala (eds), *Immigration into Western Societies: Problems and Policies*. London: Pinter, pp. 281–309.

Walker, N. (1998) 'Justice and Home Affairs', *International and Comparative Law Quarterly*, vol. 47, pp. 231–8.

PART 4

Key Issues

14

Enlargement

MICHAEL BAUN

Along with monetary union, the Eastern enlargement of the European Union is one of the defining issues of European integration in the 1990s and into the new millennium. The addition of up to 11 applicant countries – ten Central and Eastern European countries (CEECs) plus Cyprus – will have a profound impact on the character and functioning of the EU. Enlargement will affect the structure and operation of the EU's decision-making institutions, the Union's budgetary framework, and the design of key policies such as the Common Agricultural Policy (CAP) and the Structural Funds. It will also affect the EU's internal political cohesion and balance and its overall identity and sense of purpose. The precise impact of Eastern enlargement on the EU will be determined by a number of crucial decisions regarding whom to admit, when, and how, and internal institutional and policy reforms. As the chapter was written many of these decisions remained to be made, yet the process of debate and negotiation was well underway.

The chapter examines some of the key issues of Eastern enlargement. It begins by looking at the unique challenge posed by Eastern enlargement for the EU. The following two sections describe how Eastern enlargement moved to the top of the EU agenda, beginning with the revolutionary events of 1989 and leading to the key decisions of the Luxembourg European Council in December 1997. The actual launching of accession negotiations in early 1998 is also discussed. The chapter then examines the debate over the internal policy and institutional reforms that are a necessary precondition for enlargement. Included in this section are discussions of the Amsterdam Treaty and the Commission's *Agenda 2000* proposals which were in large part accepted by the member states at the March 1999 Berlin European Council. The chapter concludes by considering the impact of enlargement on the future functioning and direction of the EU.

The Challenge of Eastern Enlargement

Enlargement is an important feature of the EU's historical evolution and development. Since its founding as the European Economic Community in 1958, the EU has experienced four enlargements. In 1973, the United Kingdom, Ireland and Denmark joined the original six members of the Community. This was followed by Greece's admission in 1981, and the accession of Spain and Portugal in 1986. The most recent enlargement took place in 1995, with the entry of Austria, Finland and Sweden.

None of these enlargements were without problems or controversy. The UK only succeeded in joining in 1973 after having been rejected in its previous bids for membership by French President Charles de Gaulle. Even after de Gaulle, French doubts about the impact of UK membership on the Community's character and functioning remained. Greece was admitted despite concerns about its conflictual relations with Turkey and strong doubts about its economic preparedness for membership, while the Spanish and Portugese accessions spawned conflicts over agriculture and the budget. Even the entry of Austria, Finland and Sweden – three economically prosperous and democratically stable countries – raised concerns about the impact of enlargement on the EU's internal cohesion and political balance, and entry negotiations were threatened at the eleventh hour by objections over new procedures for qualified majority voting.

However, none of these enlargements posed the sort of massive challenge presented by Eastern enlargement. One important difference with previous enlargements is the sheer number of countries attempting to join in the present enlargement wave. Altogether, 11 applicant countries have been deemed eligible for membership by the EU: ten CEECs – Poland, Hungary, the Czech Republic, Slovakia, Romania, Bulgaria, Slovenia, Estonia, Latvia and Lithuania – and Cyprus. One additional applicant, Turkey, has been judged not ready for membership talks. This compares with a much smaller number of applicants – three or four, if Norway is included – in previous enlargement rounds. The number of prospective new members, and the fact that all except Poland are relatively small countries, has profound implications for the structure and operation of EU decision-making institutions. It will also ensure a much more heterogenous EU in terms of cultural values and economic and political interests.

Another important difference with previous enlargements is the relatively poor economic condition of the current applicants. As a group, the ten CEEC applicants have a per capita GDP that is less than one-third the EU average, and less than half that of the EU's four poorest current members. While previous enlargements also admitted countries that were far below the EU's economic level, what is different about this enlargement is the number of applicants and their combined population, meaning that the economic impact on the EU will be much larger. Whereas the three-country Mediterranean enlargement of the 1980s had the effect of reducing the EU's per capita GDP by 6 per cent, enlargement to 26 members is projected to lower this average (for a much larger EU) by 16 per cent (Commission, 1997a, pp. 109–10).

The economic status of the current applicants means that substantial reform of EU policies is a necessary precondition for enlargement. With more than 22 per cent of their labour force employed in agriculture (compared to 5 per cent in the current member states of the EU), the CEECs would be major recipients of CAP assistance. At the same time, expansion to 26 would more than double the EU population eligible for assistance under Objective 1 of the EU's Structural Funds (Commission, 1997a, pp. 111–13). Given the resistance of current member states to expanding the budget to accommodate increased spending on enlargement, it is apparent that both the CAP and the Structural Funds must be reformed before new countries can join. By contrast, previous enlargements had less of a budgetary impact because they were smaller, involved more economically developed countries, or took place in the context of economic growth and in the absence of budgetary constraints imposed by Economic and Monetary Union (EMU).

Also different from previous enlargements is the more extensive *acquis communautaire* which new member states will be required to accept. The accumulated laws, regulations and standards of the EU have grown substantially over the years, and now run to about 100,000 pages. Since 1990, when the CEECs first expressed an interest in joining the EU, European integration has deepened even further, not least because of the Treaty on European Union (1992) and the Amsterdam Treaty (1997). The CEECs will thus be joining an EU which is much more integrated and complex than the one joined by previous applicants, making their task of adjustment more formidable and the accession process more difficult. Moreover, in adopting the *acquis communautaire* the CEECs must overcome the handicap of their 40-year communist heritage and limited experience with the market economy and Western legal norms.

Another complicating factor is EMU. EMU was on the agenda before the 1989 revolution, but it took on added geopolitical urgency and significance after the fall of the Berlin Wall and German unification. As a result, EMU – and deepening more broadly – was given priority by the EU in the 1990s, and further enlargement will not occur until EMU is fully implemented in 2002. The EU is thus faced with the difficult challenge of balancing enlargement with its EMU agenda. Among other things, the restrictive economic requirements for EMU membership, and the post-EMU 'stability pact', have placed severe limits on public spending, including on enlargement.

Another factor differentiating Eastern enlargement from previous enlargements, and making it to some extent more problematic, is its geopolitical or security dimension. While previous enlargements occurred within the stable geopolitical context of a bipolar Europe, and within the Western half of Europe, Eastern enlargement is taking place in a less stable post-Cold War environment, and is itself part of the effort to redesign Europe's political and security architecture. EU enlargement is thus necessarily linked to broader security and geopolitical issues, including NATO expansion and Western relations with Russia. It is not surprising, therefore, that security and geopolitical considerations have affected decision-making on Eastern enlargement. Another area of important security and geopolitical implications concerns the Cypriot application and the question of EU relations with Turkey.

Finally, there is the 'German question'. Many of the applicant countries have close geographical, historical and cultural ties to Germany, and Germany is generally viewed as the chief economic beneficiary of Eastern enlargement. Thus, the common perception is that enlargement will enhance German power and influence within the EU. France in particular has worried that enlargement, by shifting the EU's centre of gravity eastwards, will diminish its own weight in the EU and weaken the crucial Franco-German partnership. Paris has therefore countered Germany's push for Eastern enlargement with efforts to strengthen the EU's Mediterranean policy. The desire of France and other member states to integrate a united Germany more closely into the EU has also been an important motive behind EMU and further deepening. The salience of the German question, and the impact of enlargement on the internal political balance of the EU, is thus another factor differentiating Eastern enlargement from previous enlargements.

The Promise of Membership

Before 1989 the EC's eastern boundary was determined by the Cold War and Soviet domination of Central and Eastern Europe. The collapse of communism removed this geopolitical barrier to EC enlargement, and the newly independent CEECs soon made it clear that membership in the EC was key to their goal of 'rejoining Europe'.

The EC's initial response focused on economic and technical assistance. Through its PHARE programme, the EC dispensed grants to promote economic reconstruction and transformation in the CEECs. The EC also sponsored the establishment of the European Bank for Reconstruction and Development (EBRD) in 1990 to foster development of the private sector and market economies in the reforming countries. Assistance in educational development was provided through the TEMPUS programme and in vocational training through the European Training Foundation (ETF). The EC also signed trade and cooperation agreements with the CEECs and reduced some restrictions on imports.

By early 1990, pressure from the CEECs for closer economic and political ties, and within the EC from certain member states (especially Germany, the UK and Denmark), led the Commission to propose a 'new approach' towards the CEECs. In August 1990, the Commission presented its proposal for association agreements ('Europe Agreements') with CEECs that made sufficient progress in economic and political reforms (Commission, 1990). Negotiations were soon begun with Poland, Hungary, and Czechoslovakia. Following a year of difficult bargaining, Europe Agreements were signed with these three countries in December 1991. Similar agreements were subsequently signed with other CEECs, and agreements were renegotiated with the Czech Republic and Slovakia after they became separate entities in 1993.

The Europe Agreements provided for an asymmetrical transition to free trade, with the EC lowering its barriers more quickly than the CEECs were required to do. They also provided for increased EC economic and financial assistance to the CEECs, and for the establishment of a bilateral 'political dialogue' and institutionalized consultation between the EC and associated countries. The trade provisions of the Europe Agreements were marred, however, by numerous exceptions and safeguard measures aimed at protecting 'sensitive industries' in the EC, such as coal and steel, textiles, and agriculture. These were precisely the industries of most importance to the CEECs, and the ones in which they had the greatest comparative advantage. Even more distressing for the CEECs was the absence in the Europe Agreements of any commitment to CEEC accession, or any clear indication that association was linked to eventual membership. Instead, the preamble of the Europe Agreements merely recognized the goal of membership as a 'final objective.' Even this limited statement met the strenuous objections of some member states.

One reason for the member states' reluctance to discuss accession was their preoccupation with internal reform at that time. In June 1989 the European Council had decided to launch a new intergovernmental conference (IGC) on monetary union. Both EMU and further political deepening then acquired greater importance with the opening of the Berlin Wall and the political changes in Eastern Europe. A common – although not unanimous – view in the EC was that internal deepening should have priority over enlargement, and that deepening was itself a necessary precondition for widening and the effective functioning of a larger EC. Thus, at the Dublin summit in April 1990 the European Council decided to begin parallel IGCs in December on EMU and political union. These would conclude at Maastricht in December 1991 with agreement on the TEU. This preoccupation with internal developments deflected the member states' attention from Central and Eastern Europe, and led the EC to view the CEECs largely as an 'external problem' (Rollo and Wallace, 1991).

Nevertheless, after Maastricht policy towards the CEECs began to change. In Lisbon in June 1992, the European Council endorsed the Commission's report on 'The Challenge of Enlargement', which examined the prospects of an EU of 20 or more members and called for a new form of 'partnership' with the CEECs (European Council, 1992a). The Lisbon European Council also instructed the Commission to report on the economic and political progress of the CEECs. The first official indication that the CEECs could eventually become members came at the December 1992 Edinburgh summit, where the heads of state and government declared that the next scheduled European Council in Copenhagen would 'reach decisions on the various components of the Commission's report in order to prepare the associate countries for accession to the Union' (European Council, 1992b, p. 94).

At the June 1993 Copenhagen summit, the European Council 'agreed that the associated countries in Central and Eastern Europe *shall* become members of the European Union' (emphasis added).

According to the European Council, 'Accession will take place as soon as an associated country is able to assume the obligations of membership by satisfying the economic and political conditions required.' These so-called 'Copenhagen' conditions included the achievement of stable institutions that guaranteed 'democracy, the rule of law, human rights and respect for and protection of minorities, the existence of a functioning market economy as well as the capacity to cope with competitive pressure and market forces within the Union'. A further condition was 'the Union's capacity to absorb new members while maintaining the momentum of European integration' (European Council, 1993, p. 86).

The Copenhagen summit was a major turning-point in EU policy towards the CEECs. Eastern enlargement was now on the agenda, although important decisions remained to be made about who would be admitted and when and how enlargement would occur. Supporting this change in policy was a coalition of actors which included: advocates of a more open policy within the Commission; pro-enlargement member states such as Germany, the UK, and Denmark; academic and policy experts who criticized the restrictive and short-sighted nature of the Europe Agreements; and business interests who saw economic opportunity in a more stable and integrated Central and Eastern Europe. Pressure also came from the CEECs themselves. In April 1994, Poland and Hungary became the first CEECs to formally apply for membership.

Following Copenhagen, and at the request of the June 1994 Corfu European Council, the Commission began work on devising a strategy to prepare the CEECs for accession. This effort was strongly supported by the German Government, which made integration of the CEECs a key goal of its EU presidency in the second half of 1994 (Kinkel, 1994). At the Essen European Council in December 1994, a 'pre-accession' strategy for Eastern Europe was accordingly approved. A key feature of this strategy was the establishment of a multilateral 'structured relationship', consisting of regular meetings between the EU and CEECs at different levels, from the heads of state and government down. The EU also promised to give prospective members a detailed set of guidelines for aligning their economies and legal systems with those of the internal market, and promised financial assistance for these necessary adjustments (European Council, 1994).

In May 1995, the Commission presented its White Paper detailing the specific administrative and legal reforms that the CEECs would have to make in preparation for accession (Commission, 1995a). The European Council approved the White Paper, along with new financial assistance for the CEECs, in Cannes in June 1995. The Cannes summit also approved a Mediterranean aid package directed primarily at Northern Africa as part of the internal EU political bargain underlying the pre-accession strategy (European Council, 1995a).

The Negotiations Begin

With the pre-accession strategy approved, attention turned to the questions of a timetable for Eastern enlargement and the countries to be included. The German Government favoured a relatively quick enlargement that involved only a few countries. During a visit to Warsaw in July 1995, Chancellor Kohl declared that Poland, Hungary, and the Czech Republic would be in the EU by 2000, thus becoming the first European leader publicly to set a date for enlargement (Economist, 1995). Germany argued that negotiations with these three countries should begin six months after the conclusion of the 1996 IGC, to coincide with the beginning of entry negotiations with Cyprus (Barber, 1995a). The decision on a starting date for negotiations with Cyprus had been made in March 1995, as a concession to Greece in return for its approval of an EU customs union agreement with Turkey.

Germany's push for an enlargement limited to the countries on its eastern border provoked a response from the Nordic member states, especially Sweden and Finland, who had their own political and economic reasons for wanting the three Baltic countries included in the next enlargement wave. They argued that rather than allowing Germany's geopolitical preferences to determine the extent of enlargement, new members should be admitted on the basis of their adherence to objective entry criteria. In their demand that all applicants should be treated equally, the Nordic countries drew important support from the French Government (Barber, 1995b; Barber and White, 1995).

At the Madrid summit in December 1995, the European Council agreed to begin accession negotiations with the CEECs soon after conclusion of the IGC due to begin in March 1996, to coincide with the launching of negotiations with Cyprus. The European Council asked the Commission to prepare detailed opinions on each of the

CEECs' applications, and promised that all applicants would be treated equally. The European Council also asked the Commission to prepare a report on the impact of enlargement on the CAP and structural policies, and on the EU's future financial framework (European Council, 1995b, pp. 47–8). With the IGC expected to end sometime in early or mid 1997, the Madrid decisions opened the prospect of accession negotiations beginning in early 1998 at the latest.

An important question for the EU was how to treat applicant countries that were not deemed ready to begin entry negotiations at that time. Specifically, the EU wanted to ease the 'dual rejection shock' for CEECs not included in the first wave of either EU or NATO enlargement, with the latter organization moving towards a decision to admit Poland, Hungary and the Czech Republic in 1999. One solution, initially advanced by the French Government, was to create a standing 'European Conference' that would include all EU member states and all applicant countries. This conference would exist in parallel to actual accession negotiations with a smaller group of countries that were deemed better prepared for membership and, in the words of German Foreign Minister Klaus Kinkel, would allow the EU to 'differentiate without discriminating' among the applicant countries (Kinkel 1996).

Various models for the accession negotiations were proposed. In addition to the possibility of beginning negotiations with only a select group of countries, the 'regatta' or 'starting line' model was suggested, whereby all applicant countries would begin negotiations together, although negotiations with some of the applicants would proceed at a faster pace. Kinkel also proposed something called the 'stadium' model, in which negotiations would begin with a smaller group of countries, yet those applicants not chosen as part of the first group could later join or even overtake the fast-track group if they made sufficient progress with their economic and political reforms (Urban, 1997).

In July 1997, the Commission presented its report on enlargement, entitled *Agenda 2000*, along with its opinions on the individual applications (Commission 1997a, 1997b). On the basis of these opinions, which assessed the preparedeness of applicant countries in accordance with the Copenhagen conditions, the Commission recommended that accession negotiations be initiated with five CEECs – Poland, Hungary, the Czech Republic, Estonia and Slovenia – and Cyprus. The selection of the first three CEECs was expected, as they were generally considered to be the most advanced in their economic and political reforms. The decision to include Estonia and Slovenia in the 'fast-track' group was somewhat more surprising, and was made only after considerable debate within the Commission. While both of these countries were deemed to have met the Copenhagen conditions, their selection also reflected geopolitical considerations. By including them in the first group, the Commission sought to counter the possible negative effects of the limited NATO enlargement, and to make EU enlargement more geographically balanced by giving it both a northern and southern dimension (Avery and Cameron, 1998, p. 43; Grabbe and Hughes, 1998, p. 58).

To prepare these six and the other applicants for membership, the Commission proposed reinforcing the pre-accession strategy through increased aid for agriculture and infrastructure development and the approval of bilateral 'Accession Partnerships'. The latter would involve commitments by applicants to meet political and economic goals by specific deadlines and a precise timetable for adoption of the *acquis communautaire*, coupled with increased EU financial and technical assistance. The Commission also endorsed the idea of a standing European Conference that would include all current and aspiring member states and would meet yearly (Commission, 1997a, pp. 39–59).

With the Commission's report and recommendations in hand, the European Council had to decide when to begin accession negotiations and with whom at its December meeting in Luxembourg. In the run-up to the Luxembourg summit, debate focused on two issues. The first was the concern of applicant countries not recommended for inclusion in the first group that they would be excluded from accession negotiations or permanently relegated to a slow track for membership. In particular, the two remaining Baltic states and Romania pressed their case for inclusion. The second issue was the question of what to do about Turkey, which had applied for membership in 1987 but had since been held at arm's length by the EU. For a variety of economic, political, and cultural reasons, most member states had little interest in admitting Turkey, and Greece was particularly opposed to Ankara's inclusion in the enlargement process. Before the Luxembourg summit, the Greek Government even threatened to block plans for the European Conference if Turkey was invited to attend (Barber, 1997).

At the Luxembourg summit, the European Council made a number of historic decisions regarding Eastern enlargement. Foremost among these was its decision to begin the accession process in late March 1998, with a meeting of the foreign ministers of the 15 EU member states and the ten CEEC applicants and Cyprus. Following this largely symbolic event, bilateral intergovernmental negotiations would begin with each of the five CEEC applicants recommended by the Commission, and with Cyprus. For the remaining five applicants, a slower track for membership was agreed that would involve participation in a screening process to assess compliance with the *acquis communautaire* and a yearly review of progress. For these countries, the possibility existed of joining the formal accession negotiations once sufficient progress in adopting economic and political reforms was made. The European Council also endorsed the Commission's proposals for pre-accession partnerships and increased pre-accession aid for the CEECs (European Council, 1997).

The Luxembourg summit was clouded by the dispute over Turkey. While the European Council affirmed Turkey's eligibility for EU membership, it nevertheless declared that Turkey would not be allowed to join the enlargement process because it did not yet meet the necessary economic and political conditions for membership. The EU sought to assuage Turkey by inviting it to attend the inaugural meeting of the European Conference – this now being the conference's chief purpose – and by drawing up a new strategy to prepare Turkey for future accession (European Council, 1997). However, these measures did little to diminish Turkey's anger at being excluded from the enlargement process. Instead, the Turkish Government harshly criticized the Luxembourg decisions, and subsequently boycotted the European Conference, which was held in London in March 1998. Turkey's anger with the EU also threatened to inflame the Cyprus situation and further complicate accession negotiations with Cyprus.

As planned, the enlargement negotiations were offically launched at a foreign ministers' meeting on 30–1 March 1998 in London. On the first day of this meeting, the ten CEEC applicants were presented with their individual accession partnerships. On the following day, accession negotiations between the EU and the fast-track (or '5 + 1') group of countries were formally begun. In April the screening process was launched, to assess each applicant country's compliance with specific chapters of the *acquis communautaire*. After an initial meeting with all 11 applicants, screening for each of the two groups proceeded separately. By late summer 1998, the screening of 11 out of 29 chapters had been completed for the 'fast-track' group, and the actual intergovernmental negotiations on some of the screened chapters began in November (*Agence Europe*, 1998a).

While the exact timetable of entry negotiations remains uncertain, the talks are sure to be lengthy and difficult. Among the contentious issues to be discussed will be the demands of the applicant countries for temporary derogations from EU laws and regulations, particularly those pertaining to the environment, social policy, and state supports for industry. The CEECs will also insist on early inclusion in the CAP and the immediate applicability of EU laws governing the free movement of labour. For their part, the current member states will seek to protect jobs and national shares of EU financial assistance – for instance, by demanding temporary restrictions on labour migration and lengthy transitional periods for CEEC participation in the CAP. Another contentious issue is certain to be the control of borders with non-member states, such as Poland's border with Ukraine.

Preparing the EU for Enlargement

Whereas in all previous enlargements the burden of adjustments was borne by the new members, Eastern enlargement also requires substantial internal EU reform. One such reform involves decision-making institutions, not least because the present EU of 15 countries operates with an institutional system originally designed for six member states. The view that institutional reform was necessary for a larger EU to function effectively was first expressed in the Commission's 1992 study on 'The Challenge of Enlargement' (Commission, 1992), and was repeatedly stressed by the European Council.

The question of institutional reform was in any case high on the agenda of the 1996 IGC. Among the possible reforms under discussion were: reducing the size of the Commission; the re-weighting of votes in the Council; and the extended use of qualified majority voting. In the end, however, the IGC failed to reach agreement on the key issues. Instead, a protocol was attached to the Amsterdam Treaty which specified that a new IGC on institutional reform must be called 'At least one year before the membership of the European Union exceeds twenty' (Treaty of Amsterdam, 1997, p. 111). In this manner, resolution of this contentious issue was put off for later. This failure was greeted with considerable dismay by the Commission, which in its *Agenda 2000* report proposed that a new IGC 'be convened as soon as possible after 2000 to produce a thorough reform' of the EU's institutions (Commission, 1997a, p. 13).

Also requiring adjustment in advance of further enlargement are the CAP and structural policies. Without such reform, the admission of relatively poor and farm-intensive CEECs could bankrupt the EU budget. Thorough reform of these policies, which together absorbed 80 per cent of EU spending in 1998, is even more necessary in view of the refusal of current member states to expand the size of the EU budget to pay for enlargement.

In its *Agenda 2000* report, the Commission proposed reducing support prices paid to farmers for grain, beef, dairy, and other products by up to a third, thereby forcing European farmers to be more competitive in world markets. It also proposed shifting EU assistance from price subsidies to direct income payments, with a limit on the amount of aid that individual farmers could receive. The Commission also favoured incorporating agriculture policy into a more coherent rural aid policy, by integrating it with environmental and structural policies, and allowing individual member states greater freedom in deciding how to allocate aid in keeping with the subsidiarity principle. The Commission argued, however, that even with these reforms new CEEC entrants would require a lengthy transition period before their full integration into the CAP. During this period, the new members would receive assistance to help them modernize their agricultural sectors (Commission, 1997a, pp. 29–33).

The Commission's proposals for reform of the structural policies were equally far-reaching. The Commission proposed consolidating structural operations by reducing the seven 'objectives' for structural spending to three and tightening up the eligibility requirements for assistance. Altogether, the Commission's plans would reduce the percentage of the EU population receiving structural assistance from around 50 per cent to between 35 and 40 per cent. The Commission also proposed shifting funding away from projects in poor regions and towards the broader struggle against unemployment, although it recommended maintaining Cohesion Fund assistance to the poorest member states. According to the Commission's plan, by 2006 the percentage of structural assistance going to new member states would grow to around one-third of the total. Seeking to prevent conflict over Structural Funds reforms from generating opposition to enlargement, the Commission argued that such reforms were not necessitated solely by enlargement, but would have been required in any case (Commission, 1997a, pp. 21–6).

In presenting its proposed financial framework for the period 2000–6, the Commission argued that Eastern enlargement could be accomplished without any increased budgetary contributions from member states. Instead, EU spending could be kept within the 1.27 per cent of GNP limit established by the Edinburgh European Council in 1992. The Commission's financial perspective included spending on agricultural and structural assistance for new members and pre-accession aid for CEECs not included in the first enlargement wave. The Commission also argued that, while the next enlargement would 'inevitably provoke a deterioration in the budgetary positions of all the current Member States', it should not 'lead to major changes in [their] relative budgetary positions', nor to increased national contributions. Neverthless, the Commission warned that further enlargement, beyond the first wave of six, would probably require raising the EU spending ceiling and reforming more fundamentally the financial system (Commission, 1997a, pp. 66–9).

The Commission's *Agenda 2000* proposals were criticized by both national governments and interest groups. Farmers' organizations and the agriculture ministers of most member states complained about the reduction of quotas and price supports and the limits on direct payments called for in the Commission's report. Many national and regional governments were also concerned about losing Structural Fund assistance. Spain and other poor member states were sceptical about the Commission's claims that enlargement could be financed within the existing budgetary framework, and expressed concern that enlargement would lead to a reduction in their own Structural and Cohesion Fund assistance. Wealthy member states, such as Germany and the Netherlands, responded by demanding a reduction of their contributions.

In March 1998, the Commission published its detailed legislative proposals for achieving the *Agenda 2000* goals. In doing so it expressed the hope that the necessary reforms could be agreed to by the end of 1999 so that enlargement negotiations could proceed (Commission, 1998). In June 1998 in Cardiff, the European Council agreed on the necessity of adopting the *Agenda 2000* reforms before the next European Parliament elections in June 1999, and discussed holding a special European Council under the German Presidency in early 1999 to reach agreement on the reform package (*Agence Europe*, 1998b, pp. 2 and 5; European Council, 1998, p. 8). A special summit was duly held in Berlin in March 1999 and agreement was reached on an overall *Agenda 2000* package.

Eastern Enlargement and Integration

All previous enlargements have affected the basic character and identity of the EU. The admission of Britain, Ireland and Denmark added a more liberal and sceptical dimension to the EU, bringing in two countries (the UK and Ireland) that valued their transatlantic ties and, two that did not wholly accept the political goals of European integration (the UK and Denmark). The 1980s enlargements gave the EU a decidedly more Mediterranean and Southern European profile, while also making it relatively poorer and more agricultural. The addition of Greece also imported potential problems with Turkey. The accession of Sweden, Austria and Finland countered the economic impact of Southern enlargement to some extent, while adding countries which favoured free trade and possessed strong social-democratic traditions. By adding countries with strong geographical and historical ties to Central and Eastern Europe, the latter enlargement also expanded the internal coalition for Eastern enlargement.

Eastern enlargement will likely have an even more profound impact on the EU than previous enlargements, however. With the addition of the CEECs, the EU will become relatively poorer and more agricultural. In addition, the EU's political centre of gravity will shift eastwards, with profound implications for the Union's internal political balance. Eastern enlargement will also bring into the EU new external problems and concerns, affecting, for instance, relations with Russia. Most importantly, because of the number of new members and their specific economic and political conditions, as a result of further enlargement the EU will be much larger and more heterogenous in terms of its cultural values and political and economic interests. In a Community of 21 or more member states, achieving agreement will be necessarily more difficult and intra-EU bargaining more complex.

A key question regarding Eastern enlargement, therefore, is whether it will lead to a looser and more intergovernmental EU, thus ending forever federalist dreams of an 'ever closer union'. History suggests that this may not be the inevitable result, since previous enlargements also served as catalysts for further institutional innovation, thus proving that widening and deepening of the EU are not necessarily contradictory processes. The United Kingdom's entry was linked to the creation of the European Regional Development Fund (ERDF). The Mediterranean enlargement of the 1980s helped bring about a budgetary compromise at Fontainebleau in 1984 that paved the way for the single market project and the Single European Act (SEA), while also resulting in an expansion of regional policy. The more recent Northern enlargement, together with the prospect of Eastern enlargement, has stimulated discussion of the institutional reforms necessary for a larger EU to function effectively, including the greater use of majority voting.

Nevertheless, in an EU of up to 26 countries the sheer number and diversity of national and regional interests could make further integration more difficult. For this reason, the prospect of Eastern enlargement has sparked renewed discussion of the concept of a multi-speed or two-tiered Union. Such ideas have been in circulation since the 1970s, in response to the EC's first enlargement. They have attracted growing attention more recently, however, particularly with the publication in September 1994 by Germany's governing Christian Democratic Union/Christian Social Union (CDU/CSU) of a paper proposing the creation of a 'core Europe'. According to this paper, a select group of the economically able and politically willing member states, led by France and Germany, would proceed with further economic and political union, leaving other countries to catch up later (CDU/CSU, 1994). Former Commission President Jacques Delors has also advocated the creation of 'two Europes': a broader one in which all members share in the benefits of the single market and subject themselves to certain basic economic regulations; and a narrower one 'restricted to a few countries whose ambitions would be higher and which would like Europe to play a role in the world that conforms to its vocation of universality' (*Agence Europe*, 1998c, p. 2). The potential for greater differentiation within the EU is also inherent in provisions of the Amsterdam Treaty which institutionalize the principle of 'flexibility' (Stubb, 1998).

The emergence of a two-tier Europe is one way in which Eastern enlargement, rather than contributing to a looser and more intergovernmental EU, might instead promote deeper integration among a core group of countries and accelerate the integration process overall. In any case, the future shape of the EU – whether two-tier, 'variable geometry', or some other pattern – will be greatly affected by the outcome of accession negotiations with the CEECs and Cyprus. Indeed, the efforts of the EU simultaneously to widen and deepen, together with the less-developed economic status of the CEECs and the extensiveness of the acquis communitaire, pose the question of whether Eastern enlargement can be accomplished using the 'classical Community method' (Preston, 1997), entailing full membership with only limited transitional periods or derogations in certain areas before full adherence to EU regulations and standards. Whereas previous enlargements have followed this approach, the special circumstances and problems of Eastern enlargement raise the question of whether an alternative method, perhaps involving accession in stages or a variable geometry approach, might not be more appropriate. Such alternatives have thus far been rejected by the applicant countries – who do not want to be accorded second-class status – and by current member states – who fear a dilution of EU institutions and of the *acquis communautaire*. Thus far the EU has ruled out any partial adoption of the *acquis communautaire* (Commission, 1997a, pp. 44–5). Nevertheless, the difficulties of the current accession process and the potential irreconcilability of widening and deepening could force reconsideration of alternative approaches and result in new patterns of integration in the future.

Conclusion

There is no doubt that Eastern enlargement will have important long-term consequences for the EU. Nevertheless, the EU is committed to further enlargement and has formally begun accession negotiations with five CEECs and Cyprus. Five additional CEECs are engaged in accession preparations with the EU, and hope to join the negotiations soon. No official target date for entry has been given, although it is commonly accepted that new members could join sometime between 2003 and 2005.

While the enlargement process is moving forward and has assumed an air of inevitability, there are numerous potential obstacles that could delay the accession of new members or threaten enlargement altogether. One of these is the Cyprus issue and the EU's relations with Turkey. The EU has begun accession talks with the Cypriot Government, yet most member states are against admitting a divided Cyprus, or a Cyprus whose internal tensions remain unresolved. In fact, while the EU has initiated accession talks with Cyprus, it has warned both the Cypriot and Greek Governments that EU entry is not automatic, and that a political settlement for the island is essential. The EU thus clings to the hope that accession negotiations will spur progress toward a settlement. The Greek Government has threatened to block any further enlargement if Cyprus is not admitted, however, thereby holding Eastern enlargement hostage to the

Cyprus question. An important key to a political settlement for Cyprus is held by Turkey, which could seek to further escalate tensions on the island if its demands for closer ties are not granted by the EU. In other words, the Cyprus issue has the potential to impede, or at least greatly complicate, the entire enlargement process.

Another potential obstacle is the issue of institutional reform. After the failure to agree on institutional reform at Amsterdam some member states, including France and Belgium, demanded that institutional changes be agreed before any new members are admitted, not before EU membership expands to more than 20 countries, as stipulated in the Amsterdam Treaty. Although they agree on the need for institutional reform before enlargement, the French and Belgian Governments have very different views on the nature and direction of these reforms. Nevertheless, their demands raise the prospect that France and other member states could block enlargement unless they get a satisfactory deal on institutional reform.

A further obstacle is whether the *Agenda 2000* reforms will be enough for the challenge of enlargement. The possibility exists that the debate over these reforms could become increasingly entangled with domestic politics. Accession negotiations will also have to overcome popular fears about increased foreign competition and labour migration – especially in border states like Austria and Germany – which could fuel domestic opposition to enlargement in some member states. Thus far domestic politics have not been much of a factor in the enlargement debate, but they have the potential to suddenly become one.

Also posing a potential problem for enlargement is EMU. The single currency was launched in January 1999, with 11 participating countries. Euro notes and coins will come into circulation in January 2002, and will be sole legal tender in EMU countries from 1 July 2002. From the outset it has been clear that EMU has priority over Eastern enlargement, and that a precondition for further enlargement will be the successful implementation of EMU. Despite satisfactory progress to date, however, EMU remains a highly problematic enterprise, with uncertain prospects for success. Because of its importance for the EU, an EMU crisis or failure would have a tremendous impact on the enlargement process, although it is impossible to say exactly what the full implications for enlargement of such developments would be.

The applicant countries, in the meantime, will no doubt experience problems in adopting the voluminous and detailed *acquis communautaire*. The upcoming negotiations over the nature and length of derogations and transitional periods, both those requested by the applicants and those demanded by member states, are also certain to be lengthy and difficult. For a number of reasons, therefore, while Eastern enlargement is on the EU agenda, it is still far from an accomplished fact.

Guide to Further Reading

For historical and theoretical overviews of EU enlargement, see Preston (1997), Miles, Redmond and Schwok (1995), and the chapters in Laurent and Maresceau (1998). Michalski and Wallace (1992) portray the challenge of impending enlargement for a deepening Community of twelve, while Redmond and Rosenthal (1998) examine the impact of past and future enlargements on EU institutions and policies. Sedelmeier and Wallace (1996) give a detailed account of the development of EU policy towards the CEECs after 1989, while Grabbe and Hughes (1998) examine the issues behind the EU's 1997 decisions on enlargement. Avery and Cameron (1998) provide an insiders' account of those decisions. For analysis of the Cyprus application and the problems it presents, see Nugent (1998).

References

Agence Europe (1998a) *Europe Daily Bulletin*, no. 7270, 25 July, p. 4.

Agence Europe (1998b) *Europe Daily Bulletin*, no. 7243, 17 June, pp 2–5.

Agence Europe (1998c) *Europe Daily Bulletin*, no. 7215, 6 May, pp 2–3.

Avery, G. and Cameron, F. (1998) *The Enlargement of the European Union*. Sheffield: Sheffield Academic Press.

Barber, L. (1995a) 'Kohl Draws Line Across Europe', *Financial Times*, 14 December, p. 1.

Barber, L. (1995b) 'Union Struggles to Regain its Sense of Direction', *Financial Times*, 15 December, p. 2.

Barber, L. (1997) 'Greece Threatens to Block Meeting', *Financial Times*, 9 December, p. 2.

Barber, L. and White, D. (1995) 'Partial Success for Kohl over EU Enlargement', *Financial Times*, 18 December, p. 18.

CDU/CSU-Fraktion des Deutschen Bundestages (1994) 'Reflections on European Policy', Bonn, 1 September.

Commission (1990) *Association Agreements with the Countries of Central and Eastern Europe: A General Outline*, COM (90)398 final, 27 August.

Commission (1992) *Europe and the Challenge of Enlargement*, Bulletin of the European Communities, Supplement 3/92.

Commission (1995a) *White Paper: Preparation of the Associated Countries of Central and Eastern Europe for Integration into the Internal Market of the Union*, COM (95) 163 final, Brussels, 3 May.

Commission (1995b) *The European Councils: Conclusions of the Presidency 1992–1994*. Brussels: European Commission.

Commission (1997a) *Agenda 2000: For A Stronger and Wider Union*, Bulletin of the European Union, Supplement 5/97.

Commission (1997b) *Commission Opinions*, Bulletin of the European Union, Supplements 6–15/97.

Commission (1997c) *Treaty of Amsterdam*, Luxembourg: Office for Official Publications of the European Communities.

Commission (1998) 'Agenda 2000: The Legislative Proposals', IP/98/258, Brussels, 18 March.

Economist (1995) 'Just Do It: Germany and Eastern Europe', 15 July, pp 35–6.

European Council (1992a) 'Presidency Conclusions: European Council in Lisbon, 26–27 June 1992', in *The European Councils* (1995), pp 5–29.

European Council (1992b) *Conclusions of the Presidency: European Council in Edinburgh, 11–12 December 1992*. Luxembourg: Office for Official Publications of the European Communities.

European Council (1993) 'Presidency Conclusions: European Council in Copenhagen, 21–22 June 1993', in *The European Councils* (1995), pp 81–98.

European Council (1994) 'Presidency Conclusions: European Council in Essen, 9–10 December 1994', in *The European Councils* (1995), pp 139–64.

European Council (1995a) 'Presidency Conclusions: Cannes European Council, 26–27 June 1995', in *The European Councils* (1995), pp 5–36.

European Council (1995b) 'Presidency Conclusions: Madrid European Council, 15–16 December 1995', in *The European Councils* (1995), pp 37–103.

European Council (1997) 'Presidency Conclusions', Luxembourg European Council, 12–13 December 1997.

European Council (1998) 'Presidency Conclusions, Cardiff European Council, 15–16 June 1998', in Europe Documents, no. 2094–2095, 18 June 1998.

Grabbe, H. and Hughes, K. (1998) *Enlarging the EU Eastwards*. London: RIIA.

Kinkel, K. (1994) 'Germany in Europe: The Aims of the German Presidency of the European Union', *Statements and Speeches*, vol. 17, no. 7. New York: German Information Center.

Kinkel, K. (1996) 'Ost-Erweiterung der Europäischen Union-Chance und Herausforderung', Speech on 12 November 1996 in Hamburg, German Foreign Ministry Web page at www.auswaertiges-amt.government.de/de/europa/r961114.htm

Laurent, P.-H. and Maresceau, M. (eds) (1998) *The State of the European Union*, Vol. 4: Deepening and Widening. Boulder and London: Lynne Rienner.

Michalski, A., and Wallace, H. (1992) *The European Community and the Challenge of Enlargement*. London: RIIA.

Miles, L., Redmond, J., and Schwok, R. (1995) 'Integration Theory and Enlargement of the European Union', in C. Rhodes and S. Mazey (eds), *The State of the European Union, Vol. 3: Building a European Polity?*. Boulder: Lynne Rienner, pp 177–94.

Nugent, N. (1998) 'Cyprus and the European Union: A Particularly Difficult Membership Application', *Mediterranean Politics*, vol. 2, no. 3 pp. 53–75.

Preston, C. (1997) *Enlargement and Integration in the European Union*. London and New York: Routledge.
Redmond, J., and Rosenthal, G. G. (eds) (1998) *The Expanding European Union: Past, Present, Future*. Boulder, CO and London: Lynne Rienner.
Rollo, J. and Wallace, H. (1991) 'New Patterns of Partnership', in G. Bonvicini *et al.*, *The Community and the Emerging European Democracies*. London: RIIA, pp 53–64.
Sedelmeier, U., and Wallace, H. (1996) 'Policies Towards Central and Eastern Europe', in H. Wallace and W. Wallace (eds), *Policy-Making in the European Union*, 3rd edn. Oxford: Oxford University Press, pp 353–87.
Stubb, A. C.-G. (1998) 'The Amsterdam Treaty and Flexible Integration', *ECSA Review*, vol. XI, no. 2, pp 1–5.
Urban, T. (1997) 'Neues Konzept für die Erweiterung', *Süddeutsche Zeitung*, 20 October.

15

Treaty Change in the European Union: The Amsterdam Experience

DESMOND DINAN

This chapter explores the origin, preparation, negotiation and conclusion of the Amsterdam Treaty in 1997, the most recent instance of treaty change in the European Union (EU). Treaty changes are major events in the EU, involving a complicated and protracted interplay among member states, institutions, issues, interests and individuals. The Amsterdam Treaty is the culmination of a series of major treaty reforms that began with the Single European Act (SEA) in 1986 and continued with the Treaty on European Union (TEU) in 1992. Together, these treaty changes have fundamentally recast the EU bargain, extended the EU's scope and altered the EU's decision-making dynamics. The Amsterdam Treaty foresees further treaty change, but not of the multifaceted kind that characterized the SEA, TEU and the Amsterdam Treaty itself.

Method and Significance of Treaty Change

Changes to the EU's founding treaties – the Treaty Establishing the European Community (TEC) and the TEU – are made in accordance with Article 48 of the TEU (ex Article N, TEU and Article 236, TEC). In essence, Article 48 stipulates that any member state or the Commission may suggest a treaty amendment to the Council; if the Council, having consulted the Commission and the European Parliament (EP), decides to pursue the matter, the Council Presidency may convene 'a conference of representatives of the governments of the

Member States' (that is, an intergovernmental conference) to negotiate and agree 'by common accord' (that is, unanimity) changes to the treaties. The changes become effective once ratified by the member states in accordance with their respective constitutional requirements. Depending on the country and on the nature of the proposed change, ratification may require a referendum.

An intergovernmental conference (IGC), whose duration is not limited under the terms of the treaty, is the central event in the process of treaty change, bracketed on one side by a preparatory stage and on the other by a ratification stage (both of indeterminate length). Originally, IGCs were discreet affairs, quietly prepared by a Council sub-committee, quickly negotiated by the Council itself, and effortlessly ratified by member states. The issues they dealt with were sometimes insignificant for the Community as a whole, like the convention relating to the Netherlands Antilles (1962), and sometimes important, like the treaty modifying certain budgetary provisions (1970). Either way, these early treaty changes were expeditious, uncomplicated, and attracted little public interest.

Today, by contrast, IGCs are major events in the political life of the EU. Beginning with the 1985 IGC that resulted in the SEA and culminating in the 1996–7 IGC that brought about the Amsterdam Treaty, IGCs have been transformed into lengthy, complex, factious bargaining sessions, subject to scrutiny by a sceptical public. Not only do IGCs require extensive preparation, but ratification has become contentious and unpredictable in many member states, thereby risking nullification of the proposed amendments.

Treaty change has assumed such importance in the EU because the political stakes of European integration are so much higher than in the past, thanks in large part to IGCs themselves. The point is somewhat circular: the SEA deepened European integration by extending the EC's scope and strengthening its supranational institutions; as a result, public unease about the EC increased and some member states became more Eurosceptical; the TEU, which emerged from the 1991 IGCs on monetary union and political union, further deepened European integration; the ensuing ratification crisis of 1992 and 1993 demonstrated the extent of public dissatisfaction with the emerging EU; by the time the 1996–7 IGC opened, an increasingly wary public, and an increasingly recalcitrant UK and Denmark, greatly constrained the IGC's potential. It was little wonder that, compared to the SEA and the TEU, the Amsterdam Treaty contained few major innovations or advances for European integration.

Of course, IGCs are an expression, not a cause, of member states' efforts to strengthen integration procedurally and/or substantively. The impetus for IGCs comes from changing political and economic circumstances, regionally and globally, to which a majority of member states believe that they can respond best by strengthening the EU's decision-making procedures and policy competence. Yet the outcome of IGCs is often messy and confusing, reflecting the participants' diverse interests and preferences and the dynamics of the negotiations themselves.

The complexity of IGCs also reflects the complexity of the broader EU system. Although unique in many respects, IGCs are characteristic of general EU bargaining and decision-making. Supranational actors – the Commission and EP – play an increasingly prominent role in agenda-setting and decision-shaping, either alone or, more likely, in alliance with each other and with sympathetic member states. The incursion of supranationalism into an avowedly intergovernmental process reflects the blending of supranationalism and intergovernmentalism throughout the EU system. It also casts doubt on the liberal intergovernmental view of treaty change, which dismisses the importance of supranational actors in shaping large interstate bargains.

Origin and Impetus

The origin of the 1996–7 IGC differed markedly from those of 1985 and 1991. The 1985 and 1991 IGCs came about because of a momentum toward deeper integration, driven initially by global economic challenges and later also by profound geostrategic changes (the end of the Cold War and German unification). The increasing intensity and complexity of integration called for institutional and decision-making changes to improve the EU's efficiency and legitimacy.

By contrast, the 1996–7 IGC took place because it was mandated under the terms of the TEU, Article N.2 of which stipulated that an IGC would be convened in 1996. This stipulation was made mainly at the behest of Member states which were dissatisfied with the outcome of the 1991 IGC. Amongst other things those member states that had failed in 1991 to persuade the others to incorporate the Western European Union (WEU) into the EU hoped that they might succeed in doing so five years later, not least because of the expiration of the WEU Treaty in 1998.

The TEU ratification crisis quickly dispelled any hope that a review conference in 1996 would be a good opportunity to deepen European integration either substantively or procedurally. Given the unpopularity of the TEU, talk of a possible 'Maastricht II' became less and less prevalent in the mid-1990s. Under the circumstances, it seems surprising that the IGC went ahead at all. However, because Article N.2 was one of the TEU's most explicit provisions, member states and EU institutions feared that abandoning the follow-up IGC was not only legally impossible, but also more risky politically than proceeding with it.

In the meantime, the IGC had acquired new functions when the European Council decided to confirm or amend at the IGC an inter-institutional agreement of October 1993 about the distinction between compulsory and noncompulsory expenditure, and to re-examine at the IGC an inter-institutional modus vivendi of December 1994 on comitology. This illustrates an important, although generally overlooked purpose of recent IGCs: to formalize inter-institutional agreements which themselves constitute informal treaty changes.

It was the far-reaching institutional implications of enlargement, however, rather than these relatively minor procedural issues, that emerged in the mid-1990s as the main rationale for another IGC. In the early 1990s EU enlargement into Central and Eastern Europe had seemed likely but remote; by the mid-1990s it seemed inevitable and relatively imminent. An EU of up to ten new Central and Eastern European member states, plus Cyprus and Malta, would presumably be unworkable without major institutional change, notably by reducing the number of Commissioners and re-weighting votes in the Council. The link between enlargement and institutional reform was apparent during the accession negotiations with Austria, Finland, Norway and Sweden in 1993 and 1994. Unwilling to undertake major reform before three of these countries joined in 1995 (Norway chose to stay outside), but aware of the looming accession of some or all of the Central and Eastern European states, the European Council decided to put institutional and decision-making change at the top of the IGC's agenda.

Asked in October 1995 why an IGC was going to be held in 1996, Carlos Westendorp, then chair of the pre-IGC Reflection Group, answered that 'it is indispensable to carry out (institutional) reforms that will allow us to admit new members without risk to them or to us' (International Herald Tribune, 1995, p. 3). Earlier, at the Group's first substantive meeting, Westendorp had asked his colleagues why they thought the IGC was necessary; all agreed that it should take place 'to make enlargement possible' (*Agence Europe*, June 6/7 1995, p. 2). Based on the recent accession of three new member states and the impending accession of many more, institutional reform ostensibly became the main impetus for the 1996 IGC.

Preparation

Of the four IGCs held since 1985, the 1996–7 conference was by far the most thoroughly – although not necessarily the best – prepared. There was a widespread feeling among member states and EU institutions that the non-economic parts of the TEU were unsatisfactory largely because the 1991 IGC on political union had not been adequately prepared. By contrast, the SEA and the EMU provisions of the TEU seemed effective because the Dooge Committee of foreign ministers' representatives had laid the groundwork for the 1985 IGC, and the Delors Committee of central bank governors had laid the groundwork for the 1991 IGC on EMU. With such a long lead time before the 1996 Conference, member states and EU institutions agreed on the indispensability of good preparatory work by senior-level politicians and officials.

Also in contrast to previous IGCs, member states agreed that preparations for the 1996 IGC would have to be as open as possible. One of the lessons of the TEU ratification crisis was the need to keep the public informed of EU developments in general, and of proposed treaty changes in particular. Such openness was alien to the behaviour of most national governments, with the notable exception of the Scandinavian countries and the Netherlands. In the event, most Europeans remained unaware of the IGC; the attitude of those who were aware was characterized by a lack of interest. Regardless of its importance, a protracted conference of government officials discussing such arcane issues as flexibility, qualified majority voting (qmv) and subsidiarity could hardly appeal to a mass audience.

The Reflection Group, as the IGC's preparatory committee came to be called, was an important agenda-setting body. Many of its members – personal appointees of the Foreign Ministers – later participated in the Group of Representatives which conducted most of the IGC negotiations. In addition to member state representatives, the Reflection Group automatically included a Commission representative because the Commission traditionally had a seat at the IGC table, thereby introducing a supranational element into an otherwise exclusively intergovernmental process. Yet the Commission's formal role was limited to presenting a report to the Reflection Group, submitting an opinion on whether the IGC should take place, presenting papers during the conference, and participating in the negotiations. Crucially, the Commission could neither vote on proposals nor block agreement.

The EP, the other main supranational actor, had traditionally been excluded from IGCs. Like the Commission and the Council, the EP was asked to contribute a report to guide the Reflection Group's work. Chafing at this limited role in the treaty reform process, the EP successfully exploited a crisis over qmv in 1994 to secure a place at least in the Reflection Group, if not in the IGC itself. Dissatisfied with the April 1994 'Ioannina Agreement', which conceded in principle Britain's demand for a higher blocking minority threshold after the 1995 enlargement, the EP threatened to withhold its assent from that enlargement unless member states agreed to involve Parliament 'as fully as possible' in the forthcoming round of treaty change. It is doubtful that the EP would have blocked enlargement, but the threat to do so gave it some leverage over unsympathetic member states. Thanks also to the support of sympathetic states, such as Germany, the EP won the right to appoint two members to the Reflection Group.

The reports of the three institutions (Council, Commission, and EP) that formed the basis for the Reflection Group's work provided a useful snapshot of the EU's functioning at the end of 1995 (European Parliament, 1996). All emphasized the need for greater openness, transparency, legitimacy, simplification, and effectiveness of decision-making procedures (especially with respect to the two intergovernmental pillars). Beyond that, however, they conspicuously lacked 'any explicit theory or conceptual framework linking the different approaches (to institutional improvement and greater legitimacy) together into a simple vision of a wider and stronger Union which might help the citizens understand the rationale of the whole endeavor' (Laursen, 1997, p. 62).

The EP had eschewed its usual propensity to make excessive demands for greater power, having earlier decided not to adopt a Spinelli-like approach to the challenge of EU reform. Instead, the EP's main demands were a revision of the TEU's structure (abolition of the three pillars), or at least greater parliamentary involvement in the second and third pillars, and an extension of the co-decision and assent procedures. In its report, the Council criticized the EP for occasionally overstepping the bounds of the TEU's new procedures, and especially for attempting to link co-decision and comitology. Finally, the Commission bemoaned the 'less-than-convincing experience with intergovernmental cooperation' and doubted that the TEU had brought the EU closer to the general public. Although rectifying these deficiencies would be the Commission's priority at the IGC, the Commission was at pains to stress that it sought extra powers neither for itself nor for the EU.

The Commission, Council and EP reports were a point of departure for the Reflection Group's work, as were shorter reports from the Court of Justice, the Court of First Instance and the Court of Auditors. In addition, national and regional governments, political parties, EP party groups, public and private interest groups, and research institutes produced hundreds of reports, think-pieces, and position papers on a host of IGC-related issues. One of these, from the conservative parties in Germany's coalition Government, became the most important and influential contributions to the pre-IGC debate. Released in September 1994 and known by the names of its authors, the Lamers-Schäuble paper was so significant because, clearly reflecting German Government thinking, it unabashedly raised the 'F' word. During the 1991 IGC, the 'F' word was 'federalism', a UK taboo; in the run-up to the 1996 IGC the 'F' word was 'flexibility', not a taboo but potentially a threat to many member states.

Prompted by UK obstructionism in the EU, by the prospect of large-scale enlargement in Central and Eastern Europe, and by the possibility that only a minority of member states (if any) would meet the criteria to participate in Stage 3 of EMU in 1999, the Lamers–Schäuble paper asserted that 'the existing hard core of countries oriented to greater integration and closer cooperation must be further strengthened', and that 'the further development of the EU's institutions must combine coherence and consistency with elasticity and flexibility'. With unusual honesty for a quasi-diplomatic document, the authors then identified the 'core' countries as Germany, France, Belgium, Luxembourg, and the Netherlands – in other words, the original EC member states minus Italy. Concerning the UK, the authors asserted their conviction that 'determined efforts to spur on the further development of Europe are the best means of exerting a positive influence on the clarification of Great Britain's relationship to Europe and on its willingness to participate in further steps toward integration' (Christian Democratic Union/Christian Social Union, 1994, pp. 3–4).

The thrust of the Lamers–Schäuble paper was not lost on the UK Government. For some time the UK Prime Minister, John Major, had spoken favorably about 'flexibility', by which he meant an *à la carte*, pick-and-choose EU. In June 1994, during the EP election campaign, Major had said he did not think 'that it threatens Europe if member states are free to do some things in their own way and at their own speed . . . it is simply (a) good old-fashioned common sense (approach), a multi-track, multi-speed, multi-layered approach to Europe' (*Agence Europe*, June 3 1994, p. 3). The Lamers–Schäuble paper reminded the UK government that flexibility and differentiation could be interpreted in a number of ways, and that there was a limit to the patience of the UK more integrationist partners. Clearly stung by the possibility of being left behind, John Major publicly rejected the idea of an EU 'in which some would be more equal than others'. He stated that he did not want a two-tier EU, but rather an inclusive EU in which member states could opt-in and opt-out of policies (Major, 1994, p. 4).

With the EU destined to become larger and more diverse, with some existing member states opposed to further integration, and with others hoping to embark on a monetary union that would require for its success closer macroeconomic policy coordination, an institutional innovation such as flexibility seemed not only logical but also essential. By raising the concept in such stark terms, however, the Lamers–Schäuble paper alarmed other member states, including the three small countries identified in it as belonging to the hard core. Few member states sympathized with Britain, but most feared that a core group, driven by France and Germany, could damage the EU by undermining its single institutional structure and eroding the *acquis communautaire*.

The circumstances were thus hardly propitious for the Reflection Group's deliberations. Apart from the Lamers–Schäuble controversy, Germany had further alienated Italy by casting doubts on Italy's ability to meet the EMU convergence criteria. In France, newly-elected President Jacques Chirac had irritated German Chancellor Helmut Kohl by threatening during the election campaign to call a referendum on EMU. Last but by no means least, the ongoing siege of Sarajevo highlighted the EU's continuing failure to broker a cease-fire in the former Yugoslavia and sapped political morale. The US-imposed Dayton peace accords and ensuing troop deployment took place as the Reflection Group prepared its final report at the end of 1995.

Under Westendorp's able chairmanship, the Reflection Group met 16 times between June and December 1995. The representatives' remit was not to negotiate on the member states' behalf, but rather to prepare the IGC by narrowing down a potentially sprawling agenda and by identifying likely areas of agreement. In its final report, the Reflection Group identified three main areas for discussion in the IGC: making the EU more relevant to its citizens in areas such as human rights, free movement of people, police and judicial cooperation, employment, and the environment; improving the EU's efficiency and accountability through institutional innovation and change; and improving the EU's ability to act internationally (European Parliament, 1996).

The Reflection Group confirmed that flexibility would be one of the most important issues at the IGC. Nevertheless the final report cautioned that, whatever form it took, flexibility should be used only as a last resort, when all other possible solutions had been exhausted, and only as a temporary solution to meet specific challenges. In fact, by the end of the Reflection Group's deliberations flexibility had become much less contentious than it had been a year earlier, at the time of the Lamers–Schäuble paper. Pleased that the paper had attracted interest from the other member states, but concerned about a possible overreaction, Kohl had clarified Germany's position on flexibility. In a letter jointly signed by Chirac and sent to the Council Presidency in December 1995, Kohl stressed the importance of flexibility in an enlarging and diversifying EU, but emphasized that states engaging in closer integration should do so inside rather than outside the EU, if possible using the EU's institutions, procedures, and mechanisms.

In general, the Reflection Group's conclusions were split along recognizable national lines (although countries were not identified by name). On a wide range of issues, the report noted a divergence between 'a large majority' or 'a majority' on the one hand, and 'one member' (invariably the UK) or 'some members' (invariably including the UK) on the other. Indeed, the performance of the UK's representative in the Reflection Group convinced most other member states that the IGC would make little progress until after Britain's next election, due by May 1997 at the latest, which the Conservative Government was widely expected to lose. The only other country to distinguish itself in the IGC was Spain, although in this case the contribution was positive. That was because, in effect, the Reflection Group was a Spanish operation: being held during the Spanish Presidency and chaired by a Spaniard.

Negotiations and Outcomes

By the mid-1990s, member states had acquired considerable experience of conducting complex IGCs. As in recent IGCs, the 1996–7 conference consisted of regular working sessions (three or four times a month) of the Group of Representatives (junior ministers or senior diplomats, plus a Commissioner); brief monthly sessions of the foreign ministers on the margins of regularly scheduled General Affairs Councils plus occasional special meetings; and meetings of the heads of state and government during three regularly scheduled European Councils and three specially convened summits. The extent to which the European Council conducted detailed negotiations, already evident during previous IGCs and proof of the high political importance of treaty change in the EU, became even more marked during the 1996–7 conference, culminating in a tense late night session at the concluding Amsterdam summit.

By definition IGCs are intergovernmental events, although, as noted above, the Commission and especially the EP had influenced the preparatory stage of the 1996–7 IGC, and the Commission had a seat at the conference table. According to a member of the Commission's IGC team, the Commission 'set its sights on the upper range of what it considered realistic'. As a group of 'mainstream' member states coalesced around the main issues, the Commission then 'set (the group's) sights as high as possible' (Petit, 1997, pp. 1–2). The Commission sought to defend its own interests while advancing what it saw as the general EU interest. As in other areas of EU decision-making, the Commission built coalitions, mediated disputes, and exhorted member states to reach agreement. Nevertheless the avowedly intergovernmental nature of the IGC, as well as a generally weak political position in the aftermath of the TEU crisis and of Jacques Delors's Presidency, limited the Commission's influence.

The EP's potential influence was more obviously limited. Having participated fully in the Reflection Group, the EP argued strongly for participation also in the IGC, but unsympathetic member states, notably Britain and France, refused to set another new precedent. Instead, the European Council agreed in December 1995 to involve the EP 'as much as possible' in the IGC. In practice, this meant regular meetings between the Group of Representatives and the two EP representatives who had participated in the Reflection Group, and between the heads of state and government and the EP President. Despite its formal non-participation, the EP's role in the IGC exceeded its involvement in previous IGCs. Judging by the outcome of the conference, the EP was also relatively influential.

The German Länder were the other non-traditional actor to play a part in the IGC, although one less prominent than the EP. Organized nationally in the Bundesrat, or upper house of parliament, whose Social Democratic majority constituted a strong opposition to Kohl's Christian Democratic–Free Liberal coalition government, the Länder have long resented the encroachment of EU powers into what they see as their constitutional prerogatives. Beginning with the SEA, the Länder acquired a limited but formal role in EU decision-making in areas touching on (subnational) states' rights. Given that the Amsterdam agenda included some of these issues, inevitably the Länder insisted on representation in Germany's IGC delegation.

This might have been insignificant but for the way in which the Länder limited the Federal Government's freedom of action at certain times during the conference. Nowhere was this more striking than at the Amsterdam summit itself when, under pressure from the Länder, Kohl blocked the extension of qmv into a new area of Community competence (visa and asylum policy). For Kohl, a long-time advocate of qmv, this was humiliating; for Germany's partners and EU observers, it demonstrated Kohl's political weakness and the Länder's growing assertiveness.

Of the traditional IGC actors, France and Germany had dominated the preparatory and negotiating stages of previous IGCs. Yet apart from the Kohl–Chirac letter of December 1995, and a few subsequent initiatives by the French and German foreign ministers on flexibility and foreign policy, the much-vaunted Franco-German tandem was absent from the 1996–7 IGC. This was partly because the IGC lacked a major, clear-cut, compelling objective or idea of the kind that had dominated other IGCs. More significantly, it was because of growing tensions in Franco-German relations due to policy differences – especially over fiscal and employment policies – and personal differences – Kohl's disharmony with Chirac and Lionel Jospin (who became Prime Minister of France in the closing weeks of the Conference) contrasted sharply with his affection for Mitterrand.

Precisely because the IGC was not dominated by a single big issue or idea, the dearth of Franco-German leadership was not as critical as it might otherwise have been. For instance, it gave other member states a better opportunity to influence the IGC's outcome. Of the other large member states, Spain was as actively involved in the IGC as it had been in the preparatory stage; Italy was weak throughout because of domestic political problems; and Britain was marginalized until May 1997, when the generally pro-EU Labour Party won the general election. The mixed fortunes of the large member states and the variety of agenda items increased the scope for smaller member states to play a more prominent role. The exception was Denmark, whose government felt constrained by domestic public opinion to operate within the narrow framework of the 1992 Edinburgh agreement on Denmark's participation in the EU, as approved in the May 1993 Danish referendum.

As in past IGCs, small countries occupied the Council Presidency during most of the negotiations (the exception being Italy, who held the Presidency for the opening three months). The frequency and duration of IGCs since 1985 has added a new element to the already onerous responsibility of the Council Presidency. Few Presidencies during the last 15 years have been uninvolved in some aspect or other of treaty change. In an IGC, as in the conduct of other EU business, the Presidency must try to strike a balance between self-interest and EU interests, between the politically desirable and politically possible. Small countries have an advantage because they are perceived to have fewer, or at least less flagrant, national interests.

First Ireland, then the Netherlands, occupied the Presidency during the intensive negotiating stage of the 1996–7 conference. The Irish helped to make progress on the IGC's less contentious items, largely by using the same approach as the Reflection Group. Based on answers to a questionnaire, the Irish produced 'successive approximations' of drafts to shape the final outcome. Prompted by France and Germany, who feared that the IGC's momentum was flagging, the Irish Presidency drew up 'a general outline for a draft revision of the treaties' for the December 1996 Dublin summit (Council Presidency, 1996). This contained draft treaty provisions for the less contentious items, but coverage of the more controversial items (flexibility, institutional reform, and Justice and Home Affairs) was vague.

It was up to the incoming Dutch to broker agreements on a number of difficult issues. Dutch chairmanship of the final six months of the

1991 IGC had been a memorable example of poor IGC management. Based largely on that experience, Dutch chairmanship of the final six months of the 1996–7 IGC was purposeful. The Dutch set about narrowing the differences between member states in a succession of 'non-papers', and by convening a special summit in Noordwijk only weeks before the Amsterdam summit. Failure to agree institutional reform in Amsterdam was less a reflection on the Dutch Presidency than on the overloaded agenda of EU summits and the exhaustion of the summiteers.

The number of issues discussed at the conference had mushroomed well beyond the few agenda items originally identified in the TEU and later by the European Council. Ironically, some of those items (like civil protection and tourism) were not addressed at the conference at all; others (like comitology) were deferred until a later date. Nevertheless the original goals of procedural reform covered a myriad of items, as did three other broad issue-areas addressed in the conference: 'freedom, security, and justice' (that is, fundamental rights and non-discrimination, internal and external frontiers, asylum, immigration, and visas); 'the Union and the citizen' (that is, employment, social policy, the environment, public health, consumer protection, subsidiarity, openness, etc.); and external relations (that is, the common commercial policy and CFSP).

Inevitably, member state and institutional preferences ranged widely. Strong member state misgivings were accommodated either by opt-outs (such as the UK, Irish, and Danish opt-outs from the new Community clauses on the free movement of people) and high thresholds for supranational decision-making (such as unanimity for many of the Treaty's new free movement provisions). In contrast to previous IGCs, where bargaining and coalition-building revolved around a small number of key issues, the 1996–7 IGC 'took the form of repeated discussions at which each delegation expressed its views and positions evolved gradually. It was as if each delegation came to Brussels not so much to negotiate a text as to try to bring all the forces roughly into equilibrium and to judge whether the end product would be acceptable.' (Petit, 1997, p. 8) The reluctance of the Irish and Dutch Presidencies to produce draft texts (both were careful not to call them draft treaties) until the last moment contrasted with the approach of the Luxembourg and Dutch Presidencies during the 1991 IGCs and reflected the more diverse and less confrontational nature of the 1996–7 conference.

As expected, flexibility became a major issue at the IGC, although most of the controversy surrounding it had abated by the time the conference drew to a close. The three circumstances that had prompted the incendiary Lamers–Schäuble paper nearly three years earlier – UK recalcitrance, the possibility of a small euro zone, and the prospect of large influx of Central and Eastern European states in the relatively near future – had changed significantly by the spring of 1997 (the UK Conservatives were out of power, Stage 3 of EMU looked set to start in January 1999 with 11 member states, and, as the Commission would formally propose only one month after the end of the IGC, the first 'wave' of enlargement would likely involve no more than six countries, and was unlikely to happen before 2002).

Nevertheless flexibility remained a salient and difficult issue throughout the IGC. Discussion of it proceeded cautiously during the Irish Presidency, but was prodded along by a Franco-German initiative of October 1996. Unlike other sections in the Irish Presidency's draft text, the section on 'Enhanced Cooperation: Flexibility' did not contain suggested treaty language. Instead, it reviewed the debate so far, reiterated the member states' desire to limit flexibility to precisely defined conditions that would preserve the *acquis communautaire* and respect the EU's objectives, and outlined a number of ways in which flexibility could be incorporated into the treaties. With great skill, the Dutch Presidency narrowed the options for flexibility to both general enabling clauses (applicable to the EU as a whole for member states wishing to cooperate more closely) and particular clauses in a number of policy areas. In the end, flexibility was so hedged with conditions – not least provisions allowing member states to block voting in the Council on whether or not to allow its implementation – as to be almost unworkable. Therein lay the explanation for flexibility's survival in the IGC and inclusion in the Treaty: proponents of flexibility were satisfied because the Treaty incorporated it into the EU as a general principle; others were satisfied because, in practice, flexibility was tightly constrained.

By far the most complex, time-consuming, and far-reaching subject-matter discussed at the IGC was not flexibility, but the establishment of an area of freedom, security, and justice (covering internal and external border security, immigration and asylum). Member states were unanimous that the TEU's third pillar (Justice and Home Affairs) needed to be overhauled, and most of them wanted to bring the Schengen Agreement on the free movement of people under the

EU umbrella. Not only were these issues highly sensitive politically; they were also complicated by the size and uncertainty of the Schengen acquis and by the fact that two member states – the UK and Ireland – were not signatories to the Schengen Agreement, whilst two non-member states – Iceland and Norway – were associate members.

Under the circumstances, negotiations were slow and highly technical, but resulted in a major transfer of responsibilities to the Community. In a welcome clarification of the EU's structure, all matters pertaining to the free movement of people were grouped in the first pillar, while matters relating to criminal law and police cooperation remained in the third pillar. Although replete with opt-outs and procedural qualifications that are bound to impede effective decision-making, the first pillar's new provisions for the free movement of people represent a reassuring affirmation of the Community method (notably with respect to the Commission's right of initiative and the role of the Court of Justice).

CFSP – the EU's second pillar – was another area ripe for reform, administratively and substantively. However, member states were unable to agree on a simplification of decision-making or on a means to make the CFSP more effective. The more integrationist member states, such as Germany, Italy and the Benelux countries, failed substantially to curtail unanimity and succeeded only in introducing constructive abstentionism, a mechanism whereby member states not wishing to take a CFSP-related decision can at least allow the others to do so, subject to an 'emergency brake.' Failure to merge the EU and WEU was another disappointment for the 'progressive' member states. Faced with strong opposition from the UK and Denmark, which opposed the militarization of the EU, and the neutral member states, which opposed participation in a military organization, the IGC agreed only to 'the possibility of the integration of the WEU into the EU, should the European Council so decide'. Overall, with respect to CFSP, the IGC achieved only 'a piecemeal engineering of varying quality rather than an overall reform' (Monar, 1997, p. 435).

Apart from flexibility, the most important institutional issues negotiated in the IGC concerned the size of the Commission and qmv in the Council. Inevitably these became linked, since most large member states refused to give up their right to nominate two Commissioners without being given greater voting weight in the Council, while smaller member states refused to give up the right to nominate a sole Commissioner. Given that such institutional reforms in anticipation of enlargement had become the main reason for holding the IGC, failure to reduce the Commission's size and re-weight or overhaul Council voting – regardless of the necessity for doing so – reflected badly on the IGC and overshadowed its main achievements.

Assessment

The Amsterdam Treaty is not a new, stand-alone treaty underpinning the EU, but a treaty containing changes to the EU's founding treaties. This confusion of purpose and nomenclature reflects broader confusion about the substance of the Treaty itself. For a Treaty intended to bring the EU closer to its citizens, the Amsterdam Treaty is a caricature of all that is wrong with the EU. More than 50 pages long, littered with arcane language and unexplained references to existing treaty provisions, and including numerous protocols and declarations, the Treaty is unlikely to endear either itself or the EU to a sceptical public.

Most treaties are inherently complex and generally incomprehensible to lay readers. The Amsterdam Treaty is being judged by a different standard because of the unpopularity of the TEU and because of the EU's supposed democratic deficit. Increasingly concerned about the EU's impact on their lives, many Europeans have reacted by contrasting the EU unfavourably to an idealized version of national government. Yet the EU's system of governance is unusually complicated because of the EU's nature: a blend of intergovernmentalism and supranationalism, and of subsidiarity and centralization. Given the history and politics of European integration, it is impossible to replace the EU's founding treaties with a new, streamlined set of objectives, guiding principles and institutions – however intellectually alluring such a prospect would be.

Accordingly, the Amsterdam Treaty potentially strengthens the EU's effectiveness at the cost inevitably of perpetuating and possibly compounding the EU's complexity. For instance, new provisions in the first pillar relating to the free movement of people give the EU considerable scope to enhance its citizens' welfare, but are subject to cumbersome and complex decision-making procedures because of the prevailing realities of national sensitivities and domestic political dynamics. Similarly, flexibility seems necessary in an increasingly large and diverse EU, but concern about its possible abuse, rooted in Europe's history of 'Great Power' politics, has complicated its operability and restricted its practical usefulness. Even after Amsterdam, CFSP is a striking example of a set of objectives and procedures self-evidently in the member states' collective interest, but condemned to incoherence and ineffectualness because of different national histories, traditions and perspectives.

Ratification

Understandably in view of what had happened after Maastricht, the spectre of a post-IGC ratification crisis loomed over the 1996–7 negotiations. Accordingly, governments handled ratification carefully. Ratification procedures in most member states did not include holding a referendum, and were largely trouble-free in national parliaments. This time, the President of France did not take the unnecessary risk of putting the proposed Treaty to a vote of the people. Nevertheless, ratification proved controversial and time consuming in France because compliance with the Treaty's provisions for Justice and Home Affairs required a constitutional amendment. As a result, implementation of the Treaty was delayed beyond the target date of December 1998 to May 1999.

Despite its slow progress, ratification of the Amsterdam Treaty was never likely to be as controversial or as problematic as ratification of the TEU had been. Given the difference between the two treaties and the fact that member states had already gone through the TEU ratification crisis, there was much less at stake in 1997 and 1998. A 'No' vote in Denmark in 1998 would not have had the same impact as it had in 1992 – not least because the negotiation of special Danish opt-outs after the 1992 referendum, resulting in the successful outcome of the 1993 referendum, showed that Danish rejection of the Amsterdam Treaty could be similarly finessed. Undoubtedly a negative result in Denmark would have unsettled the EU, but it would hardly have derailed either EMU or enlargement. Nevertheless, member state and EU officials breathed a huge sigh of relief in May 1998 when the result of the Danish referendum became known: 55.1 per cent in favour; 44.9 per cent against.

A week before the Danish referendum, Irish voters had endorsed the Treaty by a vote of 61.7 per cent to 38.3 per cent. Although a majority of nearly 24 per cent was comfortable by any standard, the size of the 'No' vote – substantially larger than the 'No' votes in previous EU-related referenda – demonstrated both the Treaty's unpopularity and growing disillusionment in Ireland with the EU as a whole. Many of those who voted against the Treaty complained that they did not know enough about it. Undoubtedly the Treaty is difficult to understand, but there was a surfeit of creditable and comprehensible information on the Treaty's nature and content available to interested voters. The perception of an 'information deficit' at a time of information overload confirms the public relations problem facing the EU in the lingering post-Maastricht climate of scepticism and distrust.

Prospects for Future Treaty Change

The 1996–7 IGC may well be the last in the recent series of 'big event' IGCs. The Amsterdam Treaty is not the definitive EU treaty change, but its major achievements – incorporating flexibility into the founding treaties as a fundamental EU principle and bringing the free movement of people into the first pillar – round-off the precocious stage of European integration that began with the single market initiative and continued with the launch of EMU, CFSP, and cooperation on Justice and Home Affairs. Incongruous and untidy though they are, CFSP and police cooperation are likely to remain separate pillars for the foreseeable future.

Nevertheless, ample scope remains for procedural improvements within the pillars themselves, and in the EU's overall institutional architecture. Similarly the EU's competence is still incomplete, and pressure will likely develop as a result of EMU to harmonize the fiscal policies of euro zone countries. To the extent that such changes require formal treaty amendments, they are likely to result from a process reminiscent of the EC's early history. In other words, IGCs will probably revert to their original mode: quick, discreet, single-issue affairs. Not only are major, multifaceted items no longer on the agenda, but member states and EU institutions (with the possible exception of the ebullient EP) lack the energy and enthusiasm for further protracted rounds of treaty reform, not least because of the public's negative reaction to IGCs.

This reveals a major dilemma concerning the conduct of IGCs since 1985: member states are well aware of the need to improve the EU's image and accountability, and have attempted to do so in the context of wide-ranging treaty changes. Yet it is hard to educate the general public about the complex policy and procedural issues negotiated in IGCs, and Eurosceptical or merely Euro-weary members of the public can easily seize upon the ensuing treaties as proof that the EU is impenetrable, technocratic, and citizen-unfriendly. In those member states where IGC results need to be ratified in a referendum, voters have an ideal opportunity to try to derail the entire process.

The Amsterdam Treaty includes provision for yet another IGC, but not of the all-encompassing kind that the 1996–7 conference became. Unable to reach agreement on reform of the Commission and of qmv in the closing hours of the Amsterdam summit, the heads of state and government approved a protocol stipulating that the Commission will comprise one Commissioner per member state as soon as the next EU enlargement takes place, provided that Council votes are re-weighted in order to compensate large member states for the loss of a second Commissioner. The protocol also states that at least one year before the EU exceeds 20 member states, an IGC must be convened 'to carry out a comprehensive review of the provisions of the treaties on the composition and functioning of the institutions'. This refers particularly to the fact that the EU will then have to confront the politically charged question of allocating 20 Commissioners among more than 20 member states.

These are weighty institutional issues, but are neither as complicated nor as difficult as the outcome of the Amsterdam summit suggests. The heads of state and government came close in Amsterdam to solving the problem, and will eventually do so without conducting an IGC of the 1985, 1991, or 1996–7 variety. Instead, a future IGC on institutional reform will be a model of the kind of treaty change negotiated in the pre-SEA period. As for public interest in the process of treaty change, however, it is impossible to put the genie back into the bottle.

Guide to Further Reading

De Ruyt (1987) gives an insider's account of the negotiations that resulted in the SEA. Moravcsik (1991) analyses the SEA from a liberal-intergovernmental perspective; Sandholtz and Zysman (1989) do so from a supranationalist one. Cameron (1992) and Corbett (1987) offer solid explanations of the SEA's origin and negotiation. Baun (1996) and Mazzuchelli (1997) provide lively accounts of the conduct and outcome of the 1991 IGCs. Laursen and Vanhoonacker have compiled articles and official documentation on the negotiations that led to the TEU (1992) and on the subsequent ratification crisis (1994). Curtin, Kellermann, and Winter (1996), Edwards and Pijpers (1997) and Laurent and Maresceau (1998) provide collections of articles on the main issues being considered in the run up to the Amsterdam Treaty. Petit (1997) gives an insider's account – from the Commission's perspective – of the negotiations themselves. McDonagh (1998) gives an insider's account from the perspective of the Council Presidency.

References

Agence Europe (1994), June 3. Brussels: Agence Internationale D'Information Pour La Presse.

Baun, M. (1996) *An Imperfect Union: The Maastricht Treaty and the New Politics of European Integration*. Boulder: Westview.

Cameron, D. (1992), 'The 1992 Initiative: Causes and Consequences', in Alberta Sbragia (ed.), *Europolitics: Institutions and Policymaking in the 'New' European Community*. Washington, DC: Brookings Institution, pp. 23–74.

Christian Democratic Union/Christian Social Union Group in the German Lower House (1994) 'Reflections on European Policy', Bonn, 1 September.

Corbett, R. (1987) 'The 1985 Intergovernmental Conference and the Single European Act,' in Roy Pryce (ed.), *The Dynamics of European Union*. London: Croom Helm, pp. 238–72.

Council Presidency (1996) 'The EU Today and Tomorrow: Adapting the EU for the Benefit of Its Peoples and Preparing it for the Future: A General Outline For a Draft Revision of the Treaties', Dublin: Department of Foreign Affairs.

Curtin, D., Kellermann, A. and Winter, J. (1996) *Reforming the Treaty on European Union: The Legal Debate*. The Hague: Kluwer Law International.

De Ruyt, J. (1987) *L'Acte Unique Européen: Commentaire*. Brussels: Editions de l'Université de Bruxelles.

Edwards, G. and Pijpers, A. (1997) *The Politics of European Treaty Reform: The 1996 Intergovernmental Conference and Beyond*. London: Pinter.

European Parliament (1996) *White Paper on the 1996 IGC*, vol. 1, *Official Texts of the EU Institutions*. Luxembourg: European Parliament.

International Herald Tribune (1995), 21/22 October.

Laurent, P.-H. and Maresceau, M. (eds) (1998) *The State of the European Union*, vol. 4, *Deepening and Widening*. Boulder, CO: Lynne Rienner.

Laursen, F. (1997) 'The Lessons of Maastricht,' in Edwards and Pijpers, *The Politics of European Treaty Reform*, pp. 59–72.

Laursen, F. and Vanhoonacker, S. (eds) (1992) *The Intergovernmental Conference on Political Union*. Maastricht: European Institute of Public Administration.

Laursen, F. and Vanhoonacker, S., (eds) (1994) *The Ratification of the Maastricht Treaty: Issues, Debates, and Future Implications*. Maastricht: EIPA.

Major, J. (1994) 'Europe: A Future That Works,' William and Mary Lecture, Leiden University, 7 September.

Mazzuchelli, C. (1997) *France and Germany at Maastricht: Politics and Negotiations to Create the European Union*. New York: Garland.

McDonagh, B. (1998) *Original Sin in a Brave New World: An Account of the Negotiations of the Treaty of Amsterdam*. Dublin: Institute of European Affairs.

Monar, J. (1997) 'The European Union's Foreign Affairs System After the Treaty of Amsterdam: A "Strengthened Capacity for External Action"?', *European Foreign Affairs Review*, vol. 2, no. 4, pp. 413–36.

Moravcsik, A. (1991) 'Negotiating the SEA: National Interest and Conventional Statecraft in the European Community', *International Organization*, vol. 45 (Winter), pp. 19–56.

Petit, M. (1997) *The Amsterdam Treaty*, Harvard Law School Working Paper.

Sandholtz, W. and Zysman, J. (1989) '1992: Recasting the European Bargain', *World Politics*, vol. 41, no. 1, pp. 95–128.

16

The Political Dynamics of Economic and Monetary Union

KEVIN FEATHERSTONE

Of all the recent developments in the European integration process, the launch of Economic and Monetary Union (EMU) is one of the most ambitious and far-reaching. Only the enlargement of the EU to incorporate nations from the former Communist bloc in Central and Eastern Europe ranks alongside EMU in respect of the radical change involved. But enlargement will take effect later than EMU. New states are very unlikely to join the EU by 2002, and even when they do join they will face a long transition to full membership. Enlargement will also come in a piecemeal manner, with some states entering well ahead of others. By contrast, the single currency – the euro – already exists, and the changeover from national to euro banknotes and coins will be phased in over just a few months in 2002.

The move towards EMU, laid down in the Treaty on European Union (TEU), is thus the biggest single current component in the process of 'Europeanization'. This process, which has been most evident with the 'deepening' of integration that has occurred since the launch of the single market programme in 1985, has seen its effects on EU policies becoming stronger and more visible. But EMU is of a different magnitude. It has transformed the policy agendas of national governments, favoured some political actors over others, and created a new institutional framework at the EU level.

This chapter is concerned with the political dynamics of EMU. The first section, divided into two parts, explains the emergence of EMU: the first outlines how the EMU initiative developed between 1988 and 1991, focusing on the key actors and decisions; the second relates this empirical account to a set of different conceptual frameworks, through which the evolution of the EMU agreement might be explained. By connecting the empirical account to concepts and theories, a deeper understanding of how EMU emerged is possible. EMU in this period displayed much dynamism: its emergence depended on historical contingencies, structural developments in the international economy, institutional politics, strategic calculations, and a distinctive set of economic beliefs.

The second section examines the dynamic impact of EMU since the TEU was concluded. It sees EMU as creating an important new dimension in the political system of the EU. As such, a set of conventional questions from political science can be applied. The politics of EMU can be studied by asking similar questions to those raised in other areas.

The first set of questions arise from examining the stability of the EMU project during the course of its implementation since 1991. In a basic sense, of course, EMU has been an emerging and developing policy project which will only be completed in 2002. But the focus here will be largely concerned with how EMU has been kept on track, despite the pressures which threatened to delay (or even end) the process. The second set of questions focus on who has power in EMU. This involves inquiring into the impact of EMU on the policy agendas of national governments; its affect on power within national systems; and its consequences for the EU's own institutional structure. The answers to these questions help to clarify how EMU constitutes part of the 'Europeanization' process.

The final set of issues revolves around the core concept of legitimacy. The manifold repercussions of realizing EMU raise questions about the support of mass publics; the role of technocratic elites; and the democratic accountability of the system created by EMU. By establishing a new pattern of governance, EMU poses tests of legitimacy at both the national and European levels.

The Emergence of EMU

The EMU Initiative

Who, then, put EMU on the agenda, and how and why? In fact, it was a matter of EMU returning to the EU's agenda, given the long history of the issue going back to the Werner Report on EMU of 1970 and the creation and evolution of the European Monetary System (EMS), which was established in 1979.

By the late 1980s, the EMS had enjoyed much success. It had helped to reduce inflation levels in the participating states and to maintain a stable set of currency exchange rates. Indeed, the EMS was becoming a tight constraint, imposing a discipline on domestic monetary and fiscal policies. But tensions were apparent. France and Italy, in particular, objected to the dominance of the Deutschmark in the EMS. They claimed that this dominance created unfair ('asymmetrical') burdens and constraints on their own economies. Moreover, the prospect of the liberalization of capital controls across the EC, as envisaged by the single market programme, threatened to undermine the stability of the EMS system (Padoa-Schioppa, 1987).

Against this background, a new debate about the future of the EMS began at the start of 1988. French Finance Minister Edouard Balladur, and then his Italian counterpart, Giuliano Amato, issued memoranda criticizing the constraints and asymmetries of the current EMS. They were followed by German Foreign Minister Hans-Dietrich Genscher – a foreign minister acting beyond the normal diplomatic domain – and later by German Finance Minister Gerhard Stoltenberg, who both issued their own memoranda detailing their respective positions. The German lead was crucial, given the importance of the Deutschmark. It was also facilitated by Germany holding the Council Presidency in the first half of 1988.

Following Genscher's initiative, Commission President Jacques Delors and German Chancellor Helmut Kohl worked closely together to prepare an agreement to move ahead on EMU at the Hanover European Council in June 1988. French President François Mitterrand also rallied to the idea. The Hanover meeting established the ad hoc Delors Committee to study how EMU might be achieved. The Committee's composition was intriguing. The majority of its members consisted of the central bank governors of the EU and it was headed by the most assertive Commission President for decades (Delors). This was an astute tactic to identify the governors with the EMU momentum: it would strengthen the credibility of the project.

The Committee's report (the so-called Delors Report) was published in April 1989. It set out a blueprint by which EMU would be implemented in three stages. No dates were set down at this stage. But, in its basic design of EMU, much of the report found its way into the later TEU. Significantly, the report was signed by all the governors of the national central banks. The Delors Report had placed EMU firmly on the agenda as a viable proposition.

The progress of the detailed negotiations was not simple or straightforward, however. The main problem at first was that of the UK. The Conservative Government was engulfed by an internal ministerial crisis over sterling's entry into the Exchange Rate Mechanism (ERM) of the EMS, which distracted attention from discussion of EMU. Sterling did not enter the ERM until October 1990. On the bigger question of EMU, the then British Prime Minister Margaret Thatcher expressed strong opposition. Both she and her Chancellor of the Exchequer, Nigel Lawson, argued repeatedly that talk of a single currency was premature – it would not happen in their lifetime. Yet, surprisingly, Robin Leigh-Pemberton, Governor of the Bank of England, had signed the Delors Report, much to Thatcher's annoyance.

The impact of the Delors Report was to create a momentum behind EMU which the UK found difficult to stop or divert. Two separate counter-proposals from London in 1989–90, the first for a common currency and the second for a parallel currency (the so-called 'Hard ECU'), received negligible support from the rest of the EC. They were not taken up by the UK's EC partners, but both proposals distracted domestic attention in the UK. The UK misjudged the support for EMU amongst the EC's member states.

In part due to the UK's sensitivities, the EC proceeded cautiously on EMU after the Delors Report. At Madrid in June 1989, the European Council agreed in principle to an intergovernmental conference (IGC) to determine the treaty changes necessary to realize EMU. But no date was set for the IGC. Instead, a committee chaired by Elizabeth Guigou of France endeavoured to prepare the ground for the IGC by drawing up a set of questions for it to consider.

Wider developments soon demanded political attention: the collapse of communism in the East and the process of German unification in 1989–90. These developments delayed progress on EMU, as the Germans wrestled with their own new monetary union. Such developments certainly provoked a new concern amongst Germany's neighbours (notably in France) to bind Germany to the EC and to the West. In any event, the Strasbourg European Council in December 1989 decided to hold an IGC on EMU; it was to begin one year later. At its meeting in Dublin in June 1990, the European Council agreed that a second IGC on Political Union should be called. The IGCs were a means to bind Germany to the EC.

The negotiations on the detailed content could now commence. The Italian Council Presidency in the second half of 1990 acted to prepare both IGCs and to settle disputes as to their organizational structure. The negotiations opened in Rome on 9 December 1990, but began in earnest under the Luxembourg Presidency of early 1991. The negotiations took place in a distinct institutional setting. The IGC on EMU met at different levels: on 11 occasions as a ministerial IGC, but twice as regularly at the level of officials ('personal representatives'). Alongside the IGC negotiations, three 'informal' meetings of the Council of Economics and Finance Ministers (Ecofin) were important fora for the progress of the negotiations. The IGC asked the Committee of Central Bank Governors of the EC to make various technical submissions, and its papers on the European Central Bank (ECB) and a European System of Central Banks (ESCB) of November 1990 and on the European Monetary Institute (EMI) of October 1991 determined much of the final content.

The negotiations were concluded at the European Council in Maastricht on 9–10 December 1991, although the final version of the Treaty was not signed until the following February to allow for some 'polishing-up' of the text. Thereafter, due to delays in ratification at the national level, the TEU did not come into effect until November 1, 1993.

Conceptualizing EMU

To understand the political dynamics of how and why the EMU agreement emerged it is necessary to place its history within a particular conceptual framework. Concepts and theories help to interpret actions and events. They serve to distinguish the relative importance of different elements of EMU's history and enable us to understand better which factors were crucial to the outcome. A distinction can be drawn between the endogenous and the exogenous factors which have affected EMU.

The above chronology of the EMU agreement suggested the diversity of 'internal' actors and relationships relevant to an explanation of how the EMU agenda was set. Policy leadership was shown by individual politicians (notably Genscher, followed by Kohl and Delors); by the central bank governors on the Delors Committee; and, by the Franco-German axis in forging deals. The will of the major European leaders (notably Kohl and Mitterrand) to press ahead indicates how essential was the role of particular individuals (as 'agents' in the process). There are, however, a number of 'What if?' questions here. If Kohl had not been German Chancellor, or Mitterrand the French President, would an agreement on the full Maastricht package have been possible? If EMU had not been routed via the Delors Committee, would the momentum behind EMU have dissipated? If the Franco-German relationship had been in one of its colder periods (such as after 1981 or after 1995) could EMU have emerged? If Thatcher had not been Prime Minister might the UK have played a more positive role and rearranged the pattern of alliances on EMU? Such questions illustrate the historical contingencies underpinning the EMU agreement.

Leaders and their representatives had to operate within two domains – the European and the domestic – which had their own distinct, and often competing, demands and constraints. The negotiations, before and during the IGC, can be seen as structured within a complex 'two-level' bargaining game (Putnam, 1988). Those involved were acutely aware of the conflicting pressures upon them from both 'levels' – domestic and European. They played a multidimensional chess game which cut across these two levels. Kohl's ability to agree at the EC table was constrained by his need for domestic support, not least from the Bundesbank. He could use the scepticism of the Bundesbank as a bargaining lever on his European partners. Finance ministers and central bankers shared common interests which were opposed to those of foreign ministers and diplomats. This created cross-national alliances and affected how the EMU proposal emerged through different institutional channels.

The content of the EMU agreement was, indeed, affected by the nature of the EU institutions and their rules. The 'new institutionalist' approach developed by March and Olsen (1989) is relevant to the EU, as Bulmer (1994) has argued. This type of explanation would highlight the constraints accepted under the technical rules of the EMS, and the informal conventions and codes of behaviour of the European Council, ECOFIN, the Committee of Central Bank Governors, and a forum like an IGC. The institutional route followed by the EMU initiative affected its content and progress. This was most clearly the case with the Delors Committee, which brought to bear the credibility and policy values of the central bank governors on the EMU project, setting its agenda and giving it impetus.

Those involved in the EMU negotiators were also engaged in a collective process of policy learning (Radaelli, 1995). They were searching for viable solutions to complex technical issues. Building a monetary union of this sort was unprecedented in the modern period. Negotiators were travelling beyond existing knowledge in economics as to how to establish a successful single currency. Negotiations can readily be seen as an arena of conflicting bargaining positions and strategies, but it is also important to recognize that they are affected by the nature of the knowledge available and how such knowledge is inserted into the negotiating process. Negotiators were developing EMU against a background of existing economic policy beliefs: beliefs about both what was desirable and feasible. Several conceptual approaches are relevant. The concept of 'epistemic communities' (Haas, 1992) describes a relationship in which policy-makers are influenced by an external body of expert opinion. The notion of 'advocacy coalitions' (Sabatier and Jenkins-Smith, 1993) suggests that policy is the outcome of a conflict between contending structures of beliefs, knowledge and interests involving both officials and policy experts. Finally, the concept of the 'policy entrepreneur' (Kingdon, 1984) may outline how policy ideas enter the policy process by being promoted by well-placed individuals or groups. Each of these approaches emphasizes the role of knowledge in the negotiating process.

Identifying the key actors and interests in the EMU negotiations is an example of a wider controversy amongst policy analysts. Different interpretations can be given in line with conflicting schools of thought in international relations. Traditional 'realists' would highlight the key actors as being the EU national governments, and would argue that they were preoccupied with domestic interests and policy problems. Hence, EMU might be seen as being driven by the desire to 'rescue' individual nation-states from threats to their autonomy posed by the globalization of financial markets. In essence, domestic political interests in shoring up the capability of states to deliver sound monetary policies converged to make an EMU agreement possible.

Alternatively, these same states might be seen as being bound up in a process of transformation, prompted by the dynamics of the integration process itself and changes in the world economy. In this view, national actors became prisoners of the processes that they created (for example, the single market programme and the operation of the EMS) and prisoners of processes that others created for them (globalization and the deregulation of financial markets). Thus, the degree of 'control' possessed by any particular set of national or EU actors is seen as being limited by these developments. Negotiators were constrained by developments beyond their control and had to take account of other types of actors, particularly in the financial markets.

Whichever interpretation seems most plausible, it is certainly the case that national actors had different motivations and strategies. These cannot be summarized here, only illustrated. Germany sought to make its power more acceptable to its neighbours by placing itself under a European umbrella. France sought to redress the asymmetries of the EMS and to tie Germany to a European framework. Italy shared many of the French concerns, but also saw advantages for itself in accepting an external monetary discipline to overcome domestic resistance to such a course. Each accepted that their hands might be tied. The exception was the UK, which expressed its traditional desire to maintain national choice and flexibility.

However, the EMU process cannot be understood by reference to 'internal' factors alone. The EMU negotiators were also responding to a variety of 'external' pressures. The structural changes of globalized financial markets have already been alluded to. The EMS was itself a reaction to such changes, being essentially a search for monetary stability in a world still recovering from the collapse of the Bretton Woods system after 1971. The will to proceed with EMU, even after the EMS crises of 1992 and 1993, is indicative of the response to these external pressures. Moreover, attitudes towards EMU were affected by wider political developments in Europe. After 1989, the collapse of communism in Eastern Europe increased concerns over German power and future foreign policy orientation. German unification may have delayed the EMU negotiating process – given the need of West Germany to attend to the problems of a monetary union with the East – but it also renewed old concerns.

Thus, to interpret the history of the EMU agreement correctly, it is necessary to combine a diverse set of factors, both 'internal' and 'external' to the EMU debate. This makes interpretation more difficult, but it is essential if the EMU 'story' is to be placed in its appropriate historical context. Such interpretations allow the EMU case to be compared to other areas of the integration process, so as to deepen understanding of the EU system as a whole. Interpreting the progress of EMU in these ways helps to connect the study of the EU to the concepts developed in comparative politics, public policy, rational choice and international relations.

The Dynamic Impact of EMU

Is EMU stable?

As a major new venture, questions immediately arose after 1991 as to whether the EU could achieve a successful and stable EMU. The progress of EMU soon appeared to be faltering and fluctuating.

The Maastricht European Council represented a high point of optimism about the future of the European integration process. Yet, the euphoria of Maastricht was soon undermined by the problems of ratifying what was agreed in the TEU. This delay undermined market confidence that EMU would go ahead and would succeed. The first shock came when a referendum in Denmark in May 1992 rejected ratification by a wafer-thin majority. This dent to confidence compounded the increasing instability in the EMS exchange rates. Two bouts of intense currency speculation occurred which greatly weakened the EMS. In the first, in September 1992, the UK and Italian currencies were forced out of the ERM. In the second (July/August 1993), the ERM all but fell apart. On 2 August 1993, the fluctuation band for currencies in the ERM was set at +/– 15 per cent of the central rate (up from just 2.25 per cent). Between these crises, the ratification of the TEU had become increasingly problematic in France (where a referendum in September 1992 produced a very small majority in favour); in the UK (where Conservative Members of Parliament had become increasingly 'Eurosceptic'); and in Germany (where a legal challenge to the Treaty was launched). The EMU project looked increasingly 'wobbly'.

The TEU had incorporated a complex compromise over how and when Stage 3 of EMU – the final and most important phase – might begin. The initial positions adopted by the various governments had been very divergent. France and Italy had wanted to set a clear, binding timetable for Stage 3. Germany and the Netherlands only wanted Stage 3 to begin when the conditions were right. By this they meant that the EU states had achieved a sufficient degree of convergence, as measured by various indicators. The convergence they spoke of was 'nominal', rather than 'real'. No one envisaged Portugal becoming as rich as Germany. Instead, the convergence was defined in terms of monetary stability. The TEU sought to combine both a timetable and a set of convergence tests.

The timetable allowed two possible start dates for Stage 3. If sufficient convergence was achieved, the European Council could before the end of 1996 set a date for Stage 3. Failing this, Stage 3 had to begin on 1 January 1999. If the latter date was to be adopted, then the European Council had to decide before 1 July 1998 which states fulfilled the convergence criteria and were therefore eligible to enter Stage 3.

There had been much conflict in the 1991 IGC over whether the convergence criteria should be laid down in the Treaty or in an attached protocol. If they were in the Treaty, this would make them very difficult to change or ignore. In the event, the criteria appeared in both locations – Articles 104c and 109j of the TEU elaborated the criteria, whilst a protocol defined them more closely. Four tests were set down, requiring participants in Stage 3 to have:

- a stable inflation rate (within 1.5 per cent of the best three performing states in the EU);
- a low government deficit and debt level (3 per cent and 60 per cent of GDP, respectively);
- had no devaluation of their currency in the ERM for the previous two years;
- stable interest rates (within 2 per cent of the best three performing states in the EU).

After the ERM crises of 1992–3, these tests appeared more and more restrictive as national economies fell into recession.

Stage 2 of EMU began as scheduled on 1 January 1994, but the transition to Stage 3 was delayed. The complex formula by which the EU could begin Stage 3 in 1996 was not used because the required degree of convergence between the member states had not been attained. Instead, the EU opted for the alternative, and binding, start date for Stage 3 in the Treaty: 1 January 1999.

In the period until mid-1997, the signs were that few EU states met all of these tests. It seemed likely that Stage 3 would start on a very exclusive basis, leaving a number of states marginalized. The two countries experiencing the biggest problems were Belgium and Italy. Both had huge levels of government debt accumulated from the past, and neither looked able to meet the precise TEU requirement that government debt be equivalent to no more than 60 per cent of GDP. Government debt in both cases was approximately twice that level. Political leaders in both countries, however, were very anxious to gain entry into Stage 3, with the consequence that difficult domestic reforms were introduced to try to tackle the fiscal problems.

But the problems in meeting the convergence conditions were not restricted to Belgium and Italy. In 1997 both France and Germany looked likely to have government deficits above the Maastricht stipulation (3 per cent of GDP). As a result, there was much discussion about whether 3 per cent meant 3.0 per cent precisely, and in both countries 'unconventional' ways of tackling the deficit were sought. This approach was particularly surprising in Germany, given its high reputation for financial rectitude. Finance Minister Theo Waigel became embroiled in a murky dispute in May 1997 with the Bundesbank over his proposal that gold stocks be revalued, in order to defray the government debt level. In the EU's two leading states, near-desperate efforts were made to meet the criteria that had been set in 1991.

Speculation about which states might meet the convergence criteria was highly divisive. Waigel appeared to pour scorn on whether Italy could make the grade or not. Lionel Jospin, elected as French Prime Minister in May 1997, insisted that France would not enter Stage 3 without Italy. The French and German Governments were themselves accused of attempting to 'massage' their own monetary figures.

To some, the speculation also seemed somewhat artificial. The convergence criteria were being treated as if they had been handed down in tablets of stone, as immutable truths. Yet, the figures incorporated in the criteria had been set in 1991 in the belief that they were consistent with current economic trends. No theory supported these precise figures. In principle, they could be adapted in the light of new trends. But the German authorities were keen to show their domestic opponents that the new single currency would be as strong as the Deutschmark, and so they played tough.

EMU was also set to divide the EU in another respect. Some states were likely to decide to stay out of Stage 3, at least at the start, for political reasons. Chief amongst these was the UK, which was required to notify its partners whether it wished to participate in Stage 3 (or to exercise the 'opt-out' it had secured at Maastricht) before the end of 1997. While John Major's Conservative Government was in power, the UK's attitudes appeared to be hardening against the EU, with the Eurosceptics in the Conservative Party gaining increasing sway over the Government. The election of the Labour Government under Tony Blair in May 1997 heralded a 'new start' in the UK's relations with the EU, but it had a very steep hill to climb if it was to catch-up with the rest. On 27 October 1997, Gordon Brown, the Chancellor of the Exchequer, announced that the UK was not ready for EMU and so it would 'opt-out' of Stage 3 until the time was right. The Government would 'wait and see'. Economically, it had little option as the UK's 'economic cycle' was out of kilter with that of most of its EU partners: early entry would be destabilizing. Politically, however, the UK now had a government that wanted to say 'Yes' to EMU. It announced that it would hold a referendum on whether the UK should join Stage 3, but probably not until after the next general election. By contrast, the opposition Conservative Party announced that it was opposed to UK entry for at least ten years.

The decision as to which countries would be part of the single currency from the outset was scheduled to be taken during the UK Presidency in the first half of 1998. It had initially been assumed that the decision would be hotly contested, with the Germans having perhaps the most important say. But as the day of decision approached, the situation was transformed. The impetus now was for an inclusive, rather than an exclusive approach. Almost all who wanted to join were to be allowed to do so. A flexible interpretation of the convergence criteria served the interests of a majority of governments. Moreover, many of them had invested much of their political reputations in realizing EMU. Chief amongst these was Chancellor Kohl, who identified himself with 'Europe' just as firmly as had his hero, Konrad Adenauer.

A special European Council meeting in Brussels on 2 May 1998 agreed that 11 of the 15 EU states would join Stage 3 from 1 January 1999. All EU states except the UK, Denmark, Greece and Sweden were included. Of these, Greece was the most enthusiastic to join, but the least ready to do so. The transition to a single currency – the euro – was to be gradual. The exchange rates of the participating states were to be fixed and to be upheld throughout the transition. The euro notes and coins were scheduled to appear after 1 January 2002. After a short interim period of a few months, the euro would replace each of the national currencies.

The agreement on Stage 3 was marred, however, by an intense dispute over who should head the new European Central Bank. Wim Duisenberg, Governor of the Dutch Central Bank, was favoured by 14 of the EU states. He was already President of the European Monetary Institute (EMI), the forerunner in Stage 2 for the ECB, and had been expected to move over easily to the ECB post. However, in November 1997, President Chirac started moves to have Jean-Claude Trichet, President of the Banque de France, nominated for the ECB post (*Financial Times*, 5 May 1998). At the Brussels summit,

TABLE 16.1 *Chronology of key EMU decisions and the changeover to the euro, 1995–2002*

Event	*Actions*
Madrid European Council, December 1995	Decision on the changeover timetable, and the name 'euro'.
Amsterdam European Council, June 1997	Agreement on Stability and Growth Pact, EMS 2
Brussels Council, May 1998	Decision on participating member states in Stage 3 of EMU. Fixing of bilateral conversion rates. Decision on President and Executive Board of the European Central Bank.
1 July 1998	European Central Bank set up in Frankfurt, replacing the European Monetary Institute, under Presidency of Wim Duisenberg. European System of Central Banks also set up.
1 January 1999	Start of Stage 3 – irrevocable fixing of exchange rates and entry into force of relevant legislation.
From 1 January 1999	Execution of single monetary policy, foreign exchange operations in euros, operation of TARGET payment system, new public debt to be issued in euros.
1 January 1999 to 1 January 2002	Exchange at par value of currencies with irrevocably fixed exchange rates. Assistance with an 'orderly changeover'.
by 1 January 2002 at latest	Start circulation of euro banknotes and coins
by July 2002 at latest	Cancel legal tender status of national banknotes and coins

Source: D. Dinan (1999), p. 469.

Chirac was insistent: the ECB was in Frankfurt, so it was natural that it should be headed by a Frenchman. His partners were, variously, frustrated and outraged. Tony Blair, as chair of the summit, endeavoured to establish a compromise. Finally, a fudged deal was arrived at: Duisenberg would begin the eight-year term, but would decide to retire after four years, to be replaced by Trichet. It was one of the EU's shabbiest deals and Blair was criticized by several delegations for his poor handling of the dispute. The row raised questions about the degree of political direction to be given to EMU and about the smoothness of its launch.

But, above all, this murky episode was one reminiscent of the disputes of the 1960s when French President Charles de Gaulle had asserted French interests in defiance of his partners. The 1998 dispute also testified to the increasingly poor relations between the EU's two main leaders, Chirac and Kohl. The progress of EMU over the previous decade had depended on the steer given by the Franco-German axis, but the clash at Brussels in 1998 introduced an instability into this pattern. Both Kohl and Chirac had become weaker at home, whilst Blair was keen to break into their relationship.

Who has power in EMU?

After 1991, the far-reaching nature of the EMU project was reflected in a number of ways. It reconfigured the structure of power in European monetary policy and it imposed a new and severe constraint on monetary and fiscal policy at the national level. It also gave more power to some actors, and less to others. At the EU level, it created a new institutional structure governing monetary policy across the EMU states.

The economic policy agendas of national governments across the EU have been restructured by the terms of the EMU agreement. A strait-jacket has been imposed on policy options by the requirements of the 'convergence criteria' governing the entry of states into the final phase of EMU. The consequences of this strait-jacket are much disputed, but they are variously claimed to have involved cuts to welfare benefits, higher taxes and interest rates, and increased unemployment. It is also claimed to have reduced inflation, cut government borrowing, and stabilized currency exchange rates. Whatever the truth of such claims, it is clear that the economic effects attributed to EMU are significant.

Moreover, the terms of the EMU agreement have altered the balance of political forces within the EU. Structural power relations have been affected at both the national and European levels. Perhaps more generally, EMU can be seen as a process of imposing German monetary power on the EU or, alternatively, as a means of transforming that power by 'Europeanizing' it. In addition, EMU can be portrayed as changing the power relationship between EU states and global financial markets. It changes the relationship between national finance ministries, national central banks, and global financial markets, with power slipping from the first to the third. A discipline on policy is exerted that restricts the scope for discretion by national politicians and advantages those technocrats responsible for making market-sensitive judgements. The monetary orthodoxy underpinning EMU also requires central bank independence from national finance ministries.

More generally, in connecting with debates on budget retrenchment, welfare reform and labour market deregulation, EMU revises the terms of those debates to favour distinctive sets of interests. Monetary policy has traditionally had a closeted and opaque nature, being determined by elites distant from public debate. The visibility of the EMU project may act, to some extent, to lift this veil. In doing so, new challenges to the monetary orthodoxy on which EMU is based may surface, raising questions of legitimacy at both the European and national levels.

The issue of legitimacy is also affected as a result of EMU creating a new configuration in the EU's own institutional structure. The TEU created a 'three pillar' architecture for the EU, but in many respects EMU constitutes a 'fourth pillar'. It is a distinct sphere of decision-making that is marked by the authority of the new European Central Bank in Stage 3, beyond the direct control of national governments. The ECB has more political independence than was previously possessed by the German Bundesbank and it has the supreme power to determine monetary policy for the EU. The ECB is headed by a six-member executive, each of whom is appointed by the European Council for a non-renewable term of eight years. The ECB sets interest rates and can give instructions to national central banks. Alongside the ECB, the European Council and the Council of (Economic and Finance) Ministers have some scope to guide or intervene in EMU policies. But the Council's role is much less than that initially advocated by the French Government when it sought a 'gouvernement economique', with fiscal policy responsibilities, to counter-balance the monetary power of the ECB.

The EU institutions which lose out in EMU, relative to other policy sectors, are the Commission and the European Parliament (EP). On EMU, the Commission's traditional right to initiate legislation is shared with the new European Central Bank in Stage 3, and in many cases the Commission is obliged to present its initiatives in a form which facilitates amendment by the Council of Ministers. For its part, the EP is to be informed and consulted by other bodies on EMU, but there is little parallel here to the co-decision procedure found elsewhere.

Has EMU legitimacy?

EMU raises important questions concerned with legitimacy, not least because of the strength of the ECB and the weak position of the EP. These questions cut across both the European and national levels, and apply to each separately.

At the European level, EMU creates a system of governance which privileges the role of independent central bankers and creates a sphere of power which is only intermittently or indirectly accountable to elected politicians. A set of distinct economic beliefs – centring on the importance of price stability, central bank independence, and the sharing of the Bundesbank's credibility – has created the orthodoxy on which EMU is based. In doing so, this gives rise in many parts of the EU to sensitivities about democratic legitimacy, the power of technocratic elites, and the distance of the mass public from the project. In short, nowhere is the problem of the EU's 'democratic deficit' more pronounced than it is in the domain of EMU.

At the national level, the policies necessary to join EMU challenge the political commitment of governments and their publics to the European integration process. In some cases, domestic support for European unity is being used to give legitimacy to difficult and painful economic measures. This has been evident in states such as Belgium, Italy and Greece, which struggled to meet the convergence criteria for Stage 3. In addition, domestic support for the EU in the context of clear policy messages emanating from the European level can give rise to governments seeking to shift the blame for unpopular policies to the EU. In other cases, the level of domestic support for 'Europe' is much more questionable, as in the UK, Denmark and

Sweden. Here, the idea of entering Stage 3 has to be sold on different grounds. The 'legitimacy' of the proposal has to be based much more squarely on its own pragmatic, economic merits.

More generally, in establishing such a clear new EU-level competence, EMU creates a contrasting system of governance to that existing domestically. The relatively high levels of support for EMU in Greece and Italy, for example, are surely related to the problems of inflation and currency instability in those systems. Here, EMU can give the EU an image of greater efficiency and discipline, as well as appearing less corrupt. The contrast may prove to be telling. Public disenchantment with national politicians at home may give further impetus to integration.

Conclusion

The foregoing analysis shows that the dynamism of EMU has taken many forms. One of its most distinctive features has been its varying pace. At times the course of EMU has surged, whilst at others it has faltered. The completion of an agreement at Maastricht and its subsequent implementation depended on a range of contingent factors. These have included individual political leadership, strategic calculations, the institutional route followed, the globalization of financial markets, and the impact of a set of economic beliefs underpinning EMU.

The complexity of the dynamism of EMU has also been displayed in the process of implementation. This is evident when questions of stability, power and legitimacy are raised. EMU has reconfigured the pattern of monetary power within the EU, and has provoked new concerns about legitimacy at both the European and national levels. EMU deepens the process of 'Europeanization', taking the integration process into a new era.

The combination of EMU and increased flexibility in the pattern of European integration poses additional issues. The Amsterdam Treaty of 1997 may open the way to a more differentiated structure of membership in the EU. In any event, the prospect of a prolonged and gradual process of enlargement to incorporate states from Central and Eastern Europe, as well as Cyprus, may itself give a multitiered character to the EU system. The eastern states will probably enter the EU well before they enter a single currency. The difference between an 'inner core' and the 'periphery' could be starkly set.

The dynamic impact of EMU could continue to expand and 'snowball'. Already, however, it is the major component of the developing process of European integration, and its impact deserves careful attention. Often opaque in the past, monetary policy has now become of widespread political importance and it raises fundamental questions about the nature of the emerging EU polity.

Guide to Further Reading

The literature on EMU is varied, though not much is available on its recent political history. There is a vast literature on the economics of EMU, much of which is very technical. Johnson (1996) is a lucid guide, setting out the pro-EMU case. Tsoukalis (1996) covers the economic implications and considers the long-term development of EMU as a policy project for the EU. Dyson (1994) places the history of monetary union in a political science framework. Dyson and Featherstone (1999) examine the emergence and negotiation of the 1991 EMU agreement, and analyse domestic policy-making on it in the four larger member states.

References

Bulmer, S. (1994) 'The Governance of the European Union: A New Institutionalist Approach', *Journal of Public Policy*, vol. 13, no. 4, pp. 351–80.

Delors, J. *et al.* (1989) Committee for the Study of Economic and Monetary Union, *Report on Economic and Monetary Union in the European Community*. Luxembourg: Office for Official Publications of the European Communities.

Dinan, D. (1999) *Ever Closer Union* (2nd edn) Basingstoke: Macmillan.

Dyson, K. (1994) *Elusive Union: The Process of Economic and Monetary Union in Europe*. London: Longman.

Dyson, K. and Featherstone, K. (1999) *Negotiating the Maastricht Treaty: The Dynamics of Economic and Monetary Union*, Oxford: Oxford University Press.

Haas, P. M. (1992) 'Introduction: Epistemic Communities and International Policy Coordination', *International Organization*, vol. 46, no.1, pp. 1–35.

Johnson, C. (1996) *In with the Euro, Out with the Pound*. London: Penguin.

Kingdon, J. (1984) *Agendas, Alternatives and Public Policies*. New York: HarperCollins.

March, J. and Olsen, J. P. (1989) *Rediscovering Institutions*. New York: Free Press.

Padoa-Schioppa, T. (1987) *Efficiency, Stability and Equity*. Oxford: Oxford University Press.

Putnam, R. (1988) 'Diplomacy and Domestic Politics: The Logic of Two-Level Games', *International Organization*, vol. 42, no. 3, pp. 427–60.

Radaelli, C. (1995) 'The Role of Knowledge in the Policy Process', *Journal of European Public Policy*, vol. 2, pp. 160–83.
Sabatier, P. and Jenkins-Smith, H. (eds), *Policy Change and Learning: An Advocacy Coalition Approach*. Boulder, CO: Westview Press.
Tsoukalis, L. (1996) 'Economic and Monetary Union', in H. Wallace and W. Wallace (eds), *Policy-Making in the European Union*. Oxford: Oxford University Press pp. 279–99.

17

Democracy and the European Union

BRIGID LAFFAN

Democracy and legitimacy are key themes in the contemporary discourse about European integration. That there is such a discourse is significant and of profound interest to students of politics. The United Nations, the World Trade Organization and the numerous other organizations above the level of the state are not discussed in a similar vein. That these issues arise in relation to the European Union (EU) and the dynamic of integration tells us that the EU lies somewhere between politics and diplomacy, between the domestic and the international, and between government and governance. It is precisely this quality of 'betweenness' that poses a challenge for politicians and political theorists alike.

The debate about democracy in the EU is based on the twin assumptions that the Union is a polity, however part-formed, and that it impinges to a growing extent on the institutions and practices of national democracies. The debate stems from strong normative concerns about contemporary governance both at the national and European levels. Scholars addressing the question are faced with a number of inter-related challenges. First, both democracy and the related concept of legitimacy are themselves contested concepts in political theory and political science. Second, political theorists have tended to focus on democracy and legitimacy in the traditional nation-state, rather than non-state forms of political order. Democratic institutions and practices, as we know them, evolved within the sovereign nation-state. The EU is a challenge to how we conceptualize democracy, authority and legitimacy in contemporary politics. Third, the EU is crafted onto pre-existing democracies in Western Europe, which means that there is a dual democratic imperative operating in the EU.

This chapter addresses the questions of democracy in a number of stages. Firstly, a brief overview of the institutions and practices of liberal democracy will be given. Next we will consider why democracy and legitimacy should have such significance in the current phase of the integration process. Thirdly, the chapter analyses the symptoms of a democratic deficit in the Union. Finally, the various projects designed to render the EU more democratic and legitimate are assessed.

Democracy

Democracy is both a set of ideals about the exercise of political authority and a set of institutions/processes to organize government. In the contemporary world, democracy is practised through representative institutions whereby the people elect politicians in competitive elections to represent them in parliamentary institutions. Representative democracy, characterized by choice between different political parties, evolved to correspond with the scale of the nation-state. Elections exercise a key role in government formation and parliaments provide an arena of accountability and deliberation. In the liberal democratic tradition of government, executives are accountable to parliament and executive power is limited by constitutional provisions. The political community is made up of citizens who are endowed with legal, political and social rights by virtue of their inclusion in the polity. Although majoritarian institutions predominate in liberal democracies, non-majoritarian ones, such as courts, independent central banks and regulatory agencies, exercise a pivotal role. Notwithstanding diverse constitutional and institutional traditions, the member states of the EU all conform to this liberal democratic model of statehood, as outlined in Figure 17.1.

Legitimacy is a fundamental concept in political theory and a key component of democratic governance. It is important, however, to distinguish between democracy and legitimacy. A system may benefit from a reasonably high level of legitimacy while not conforming to key features of democracy and vice versa. However, in the western tradition of liberal democracy, legitimacy and democracy are closely related. On the one hand, democracy legitimates the authority of those in power and, on the other hand, the effectiveness of political

Constitutionalism: Limits to state power, rule of law, fundamental rights and freedoms, judicial review.

Popular Sovereignty: Regular competitive elections and forms of direct democracy.

Separation of Powers: different branches of authority – judicial, executive and parliamentary.

Representative Government: government accountable to parliament.

Separation of State from Civil Society

FIGURE 17.1 *Key features of the liberal democratic state*

authority must rest on a degree of legitimacy. The authority of governments to govern and the publics' acceptance of that authority rests on the assumption that governments represent the will of the people as defined by competitive elections, and that governments are responsive to the concerns of the people. For some, political institutions are deemed to be legitimate if 'people hold the belief that . . . institutions are appropriate or morally proper' (Dogan, 1992, p. 116) whereas for others, legitimacy exists when 'political institutions are better than any other that might be established, and therefore can demand obedience' (Linz, 1988, p. 65). The emphasis on obedience is not, however, a sufficient test for those who would argue that legitimacy implies that 'people follow rules and laws because they actually think them right and worthy of respect' (Held, 1987, p. 238). When addressing the questions of democracy and legitimacy in relation to the EU, we must be mindful that these are contested concepts and that theorists are only beginning to address how these might be applied to non-state forms of political order.

Why Do Legitimacy and Democracy Have Such Significance in the Present Phase of European Integration?

Questions of democracy and legitimacy are now far more salient than they have ever been in the history of the EU. This reflects the growing politicization of integration. However, the roots of the EU stem from a profoundly democratic ideal, which was to moderate inter-state relations in Europe. From the outset, the objective of the so-called founding fathers was to transform the context of inter-state relations in Europe, to tame the worst excesses of European nationalism and to contribute to peace and prosperity in Western Europe. The justification for this new approach to inter-state relations was embedded in the founding treaties, in the following terms:

> Resolved to substitute for age-old rivalries the merging of their essential interests; to create, by establishing an economic community, the basis for a broader and deeper community among peoples long divided by bloody conflicts; and to lay the foundations for institutions which will give direction to a destiny henceforward shared. (Treaty of Paris, Preamble, 18 April 1951)

This rhetorical statement embodies the key features of the EU as a political entity, notably, the references to 'essential interests' which would be worked out in common, the creation of a 'community among peoples', and the establishment of common institutions to articulate a shared destiny. To the interests and identities of each member state were added common interests, vested in common institutions and a powerful appeal to the future in terms of a shared destiny. Membership of the EU implied a willingness to accept the other member states as partners in a collective project.

At the outset of the integration process, legitimization rested on the authority of the member states consenting, in the form of international treaties ratified by national constitutional provisions, to the establishment of the then European Community. The consensual and voluntary nature of the process was and remains critical to its legitimacy. Legitimacy was also bound up in the Community's image as a peacekeeper in Europe (Kaiser *et al.*, 1983, p. 23). National actors in the Community arena brought with them the authority and legitimacy of their national systems. The European Court of Justice (ECJ) in Luxembourg set about establishing the key principles of a federal legal order. The technical nature of the 'politics of policy' meant that politics in the Community in this period was the preserve of small groups of interested parties. There was a permissive consensus among the populations of the original member states; the feeling that integration was desirable became part of the landscape of European politics (Lindberg and Scheingold, 1970).

Concern about the relationship between integration and democracy surfaced at the end of the 1960s, precisely when the transitional phase of market integration was completed and the Community was about to embark on a more ambitious programme of policy integration. In 1969, Chancellor Willy Brandt of Germany called for a Europe with a 'human face'. This was followed by the Vedel Report on the powers of the European Parliament (EP), which argued for a reinforcement of the democratic element of the Community. Proponents of a federal Europe, such as Altiero Spinelli, were always conscious of the need to enhance democracy in the Community and to increase the participation of individual citizens in its processes. Direct elections to the EP in 1979, the Parliament's Draft Treaty on European Union (1984), and the establishment of the Adonnino Committee by the European Council in 1984 all reflected a 'top-down' concern with the political dimension of integration.

The salience of the debate on democracy and legitimacy on the EC/EU agenda increased dramatically in the 1990s. This took place against the backdrop of a debate in the academic literature about a crisis of representation in Europe and growing distrust in public institutions at national level (for example, see Dunn, 1995; Hayward, 1995; Held, 1996). The following factors appear the most significant indicators of a shift to this new phase in the development of the EU:

- The EU impinges more on the member states than ever before because of the extension in the policy reach of the Union and the growing Europeanization of public policy-making. There are few areas of domestic policy that do not have a European dimension.
- Europeanisation is a question of breadth, but also of depth. With the advent of Economic and Monetary Union (EMU), and growing cooperation in pillars two and three of the Treaty on European Union (TEU), EU policy impinges more and more on core attributes of statehood – money, borders and security. The inherent tension between sovereignty and integration has been exacerbated as the stakes in integration have heightened.
- The process of Europeanization disturbs domestic policy networks and territorial politics in the member states. European matters have been internalized in domestic politics and have become politicized in a manner that was not evident in the past.
- The process of constitution-building, with three treaties in just eleven years, has imposed considerable demands on national political parties, constitutional courts, parliaments, governments and publics. Membership of the Union has implied acceptance of a developing and evolving set of institutions and policies with no end in sight.
- The growing visibility of the Union raises the question of public opinion and the level of support for the EU and its policies. It is

clear from the regular *Eurobarometer* surveys that are conducted on behalf of the Commission, that support for the EU differs significantly across the member states, and that in some member states the public is not at all at ease with Union membership. Euroscepticism is a distinct feature of contemporary Europe.

The Democracy Deficit

When a majority of the Danish electorate opposed ratification of the TEU in 1992, politicians throughout the member states responded by emphasizing the need to make Europe more transparent, accountable, and relevant to the peoples of Europe. Speech after speech and communiqué after communiqué resonated with references to the 'citizens' of Europe. The pronouncements of all EU institutions increasingly identified the need to democratize the Union. The Reflection Group which prepared the way for the 1996 Intergovernmental Conference (IGC) on treaty reform acknowledged that the Union would have to become more transparent and closer to its citizens in order to overcome their alienation from the Union (Reflection Group, 1995, p. 4). The Dublin Draft Treaty (December 1996), issued by the Council Presidency during the IGC, opened with the ringing statement that 'Europe belongs to its citizens'. It went on to emphasize that 'for the Union's institutions to retain the trust, respect and active support of its citizens in each and every Member State it will be necessary to make institutional changes which marry the desire for more efficient and effective decision-making with the need to ensure that the institutions are visibly democratic and firmly rooted in public acceptance' (Dublin Draft Treaty, 1996, p. 7). Politicians identified the need for direct mechanisms of legitimization and began to accept that the Union could no longer rely only on indirect forms of legitimization, via the member states.

Six different aspects of the democratic deficit have been identified by scholars examining democracy and legitimacy in the integration process.

Constitutional

The constitutional architecture of the Union has evolved from a series of treaties agreed by the 'high contracting parties', that is, the member states. The treaties in turn have been constitutionalized by the ECJ which fostered a federal legal order, but the system lacks constitutional clarity (Laffan, 1996a). The treaties have been ratified by the member states according to domestic constitutional provisions, but they have not received the direct consent of citizens at national level, except in those few member states with a tradition of direct democracy. Moreover, the dynamic of legal integration has led to an ever-widening policy competence at EU level.

Institutional design

The creation of a set of common institutions at EU level has been one of the most characteristic features of European governance. The functioning of the Commission, European Council, Council of Ministers, Parliament and Court of Justice provides the institutional framework for collective action by the member states. However, the Union's institutional design does not conform to the traditional separation of powers between legislative, executive and judicial branches of government. Rather, decisions evolve from intense bargaining within and across the policy-making institutions, operating within a delicate institutional balance. The Union is not a traditional hierarchy with a clearly defined centre of political authority, such as a government. As a result, Europe's citizens have difficulty in identifying 'who governs' in the Union and cannot exercise their own perogative to dismiss them at elections (Weiler, 1996).

During the 1990s, the legitimacy of each of the institutions has been questioned. Firstly, the Commission, which exercises a number of very important roles including policy initiation and law-making power (the latter albeit of a secondary character), has no direct democratic mandate. The Commission was conceived as a powerful 'think-tank', a technocratic body at the heart of the institutional system which would depoliticize issues and frame policy in a rational environment. In the 1990s, caricatured as the Brussels bureaucracy, it faced sustained criticism from politicians in a number of member states. The allegations of fraud and corruption culminating in the resignation of the College of Commissioners in March 1999 have undermined its legitimacy and exposed its shallow political roots. Secondly, the Council of Ministers, as the main law-making body, has increasingly been regarded as lacking in accountability as a collective entity. Accountability could only be exercised through national parliaments, which have found it difficult to keep up with EU affairs. The increased use of qualified majority voting in the Council has meant that the member states have had to transpose and enforce laws with which they do not agree. The secrecy of the Council when making decisions and passing laws has also been highlighted. Thirdly, the European Parliament, directly elected since 1979, has used its democratic credentials to press for more power in the system. However, the EP has suffered from a number of problems, notably high levels of absenteeism and low turnout in EP elections, which have served to undermine its assertion of legitimacy. Furthermore, an undoubted tension developed between the EP and national parliaments in the 1990s.

Process

The EU has spawned a complex set of governing institutions, a myriad of decision rules and an inchoate constitutional framework. Each additional treaty has brought additional competencies and rules encapsulated in the pillar system established by the TEU. Governance in the EU is opaque and inaccessible which exacerbates the problems of accountability identified above.

The Union has fostered an intensification of institutional linkages between Brussels and the member states in a form of *engrenage* which has brought more and more national actors into the Brussels arena. At the core of the process is the growth of committees and working groups attached to the Commission services and in the Council (Wessels, 1997). As part of this growth, the Commission has enhanced its weak bureaucratic resources by co-opting national officials into a burgeoning world of comitology committees. The system privileges administrative, technical and expert knowledge over political power and represents a system of government by committee. Middle-ranking Commission officials and their national counterparts play a pivotal role in agenda-setting, in framing the terms of debate on precise regulations, and in taking decisions before the final 'political' decisions are taken at ministerial level. This world is the preserve of Brussels 'insiders' who can find their way through the labyrinthine decision maze. This dominance of technical experts, and the Euro-jargon which they have spawned, has been important in serving to obfuscate the big political choices that must be faced in Europe.

Public Opinion

Individual Europeans are subject to European law and have gained rights under the new legal order, but they are more actively engaged in the system as consumers or workers then as citizens. EU institutions suffer from a distinct remoteness from Europe's peoples, which was most dramatically demonstrated by the Danish 'No' and the narrow French 'Yes' for the ratification of the TEU in two referendums in 1992. Yet the drafters of the Treaty had insulated themselves from public opinion, secure in the conviction that there was diffuse support for European integration.

From 1981 to 1991 support for the Union rose steadily, with 72 per cent of respondents claiming that their country's membership was a good thing in 1991. The proportion was 49 per cent in autumn 1997, having recovered from a low of 46 per cent recorded earlier that year (*Eurobarometer*, 48, 1997). This figure disguises considerable cross-national variation. For example, there are reasonably high levels of support for European integration among most of the founding member states and among a number of latecomers – notably Ireland, Spain, Portugal and Greece. By contrast, following German unification in 1991, support in Germany began to fall and it was the only founding member state with less than 40 per cent of respondents claiming that EU membership was a good thing in 1997 (*Eurobarometer*, 48, 1997). Public support in the UK, Denmark and the new EFTA members is also comparatively low – for instance, 46 per cent of Swedes did not think that their country's membership was a good thing in 1997 (*Eurobarometer*, 48, 1997).

When asked if they were satisfied with democracy in the EU, less than half of the respondents in 1997 replied in the affirmative. Dissatisfaction was particularly high in Sweden, Germany, Belgium, Finland, Denmark and the Netherlands. This was a significant finding because a majority of respondents felt that the Union would play a more important role in their daily lives (46 per cent), or at least the same role (34 per cent) in the next century (*Eurobarometer*, 48, 1997).

Political Community

The European Union is not, and cannot be, a political community in the way that national democracies are. The public space in Europe is fragmented into separate national spheres. The EU lacks the transmission belts, such as strong European political parties and a European-wide media, that animate deliberation and enlightened understanding at national level. The profusion of administrative and governmental ties in the EU is not matched by strong linkages between other parts of the national political systems. The Europeanization of public policy-making has not been accompanied by a Europeanization of politics. Political community rests on feelings of solidarity and a sense of belonging which develop from a sense of common identity and a commitment to the commonweal. Political development in the nation-state is underpinned by nationalism and national identity.

There is now a debate about the desirability and feasibility of a European identity which may be necessary if the EU is to enhance its identity and become a genuine political realm. Because of the challenge of scale, democracy and solidarity in the contemporary world may need to be redefined in a larger political space than the nation state (Held, 1996).

Scale

Robert Dahl, a seminal scholar of democracy, identified the growing problem of scale in contemporary government which may transform the possibilities and limits of democratic politics. He has suggested that the transformation of political order in the world today may be akin to the shift from city-state democracy in ancient Greece to representative democracy in the nation-state. There is an increase in the scale of decision-making and growing limits to the autonomy of the national democratic state (Dahl, 1989, p. 319). In large-scale political systems, it is more difficult to allow for the effective participation of citizens and to ensure that the political process is responsive to the preferences of the people. This produces a dilemma because the benefits of participating in integration may come at the cost of submerging national democratic government into larger and less democratic transnational political spaces (Dahl, 1994, p. 23). Citizens are faced with a trade-off between the need to participate in structures that manage interdependence and the impact of these structures on national democracies. In the Union, national electorates vary greatly in their attitude to the trade-off between effectiveness and participation (Laffan 1996b, p. 95).

The democratic deficit in the EU stems from structural features of the decision making system, barriers to participation in the system and the key challenge of democratizing political space above the level of the state. The word 'deficit' implies an inadequacy or insufficiency, but what is the appropriate bench-mark against which to test the EU?

From the perspective of traditional international organizations and diplomacy, 'With all its imperfections the Community domesticates the balance of power into something which , if not as "democratic" as domestic norms, has made the international system in Europe take a huge step in their direction' (Duchêne, 1994, p. 405). The Union is bound by laws, rules and mutual obligation. Yet from the perspective of national representative democracy, the Union is deficient in terms of democratic practice and accountability. How then can these deficiencies be addressed?

Students of political development should not be surprised at the debate in the Union on democracy and legitimacy. National democracies and political communities emerged from war and struggle about different ideals of democracy, different democratic practices and different institutional models. It would be surprising if the new and emerging governance structures in the EU were rendered democratic without conflict. The habits of diplomacy are difficult to dislodge. It would be even more surprising if the Union evolved as a political community in the national sense in such a short timeframe. The feeling of belonging to the nation-state and the solidarity it engendered was fostered over long periods by statebuilders and by war.

What then are the prospects for a transnational democratic polity at EU level? What ideals, democratic practices, institutions and community should animate such a polity? Can the incipient institutions of a transnational political community, identified by Dahl (1989, p. 320), become rooted in Europe? Can the EU be transformed from a system of democratic governments into a democratic system of governance (Chryssochoou, 1996, p. 788)?

Two-level Democracy in Europe: Addressing the Democratic Deficit?

Democracy in the EU cannot be seen as distinct from democracy in the member states. If the Union is to transform itself from a system of democratic states into a democratic system of governance, it must first crucially remain a system of democratic states. For governments, individuals and interest groups, democratic participation, channels of influence, identity and rights may begin within their national polities but they do not end there; there is now a wider European arena. Democratization of the EU is following the well-worn path of

Founding Values: Embedding deep values in the Treaty of Amsterdam

Constitutionalism: Importance of legally binding treaties, the rule of law and judicial review to the process but public power mediated by states rather than the people.

Institutional Reform: Enhanced role of the EP, the role of national parliaments, the establishment of the Committee of the Regions, the Ombudsman.

Procedural Principles: Subsidiarity, transparency and openness.

Citizenship and Identity Building: Establishment of legal and political rights, symbols of belonging.

Associative Democracy: Transnational linkages of all kinds.

FIGURE 17.2 *Democratizing the EU in bits and pieces*

incremental change and pragmatic adaptation, not unlike the process of market creation. As Figure 17.2 shows, we can detect a mixture of old- and new-style politics and strategies, but a very ill-defined political form.

Embedding liberal values

A significant development in the 1997 Treaty of Amsterdam was the inclusion of the founding values of the EU system. Article 6 of the post-Amsterdam consolidated TEU states that 'the Union is founded on the principles of liberty, democracy, respect for human rights and fundamental freedoms, and the rule of law, principles which are common to the Member States'. Hence these universal values, which were rooted in the particular contexts of the member states, are to be given a wider European context. European states which respect these principles may become members of the Union. Moreover, the Treaty implies a standard of conduct to the extent that the Treaty includes a provision that the Council may suspend certain rights under the Treaty if a member state engages in a serious or persistent breach of these principles. The Treaty makes more explicit what was implicit in the Communities from the outset and its powers to ensure that these values are respected by existing and new member states. The Treaty underlines the historic mission of the Union to extend a liberal order throughout Western Europe and the wider continent. Embedding these values in the continental order adds another layer to their protection.

National Parliaments

It is important to distinguish between those member states for whom membership of the EU protects democracy and those for whom membership is seen as a dilution of a vibrant and self confident national democracy. On the one hand, for Greece, Spain and Portugal membership of the Union was significant in the process of democratization. On the other hand, for the Scandinavian states EU membership was perceived as a threat to the institutions and practices of national democracy. The concerns in many of the member states, not just in Scandinavia, about the impact of integration on their national democracies must be taken seriously.

These concerns can be partially met by enhancing the role of national parliaments in the EU system. A marked feature of this phase of integration is the mobilization of national parliaments on EU matters. The Treaty of Amsterdam's protocol on the role of national parliaments is a beginning. The Conference of European Affairs Committees (COSAC) provides an important transnational link for national parliamentarians, and the domestic European committees provide an arena of deliberation on the national dimension of integration. Their effectiveness depends on national parliamentary culture and competence. The principle of subsidiarity, enshrined in the TEU, acts as a necessary break against the tendency of EU legislation to spread its tentacles into ever-widening areas of activity. National governments must communicate more effectively on European matters. Political players within the member states have so far not communicated the realities of power in contemporary Europe to their electorates. They persist with an old language of national interest when in reality, janus-like, they serve both the national governments and collective European government. National politicians, to a far greater degree than hitherto, need to engage their electorates in a dialogue about internationalisation and its consequences for political order.

The European Parliament

The debate on democratizing the Union's decision-making process has been dominated by a discussion of the powers of the EP. Armed with enhanced democratic credentials following the first direct elections in 1979 and unhappy with its place in the Union's institutional order, the Parliament has persistently argued for more power. In so doing it has engaged in advocacy politics and has co-opted friendly national governments to its cause.

On the question of Parliament's power, the member states have tended to fall into three camps. First, Germany, Italy, and the Benelux countries have strongly supported an enhanced role of the EP, seeing this in terms of a federalizing process. Second, a number of member states, particularly Denmark and the UK, have opposed increased powers for the EP on the grounds that this represents a dilution of the role of national parliaments and hence national democracy. Third, there are states such as France and Ireland that have opposed increased powers for the Parliament on the grounds that this dilutes the power of national governments in the Council.

These different national positions have framed much of the context in which the EP, like all relatively young institutions in a radically changing institutional landscape, has had to struggle to establish its influence and presence. As Chapters 4 and 7 show, treaty reforms have steadily strengthened its powers, and it has further managed to insert itself in the Union's 'politics of policy' by using its legislative powers and through the work of its committees. The growing role of the Parliament may be gleaned from the attention its receives from lobbies of all kinds. Its ability to hold open fora and to conduct committees of inquiry provide important arenas for deliberation on the 'big issues' of European politics. It is capable of holding the Commission accountable for its activities, but not the Council. Importantly, it is the main forum for party politics at European level. The Parliament's links to its electorates are less secure than its place in the 'politics of policy'. Turnout in European elections is low (58 per cent in 1994), with considerable cross-national variation in turnout figures. To date, European elections are manifestly less salient to national electorates than national general elections. They are dominated by national campaigns – a fact which undermines the EP's claims to be the main channel of democracy in the Union. We will return below to a discussion of how further avenues of participation might open up.

Mobilization of National Actors

A striking feature of European integration from the mid-1980s onwards has been the extensive mobilization of national actors seeking voice and presence in the European arena. This wave of mobilization was initially dominated by producer groups, but the

Commission quickly moved to create opportunities for countervailing groups such as women's groups, environmentalists, the unemployed, and many others. The latter have used EU finance to attend conferences in Brussels and to develop transnational ties.

As James Mitchell and Paul McAleavey show in Chapter 9, regional actors have been amongst the foremost mobilizers of recent years, with European regions and subnational entities increasingly active in the European arena, opening offices in Brussels and campaigning for direct representation. This direct representation materialized in the form of the Committee of the Regions, established by the TEU as a formal consultative voice for the regional and local tiers of government in Brussels. The growing voice of Europe's regions reflected processes of constitutional reform and devolution in many member states.

The mobilization of actors in the Brussels arena reflects the growing salience of EU politics. Those groups and interests that are affected by EU policy make their way to Brussels or bring Brussels into the national arena and are actively engaged in transnational partnerships of one kind or another. This represents the emergence of associative democracy in the Union.

The Establishment of Rights

The mobilization of groups has been accompanied by a strengthening of the rights of individuals in the system. Since the 1950s, EC provisions on the free movement of workers have gradually increased the rights of workers and their families as they move from one member state to another. Advocacy by the Commission and activism by the ECJ has established the principle of nondiscrimination on the basis of nationality in the EU system. The extent of these rights has been greatly enhanced over time. In 1992, the Treaty on European Union made provision for citizenship of the Union which entailed, in addition to pre-existing free movement rights, further political rights. The development of citizenship as an additional layer has been highly contentious in some member states – notably in Denmark, where the electorate fundamentally opposed the whole concept of European citizenship. Since Maastricht, it has not proved possible to add to the citizenship provisions in any substantial way because of this opposition in some member states, which remains wedded to citizenship rooted in the nation state.

Transparency

Since the shock of the Danish 'No' in 1992, Europe's political leaders have attempted to tackle the problems of the Union's decision-making process by focusing on transparency, openness and access. Changing the culture of decision-making in the Union is likely to be a slow and tortuous process given the ingrained culture of secrecy in the Council and the traditions of secrecy in many member states. Membership of the Nordic states, however, with their strong tradition of open government, has altered the political balance in favour of greater openness. Their presence at the 1996 Intergovernmental Conference resulted in new provisions on transparency being incorporated into the EC Treaty (Article 255) which allow any citizen of the Union access to documents subject to certain limits. The provisions on transparency in addition to the protocol on subsidiarity, already mentioned, serve to alter the norms and procedures of the policy process in a more democratic direction. Provision for an Ombudsman also strengthens mechanisms for accountability in the system.

Together the steps taken to enhance and reinforce the democratic element in the Union add basic democratic ideals, processes and accountability to the EU system which can contribute to the emergence of a transnational democratic polity at EU level. However, they are not sufficient in themselves. This brings us back to the question of political community.

Political Community

The borders of nation-states are not just territorial borders but define national societies and political communities. Within national borders, political communities operate on the basis of majoritarian rule through competitive elections. The national polity is constituted by the demos, the people with rules of inclusion and exclusion. This model

> presupposes the existence of a 'community' with a collective identity, which implies that in regard to particular issues citizens are in principle prepared to treat their fellow citizens' interests as their own. It is only where this is the case that the minority need not fear exploitation, oppression or annihilation by the ruling majority, and it is only where this is the case that measures amounting to redistribution at the expense of individual interests will be considered acceptable. (Scharpf, 1996, p. 137)

The Union is not constituted by a demos with a collective identity but consists of the multiple demoi of the member states. Scholars are deeply divided about the consequences of this for political community and democracy in the EU. The German Constitutional Court, in its ruling on the TEU in 1993, expounded a 'no demos' thesis which essentially argued that European democracy had to be based on 'certain pre-legal conditions, such as continuous free debate between opposing social forces, interests, and ideas, in which political goals become clarified and change course and out of which public opinion emerges which starts to shape political will' (German Constitutional Court Ruling, 1993, p. 28). In the absence of these conditions in the Union at present, 'democratic legitimisation comes about through the feed-back of the actions of the European institutions into the parliaments of the Member States' (ibid). According to Weiler *et al.*, (1995) the rigorous implication of the no demos thesis is that in the absence of a demos there cannot be a democracy or democratization at EU level. Other scholars, such as Hix (1998) and Chryssochoou (1996), are far less pessimistic but differ in their prescriptions for democracy in the Union.

Hix argues for the need to inject traditional majoritarian competitive politics into the system while rejecting the standard recipe of institutional reform. He advocates electoral competition based on European not national issues and suggests two institutional devices, namely, European-wide referenda and direct election of the President of the Commission. The idea of European-wide referenda as a means of injecting an element of direct democracy into the system may have some merit. The direct election of the Commission President would represent a competitive election on a European-wide basis and would alter the opportunity structures for political parties at the European level. Traditional political competition would help construct new democratic identities and hence would contribute to solving the no-demos problem (Hix, 1998, p. 53).

The no-demos thesis also exercises Chryssochoou, but his analysis leads him an a different direction. He is essentially optimistic about the construction of what he calls Europe's could-be demos which is the core source of transnational political authority. The challenge is to transform this nascent and highly fragmented demos into more than an incipient political community and to provide it with the means of making its mark on the central processes of government. The aim is 'the gradual building of a European civic order among a cluster of democratic entities, allowing for the forging of new collective political identities out of a rich spectrum of pre-existing ones' (Chryssochoou, 1996, p. 790). The civic order would be based not on traditional nation or statebuilding but would seek to harness the democratic ethos of the existing demoi at the European level. He argues strongly for Union citizenship as the pathway to a transnational demos and a civic weapon for creating new and better politics in the Union (ibid.). But Union citizens would have to be able to mobilize in some form of European political contest to transform the existing rights base of European citizenship into democratic 'praxis'. Hence the need to combine the approaches of Hix and Chryssochoou to inject some politics into the EU system beyond the 'politics of policy'.

Conclusions

The European Union is not suffering from a crisis of democracy or legitimacy. The claim that the EU is undemocratic is fallacious. Rather in the present phase of integration the Union has become a far more salient and visible arena of politics for Europe's political elites and publics. Increased saliency has been accompanied by a level of politicization never before experienced by the EU. Politicization brings growing numbers of actors into the EU forums, each of which is seeking voice and representation in this emerging arena of politics. Politicization also brings opposition to the European project itself and to the programmes of the EU. An intensive process of constitution-building brings to the fore deep divisions among the member states about their preferred model of integration. Individual citizens are faced with the growing importance of the EU and the speed of change in integration. The traditional moorings of political order are changing.

The process of democratizing the EU is animated by caution rather than big ideas and heroic struggle. It is being built on the spread of civic statehood throughout Western Europe and the wider continent and involves the incremental addition of institutional and procedural mechanisms to enhance accountability and transparency in EU decision-making. The spread of Union citizenship and symbols of European identity all add to the political fabric of integration. Just where this piecemeal process of democratization will take the system is far from clear. It is likely, however, that it will produce a system with less substantial institutions and processes of democracy than is customarily found at national level. This may well be wholly appropriate because the system should continue to rest on national democracies. However, it is a development at odds with the traditional federalist view, which advocates the creation of a state-like Union in the form of a traditional federation.

Guide to Further Reading

For an analysis of the main issues concerning democracy and the global system, see chapter 10 of Held (1996). Dahl (1994) provides a succinct analysis of the tension between national democracies and integration. Hix (1998) adopts a traditional comparative politics approach to politics in the EU. Dehousse (1995) offers a set of interesting arguments about majoritarianism and the EU.

References

Chryssochoou, N.D. (1996) 'Europe's Could-Be Demos: Recasting the Debate', *West European Politics*, vol. 19, pp. 788–801.

Dahl, R. (1989) *Democracy and its Critics*. New Haven: Yale University Press.

Dahl, R. (1994) 'A Democratic Dilemma', Political Science Quarterly, vol. 109, pp. 23–35.

Dehousse R. (1995) 'Constitutional Reform in the European Community: Are there Alternatives to the Majoritarian Avenue?, *West European Politics*, vol. 18, no. 3, pp. 118–36.

Dogan, M. (1992) 'Conceptions of Legitimacy', in M. Hawkesworth and M. Kogan (eds), *Encyclopaedia of Government and Politics*. London: Routledge, pp. 116–26.

Duchêne, F. (1994) *Jean Monnet: The First Statesman of Interdependence*. London: W.W. Norton and Co.

Dunn, J. (ed.) (1995) *Contemporary Crisis of the Nation State?* Oxford: Blackwell.

Eurobarometer (1997) *Public Opinion in the European Union*, no. 46, Autumn.

European Community (1972) *Vedel Report on the Enlargement of the Powers of the European Parliament, in Selection of Texts Concerning Institutional Matters of the Community from 1950 to 1982*. Luxembourg: European Parliament.

Featherstone, K. (1994), 'Jean Monnet and the "Democratic Deficit" in the European Union', *Journal of Common Market Studies*, vol. 32, pp 149–70.

Franklin, M., Marsh, M. and McLaren, L. (1994) '"Uncorking the Bottle": Popular Opposition to European Unification in the Wake of Maastricht', *Journal of Common Market Studies*, vol. 32, pp. 455–72.

German Constitutional Court (1993), Ruling on cases 2 bvR 2134/92 and 2 BvR 2159/92, 12 October.

Hayward, J. (1995) 'The Crisis of Representation in Europe', Special Issue of *West European Politics*, vol. 18.
Held, D. (1987) *Models of Democracy*. Cambridge: Polity Press.
Held, D. (1996) *Models of Democracy*, 2nd edn, Cambridge: Polity Press.
Hix, S. (1998) 'The Study of the European Union 11: The "New Governance" Agenda and its Rival', *European Journal of Public Policy*, vol 5, pp. 38–65.
Irish Presidency (1996) *Outline for a Revision of the Treaties*, Dublin, 5 December.
Kaiser, K., Merlini, C., Montbrial, T. de, Wellenstein, E. and Wallace, W. (1983) *The European Community: Progress or Decline?*. London: Chatham House.
Laffan, B. (ed.) (1996a) *Constitution-Building in the European Union*. Dublin: IEA.
Laffan, B. (1996b) 'The Politics of Identity and Political Order in Europe', *Journal of Common Market Studies*, vol. 34, pp. 81–102.
Lindberg, L.N. and Scheingold, S. (1970) *Europe's Would-Be Polity*. Englewood Cliffs, NJ.: Prentice-Hall.
Linz, J. (1988) 'Legitimacy of Democracy and the Socio-Economic System', in M. Dogan (ed.), *Comparing Pluralist Democracies: Strains on Legitimacy*. Boulder, CO: Westview Press.
Neidermayer, O. and Sinnott, R. (eds) (1995) *Public Opinion and Internationalised Governance*. Oxford: Oxford University Press.
Reflection Group's Report (1995), Brussels: General Secretariat of the Council.
Scharpf, F.W. (1996) 'Democratic Policy in Europe', *European Law Journal*, vol. 2, pp. 136–55.
Weiler, J., Haltern, U.R. and Mayer, F.C. (1995) 'European Democracy and Its Critique', *West European Politics*, vol. 18, pp. 4–39.
Weiler, J. (1996) *The Selling of Europe: The Discourse of European Citizenship in the IGC 1996*, Harvard Jean Monnet Working Paper 3/96.
Wessels, W. (1997) 'Ever Closer Fusion? A Dynamic Macropolitical View on Integration Processes', *Journal of Common Market Studies*, vol. 35, pp. 267–308.

PART 5

Conclusions

sidelines confined to consultation, has been replaced, especially where legislation is concerned, by a Commission–Council–Parliament triangle. This triangle has emerged mainly as a result of treaty reforms contained in the Single European Act (SEA), the Maastricht Treaty, and the Amsterdam Treaty. The reforms have been both direct and indirect in their impact. They have been direct in that they have, for example, given the EP a veto over the majority of legislative proposals and have also given it the power to request the Commission to submit proposals on specific matters. They have been indirect in that they have fostered an attitudinal change in the Commission and the Council, both of which have come to regard the EP as an almost equal partner in some respects.

At the same time, the increasing assertiveness of traditionally 'quiescent' member states like Germany and the Netherlands – one of the most striking developments in the EU today – can be seen as evidence of the EU's maturation. As the stakes of European integration increase, national positions are less likely to wither away than to be cast in sharper relief. This may make big decisions harder to reach, but it does not necessarily herald a radical reconfiguration of the institutional system. A more explicitly intergovernmental approach enhances the importance of the Council of Ministers and the European Council. The EP's position is protected to a great extent by the enhanced institutional role that it has acquired during successive rounds of treaty change. As for the Commission, the 1999 resignation of the Santer College was clearly a blow to its esteem. Moreover, it may become more vulnerable to resurgent national interests because much of its political influence depends on informal or circumstantial considerations. However, in an EU defined by more assertive and sharply defined national positions, the Commission's role as an arbiter and broker of compromise agreements may be strengthened.

The EU's institutional development is likely to be profoundly affected by enlargement. Although minor institutional modification has been a feature of all enlargements, the limits of a system of institutional representation designed for six member states became glaringly obvious in 1995, when the accession of three member states increased the EU to more than double the EC's original size. Member states ducked the contentious issue of institutional reform at that time, knowing that they would have to confront it at the 1996–7 IGC in the run up to the Central and Eastern European enlargement.

But, the member states failed during the IGC to resolve the two major institutional problems of representation in the Commission and voting weights in the Council. Nevertheless the Amsterdam Treaty included a protocol stipulating that the Commission will comprise one Commissioner per member state as soon as the next enlargement takes place, provided that Council votes are re-weighted in order to compensate large member states for the loss of a second Commissioner. The protocol also states that at least one year before the EU exceeds 20 member states, an IGC must be convened 'to carry out a comprehensive review of the provisions of the treaties on the composition and functioning of the institutions'. Institutional change is thus very much on the horizon and may be advanced before it is strictly necessary to allow for Amsterdam 'leftovers' to be resolved, to provide for further extensions of qmv, and to enable the CFSP pillar to be strengthened in the wake of the experience of the Kosovo conflict.

Politics and Policies

The range of policy issues and areas embraced by the EU is broader than ever before. So too is the political impact of EU membership. National politics and European politics are inextricably intermeshed. National political actors operate at the European level, and European policies and procedures have a direct impact on national political life. The intensification of European integration since the landmark SEA has left few political actors or actions without a European dimension.

The importance of this European dimension may be illustrated by looking briefly at EU politics and policies with respect to three key areas of current debate and development: EMU and employment; enlargement and expenditure; and external and internal security.

EMU and Employment

The launch of the final stage of EMU by eleven member states in January 1999 was one of the most important political and policy developments in the history of European integration. A single currency was created and the key macroeconomic policy instruments of external exchange controls and interest rates were pooled. For many practitioners and observers, EMU provides irrefutable evidence that a state of some kind is emerging at the European level.

EMU may also be said to provide evidence of the seemingly remorseless incrementalism of the integration process. It was itself largely a spillover from the single market programme, with much of the impetus behind it stemming from a belief held by many EU decision-makers that the single market could never be fully integrated or work to maximum effect as long as there were separate national currencies and competing national monetary policies. In its turn, EMU is now prompting a further spillover, with many EMU participants pressing for the further development of EU macroeconomic policies, including fiscal policy. The intensifying debate about whether, and to what extent, the EU should tackle the politically-charged issue of tax harmonisation demonstrates how pervasive economic integration has become.

Like the single market programme, EMU is intended to boost European competitiveness and economic growth. By extension, both are also supposed to increase employment. In fact, job losses in Europe rose steadily during the EMU-dominated decade of the 1990s, fuelling the popular perception that economic integration and high employment are mutually incompatible. The EU's inability to generate new jobs is certainly one of the most disappointing aspects of integration, and one of the most difficult problems with which politicians must deal. Commission and member state efforts to counter the impression that integration generally, and EMU in particular, are conducive to high levels of unemployment resulted in the inclusion of a title on employment in the Amsterdam Treaty and in a special jobs summit in Luxembourg in November 1997. Both measures were largely symbolic, however, leaving responsibility for job creation largely at the national level.

The increasing emphasis on the problem of unemployment is a reflection also of the new political climate in Europe. The Labour Party's victory in the British general election in May 1997 was a harbinger of political change in the EU, although it was less portentous for the conduct of economic policy than it first appeared to be. Despite their left-of-centre political orientation, Tony Blair, the Prime Minister, and Gordon Brown, his Chancellor of the Exchequer, epitomized the new economic orthodoxy of central bank autonomy (hence their decision to make the Bank of England independent) and public spending discipline (hence their determination to reduce borrowing and deficits). Blair's election seemed more significant for the direction of EU economic policy than did the almost simultaneous election of Lionel Jospin, a more traditional socialist, as Prime Minister of France, although Jospin's socialism was strongly tempered by pragmatism. The election of Gerhard Schröder, another presumed pragmatist, as Chancellor of Germany in September 1998 seemingly set the seal on the emergence of centre-left, 'third way', governments in Britain, France, and Germany, the EU's largest and most influential member states.

National governments blamed EMU in the 1990s for unpopular decisions to cut public spending in order to meet what came to be seen as the most important of the convergence criteria: an annual budget deficit no more than 3 per cent of GDP. Will left-of-centre governments stick to the Stability Pact's stipulation, based on the convergence criteria, that euroland members keep their deficits lower than 3 per cent? If not, will they be able to justify their action by delivering higher economic growth and, more importantly, higher employment? Lessons from Europe's economic performance in the 1990s, and from comparisons with the situation in the United States, suggest that the solution to high unemployment lies largely in taking steps to reduce the risk and expense to employers of hiring new workers, thereby giving enterprises the flexibility to contract during an economic downturn but also to expand rapidly during an economic upturn. Because such steps, which could include tackling generous welfare systems supported by taxes on labour, or even reducing protections which make it difficult and expensive to let workers go, are unlikely to appeal to resurgent social democrats, prospects for the eradication of high unemployment in Europe are not particularly bright.

Nor does the ECB's tight monetary policy and commitment to price stability necessarily sit easily with a social democratic economic approach. As it is, the ECB will have difficulty adopting a 'one-size-fits-all' policy for such a heterogeneous economic area as euroland. A central bank makes policy for a country or – in the case of the ECB – for a collection of countries, as a whole. It cannot make policy for a particular region, no matter how disadvantaged – for example, because it suffers higher than average unemployment – that region happens to be. In euroland, disadvantaged regions are likely to be entire member states whose populations are bound to resent the impression that unemployment in their country is the price being paid for low inflation throughout euroland.

The ECB's legitimacy is already fragile. There are limits to how transparent a central bank can be, especially one that formulates monetary policy for an entity such as the EU. Similarly, the ECB's accountability is inherently questionable. Central bankers routinely appear before parliamentary committees, and ECB members will appear before the EP. But the EP is not analogous to a national parliament, especially in terms of its credibility. For most Europeans, EP committee hearings on European monetary policy will not suffice to close the ECB's accountability deficit, even if they help unwittingly to increase the EP's legitimacy.

The ECB's perceived weakness of accountability and legitimacy will only become acute, however, if euroland slips into economic recession, if unemployment rises, and if the ECB fails to cut interest rates quickly and substantially (or if the economy fails to respond to such cuts). Well before that point is reached, governments – which also have responsibility for economic policy management and which do not have accountability and legitimacy problems – are likely to be facing deep political difficulties. Governments, not the ECB, will first face the wrath of disaffected Europeans. Hence the incentive for governments to manage economic policy in concert rather than conflict with an ECB legally obliged to pursue price stability and culturally fixated on a tight monetary policy.

Enlargement and Expenditure

Apart from its institutional impact, the process of enlargement to the Central and Eastern European countries (CEECs) has provided a major impetus for reform of the EU's two most expensive policies: the Common Agricultural Policy (CAP) and cohesion policy. In the case of the CAP, enlargement is the latest in a series of factors over a number of years driving the reform movement. Thus enlargement is accelerating rather than initiating efforts to rein in agricultural spending as part of a package aimed also at eliminating export subsidies and devising a more environmentally and consumer friendly regime. In *Agenda 2000*, its strategy 'for strengthening and widening the Union in the early years of the 21st century', the Commission proposed that the EU continue its current CAP reform effort by shifting agricultural subsidies from price supports to direct payments (Commission, 1997). Ironically, the Commission estimated that the cost of compensatory direct payments would substantially exceed the savings from reduced price supports. However, the Commission also anticipated that CAP spending would remain within existing guidelines and continue to shrink as a percentage of overall EU spending because of higher EU revenue (linked to projected annual economic growth). The Commission's proposals were subsequently somewhat diluted when the member states reached agreement on *Agenda 2000* reforms at the March 1999 Berlin summit.

By contrast with the CAP, Central and Eastern European enlargement has been the sole impetus for member states to undertake necessary but – for some – politically unpopular reform of cohesion policy. Although in *Agenda 2000* it proposed keeping EU funding for economic and social cohesion at broadly current levels, the Commission also suggested reducing the Structural Funds' objectives and reducing the proportion of EU population covered by the Structural Funds from 51 per cent to between 35 and 40 per cent. Not surprisingly, these proposals generated controversy in both existing and prospective member states, with net contributors to the Structural Funds wanting to pay less, recipients of large-scale payments wanting to maintain or increase their share, and prospective member states wanting to get more than the EU was likely to offer. The Commission's proposals were endorsed at the Berlin summit.

The financial impact of enlargement triggered widespread debate not only about reform of agricultural and cohesion policies, but more generally about reform of the entire EU budget. Overall, the Commission estimated that enlargement would cost the EU up to 75 billion Ecu, spread out over several years. Yet the Commission also concluded in *Agenda 2000* that enlargement would not require an increase in the EU's current level of 'own resources' (1.27 per cent of GDP), assuming an average growth rate of 2.5 per cent in the EU and 4 per cent in the applicant countries during the period of enlargement. These optimistic assumptions exposed the Commission to criticism that it deliberately underestimated the likely costs of enlargement in order to assuage member state sensitivities and avert a bruising battle during the negotiations which led to agreement on a new multi-year financial perspective (covering the years 2000–6) at the Berlin summit.

By contrast with previous negotiations on financial perspectives (covering the years 1988–2 and 1993–9), the 1999 negotiations were dominated by demands from the EU's biggest net contributors – those member states, notably Germany and the Netherlands, that pay more into the EU than they receive back through various forms of financial transfers – for a more equitable system. A Commission paper on budgetary reform acknowledged the unfairness of the current arrangement and discussed a number of possible reforms (Commission, 1998). One of these was the surprising suggestion that 25 per cent of CAP expenditure (covering direct income supports) be switched back to member states, thereby removing some of the transnational subsidization that is a major source of the budgetary imbalance. The option was politically appealing because it could have been implemented by a qualified majority vote in the Council, but was politically risky because it raised an EU taboo: the prospect of renationalizing, however partially, one of the EU's few truly 'common' policies. The Berlin summit did not take up the option.

The 1999 budgetary negotiations were unusually tense because of the EMU-induced climate of financial retrenchment, an unexpected decline in economic growth, the resentment of the net contributors, and a realization of the high cost of enlargement. Inevitably, the negotiations exposed deep cleavages between rich and poor member states and between those who benefit most and least from the CAP's largesse. The stakes were especially high for the EU because, without a new budgetary agreement, accession negotiations with the Central and Eastern European states and Cyprus could not have begun in earnest. Resistance to further CAP reform and to cohesion reform, and failure to reach a new budgetary agreement, could have thwarted enlargement.

The Commission's proposal to switch some of the responsibility for CAP expenditure back to the member states demonstrated the profound impact of enlargement on positions and principles hitherto thought to be sacrosanct. The most striking changes were in the positions of Germany and the Netherlands, two member states renowned for their unswerving support of European integration and for their willingness to bear a disproportionately high budgetary burden. Although politically supportive of EU expansion, the financial implications of enlargement became a focal point for their discontent with the EU, a discontent that had been building up since the 1991 IGCs. In Germany's case, the change of government in October 1998 symbolized a transition to a more assertive EU bargaining position based unapologetically on perceived national interests.

Despite the necessity for – and difficulty of achieving – internal policy reform, the EU cannot afford to let the accession negotiations languish or fail. As EU officials often points out, promoting democracy and prosperity in Central and Eastern Europe is the EU's primary foreign policy goal, and enlargement is the primary means of achieving that goal. If enlargement were to be unduly delayed by the EU's failure to make internal policy and institutional reforms, the damage to the EU's already fragile political image and international credibility would be grave.

The substantive stages of the accession negotiations themselves will not be easy. Although the five CEECs earmarked for early membership have made great advances economically and administratively since the early 1990s, much restructuring remains to be done, especially with respect to deregulation, privatization, and macroeconomic policy-making. As the talks progress, applicant countries will fight tenaciously for concessions and derogations in troublesome areas such as agriculture, environmental policy, and services. The EU will drive a hard bargain, and the CEECs seemingly have little leverage. However, the political importance for the EU of successfully accomplishing eastward enlargement is likely to be a strong card for the applicant states.

External and Internal Security

The end of the Cold War gave rise to great insecurity in Europe, with the outbreak of war in the Balkans, instability in Russia, and growing concern in the EU about illegal immigration and international crime. Member states responded in the 1990s by strengthening the EU's fledgling external and internal security policies.

On the external security front, the Maastricht Treaty launched the Common Foreign and Security Policy (CFSP), including 'the eventual framing of a common defence policy, which might in turn lead to a common defence.' One of the original purposes of the 1996–7 IGC was to strengthen the CFSP procedurally. However, just as the architects of the Maastricht Treaty recognized the weakness of the CFSP even before their treaty was implemented, so too did the architects of the Amsterdam Treaty realize the inadequacy of the CFSP reforms before their treaty came into effect.

The EU's continuing inability to craft a CFSP capable of meeting the challenges of the post-Cold War world is an embarrassment for proponents of deeper European integration. Given the EU's enormous economic strength around the world, and the likely global impact of EMU, the EU's failure to become an effective international political actor is striking. Future prospects are not particularly bright. Having failed to fashion a coherent and effective CFSP initially in the Maastricht Treaty, and later in the Amsterdam Treaty, there is no reason to hope or expect that the situation will change in the near future. The kinds of pressures that brought about the Common Commercial Policy and EMU are absent in the traditional foreign policy sphere. Public opinion may deplore the EU's failure to 'do something' in Bosnia and Kosovo, but national governments are still reluctant to transfer responsibility for foreign and security policy to the European level.

Nevertheless current defence-related developments – the restructuring of the European defence industry and British support for a European defence initiative – suggest that a European defence policy may be in the offing. While these developments unfolded in 1998, however, successive Iraqi crises – culminating in the Anglo-American bombardment in December – showed how far the major member states are from formulating a common position on international conflict, let alone from acting militarily together. Britain, France and some other member states may have been able to agree to intervene militarily in Kosovo, but their response was ad hoc, entirely intergovernmental, channelled through NATO, and outside the EU's CFSP mechanism. Such action may be called 'European', but it can hardly be characterized as 'EU'.

Prospects for internal security integration look more promising. The Amsterdam Treaty is widely criticized for what it did not include – major institutional reform – but it is praised for having made significant progress by moving six areas of common interest (covering asylum, immigration, etc.) from the third pillar (Justice and Home Affairs) to the first pillar of the EU. By promising to establish an area of 'freedom, security, and justice', member states committed themselves to a more concerted EU response to the problems associated with the free movement of people, one of the fundamental freedoms associated with the single market programme. Yet the use in the first pillar, for at least five years after implementation of the Amsterdam Treaty, of intergovernmental decision-making for the establishment of the area of freedom, security and justice shows how sensitive member states remain to sharing sovereignty in these areas. The inclusion of an intergovernmental regime, however temporary, in the supranational first pillar also sends a mixed signal about the future direction of European integration. Does truncating the third pillar mean a weakening of intergovernmentalism and a strengthening of supranationalism? Or does it merely symbolize such a development while, in fact – by inserting an intergovernmental policy area into the first pillar – maintaining or even strengthening intergovernmentalism in the EU?

Involvement of the Citizenry

Clearly, EU citizens are increasingly affected by EU politics and policies. Yet the gap between citizens and policy-makers – between the consumers and producers of EU public policy – seems wider than ever before. The Amsterdam Treaty may have been more of a hindrance than a help. Despite its provisions for greater decision-making transparency and institutional openness, a glance at the consolidated versions of the Treaty on European Union and the Treaty Establishing the European Community shows that the post-Amsterdam EU is even more arcane and complex than its already impenetrable predecessor.

The prevailing sense of popular alienation from the EU is due in part to the nature of the EU itself. More generally, rapid economic, social, and technological change – known colloquially as 'globalization' – is undermining confidence in well-established political procedures and institutions. The ensuing challenge for the EU is especially acute because of the EU's novelty and the threats to national sovereignty and identity.

So far, the EU has responded to this challenge along predictable lines, focusing especially on the role of the EP and on greater institutional openness and transparency. Although much work remains to be done to open the institutions – especially the Council – to greater scrutiny, there is no shortage of high-quality public information on the EU, thanks in large part to the Internet. Despite an EU information surplus, however, there is and will always be a knowledge deficit, given limited public interest in political processes and policy-making. Arguably the EU is subject to particularly harsh criticism both because of its obvious foibles and failings, and because it epitomises for many people unprecedented and unfathomable global change.

The EU Polity

It has always been difficult to characterize the nature of the EU: its structural mix makes it 'neither a state nor an international organization' (Sbragia, 1992, p. 205). Yet, it is not enough simply to state that the EU is unique (or sui generis) and to abandon our analytical effort at this first hurdle. As the various chapters in this volume have shown, there are many aspects of the functioning of the EU institutions and policy processes that are highly reminiscent of government bodies and their interactions with the wider public at the national and local level. These aspects can only benefit from comparative analysis. At the same time it has become clear that many of the tasks of government that are traditionally carried out at the national level are increasingly being influenced, if not usurped, by the institutional processes at the EU level. Thus, the study of the EU may also help to raise questions about our traditional assumptions about the role of national governments and the role of the nation-state more generally. Sbragia made precisely this point in 1992 when discussing the then EC: 'Perhaps the study of the Community will stimulate scholars of politics within unitary states and federations to rethink what they have so far taken as givens' (Sbragia, 1992, p. 267).

One of these 'givens' is the concept of the state. While subject to extensive scrutiny by scholars more generally, this concept has tended to be presented rather statically in the literature on the EU. Although it is generally agreed that the EU is not a state, there have been few attempts to examine how the changing capacities of the European state might impact upon our evaluation of the EU's 'statehood'. The role of the European state has been transformed in recent years, in part as a result of membership in the EU: 'the centrality of the European state has been progressively reduced both by the transformational effects of technological, economic and social change and by the reluctant response of national governments in transferring some previously core functions of national sovereignty to the European level' (Wallace, 1996b, pp. 453–4). Crucially, Helen Wallace (1996a, p. 16) has argued: 'Globalization makes the traditional state level of governance particularly inadequate for a number of important issue areas, including – and this is troublesome – some policy issues traditionally defined as core prerogatives of statehood or the stuff of high politics'. So if European states no longer monopolize the attributes traditionally ascribed to them and the EU is increasingly encroaching into policy areas such as monetary policy, defence and immigration (crucial for establishing the 'us and them' of a territorial entity), how unique is the EU and how different from those bodies at the national level which we continue to call states?

Symbolically and practically, EU institutions are increasingly reaching out into areas of activity that have long been associated with the functions of the state: issues of citizenship, welfare, border control, and defence and security are increasingly accepted as legitimate areas of EU activity. Although the EU's capacity to perform these tasks and the adequacy of its existing policies are often questioned, the ability of states acting by themselves to perform the tasks is also increasingly doubted.

A 'European people' is the one key aspect often associated with the concept of statehood that the EU lacks. However, historically not all states have been nation-states. Moreover, as was shown in Chapter 17, the prospect of an emerging demos in the EU is not so unlikely. As the capacities of the traditional European state continue to decline; as more policy competences are transferred from the national to the EU level; and as a wider range of actors begin to interact with one another at the EU level, the utility of the very concept of the state in this context comes into question. Insofar as the traditional concept of a European state has begun to be redefined, it seems increasingly possible to characterize the EU as, at the very least, a could-be state.

References

Commission (1997) *Agenda 2000: For a Stronger and Wider Union* Com (97)2000, Brussels.

Commission (1998) *Financing the European Union*. Brussels: European Commission.

Sbragia, A. (1992) 'Thinking About the European Future: The Uses of Comparison', in A. Sbragia (ed.), *Euro-Politics*. Washington: The Brookings Institution, pp. 257–89.

Wallace, H. (1996a) 'Politics and Policy in the EU: The Challenge of Governance', in H. Wallace and W. Wallace (eds), *Policy-Making in the European Union*. Oxford: Oxford University Press, pp. 3–36.

Wallace, W. (1996b) 'Government without Statehood: The Unstable Equilibrium', in H. Wallace and W. Wallace (eds), *Policy-Making in the European Union*. Oxford: Oxford University Press, pp. 439–60.

Index